Every Chart-Topper Tells a Story:
The Seventies

A native of East Sussex, Sharon Davis was a devoted admirer of black American music from an early age, particularly that emanating from Motown Records in Detroit. Early in her career she worked for EMI Records, running the British Motown fan club in her spare time. She then became publicity manager for three American labels, followed this by working at Motown Records and then spearheaded her own press and promotion company, Eyes and Ears. She has written for several publications, including the prestigious *Blues and Soul* magazine where she is currently a features writer. Her previous books include *Marvin Gaye, Motown: The History* and *I Heard It through the Grapevine*. She worked with Diana Ross on the writing of Diana's autobiography, *Secrets of a Sparrow,* and penned, among others, the CD sleeve notes for the successful series *Early Classics,* released by Spectrum Records, and the forthcoming Britannia mail order series and 'Master Series' to issued by Phonograph Records. *Every Chart-Topper Tells a Story: The Seventies* is the second in a series which also includes *The Sixties. The Fifties* and *The Eighties* will later be incorporated into the 'Chart-Topper' series, as will books on soul and dance music covering the same decades.

Every Chart-Topper Tells a Story
THE SEVENTIES

SHARON DAVIS

MAINSTREAM
PUBLISHING

EDINBURGH AND LONDON

The moral right of the author has been asserted

First published in Great Britain in 1998 by
MAINSTREAM PUBLISHING COMPANY (EDINBURGH) LTD
7 Albany Street
Edinburgh EH1 3UG

ISBN 1 85158 837 X

A catalogue record for this book is available from the British Library

Typeset in Plantin by Brinnoven, Livingston
Printed and bound in Finland by WSOY

This Book Is Dedicated to the
Memory of my Father

Douglas Spreadbury

BRITISH No. 1 SINGLES

1970–79

CONTENTS

CONTENTS

INTRODUCTION

If the sixties were free, then the seventies were adventurous. The new decade began with the sixties' overflow until a new league of acts made their presence felt and gradually took over. Known as the era of change, both in music and dress style, the seventies will probably be remembered for the disco explosion. Mind you, at the start of the decade Rolf Harris's 'Two Little Boys' wasn't exactly an indication of what the future held! If it comes to that, neither was Pink Floyd's 'Another Brick in the Wall (Part II)' which closed the decade. It was the in-between years that were the most exciting.

With beat replaced by dance, disco music gripped both Britain and America courtesy of artists like one-hit wonder Anita Ward, Gloria Gaynor, Donna Summer, The Village People and The Bee Gees who, many believe, took dance to the limit. In some respects, The Bee Gees and the biggest box office movie ever, *Saturday Night Fever*, were instrumental in the demise of disco because of huge overdoses of familiarity.

With the dance came glitter, and not only Gary, who, of course, certainly proved to his public that music was f-u-n! Alongside this extremely colourful character (who, incidentally, at the time of writing still pulls capacity audiences at Christmastime) Slade, Sweet, Mud, Wizzard and Showaddywaddy outshone each other, dressed in their silks and sequins, jewellery and platform boots. Their music matched their colours. However, those bands walked in the footsteps of T Rex's Marc Bolan, who spearheaded the glam-rock movement, which went on to introduce David Bowie and his cast of fantasy characters to the world. Yes indeed, the sparkling carnival of talent is all here! Punk music made a razor-sharp impact more through headlines than chart music. The most notorious group was The Sex Pistols, whose 'God Save the Queen' narrowly missed chart-topper status. Pure, hardcore punk seemed to remain underground, although some acts enjoyed hits with a watered-down punk style, or by swiping riffs, hooklines, safety pins and swearing.

Then there was Abba, the Swedish quartet who spoke limited English, and won the Eurovision Song Contest with 'Waterloo', before reaching and surpassing musical peaks not previously thought of, only to eventually disband in bewilderment. They too started their hit career with silks and satins, with just a discreet sprinkling of glitter. The decade was cluttered with teenybopper idols, from Donny Osmond and Michael Jackson to David Cassidy, who all broke many young hearts which were awash with the wild frenzy of fan worship. So did Jimi Hendrix, the wild man of rock, but for different reasons. The American contingent also included Diana Ross and Chuck Berry, while Big Bad Barry White introduced his own brand of growling love to British ears, leaving The Tymes to be more respectable. The seductive Commodores and the whispery pleasantries of Simon and Garfunkel introduced a little sanity into a decade that then rapidly lost control in its determination to pack dancefloors and sustain the glitzy world of glamour and dual sexuality.

Of course, like any decade, there were the oddities, or the singles that got away for no particular reason. How's about Clive Dunn's 'Grandad' for starters? Or Lieutenant Pigeon and Demis Roussos? Well, someone must have bought the records! More seriously, principal British charters included the innovative Kate Bush, with her soprano 'Wuthering Heights' and George Harrison's costly 'My Sweet Lord', while groups like Middle of the Road and Chicory Tip couldn't surely have taken their singles that seriously – 'Chirpy Chirpy Cheep Cheep' indeed! And then someone handed actor Lee Marvin a microphone. Ah well, it was all part of the unpredictable decade. However, sanity was probably saved by 'Bohemian Rhapsody', the greatest 'pop' song of all time, which remains as popular two decades on as it did when originally issued.

Does it really matter?

As the title suggests, this book is devoted to the No. 1 singles (chart-toppers) of the seventies. It is the sister book to *Every Chart-Topper Tells a Story: The Sixties* and *Every Chart-Topper Tells a Story: The Eighties*. When more than one single reached the top during a particular month, the most topical has been included. This is also the case when, say, Abba had a consecutive run of chart-toppers. Other artists' singles have been included to break the (possible) monotony of both writing and reading about the same act.

Once more, I've raided a million-plus newspaper clippings and articles from both British and American publications, including *Disc*, *Melody Maker*, the *New Musical Express*, *Music Week*, *Record Collector*, *Cashbox*, *Rolling Stone*, *Billboard* and *Blues and Soul* magazine, whose pages are a wealth of information. Fanzines have also proved indispensable this time round. Reading artists' biographies was a time-consuming but wonderful chore; there are so many excellent books available. Those of particular interest and help are credited at the close of each chart-topper section. My thanks indeed; excellent fodder. Reference books also came high on the list to consult, including the *British Hit Singles – Volume 9* published by Guinness and compiled by Paul Gambaccini, Jonathan Rice and Tim Rice, and *Top R. & B. Singles 1942–1988* by Joel Whitburn.

As with the sixties volume, my grateful thanks to project researcher and co-ordinator Gerry Constable who, among other things, organised a particular brand of tidyness in my otherwise cluttered mind. Other researchers to be thanked are Chris Williams, Phil Symes, Andy Hill, Jayne Jollife and Tina Llewellyn – your assistance here is very much appreciated. An extended thank-you too goes to the staff at the Harrow Lodge Hotel, Shanklin, Isle of Wight, where this volume was completed. Food was excellent, you guys!

Back with Mainstream Publishing too. Thanks Bill for your faith in this off-the-wall project. Happy sales!

That's it, except a big thank-you to all the artists who made this volume possible. Wasn't it fun?

Sharon Davis
1997

ROLF HARRIS

Two Little Boys

He doesn't rate himself as a singer, rather a performer. Indeed, when he first performed on stage he was booed off! At the time of writing, though, Rolf Harris is the frontman of the BBC TV weekly programme *Animal Hospital,* often sad, but definitely rewarding.

Rolf Harris, born during 1930 in Perth, Australia, is one of today's most established entertainers and television hosts. However, as a singer he seriously became a competitor. Before embarking on his showbusiness career, Harris was a noted swimmer, teacher and artist. It was his extraordinary talent as a presenter of a children's television show, where he excelled as a cartoonist and later painted giant-sized screen pictures with large brushes and a wild selection of vivid colours, that secured him in the public eye.

As a singer, Harris enjoyed his first British hit with a slice of Australian nonsense titled 'Tie me Kangaroo Down Sport' during July 1960. Released via the EMI Records' Columbia label, the single soared to No. 9 in the chart. Harris told journalist John Perry from the *New Musical Express* in 1996: 'I only get worried [about that single] if people think I'm taking the mickey out of Australia. "Tie me Kangaroo Down Sport" was just an exercise in getting as many funny Australian words in there as possible. At the time I didn't even know what a didgeridoo was.'

In 1962 'Sun Arise', ably assisted by his faithful didgeridoo, soared into the British Top Three, converting the public to an incessant Aboriginal drone which Harris later claimed was twenty years ahead of 'this ambient earth music you have at these hippy raves today'. The follow-up single to this runaway hit was 'Johnny Day', which struggled into the Top Fifty during 1963.

Harris toured the world as a singer and entertainer for several years. Through his travels, particularly his treks to Australia, he searched for the lyrics to a track he had first heard in 1963. That year, he had been partway through an Australian tour when, one evening, prior to his performance, he went to the cinema to see Cliff Richard's block-busting movie *Summer Holiday* with the support movie *Down Under*. Harris said,

17

'It was a documentary on the Queen's visit, including her day at the Australian version of a rodeo. At the rodeo there were some Aborigine boys, and they sat on the grass in two lines forming the body of a canoe and sang a folk song. Some of the boys were singing the words while the others were making sounds imitating the noise of oars sweeping through the water. I tried hard for two years to get the words, but had no luck at all. I was hoping to translate them into English.' Eventually, Harris wrote his own lyrics and released the song under the title 'War Canoe'. Regrettably, his two-year search resulted in a single which bombed.

It was a minor setback; in 1966 Harris released his much-loved song 'Jake the Peg' as the flipside to 'Big Dog'. When performing the novelty track, the singer connected up a third leg to strut across the stage with relative ease. His routine still stands (!) three decades later.

It was six years before Harris returned to the British chart with the title 'Bluer Than Blue', which peaked in the Top Thirty, paving the way for his first and only chart-topper, in January 1970. Written by Theodore F. Morse and Edward Madden in 1903, and titled 'Two Little Boys', the single told of two lads, Jack and Joe, and their friendship through to adulthood. The story, warm and sensitive, lovingly told by Harris was, of course, the perfect Christmas single, dominating the chart's top spot for a staggering six weeks. Six months on, 'Two Little Boys' was reissued to peak in the Top Fifty.

Novelty and straight tracks formed the basis of Harris's singing career, although he secretly harboured the ambition to become a rock 'n' roll singer, for both the music and the groupies. In fact, he eagerly followed Bill Haley's British triumph, and went on to tour with artists like Billy Fury. However, by not pursuing his instincts, Harris believed he missed out on the swinging sixties: 'All the girls! All the drugs! They were for all those young rockers really. I just sat there and tried not to look!'

Leaving rock 'n' roll to others, Rolf Harris went on to become a familiar contributor to daytime television, where his talent as an artist led to guest spots on quiz and variety shows. His growing popularity naturally won him several entertainment awards and honours, culminating with the OBE.

More recently, though, in 1993 Harris switched record companies from EMI to Vertigo to release the Top Seven single 'Stairway to Heaven' and, during 1996, recorded a track which many believed to be an unthinkable move – a version of Queen's 'Bohemian Rhapsody'. It was the Australian's intention to transform the operatic fantasy into a comedy single. However, the Freddie Mercury estate forbade it. Harris said: ' "Bo Rhap" is in everyone's Top Ten rock songs of all time . . . I was so nervous about doing it . . . I'm such a big fan of Freddie Mercury that I wanted to do it right.' Subsequently, on his version, which viewers saw him perform during the television special *Rolf!*, screened in December 1996, Harris accompanied himself on the wobble board which, he said, was 'a real bugger to play'. Released via Living Beat Records, the single peaked in the Top Fifty.

Also in 1995–96, he turned his back on music to host the BBC TV programme *Animal Hospital,* a thirty-minute look into the daily routine of a London PDSA surgery. This later gave birth to *Animal Hospital on the Hoof,* a series of visits to Whipsnade Zoo where behind-scenes filming included deer giving birth and elephants being X-rayed. Further spin-offs included *Animal Hospital Goes West,* among others. It was Harris's sensitive approach to the desperate and sick animals and their owners which made the series compulsive viewing during 1996 and 1997. He believed these programmes were so successful with television viewers because they dealt with real people and their animals' problems. More importantly, there were no scripts. He told journalist Hilary Kingsley, 'We warn people of things that can go wrong for their pets that they shouldn't leave untreated. And it gives people a chance to release their emotions, which is important.'

Combining two careers now, entertainer and animal host, Rolf Harris will be gracing television screens for years to come. In his own way, perhaps he'll be able to prevent the horrendous cruelties people inflict on animals which, he said, often made him cry. If so, his version of 'Bohemian Rhapsody' then wouldn't sound so . . . um . . . different!

(Quotes: *New Musical Express,* interview by John Perry, 1996)

February 1970

EDISON LIGHTHOUSE

Love Grows (Where my Rosemary Goes)

'Daa, da-da-da-da, da-da-daa . . .' The perfect 'pop' song. Light and spontaneous with lyrics everyone could remember. The downside was there was no group to promote the single!

Edison Lighthouse was a group of session musicians headed by studio singer Tony Burrows. They recorded the Tony Macauley and Barry

Mason composition 'Love Grows (Where my Rosemary Goes)' quite by chance. In the right place, at the right time.

The track was then offered to Bell Records, who believed it was destined to be a million-seller. The company was right; the single shot to the top of the British chart during February 1970 within days of being released. A remarkable achievement for a new 'act', particularly as it went on to dominate British record sales for a staggering five weeks. However, while the single was climbing the chart, Bell Records needed a group to promote it. Edison Lighthouse was quickly assembled, but minus lead singer Tony Burrows, who had commitments elsewhere. Subsequently his distinctive vocals which graced the million copies sold were sadly missed and performances suffered. The buying public remained ignorant of this.

This deception failed to deter Edison Lighthouse, who went on to follow their chart-topper with 'It's Up to You Petula' in January 1971. It stalled in the Top Fifty and more or less marked the demise of the faceless Edison Lighthouse.

March 1970

LEE MARVIN

Wand'rin' Star

No one in their right mind could have called this single a song! It was a deep-throated growl that held a mild tune at the very best. On reflection, perhaps this was its fascination.

The white-haired, rugged-faced American actor Lee Marvin was born in 1924. While convalescing from an injury received during the Second World War, his interest turned from fighting to acting. His future career saw him in a variety of roles but he excelled as a villain, or a hard-nosed hero. The more brutal the role, the better he was.

During the fifties, Marvin appeared in movies like *You're in the Navy Now, The Wild One* and *Raintree County,* and starred in the American television series titled *M Squad.* Two decades on, he grew in status as an actor to star in such classic movies as *Donovan's Reef, Cat Ballou, The Dirty Dozen, Hell in the Pacific* and, of course, *Paint your Wagon.*

'Wand'rin' Star', sung by Marvin's character Ben Rumson, a white-whiskered, hard-drinking, loud-mouthed Californian gold prospector (who looked suspiciously like Jimmy Edwards), was one of numerous musical sequences included in the Jay Lerner and Frederick Loewe musical *Paint your Wagon*. Marvin's co-stars were Clint Eastwood as Pardner and Jean Seberg as Elizabeth. Eastwood also 'sang' in the movie; his 'I Talk to the Trees' was the flipside of 'Wand'rin' Star', one of two he talked through during the film. 'Wand'rin' Star' shot to the top of the British chart in March 1970 to enjoy a three-week stay. The movie *Paint your Wagon,* on the other hand, struggled for life.

By the time Paramount Pictures purchased the film rights to the 1951 Broadway play, the storyline was already dated. A rewrite resulted in a more acceptable tale of a ménage à trois between the three major actors. Paramount then financed the movie with an initial $14 million which quickly soared to almost twice that amount.

Five months of shooting in Baker, a village in the mountains of Oregon, was, the cast and crew confirmed, not a wise move. People and supplies had to be flown in by helicopter, at great expense. Some actors would commandeer this means of transport for their own personal use when boredom set in between episodes of filming – and this was often. However, Lee Marvin spent this down-time with Clint Eastwood, who had rented a 40-acre farm in Baker, where frequent visitors were Eastwood's (then) wife Maggie, and their son Kyle.

The loud, colourful *Paint your Wagon* was released at the close of 1969 to mixed reviews, ranging from 'a big, bawdy, rip-roaring Western musical' to 'a monument to unparalleled incompetence . . . They bought an expensive musical property and hired actors who can't dance or sing. Absolutely nothing happens.'

Despite its troublesome filming period and scathing reviews, *Paint your Wagon* went on to gross $14,500,000 by 1988 in America and Canada alone. Certainly, the cash collected from video and television rights must be useful, as the movie can generally be seen once a year on the small screen.

April 1970

SIMON AND GARFUNKEL

Bridge over Troubled Water

They were an unlikely looking duo – the small, dark-haired one and the tall curly blond. They barely acknowledged each other on stage, giving the impression of total disinterest. However, Garfunkel possessed the voice; Simon the composing pen. Together they were perfect.

Born in Newark, New Jersey, on 13 October 1941, Paul Frederic Simon was the son of established bass player Louis, and Belle, a school teacher. Shortly after Paul's birth, the family moved to Kew Gardens, Forest Hills. Born in Forest Hills, New York, on 5 November 1941, Arthur Garfunkel was the second son of a travelling salesman and a housewife.

The Simon family lived in the same street as the Garfunkels; Simon first met Garfunkel at the Forest Hills High School. Both were sixth-grade students and both were appearing in the school production of *Alice in Wonderland*. Together they transferred to Parsons High School where, during the mid-fifties, they started dabbling in music. Their first copyrighted composition was titled 'The Girl for Me', written with The Everly Brothers in mind. This led to the couple recording a demo tape of another track, 'Hey Schoolgirl', at the Sanders Recording Studio in Manhattan; there they met Sid Prosen, who released the track, with the title 'Dancing Wild' on the flipside, on his newly-formed label Big Records.

The single, credited to Tom and Jerry (Tom Graph – Garfunkel – and Jerry Landis – Simon) sold sufficient copies, thanks to Alan Freed's radio exposure, to guarantee the duo a spot on the teenage television programme *American Bandstand*. This, in turn, led to further live dates. Garfunkel told authors Joseph Morella and Patricia Barey, 'I never thought I was seriously going to make my living this way. I thought sooner or later I would do something more reputable. But I sure did always want to be famous.' 'Hey Schoolgirl' was Tom and Jerry's first and only hit, although they issued further titles that included 'Don't Say Goodbye' and 'Baby Talk', emulating their musical peers The Everly Brothers. Paul Simon also released a solo single titled 'True or False' under the name True Taylor, together with a pair of instrumentals. With no further success, despite Sid Prosen leasing material to other record companies, the duo disbanded during 1959. Paul Simon studied English at Queen's College, while Art Garfunkel became a liberal arts student at Columbia University in Manhattan.

While studying, Simon maintained his musical interests by recording demo titles for third-party artists, and working with Carole Klein, later known as Carole King; she went on to compose and produce with fellow student Gerry Goffin, whom she also married. Simon also resurrected the name Jerry Landis for recording purposes, to touch the American chart with 'The Lonely Teen Ranger' while other titles like 'Searchin''' were poor sellers.

The next decade saw Paul Simon continuing his solo career with

Warwick Records, before signing a contract with Madison Records, using the name Tico and the Triumphs. His most notable release was the 'Motorcycle' single, an American Top One Hundred hit in 1963. When Amy Records purchased Madison, Simon moved too. All the while, though, he continued to record demo tracks and, whenever he got the opportunity, performed on the local club circuit.

During this time, Art Garfunkel likewise returned to the music business by composing tracks like 'Private World', which he sold to Octavia Records, and by recording titles that included 'Beat Love' under the name Artie Garr, for the Warwick label. As he completed his mathematics degree, he met Paul Simon again, who was now at law school, and they performed for the first time as a duo. Garfunkel said, 'We wrote rock 'n' roll songs together, but suddenly one of us could write poetic folk songs. I really connected with that . . . so the rejoining after several years was on the basis of the two of us as singers and Paul as the songwriter.'

During 1964, Simon left law school and went to Britain to test his talent on the London folk club circuit. He took up residence with Judith Piepe, a social worker, and secured a recording deal with the British company, Oriole Records. His only significant release there was 'He Was my Brother', recorded under the name Paul Kane; a poor seller. With no success, Simon returned to America where he and Garfunkel signed as a singing duo to CBS Records' Columbia offshoot. In October 1964, they issued *Wednesday Morning 3 a.m.*, their debut album, crammed with folk material.

Early in 1965, Simon once more returned to Britain where he again provided the music for Judith Piepe's religious programmes on BBC Radio, before performing with fellow American folk singers in British clubs. Mid-1965, he returned to the studio to record *The Paul Simon Songbook* album for CBS Records in London. Some while after the album's release, a CBS executive, Tom Wilson, lifted the track titled 'The Sound of Silence'. Unhappy with the title as it stood, Wilson restyled it, adding drums and percussion, and the single's most endearing feature, the electric guitar. Satisfied with the result (which, incidentally, later horrified Simon), Wilson released 'The Sound of Silence' as a single with the name Simon and Garfunkel on the disc's label. Neither artist was aware of the release, let alone their performing credit. When the single began climbing the American chart, Simon quickly returned to America to persuade Garfunkel to join him on the promotion bandwagon. Their efforts paid off. 'The Sound of Silence' shot to the top of the American chart in January 1966 and stayed there for two weeks, while in Britain the title bombed. All was not lost though; the song grew legs to be rerecorded by The Bachelors, who enjoyed a British Top Three hit in March 1966.

The Paul Simon composition 'Homeward Bound', also issued during 1966, represented the duo's first British hit, reaching No. 9 that April. Two months on, their next single, 'I Am a Rock', peaked at No. 17 in Britain, but reached the Top Three in America. This title was, incidentally, first recorded by Simon solo and issued as an album track on *The Paul Simon Songbook*.

With a steady track record to date that had catapulted Simon and Garfunkel from obscurity into stardom, their recording future looked secure. Then the unthinkable happened. In September 1966, midway through the Flower Power era of peace and drugs, following a short British promotional trek, the single 'The Dangling Conversation' bombed. Simon said, 'Why it wasn't a big hit is hard to know. It probably wasn't a good song. It was too heavy.' Aside from the music, during 1967 Simon admitted to the media he had dropped LSD, while Garfunkel experimented with several drugs because it gave him 'interesting musical insights'. 'The Dangling Conversation' was the first of several titles to bomb, until 'Mrs Robinson' established them as successful artists in Britain, where it reached No. 4 in 1968, and as a chart-topping act in America. 'Mrs Robinson' was part of the soundtrack for the Mike Nichols movie *The Graduate* co-starring Anne Bancroft and Dustin Hoffman, and was one of five Simon and Garfunkel titles to be included. A reworked version of the title was later featured on the duo's *Bookends* album, which, during August 1968, topped the British chart. 'Mrs Robinson' went on to scoop a handful of 1969 Grammy Awards, including Record of the Year.

Late in 1968, *The Graduate* hit the British cinema circuit, garnering high critical acclaim and public success with its strong theme of mature seduction. The film's presence encouraged the release of the soundtrack which soared to No. 3 in the British album chart. Indeed, Simon and Garfunkel would remain synonymous with the movie for years to come and, of course, every Mrs Robinson had a tailor-made song!

By now, Simon and Garfunkel had accumulated vast earnings, although Simon received the most; he owned his compositions, which earned a writer's royalty, and had negotiated for 75 per cent of the duo's performing income. Originally, Simon was quite content to publicly credit Garfunkel as his equal musical partner, but in later years he regretted the admission: ' "We're Simon and Garfunkel. I write the songs. Artie arranges them." It was a joint statement all through the sixties. Everyone believed it and, of course, it was never true.' Garfunkel, on the other hand, was less pointed: 'People always asked why I didn't write the songs. It was because Paul was so good.' This situation would, it appeared, continue to cause hostility between them throughout their career.

During 1969, the solitary single 'The Boxer' became a Top Ten entrant on both sides of the Atlantic. Simon and Garfunkel, both now heavy marijuana users, were growing apart, diversifying in other areas, away from their recording commitments as a duo. Garfunkel, having tasted the movie world from the periphery, took his first steps towards an acting career. The separation was short-lived; the next year saw the return of the singing duo with a vengeance. Written by Simon during 1969 and sung by Garfunkel, the whispery, haunting 'Bridge over Troubled Water' was issued. The title crashed into the American chart to dominate the top spot for a staggering six weeks. Interestingly, Simon composed the track on his guitar in the key of G, before transferring it to the piano to Garfunkel's key of E-flat. Garfunkel: 'Paul showed me "Bridge over Troubled Water" and he felt it was his best song. I felt it was something less than his best, but a great song.' In reality, after hearing Simon's version, he did not want to sing it. Simon insisted. Only two verses were completed when the couple went into the studio; the third was added partway through the session. Connoisseurs believe the final verse to be alien to the song's overall theme.

Already on British release and a No. 1 seller, the *Bridge over Troubled Water* mother album hotly followed the American chart-topper to push its sales over the five million mark.

The single was the decade's most meaningful of songs; it broke all barriers, selling as quickly as CBS Records' plant could manufacture it. However, the astonishing success had a downside. The entire album project had taken Simon and Garfunkel three months of intensive recording to complete. This, in turn, wore down their tolerance of each other. Such was the strain on their relationship that, unbeknown to the public, the duo admitted they could no longer work together. According to Garfunkel, 'We were a perfect case of two people who communicate poorly about sensitive issues.' He wanted to concentrate on his acting career, while Simon intended to pursue a solo career with CBS Records, a move he had wanted to make for some months, but due to his security with Garfunkel was afraid to do so. According to Simon, 'We didn't say that's the end. We didn't know if it was the end or not.'

Meanwhile, in the public eye, their success continued to expand at an alarming rate. 'Bridge over Troubled Water' was issued in Britain as a single during April 1970, whereupon it soared to the top of the chart, a position it held for three weeks. The single went on to win Song of the Year and Record of the Year at the Grammy Awards in 1971, while the album won, and rightly so, the Album of the Year category. Backstage, however, Simon was privately seething, regretting he had insisted Garfunkel be the song's vocalist. As Simon said, 'Everybody treated Artie like a star . . . fame and attention are really a hothouse for feelings.'

Before Simon and Garfunkel could cull further album tracks for single release in Britain, Julie Felix and Marsha Hunt pinched 'El Condor Pasa (If I Could)' and 'Keep the Customer Satisfied' respectively: both were single hits during 1970. However, before the close of the year, the duo issued their own version of 'El Condor Pasa (If I Could)' to enjoy a Top Twenty hit, while the *Bridge over Troubled Water* album re-established itself at the top of the British chart. The album continued its yo-yo chart life for nearly two years and (to date) remains an active seller.

Midway through 1972, Simon and Garfunkel reunited on stage in support of Senator McGovern in his run for presidency at Madison Square Garden in New York. Other participating acts included Dionne Warwick, Burt Bacharach and Peter, Paul and Mary. It was a solitary performance which their record company capitalised upon by releasing the album *Simon and Garfunkel's Greatest Hits* while Simon's eponymous solo album was at the top of the American chart. Lifted from that album as its debut single, 'Mother and Child Reunion' became a British No. 5 hit, reaching one position higher in America. Simon would remain a consistent record seller through to the nineties. *Simon and Garfunkel's Greatest Hits* album likewise spawned a single. Titled 'For Emily, Whenever I May Find Her', it faltered in the American Top Sixty, and when flipped for British release, its B-side 'America' peaked in the Top Thirty.

Simon and Garfunkel were once more persuaded to perform together in public. This time they agreed to guest on the American television variety show *Saturday Night Live,* screened late in 1975; the first part of the act featured solo Simon, who then duetted with Phoebe Snow before announcing Garfunkel was to join him to sing a medley of their hits. Following this, the duo recorded the single 'My Little Town' together, which returned them to the American Top Ten.

Of course, by now, Paul Simon and Art Garfunkel had carved solo careers. However, they would continue to perform together when the occasion warranted until 1987 when they embarked upon a fully fledged tour of Europe which included sell-out concerts at Wembley

Stadium. It was intimated that when the trek ended, they would record together once more as a duo, but Simon quashed any hope when he told the American magazine *Newsweek,* 'I can't go back and do anything with Artie. That's a prison. I'm not meant to be a partner . . . But I wouldn't mind being in the position of doing something like a single again.' By the nineties, their public appearances were slashed to charity functions and fundraising benefits including one in 1993 for the American Children's Health Fund Project.

'Bridge over Troubled Water' was an ethereal composition, rerecorded approximately 200 times by various artists including Aretha Franklin, Elvis Presley and The Supremes. To give an indication of the title's monetary worth, Paul Simon earned $7 million in composer's royalties during its first year of release. Surely that must compensate for not being the lead vocalist!

(Quotes: *Simon and Garfunkel: Old Friends* by Joseph Morella and Patricia Barey)

May 1970

NORMAN GREENBAUM

Spirit in the Sky

What made 'Spirit in the Sky' so compelling was its dazzling fuzz guitar work. Or was it the sharp melody and shrill vocals? Perhaps having religious overtones might have had something to do with it? Whatever it was, this magnificent 'pop' track was one of the most significant releases of the decade.

Born on 20 November 1942 in Massachusetts, Norman Greenbaum performed as a folk singer while studying at Boston University. When he moved to Los Angeles he formed Dr West's Medicine Show and Junk Band, which included percussionist Evan Engber, and guitarists Jack Carrington and Bonnie Wallach, and which recorded 'The Eggplant that Ate Chicago'. This nonsensical single reached the Top Fifty in America, encouraging the band to tour. It was reported that audiences had mixed reactions, not able to accept the psychedelic presentation of the group's painted faces and the blinding light shows. When no further success was in the offing, the group disbanded during 1967.

Greenbaum retired from the music business to tend a dairy farm, but in 1968 he met Eric Jacobson, who persuaded him to return to the recording studio. This resulted in the *Spirit in the Sky* album, whose title track became an unexpected Top Three American hit. When released in Britain on the Reprise label, the single shot to No. 1 in May 1970, where it remained for two weeks. 'Spirit in the Sky' then took Europe by storm, selling several million copies on the way.

The follow-up was the poor 'Canned Ham' single, while Greenbaum's second album, *Back Home,* issued during 1971, struggled for sales. A year on, Warner Brothers released his third album *Petaluma,* another bomber. Once more with no success, Greenbaum left the music business.

However, 'Spirit in the Sky' grew legs when the British psychedelic group Doctor and the Medics rerecorded it and enjoyed a chart-topper in May 1986. In all honesty, the original version is the one the public remember. During early 1997, 'Spirit in the Sky' was used as the musical backdrop to a television commercial for Kelloggs Bran Flakes. The connection between the two was debatable!

June 1970

CHRISTIE

Yellow River

Despite public belief to the contrary, Christie was a British trio, not American, and like so many other groups on the periphery of seventies glam-rock, they lasted only a short time.

Jeff Christie, born on 12 July 1946, and late of two groups, The Outer Limits and The Epics, formed Christie during the late sixties. He recruited drummer Mike Blakely and guitarist Vic Elmes, and it was this trio that chanced to record 'Yellow River' via a recording contract with CBS Records.

Christie wrote 'Yellow River' for The Tremeloes because Mike Blakely's brother Alan was a member of the group. However, when they passed on it, Jeff Christie decided to record it with Elmes and Blakely, persuading The Tremeloes' producer Mike Smith to oversee the recording session. 'Yellow River' shot to the top of the British chart in June 1970. Christie's gain; The Tremeloes' loss!

Four months on, the chart-topper's clone 'San Bernadino' was issued to reach the British Top Fifty, and upon re-entry reached the Top Ten. Early in 1972, the 'Iron Horse' single was the trio's last hit as it struggled into the Top Fifty. Nothing Christie did could turn their career around.

So they accepted the inevitable. The hit run was over. If it's any consolation, though, by this time The Tremeloes were in the mire. Bet they're still kicking themselves for their hasty rejection!

July 1970

MUNGO JERRY

In the Summertime

Known as the carefree jug/blues band, Mungo Jerry recorded one of Britain's most loved songs. No idle statement that, because every summer radio stations programme it, while television advertisers sell their wares with it! 'Dee, dee, dum-de-dum . . . in the summertime . . .'

Ray Dorset, founder of Mungo Jerry, was born on 21 March 1946. He first became interested in music during 1957 when, influenced by the British skiffle boom, he formed his first group, The Blue Moon Skiffle Group. Expelled from school for breaking the uniform rule in 1960, he didn't turn to music full time but became a hairdresser based in Egham. With a regular daytime job, Dorset followed his love of music as a hobby as a member of The Buccaneers, whose line-up included Derek Sermon and Dave Hutchins. With a name change to The Conchords they recorded their first demo discs which included 'Wow-Ho-Oh'. This in turn led to a residency at the Station Hotel, Richmond, where The Rolling Stones also performed. As The Tramps they performed regularly as a support act before becoming The Sweet and Sour Band, a back-up unit for artists like Millie Small. In fact, Dorset contributed to her No. 2 hit 'My Boy Lollipop' during March 1964, released on the Fontana label.

In 1967, following countless line-up changes, Dorset's group, now known as Memphis Leather, secured a recording contract with Saga Records. At the company's insistence, Memphis Leather became Good Earth and as such released the album *It's Hard Rock and All That* containing several Ray Dorset compositions. They progressed to The Good Earth Rock 'n' Roll Band, playing both rockers and jug band blues. While their live work was well supported, their recorded material struggled, leaving Saga Records no option but to drop them from its artist roster. A minor hiccup.

Pye Records' producer Barry Murray signed them to the recently formed offshoot Dawn, where they became Mungo Jerry, borrowed from Mungo Jerrie, a wily character in *Old Possum's Book of Practical Cats* by T.S. Eliot. At this juncture, Mungo Jerry's line-up consisted of bassist John Godfrey, pianist Colin Earl, instrumentalist Paul King and guitarist/lead vocalist Ray Dorset. Among the first tracks to be recorded for the Dawn label were 'In the Summertime' and 'Mighty Man'. Barry Murray believed 'In the Summertime' was the stronger track; he was right. Within two weeks of its release date, the single shot to No. 1 in the British chart during July 1970. It dominated record sales for a staggering seven weeks, before repeating the success in over twenty countries, selling in excess of six million copies and earning the distinction of being 1970's top-selling single.

The remarkable success of 'In the Summertime' was attributed to Mungo Jerry's blinding performance at the Hollywood Music Festival held in Staffordshire when they supported acts like The Grateful Dead. Ray Dorset, on the other hand, thought differently when he said the song appealed to everyone as it represented the old American image of 'cruising round in an open-top car, with a girl in the passenger seat and a bottle of Coke or something in your hand . . . those guys would always pull into a lay-by and give their girls a good seeing-to, so I wrote a song about it.'

Hot on the single's tyre tracks came the *Mungo Jerry* album, expensively packaged in a 3D sleeve complete with the special glasses needed to see the effect. In actual fact, 'In the Summertime' was absent from the album, and no further singles were lifted from it either. As the album was released, the group was touring America. In between performances they recorded material at New York's A. & R. Studios, where 'Have a Whiff on Me' was earmarked as their next single. That was not to be.

Also see: 'Baby Jump', March 1971

August 1970

SMOKEY ROBINSON AND THE MIRACLES

Tears of a Clown

'I believe in God and I believe He sent me a message to do this – the melody and the words . . . There are a lot of songs I write which I never record but I don't necessarily feel I am recording the cream of my compositions.' – Smokey Robinson

Born William Robinson, on 19 February 1940 in Detroit, Michigan, he lived in the North End of the city with his mother. Naturally, he lived in a musical environment, ranging from jazz to gospel, and at the age of three years, he performed for the first time. Emulating (as best he could) Billy Eckstine, Robinson sang for a train-load of soldiers destined for Europe and the Second World War. Three years on, the youngster sang 'Ragtime Cowboy Joe' at the Michigan State Fair.

By listening to the radio and by fooling around on his mother's piano, Robinson developed a growing interest in music. However, his contented childhood was tragically shattered when his mother died from a cerebral haemorrhage at the age of forty-three, whereupon his sister Geraldine became his legal guardian.

With encouragement from one of his schoolteachers who formed a Young Writers' Club, Robinson experimented with verse. He told author David Ritz: 'I had me a Big Ten notebook where I'd . . . be jotting down songs. Mrs Harris was one of the first to make me see the value of writing.'

His jotting at Northern High School led to him forming a group called The Five Chimes, with the membership of Warren 'Pete' Moore, born on 19 November 1939 in Detroit; James Grice, Donald Wicker and Clarence Dawson. When Wicker and Dawson later departed the line-up, they were replaced by Ronnie White, born on 5 April 1939 in Detroit, and Sonny Rogers; and as such they won the local, but prestigious, Ed McKensie television talent contest. James Grice was the next to leave the group, whereupon Bobby Rogers, born on 19 February 1940 in . . . yep . . . Detroit, replaced him. With Robinson the lead vocalist, The Five Chimes became The Matadors.

In June 1957, Robinson graduated from Northern High School; instead of continuing his education at the Highland Park College, he opted to plough his energies into The Matadors. College could wait a year. Sonny Rogers was then drafted into the Army to be replaced by Bobby's sister, Claudette Rogers, born on 20 June 1942. The group's new membership then auditioned for Jackie Wilson's manager, Nat Tarnopol, singing a selection of Robinson's compositions. They were told, 'You're not bad, but you got the same set-up as The Platters, and who needs another Platters?' However, before leaving the audition room, Robinson met Berry Gordy Jr, who, unbeknown to the young singer, had also heard the audition. (At this juncture, Gordy was Jackie Wilson's songwriter; Robinson told Gordy he had stockpiled 100 songs –

which would later all be discarded by Gordy.) Gordy asked The Matadors to sing a (then) current track, believing any true potential had been lost in singing Robinson's material. Impressed with what he heard, Gordy agreed to work with the group.

As Gordy's success with Wilson had been limited, he kept his day job working on the assembly line in the Ford Motors Factory, but he was able to secure local dates for The Matadors before negotiating a recording contract for them with End Records. What to record? Robinson's first composition of note titled 'Got a Job' was his 'answer' to The Silhouettes' single 'Get a Job'. Gordy assisted Robinson in the song's completion, The Matadors recorded it and its flipside, 'Mama Done Tole Me', at the United Sound Studio during November 1957. The group now had a single and a new name – The Miracles.

'Got a Job' was a local Detroit hit during 1958, which encouraged End Records to release a second single, titled 'Money' (not to be confused with the later Motown hit recorded by Barrett Strong 'Money (That's What I Want)'. Robinson: 'For these first four sides – and this includes producer's fee, publishing income, writers' and artists' royalties – Berry got a cheque for $3.19. And keep in mind, "Got a Job" was something of a hit.' Gordy framed the cheque rather than cash it, claiming it was the first and last because he intended to open his own record company, Motown. With $800 borrowed from his family and royalties received from Jackie Wilson's recordings, Gordy formed his company in Detroit during 1959. The Miracles were his first group.

In the meantime, The Miracles' next pair of singles were issued via Chess Records, namely, 'Bad Girl', the group's debut mainstream American hit, albeit only in the Top Ninety, followed by 'I Need a Change'. On the personal front, Robinson married Claudette Rogers in November 1959.

All future Miracles' singles would be released on Motown's Tamla label, starting with 'Way over There'. The group's wait for American success was short. The single 'Shop Around', composed by Robinson and Gordy and released during February 1961, earned Motown its first million-selling disc by soaring to No. 2 in the chart. Robinson: 'This was the song that established Motown and The Miracles and, along with "Money (That's What I Want)", sent the company into orbit. We were flying high.'

'Shop Around' was lifted from the group's debut album *Hi! We're The Miracles,* while 'Ain't It Baby' was the follow-up single, which faltered in the American Top Fifty that April. A further pair of titles – 'Mighty Good Lovin'' and 'Everybody Gotta Pay Some Dues' – stalled in the

Top Sixty. However, these early releases helped cement Motown's future; the music at this time was categorised as commercial R. & B. with an underlying blues element. In time, with outside composers and producers being recruited into Motown's family, commerciality would be a song's prime ingredient.

Although he spearheaded The Miracles' recordings, Robinson also became a valued composer/producer with Berry Gordy at Motown. Indeed, Robinson was responsible for countless hits by Motown artists, prompting Gordy to give him a vice-presidency within the company.

Three singles charted during 1962, namely, 'What's So Good about Goodbye', 'I'll Try Something New' (lifted from the album of the same name) and a reworked version of 'Way over There'. All titles were semi-hits, flying the Motown flag even higher. To close 1962, The Miracles joined the first Motown Revue to tour America. This trek would be the first of several touring revues; the only method Gordy was permitted to use to present his black acts to the public. As promoters were reluctant to represent solitary black acts, concerts were usually limited to the chitlin circuit (supper clubs). However, in time, Gordy introduced his own promotion department at Motown.

'You've Really Got a Hold on Me' soared into the American Top Ten singles chart early in 1963. This track went on to be rerecorded by countless acts during the next two decades, including The Beatles as an album track. The title 'A Love She Can Count On' was issued as follow-up to reach the Top Forty, while the evergreen dance single 'Mickey's Monkey' jumped to No. 8 that August. Before the year closed, The Miracles had released a further trio of albums, namely, *The Fabulous Miracles*, *The Miracles on Stage* and *Christmas with The Miracles*.

During 1964, the group membership was reduced to a quartet when Robinson's wife Claudette retired from live performances, preferring to remain a full-time wife. (In 1968 their son Berry was born; two years on, their daughter, Tamla.) She did, however, continue to record with The Miracles for a time. In 1964 Robinson successfully branched out as a composer/producer with The Temptations, who enjoyed a No. 11 American hit with his 'The Way You Do the Things You Do', and Mary Wells with 'My Guy', which soared to the top of the American chart. Robinson would continue to work with these two acts, while writing for and fronting The Miracles. Meantime, his group charted three times during 1964 with '(You Can't Let the Boy Overpower) The Man in You', 'I Like It Like That' and 'That's What Love Is Made Of'.

Despite not cracking the mainstream British market, appealing to a cult following in much the same way as other black American acts at this time, The Miracles visited the country for a short promotional trek, appearing on Rediffusion's premier Friday night music programme *Ready, Steady, Go!*

Through to the end of the decade, The Miracles remained one of Motown's foremost groups. As a composer, Robinson enjoyed a variety of hits with other acts; in fact, it was ironic that these songs fared much better than those he cut with The Miracles. However, that situation was to change quite unexpectedly.

During March 1965, the Motown Revue toured Britain; participating acts included The Miracles, The Supremes, The Temptations and Martha and The Vandellas. The tour was a financial bomber, yet no one could fault the performances or the music. While the artists were in London, Dusty Springfield arranged for them to be featured in their first television programme. Titled *The Sound of Motown,* screened by Rediffusion, the show, hosted by Springfield, was the first to feature one record company's artists – and black at that!

A series of single releases sustained The Miracles' career, but by 1966, Robinson had branched out from the ballad in which he excelled, to more beaty tracks, like 'Going to a Go-Go', a Top Fifty hit in Britain, and '(Come 'Round Here) I'm the One You Need', a Top Forty hit. Mind you, the slow titles he did compose were excellent: Robinson's gift as a lyricist could not be matched, prompting Bob Dylan to call him 'the world's greatest living poet', with titles that included 'Ooh Baby Baby', 'The Tracks of my Tears' and 'My Girl Has Gone' – faultless, pure magic.

From this juncture, the group would establish itself on the British music scene; regrettably never joining the high-ranking success of fellow Motown acts like the Four Tops and Diana Ross and The Supremes. Back in America and also during 1966, Robinson added Marvin Gaye (nicknamed 'dad' by Robinson) to his roster of acts by producing his 'Ain't that Peculiar'. One wonders when Robinson actually had time for himself!

A year on, the group became known as Smokey Robinson and The Miracles; Gordy wanted to highlight the lead singer. In 1968, the single 'I Second That Emotion' marked their highest British success to date – in the Top Thirty, while in America the title had previously shot to No. 4. The titles 'Yester Love' and 'Special Occasion' followed; both American semi-sellers.

Smokey Robinson and The Miracles next cracked the British chart mid-1969 with 'The Tracks of my Tears', which soared into the Top Ten. However, it was the group's next release which catapulted them to the top of the British chart in August 1970. Originally recorded during 1967 and included on the *Make It Happen* album, 'Tears of a Clown' was swiped for British release to sell in excess of 950,000 copies. Due to this unexpected (but welcomed!) success, the single was hastily released in America where it likewise shot to the top of the chart during December. Robinson was startled at the single's sudden climb; if the public wanted his old, uptempo material instead of the current ballad, he would seriously rethink The Miracles' musical future. To this end, he hastily composed the official follow-up titled 'I Don't Blame You At All', a clone of 'Tears of a Clown'. However, before the title could be released, Motown/EMI in Britain had reissued '(Come 'Round Here) I'm the One You Need', which peaked at No. 13 in February 1971. 'I Don't Blame You At All' followed, a No. 11 British hit; No. 18 in America. The group's British hit run was now ended.

In the new decade, Smokey Robinson and The Miracles struggled for their American hits, as their lead singer spent his time elsewhere within Motown's operation. The situation changed at Robinson's instigation when, following a lengthy American farewell tour, he left the group during July 1972, citing his intention to retire from the music business to concentrate on his family life. He had been planning the departure for some time, but since the group's financial situation was unstable, he had agreed to stay until their standing was more positive.

William Griffin, born on 15 August 1950 in Detroit, Michigan, replaced Robinson. Meanwhile, 'I Can't Stand to See You Cry', released early 1973, which faltered in the American Top Fifty, marked Robinson's final single with The Miracles, while a double album tracing their career titled *1957–1972* struggled into the Top Eighty. Not an ideal epitaph for one of Motown's premier groups.

The 'new' Miracles' debut single in September 1973, titled 'Don't Let It End ('Til You Let It Begin)' failed abysmally in the American Top Sixty. The group struggled on until March 1976 when their single 'Love Machine' topped the American chart, the same month as it soared into the British Top Three. The title marked The Miracles' final hit. When their recording contract with Motown expired, they switched to CBS Records, to plummet to further commercial depths. Eventually, the group disbanded; to retire from the music business until the nineties, when the London-based Motorcity Records, headed by Ian Levine, signed them to his artist roster. The new liaison proved fruitless for The Miracles, whereupon they returned to their daily lives. On 26 August 1996, Ronnie White died from leukaemia at the Henry Ford Hospital in Detroit.

Returning to 1973, Smokey Robinson's retirement was short-lived. Released during September, his debut solo single 'Sweet Harmony' became a Top Fifty American entrant. Early the next year, he enjoyed his first Top Thirty hit with 'Baby Come Close', while 'Just my Soul Responding' marked his debut solo British hit in the Top Forty during February. The next time the soloist appeared in the British chart, he was joined by fellow artists Marvin Gaye, Stevie Wonder and Diana Ross, on the tribute single for Berry Gordy's father, titled 'Pops We Love You'. The title reached the Top Seventy; Top Sixty in America during February 1979.

Like the majority of Motown acts, Robinson was, by now, a regular visitor to Britain. During 1976, he embarked upon a lengthy British tour, where his performances comprised material requested by his audiences. Remarkably, Robinson was rarely caught out with a song he didn't know! Two years on, he toured once more, closing the trek with a concert at London's Royal Albert Hall.

As the new decade loomed, Robinson's recorded work became more commercial; his style had altered due to him working with outside influences. He broadened his musicianship by composing the soundtrack for the movie *Big Time,* which he also financed, and issued a series of albums, all critically acclaimed, notably *A Quiet Storm, Deep in my Soul* and *Where There's Smoke.* With the advent of the eighties, Robinson's career was on the upturn. 'Cruisin' ', his first single lifted from the mother album *Where There's Smoke,* shot to No. 4 in America. Despite a mammoth hype by Motown's British office, all attempts failed to repeat the American success. In mid-1980 Robinson released the *Warm Thoughts* album, from which the track 'Let Me Be the Clock' was swiped reaching the American Top Forty. The next year, as Robinson celebrated his twenty-fifth anniversary in the music business, he struck gold. He released 'Being with You' as a single, originally written for Kim Carnes. In May 1981, the title shot to No. 2 in America, while a month on it catapulted to the top of the British chart, a position it held for two weeks. The album *Being with You* hotly followed, earning the distinction of becoming the singer's debut British charter in the Top Twenty. Before the year closed, 'You Are Forever' peaked in the American Top Sixty singles chart; Robinson hosted the ABC TV special *Smokey Robinson – 25th Anniversary Special,* and issued the album *Yes It's You Lady.*

During 1983 when Motown itself celebrated its twenty-fifth anniversary by way of a musical gala, Robinson and The Miracles re-united to perform, alongside numerous other company acts, past and present. That August, the singer duetted with High Inergy member,

Barbara Mitchell, on the 'Blame It on Love' single, a Top Fifty American hit, before duetting with Motown funk-master, Rick James on the 'Ebony Eyes' single.

On the personal front, Robinson's life was in turmoil. Following two affairs during his marriage to Claudette, and the birth of his son Trey in 1984 by his second lover, it was decision time. His marriage had been troubled for several years but he chose to stay with his wife and family. Now, with a third child, he was unable to either sever his family ties or disown Trey. So he chose drugs; preferring rock cocaine cigarettes to his family home. He began to live alone in 1985, and his self-destructiveness spanned two miserable years. He was unable to work, and touched death's door more than once. Following pressure from a desperate friend, Robinson became involved with the Ablaze Ministry, attended their meetings, and cleaned his system, saving his life.

It took Robinson until 1986 to hit the headlines once more, this time as a contributor to the 'We Are the World' project, recorded by USA for Africa, a conglomeration of artists, inspired by Bob Geldof's success with Band Aid. A year on, he re-entered the British chart with the single 'Just to See Her', a No. 32 entrant, while in America the title soared into the Top Ten. The track went on to win a 1988 Grammy Award for the Best R. & B. Vocal Performance – Male.

To start the nineties, and following his unexpected departure from Motown Records, Robinson released the album *Double Good Everything* for SBK Records. The album's title track was swiped for single release in November 1991; it bombed.

Regarded as one of music's foremost composers, Smokey Robinson was constantly in demand. Sure, his recording career had fizzled out, but his compositions and presence helped and encouraged others. He continued to tour Britain, although in America his performances were restricted to special occasions or charity earners, like performing with Aretha Franklin (his life-long friend) to help the Gay Men's Health Crisis; or joining the 1993 celebrations of 'An American Reunion' staged at The Lincoln Memorial, Washington.

As recently as 1996, Robinson supported a tribute concert for the late Ella Fitzgerald, and was the recipient of yet further honours for his vast contribution as composer, producer and singer during the past three decades.

(Quotes: *Smokey: Inside my Life* by Smokey Robinson with David Ritz; *Motown: The History* by Sharon Davis)

ELVIS PRESLEY

The Wonder of You

'Elvis Presley is a God-loving, jelly-kneed kid who has taken rock 'n' roll out of the category of race or R. & B. music and made it into pop. Elvis is still a country boy at heart and he's not fixin' to change.' – Colonel Tom Parker

Elvis Aaron Presley was born on 8 January 1935 in East Tupelo, Mississippi, to Vernon and Gladys. His twin Jesse died at birth. He grew up in an impoverished neighbourhood said to be 'the poorest place that white folks could live'. It was only singing together at gospel revivals and being members of the congregation of the First Assembly of God Church that helped the family survive.

While attending Lawhon Grammer School, his teacher, Mrs Grimes, encouraged the young Presley to enter the annual music festival, the Mississippi-Alabama Fair and Dairy Show, held in Tupelo. Ten-year-old Presley won the runner-up prize singing 'Old Shep', a sad tale about the relationship between a boy and his dog.

During 1948, Presley and his family moved a hundred miles to Memphis, where his mother worked as a nurse's aide while his father joined the United Paint Company. Outside school hours, Presley contributed to the family finances by gardening for the neighbours, although he managed to save $12.95 to buy his first guitar, enabling him to emulate the country and western and R. & B. music that was so much a part of his adolescence.

Presley said, 'My upbringing was pretty quiet. I was never out of my mother's sight until I was sixteen. All the kids would go swimming in the creek but my mother wouldn't let me go . . . When I was fifteen I got crazy about football, but my folks thought it was too dangerous and tried to stop me. After school the white boys would team up against the coloured boys and they'd all come home with their clothes torn . . . I was always taught the difference between right and wrong. I remember once when I was five, I took two empty Coke bottles from a neighbour's porch, and got a spanking from my dad.'

With no academic qualifications, Presley worked as a truck driver for the Crown Electric Company. While driving around he would often visit the Memphis Recording Service which guaranteed it could record anything anytime for $4. Sam Phillips, who owned the company and its offshoot Sun Records, regularly saw Presley using the facilities but took little notice of him. Yet, for some reason, his office manager, Marion Keisker, secreted a tape of Presley singing 'My Happiness' and 'That's When your Heartaches Begin' which he played to Phillips. The next time Presley visited the studio, Phillips asked him to record with a couple of musicians. The original material Phillips had prepared was discarded when Presley sang 'That's All Right, Mama'. This track, with 'Blue Moon of Kentucky' became Presley's debut single on the Sun label. Within days, DJ Dewey Phillips on WHBQ, Memphis' premier radio station, aired 'That's All Right, Mama' and before the track had finished the station's switchboard was jammed by callers wanting to purchase the disc. Within a week, Sam Phillips was desperately trying to press records to fulfil the 6,000 advance orders! Within a month, Elvis Presley was invited to participate in Nashville's Grand Ole Opry, where he performed 'Blue Moon of Kentucky'.

During July 1954, Presley signed a recording contract with Sun Records and returned to the studios to cut his next single 'Good Rockin' Tonight', released during September. His third release, 'Milkcow Blues Boogie', followed early in 1955. It was at this juncture that Colonel Tom Parker entered Elvis Presley's life. He recognised a raw, crude talent in the young singer and when Presley's father, Vernon, asked him to manage his son, Parker said, 'I agreed a deal with Elvis and his father to become his manager and promoter, promising to handle his record contracts, tours, personal appearances and to try to get him into motion pictures.'

Originally, Parker received 25 per cent of all Presley's income; later other deals, including merchandising, ensured he received a staggering 50 per cent of his earnings. His percentage, Parker said, depended on the type of deal he negotiated; in time, he (not surprisingly) became the richest manager in the history of the music business.

Parker's first move was to interest a major record company in his protégé. RCA Records were sufficiently impressed with the package to pay Sam Phillips $35,000 to release Presley from his contract with him. This money helped Phillips to promote other artists' careers.

In January 1956 Presley recorded his debut single for RCA Records. Titled 'Heartbreak Hotel', it was penned by Parker's public relations officer Mae Axton and Tommy Durden, who conceived the song after reading of a suicide victim's note 'I walk a lonely street'. It was released on 27 January to coincide with the singer's television debut on *Stage Show* hosted by Tommy and Jimmy Dorsey. In April Presley sang the single on NBC's *The Milton Berle Show,* televised from the aircraft carrier USS *Hancock,* moored in San Diego, before an estimated one quarter of the American viewing population. Within three weeks, 'Heartbreak Hotel' dominated the American chart, selling in excess of one million copies. During May 1956 it peaked at No. 2 in the British chart.

On Presley's second performance on *The Milton Berle Show* during June (and his first with his backing group The Jordanaires) he sang 'I Want You, I Need You, I Love You' and 'Hound Dog', causing uproar with the viewing public who instantly lodged complaints with the television company about his provocative hip-shaking and vulgar leers. It was the singer's last performance on the show for over ten years! The more certain sectors of the public continued to express their outrage at Presley's 'bumps and grinds', the more in demand he became. However, when he appeared on *The Steve Allen Show* during July 1956, he took on board the criticism to stoically perform 'Hound Dog'. This in turn prompted Ed Sullivan, Allen's greatest rival, to invite Presley to perform on his equally high-ranking show only if he would agree to be shown from the waist up. Presley conceded – and was criticised by the *New York Times* for making lewd movements with his tongue!

As Presley's eponymous album dominated the American chart, following advance orders of 350,000, 'Blue Suede Shoes' reached the American Top Forty; No. 9 in Britain in June 1956.

Behind scenes, Colonel Tom Parker beavered away ensuring his client received maximum media attention. It was not a difficult task because television, radio and press were only too willing to satisfy the public's growing demands. In between the promotional bandwagon schedules, Presley released his second American million-seller 'I Want You, I Need You, I Love You', which soared to No. 3, while in Britain it stalled in the Top Twenty.

With Presley's recording career now progressing according to Parker's master plan, it was time to approach the film world. To this end the singer did a screen test for Hal Wallis at Paramount Pictures, who told the media he possessed 'the same power, virility and sexual drive on screen as the young Errol Flynn', and signed him to a seven-year contract. By August 1956, Presley-the-actor was loaned to 20th Century Fox to star as Clint Reno in *The Reno Brothers,* a Civil War western. So strong was Presley's ballad 'Love Me Tender' in the movie, that the film's title was changed. Critics were mixed in their opinion – some believed him to be the rightful successor to James Dean, while others felt he should stick to singing. *Love Me Tender* was premiered at

The Paramount Theatre, New York, in November 1956, and despite the critics, the movie recouped $1 million of its costs within one week. The 'Love Me Tender' single, written by Ken Darby, soared to the top of the American chart and, following the film's British premiere in London, peaked at No. 11 during December 1956.

Presleymania continued to grip America; his brand of rock 'n' roll caused uncontrollable hysteria among the young and disgust among the mature. The frenzy, the unprecedented furore and excitement that was Presley-related led to countless hit singles including those which charted in Britain, like 'All Shook Up', 'Jailhouse Rock', 'King Creole', 'A Fool Such As I' and 'Stuck on You'. From the proceeds of his success, Presley bought Graceland for $102,500, a two-storey mansion which had originally been built by S.E. Toof who named it after his daughter.

Following the release of 'Don't' (his first ballad since 'Love Me Tender') in March 1958, which sold in excess of two million copies, Presley was drafted into the Army. The military actually did not expect the singer to undertake the two-year term and indeed had encouraged him to fulfil his commitment in the Special Services which would have allowed him to continue with his career. Presley agreed to this, but Parker and RCA Records' executives demanded he serve his country as a private, a move, they said, that would benefit his career in the long run.

The Army granted Presley a postponement of call-up to enable him to complete his fourth film, *King Creole,* but on 24 March 1958, a very reluctant singer reported for duty at the Memphis draft board, amid a huge publicity hype organised by Parker, who said Presley's stint in the Army would cost America $500,000 a year in lost taxes. When Presley was shipped to Fort Hood in Texas his family followed. This was the first time Presley and his mother Gladys had been parted since he was born. Such was her grief that she died on 14 August 1958 from heart and liver failure shortly before Presley was due to be shipped to Germany.

Army life bored him; the daily drudge left him eager to enjoy his social pursuits. To this end he rented a three-storey house in Bad Neuheim, in which he installed his father and grandmother. Most nights the house was crammed with select Army colleagues and hordes of young girls, one of whom was fourteen-year-old Priscilla Ann, stepdaughter of Captain Joseph Paul Beaulieu.

On 2 March 1960 Sergeant Elvis Presley left the Army. Prior to leaving Germany, and dressed in the khaki green uniform of the Third Armoured Division, he held a press conference in Friedberg where he said, 'The Army has been a great experience for me. I wouldn't have

41

missed it.' His flight to America was interrupted when the plane made an hour-long refuelling stopover at Prestwick Airport, Scotland. This was to be the first and only time Elvis Presley stood on British soil.

Once back in America, Presley was quick to see music had changed in his absence. His career needed remoulding; he was transformed from rock 'n' roller to balladeer. To spearhead the change, and to impress upon the American public that Presley was an ideal citizen, Colonel Parker arranged for him to appear on *The Frank Sinatra Spectacular,* a nationwide television special filmed in Miami. By the time viewers saw Presley arm-in-arm with Sinatra, he had already cut six tracks during an eleven-hour recording session in Nashville. From this, 'It's Now or Never' was chosen as his first single to be released since he had left the Army. (The tracks issued during his two-year stay of duty had been recorded prior to his departure.)

'It's Now or Never' buried Presley's rock 'n' roll past by becoming the first in a series of adult ballads. It topped the American chart for five weeks following its release in August 1960. The single entered the British chart at No. 1 during November 1960, a position it held for a remarkable nine weeks. Its sales were the fastest recorded anywhere in the world; it sold in excess of 750,000 copies in two weeks.

Presleymania had crossed the Atlantic to grip Britain. Record stores were jammed with customers wanting to buy the single. One shop that had queues outside only admitted those who wanted to purchase Presley's single, while another reported it was selling twelve copies of 'It's Now or Never' to one by another act. These sales earned Presley his first British gold disc. He had a series of highly successful singles (and albums) throughout the early sixties, including 'Are You Lonesome Tonight?', 'Wooden Heart', 'Surrender', 'Good Luck Charm', '(You're the) Devil in Disguise', 'Chapel of Love' and 'Crying in the Chapel'.*

During this period, films became conveyor-belt productions to fulfil public and film company demand; *Blue Hawaii* grossed $30 million though critics were quick to fault its poor storyline. Film producer Hal Wallis still believed in Presley's viability as an actor: 'It was the look of him, the eyes – with flickers of Rudolph Valentino – the way he moved. There was just an excitement about him.' There was never a problem with him on the set, he added. Presley was always on time, had learned his lines and was polite to everyone, especially his co-stars. Yet even these attributes failed to compensate for the lightweight storylines which were based more or less on the same theme of boy-gets-girl. After the excitement generated from his first roles of a rebellious young man,

*For details see *Every Chart-Topper Tells a Story: The Sixties*

Presley had slowly transformed into the acceptable all-American boy as the scripts he was expected to follow turned from boiling hot to lukewarm. But nonetheless Presley continued to outsell and outshine all competitors. His spate of movies, almost three a year, generated millions of dollars for those concerned, while his record sales maintained their staggering proportions. 'I was lucky,' he once said, 'I came along when there was no trend in music and people were looking for one.'

Between 1956 and 1962 he notched up a No. 1 single per year, a record he held until The Beatles broke loose in America. Indeed, it was to be the Fab Four and the music they represented that inadvertently heralded Presley's decline. After an incredible run of American chart-toppers, Presley's recording career began its descent. His last American No. 1 was 'Good Luck Charm' in April 1962, while in Britain he maintained his run until the following year. RCA Records were never short of Presley material because the majority of the singles and EPs issued were swiped from the constant stream of movie soundtracks. No single was recorded for a particular purpose, nor to follow a current trend. The record company had what was on offer and that was it. As public taste changed Presley was being left behind; his music rapidly became dated, and he was left to flounder.

In March 1965 Presley and Colonel Tom Parker celebrated the tenth anniversary of their partnership. Parker revealed that Presley had sold in excess of 100 million records, earning an estimated $150 million worldwide. He also confirmed that Presley's seventeen movies to date had grossed a further $130 million. Yet, by the start of the seventies, after the release of his last film in 1969, Presley was forced to return to live appearances because the bulk of his earnings had been spent. His close friend Tom Jones was his inspiration, particularly when he saw the audience reaction during one of Jones's Las Vegas shows. Women flung items of underwear (and often themselves) at the stage as he performed his 'bump and grind', with pelvic thrusts that left nothing to the imagination. Most of Jones's onstage antics were swiped from Presley anyhow, so why couldn't the originator also succeed?

To test the water, Presley had starred in an American television showcase during 1968. The response was overwhelming, encouraging him to return to the recording studios with renewed enthusiasm. After churning out so much lukewarm material, the singer was eager to record songs that were both powerful and gutsy. He chose the direction of America's most influential black singers to record at the American Sound Studios in Memphis. Within five weeks Presley had recorded sufficient material to provide a year's worth of releases for RCA Records. The most impressive of the tracks was 'In the Ghetto', penned by Mac Davis, which was the first to be issued from what was later to be called 'The Memphis Sessions'. 'In the Ghetto' re-established Presley as a Top Three American artist when it sold in excess of one million copies during June 1969 (his last million-selling single had been 'Crying in the Chapel' in 1965). When 'In the Ghetto' was released in Britain a month on, it soared to No. 2. Other Memphis tracks included 'Suspicious Minds' written by Mark James, and the Eddie Rabbitt composition 'Kentucky Rain'. Both were issued as British singles in 1970, reaching No. 2 and No. 21 respectively.

Sales were more impressive Stateside; 'Suspicious Minds' topped the chart, selling in excess of two million copies, though it was to be Presley's final American chart-topper. 'Kentucky Rain', on the other hand, peaked at No. 6.

Following the release of 'In the Ghetto', Presley hit the American stage at the International Hotel in Las Vegas during July 1969, his first live show since 1961. The four-week season guaranteed him $1 million. To prepare himself, Presley rehearsed for two weeks at RCA Sound Studios, while Colonel Tom Parker fuelled the publicity and hype until the public were fighting each other for tickets.

Elvis Presley was magnificent; his repertoire ranged from current material to his earliest recordings. The back-up group was handpicked while the support vocalists were the finest in soul circles, namely The Imperials and The Sweet Inspirations, headed by Cissy Houston, mother of Whitney. With his triumphant and spectacular return to the stage, the International Hotel secured Presley to a five-year contract.

Meantime, the album which spawned the singles that returned him to the top regions of the charts was issued. Titled *From Elvis in Memphis,* it became a British chart-topper but faltered in the American chart at No. 13.

Following his second $1 million season at the International Hotel, work was put on hold for a week during March 1970 when Presley was hospitalised suffering from glaucoma of the left eye. This was also the year when the singer contracted a colon ailment attributed to the overuse of the steroid hormone cortisone, which, in turn, meant he had little control over his bodily functions. The singer's valet James Caughley told author John Parker: 'I had to clear up the mess behind him which was at times rather embarrassing and distasteful.' Caughley also stated that Presley's drug problem at the time was mounting; it fell to Caughley to ensure prescriptions were filled. He estimated that he transported hundreds of pills to Graceland, including Percodan, Demerol and Valium, many contained within bottles and packages in his own name. Presley did not want outsiders knowing that all the drugs were intended for his personal use.

Following the Top Ten American success of 'Kentucky Rain', Presley's live recording of the Ray Peterson 1959 classic titled 'The Wonder of You' was issued. Recorded during his Las Vegas performances, the single sold in excess of one million copies in America to peak at No. 9, while in Britain it went to the top during September 1970, a position it held for a remarkable six weeks; it was his sixteenth British chart-topper.

With his stint at Las Vegas behind him Presley embarked upon his first American tour since the fifties. Midway through this lengthy trek, the movie *Elvis – That's the Way It Is,* filmed during his Las Vegas shows, premiered in America. British release followed in December 1970.

The follow-up to his British chart-topper was another cover version and another live performance. This time Presley released 'You Don't Have to Say You Love Me', previously recorded by Dusty Springfield, a British No. 1 in 1966. Presley's interpretation reached No. 11 in America; No. 9 in Britain in January 1971. In the new year, Presley once again spent four weeks in Las Vegas, while 'I Really Don't Want to Know' was swiped as a single from the album titled *Elvis Country*. It was a version of the 1954 American hit by Les Paul and Mary Ford, and reached the American Top Thirty. His next British hit, though, was yet another powerful, adult track; a reworking of Engelbert Humperdinck's No. 2 British hit from 1967 titled 'There Goes my Everything'. Presley's version soared to No. 6 in the British chart during April.

Before 1970 ended, Presley continued his run of British singles including the titles 'Rags to Riches' and 'I'm Leavin' ', Top Ten and Top Thirty hits respectively. He also undertook a further American tour; received the Bing Crosby Award for 'making creative contributions of outstanding artistic or scientific significance to the field of phonogram records', and released a boxed compilation titled *Worldwide Gold Award Hits, Volume 2,* with each set containing a small piece cut from the singer's clothing. Oh yeh!

The king had re-established himself as a performer, albeit looking somewhat like an oversized tailor's dummy in high collared, wide belted cat suits, with flared trousers and heeled boots, designed and stitched in the most elaborate of sparkling materials to conceal the mountainous man underneath. His audiences cared little about his size, contenting themselves that their king had returned. Presleymania was once again in full swing, but it would end as dramatically as it had begun.

Also see: 'Way Down', September 1977

(Quotes: *Elvis: Murdered by the Mob* by John Parker)

October 1970

FREDA PAYNE

Band of Gold

Unlike most black artists, Freda Payne was raised on jazz, not gospel: 'I wasn't raised in the Baptist church either, so I've never been considered a "shouter". Sure I missed out on a few soul injections but I think I acquired what I needed from life itself.'

Born Freda Charcilia Payne on 19 September 1945 in Detroit, Michigan, Payne's professional career started early when she sang on commercials in her hometown. It was hardly a riveting start, but it did give her the chance to later sing with the Pearl Bailey Revue, gaining valuable experience for her future career. Her stay with the Revue led to her performing on stage with jazz greats like Duke Ellington, Lionel Hampton and Sammy Davis Jr. She was quite content to remain within this musical circle until she met composer and producer Quincy Jones, who invited her to perform as a soloist with his orchestra at the prestigious Apollo Theatre in New York.

Due to her musical upbringing Payne's first love was naturally jazz and when, during 1965, she signed a recording contract with the Impulse label, a subsidiary of ABC Records, she recorded her growing art. As splendid as her work was, it only appealed to a limited audience. Broader acceptance was what she now craved, and the pull of popular music led to her joining the Invictus label during 1969. It was a wise move as it reunited her with hometown friends, Brian and Eddie Holland and Lamont Dozier, who prior to opening their own company, Invictus, were Motown's famous in-house composer/producer trio working with The Supremes, Martha and The Vandellas, the Four Tops and so on. They transformed each from so-so acts into million-selling performers. In truth, Holland/Dozier/Holland were responsible for what was later to become 'The Motown Sound'. However, when the trio became dissatisfied with the company's royalty payment system and working conditions, they left in a flurry of lawsuits to start Invictus Records, although for a time they had to work anonymously because of

46

certain stipulations included in Motown's lengthy legal action.

Freda Payne's younger sister Scherrie was already signed to the Invictus set-up as a member of the Glasshouse group, but she was later seconded to The Supremes. Indeed, Freda was asked first but turned down the offer, preferring to remain a soloist.

Once under the Invictus banner, the jazz singer immediately made a name for herself in the American R. & B. chart with 'Unhooked Generation', but it was to be 'Band of Gold', penned by Ron Dunbar and Edith Wayne, that transformed her into an international success. Apart from presenting Payne in October 1970 with her first and only British No. 1, a position it held for six weeks, the title topped the American chart, selling one million copies, before repeating the success across Europe. The track, with its instantly recognisable twangy introduction, and which, loosely speaking, told of an unconsummated marriage (or did it?), also stood the test of time, remaining popular for two decades. Numerous cover versions have also been recorded, including a sophisticated eighties dancefloor mix by the American singer Sylvester. Payne herself rerecorded the track during 1990 for the British-based Motorcity Records. However, the public remained loyal to the original. Payne said in 1978: 'It has taken me until recently to really fully appreciate just how big a record that was all around the world. My name is synonymous with that song and it will take a real monster hit for me to ever live it down. I know that has been one of the problems of my career.'

'Band of Gold' opened the way for two further British hits, although neither achieved its predecessor's success. The first was 'Deeper and Deeper', which became a Top Forty hit during November 1970, followed by 'Cherish What Is Dear to You' in March 1971, which stalled in the Top Fifty. Meanwhile, in America, the singer faced the wrath of the American government which attempted to ban her anti-Vietnam song 'Bring the Boys Home'. It was a sensitive plea that few could resist, and, with the added free publicity, it became Payne's second American million-seller. However, success had its downside. Behind the public face, her relationship with Invictus had soured. Payne: 'I always felt that Holland/Dozier/Holland used [me] as a tool. They would tell me exactly how to sing and I never really appreciated that. To me, it represented a lack of respect and a hold back on my personal freedom. But then, as a vehicle, it got me over. It worked, so who is to say what's right or wrong.' Also there was no consistency following her initial chart-topping success. Payne said, 'I stopped working with the company in June of '71 and then we didn't do anything until 1973 when I recorded the

Reaching Out album. But it was like the spark and magic had gone, so we realised that we couldn't go any further.' For some while, Payne had received recording offers from other record companies, but when Invictus found out, they insisted she was not contractually free. 'Those problems with them didn't stop me working. It just meant I couldn't work with other acts with hit records. But I was still able to play supper clubs and classrooms because my earlier training had stood me in good stead.'

In time, the singer was free to secure a recording contract with ABC Records, where she released two albums of note, namely, *Payne and Pleasure* and *Out of Payne Comes Love* during 1974 and 1975 respectively. Payne said: 'The albums were good from a musical point of view. They were well orchestrated and the songs were very good. But I admit I was disappointed with the lack of success for them . . . I accepted the fact that they weren't commercial.'

From ABC Records she moved to Capitol Records, albeit hesitantly. 'I had dealt with them through Invictus before – they distributed the label – and that whole thing had left me with a bad taste in my mouth. But checking into it further, I found that Capitol itself had been most co-operative with me.' While contracted, she released her best work to date, particularly the albums *Stares and Whispers* (which spawned the American hit 'Love Magnet'), *Red Hot* and *Supernatural High*.

Once more, itchy feet prompted the singer to move on. This time she chose Broadway, and made her acting debut understudying for Leslie Uggams in the Tony Award-winning musical *Hallelujah Baby*. This led to her playing the role of Linda in the Kurt Weil musical *Lost in the Stars* off Broadway, and performances in *Daddy Goodness, Ain't Misbehavin'* and Duke Ellington's *Sophisticated Ladies*. From the stage she turned to movies by debuting with *Miami Vice*'s Phillip Michael Thomas in the Avco Embassy film *The Book of Numbers*.

The next medium was television. Payne soon found a niche for herself in entertainment specials like *Freda Payne and The Stylistics*, HBO's *Legendary Ladies of Rock* and *Soul No. 2 America's Music*, later released on video. For two years she turned her back on music to host her own nationally syndicated television talk show, *Today's Black Woman*, where her guests included the Rev Jesse Jackson, Natalie Cole and Don King. When the series ended, music beckoned once more. With the Capitol Records deal finished, Payne recorded the 'In Motion' single for Sutra Records, available in Britain via Buddah Records. When that bombed, she turned to live performances, notably as a contributor to the 1993 'Giants of the Seventies' tour. Her trips to Britain were regular, but when she was booked to perform at holiday camp venues, she honoured a handful of disastrous dates before returning to America. Her high-calibre act was completely unsuitable for the noisy, camping audiences, and whoever booked her was either unaware of what her nightclub act was like or misled her management. Either way, the promotor should have been shot at dawn.

More recently, Payne's success has been on the musical stage. She enjoyed the leading role in *Jelly's Last Jam*, based on the career of the jazz legend Jelly Roll Morton. Playing young Jelly's grandmother, Gran Mimi, Payne performed the showstoppers 'The Banishment' and 'The Last Rites'.

Freda Payne has carved herself a name with fans of both commercial and soul/jazz music. Her stage act is engrossing and stylish and when the opening bars of 'Band of Gold' are heard, it's hard to resist joining in: 'Since you've been gone, all that's left is a band of gold . . .'

(Quotes: *Blues and Soul* magazine, 1970)

November 1970

JIMI HENDRIX

Voodoo Chile

He was the wild man of rock, crowned during the drug-hazed, revolutionary sixties. His music was aggressive and sexual, and when The Who smashed their equipment on stage, Hendrix set his on fire! With little regard for authority, the artist rarely strayed from the fast lane; nicknamed the 'Black Elvis', Hendrix died in similar circumstances.

Born on 27 November 1942 in Seattle, Washington, Hendrix was named Johnny Allen Hendrix by his Cherokee Indian mother, Lucille, a frail, sickly woman. When his father, James Allen, left the Army, he legally renamed his son, James Marshall Hendrix. Jimi's parents had separated during his father's period in the Army, but had reunited to produce their second son, Leon, during 1948. Two years on, the couple divorced. Lucille remarried in Canada, but her ill health contributed to her early death in 1958.

While the Hendrix brothers' father searched for manual jobs, they lived with an aunt based in Vancouver for two years, and spent time with their half-Cherokee grandmother, living on a reservation. She instilled into her grandsons the pride of the Indian race, and ensured they were conversant with the history of their ancestors.

Young Jimmy was an introverted youngster, who found solace in music within and without the church. Before he was ten years old, the youngster became obsessed with the rock 'n' roll innovators like Chuck Berry and The Bluesmasters; at thirteen years, he could strum the broomstick like a professional. His first experience with a guitar proper was thanks to his father's friend, who would play cards at the Hendrix home. The friend would bring his guitar, and while the men played, Jimi sneaked away with the instrument to practise. He told journalist Kevin Swift, 'I didn't know that I would have to put the strings round the other way because I was left-handed, but it just didn't feel right . . . One night my dad's friend was stoned and he sold me his guitar for $5. I changed the strings round but it was way out of tune when I'd finished.' A trip to his local music store remedied that problem. Eventually his father gave him a second-hand ukulele, a cheap acoustic guitar, later a Danelectro guitar.

The youngster's musical training consisted of listening to the radio, guitar in hand, and before long, the instrument became his voice. This, in turn, allowed him to withdraw further. Due to his musical obsession, Hendrix's education naturally suffered. While at high school he joined a group called The Rocking Wings; during their performances his introvertedness was replaced by a previously untapped confidence. In later years, this would be classed as showmanship. In 1959, Hendrix dropped out of school and within two years joined the US Army, despite objections from his father. Stationed at Fort Campbell in Kentucky, he was influenced by a richer, more sincere style of music called the blues. During his three-year stay, Hendrix was drafted into The Screaming Eagles Regiment of the 101st Airborne Paratroopers where he attained the rank of private, first class. In July 1962, the Army used the excuse of a broken ankle sustained during a parachute jump to honourably discharge Hendrix. In reality, the military was relieved to offload him; his insistence in following music, not orders, was seriously outside regulations. Three years after his discharge, The Screaming Eagles went to Vietnam.

Settling in Nashville, Hendrix and his Army musician/colleague, Billy Cox, soaked up the musical environment. While Cox was content to stay within the country heart, Hendrix was impatient to move on. To feed his lust for wandering, he performed with any group offering him a playing position. Most were short-lived because Hendrix would upstage his fellow musicians or ignore touring timetables. One such outfit was Bob Fisher and The Barnesvilles, who toured America as the support band to Curtis Mayfield and The Impressions, and The Marvelettes.

In 1963, upon his return to Nashville, Hendrix befriended 'Gorgeous' George Odell who, in turn, secured work for him with Sam Cooke, The Supremes, and Chuck Jackson, among others: all were soulsters working their way to stardom. Also that year, he worked with Steve Cropper (guitarist with Booker T and The MGs), auditioned unsuccessfully for Ike and Tina Turner, and met Little Richard, who was to be the biggest influence on Hendrix's life. Eventually, their egos clashed; the relationship ended.

Moving to New York in 1964, Hendrix teamed up with The Isley Brothers, who had a pair of hit singles to their credit, namely 'Twist and Shout' and 'Shout'. Hendrix toured and recorded with the brothers, but he stood in their spotlight and not his own, so he left to work with Curtis Knight and The Squires, a popular club circuit group. By performing with an unknown act, Hendrix could grab audience attention for himself, which was exactly what he did. Subsequently, nightclub punters flocked to watch his performances, a move not unnoticed by Curtis Knight's manager, who signed Hendrix to an exclusive contract for an advance of $1.

Hendrix and Curtis Knight went on to compose and record together, notably, the title 'Ballad of Jimi' in 1965. The young but hopeful musician moved on to tour with Joey Dee and The Starlighters, before joining The Kingpins, back-up group for King Curtis. With an image that befitted a vagrant with an attitude, rather than a musician with an ambition, Hendrix soon parted company with Curtis.

Midway through 1966, Hendrix formed his own unit called Jimmy James and The Blues Flames, playing material that included his own compositions and R. & B. classics, and performing at venues in New York's Greenwich Village. The Rolling Stones' guitarist, Keith Richard, and his girlfriend Linda Keith saw Hendrix perform at the Cafe Wha? Impressed with his act, the couple persuaded Chas Chandler, bassist with the British group The Animals, to join them the following evening. Chandler, looking for an act to manage, immediately offered Hendrix a management contract, suggesting he should move to London with him. After five years of perfecting his art, and playing one-nighters until he dropped, Hendrix was quietly confident he could embark upon a solo career. Subsequently, Chandler completed his final tour with The Animals, while Hendrix settled his affairs, and on 24 September 1966, with his worldly possessions in a suitcase and his guitar slung over his shoulder, Hendrix moved to London. Once settled, the first move towards his new career was to alter the spelling of his first name: Jimmy became Jimi. Chandler then introduced him to the British music scene. Following a series of jam sessions with British musicians both on stage and in the studios, Hendrix was booked as support act to the French singer Johnny Hallyday at the Olympia, Paris. However, Hendrix could not perform as a soloist, and with three weeks to spare, he had to recruit musical support. Hasty auditions resulted in guitarist Noel Redding, born in Folkestone, Kent, on 25 December 1945, and drummer, John 'Mitch' Mitchell, born in Ealing, London, on 9 July 1947, and late of Georgie Fame's Blue Flames, being recruited. Together they rehearsed an act that impressed Hallyday sufficiently to offer the trio further support dates in Germany.

Once back in London, Chas Chandler booked them into the recording studio, with financing from Mike Jeffrey. From the sessions, with Chandler as producer, a pair of titles emerged: 'Hey Joe', a cover version of The Leaves' hit single, and the Hendrix composition 'Stone Free'. Chandler then scouted British major companies for a recording deal; with the climate as it was, most were loathe to sign a group of any description. Meanwhile, manager and trio were penniless. To ease financial pressure, Chandler reluctantly sold his collection of guitars, bar one. Before he was forced to part with it, Polydor Records stepped in, offering to release 'Hey Joe' as a single. Under the label name, Jimi Hendrix Experience, the title soared to No. 6 in the British chart during February 1967, much to the surprise but delight of all concerned. To support the release, the trio secured television spots and performed selected concert dates, including one at the Saville Theatre in London, supporting The Who. Dates in Europe followed, including a handful at the infamous Star Club in Hamburg, Germany. In March 1967, The Jimi Hendrix Experience embarked upon their debut British tour with The Walker Brothers and Cat Stevens, among others. Audiences were introduced first-hand to the wild man of rock, with his gypsy appearance and mass of unruly hair, playing the guitar with his teeth! He was strongly criticised for his stage presence – 'I feel comfortable the way I look right now' – while on occasion the remarks were insulting. Hendrix said, 'Some reporters have the idea of hanging me from a tall tree but they don't bother me too much.'

In May 1967 the second single, titled 'Purple Haze', was issued, this time by Track Records. It was a monstrous rock sound which peaked in the British Top Three, doubtless assisted by users of LSD, as the single related to self-induced hallucinations of the floating kind. Hot on this single's heels came the debut album titled *Are You Experienced?*, which reached No. 2, followed by a fully-fledged European tour. The title 'The Wind Cries Mary', which Hendrix composed en route to an airport with Bob Dylan's music in mind, was released during June 1967 and peaked at No. 6 in the chart, while the trio embarked upon their first American tour. Record companies there had become aware of Hendrix's selling power and wild stage act, but it was Reprise Records who purchased the trio's recorded work for approximately $120,000.

Hendrix's career was progressing according to Chas Chandler's gameplan, although he had to stem the continuing criticisms regarding his artist's stage act, including the volume of his music – 'People who just hear the loudness are blind to what he's really doing' – and his showmanship. 'It all adds up to narrow-mindedness. It comes from older folk who probably go to strip clubs for their kicks . . . We're all out to build up the sheer personal excitement of Jimi.'

Meanwhile, behind scenes, a quartet of enterprising music men beavered away to launch the start of the hippie summer with the Monterey International Pop Music Festival, which was intended to outsell and outshine all previous events. Indeed it did, when during June 1967, artists including Simon and Garfunkel, The Mamas and The Papas, Otis Redding, Booker T and The MGs, Eric Burdon and The Animals, and, of course, Jimi Hendrix performed together at the County Fairgrounds in Monterey. This was the perfect showcase for the trio, who appeared on the last evening's bill. An estimated 100,000 people in total attended the five concerts that comprised the two-and-a-half-day festival. Naturally, police presence was high, but that was drastically reduced by the second concert. The constant supply of drugs ensured stoned audiences but no riots. Music ruled. The police were happy with that policy. All the concerts were filmed, and sold to ABC TV for approximately $300,000. It was a vital historical event in music's wealthy heritage. Author Gary Herman wrote, 'Jimi Hendrix, half black American and half Red Indian, "fucked" his guitar, stroking it as though it was his own member and, finally, set light to it – all the while squeezing pure rock 'n' roll from it.'

Following the love and rock, dope and roll of Monterey, The Jimi Hendrix Experience continued their American stint as support act to The Monkees. It was a worrying musical mixture; The Monkees' faithful were teenyboppers, while Hendrix attracted, well, a wilder, more mature crowd. The clash was so disturbing that Hendrix was dropped from the tour following a handful of dates. Doubtless, Monkees fans breathed easier! It later transpired, incidentally, that Hendrix had agreed to tour with the clean-cut group as a publicity ploy, knowing his act would cause outrage – and garner attention. Further American dates continued through to the middle of August 1967, whereupon the trio returned to Britain for a London concert with The Crazy World of Arthur Brown.

A month on, the next single, 'Burning of the Midnight Lamp', penned by Hendrix on a return trip from America when he was depressed, hence the sad lyrics, peaked in the British Top Twenty, while 'Purple Haze' reached the American Top Sixty. Before the year closed, Hendrix embarked upon a lengthy British tour with Amen Corner and Pink Floyd, among others, and released his second album, titled *Axis: Bold As Love*, a No. 5 seller.

The new year began badly for the trio. During a January touring trek in Scandinavia, the relaxed, introverted guitarist, topped up with LSD and alcohol, suddenly vented his doped fury on a hotel room in Gothenburg. He was subsequently handcuffed, arrested and jailed. The following morning, he reputedly had little recollection of the previous night's activities.

Although Hendrix was by now a regular drug user, their most vivid effects were yet to be seen. The more the pressure mounted, the larger his intake became. As his popularity catapulted beyond boundaries, so did his female following. It was, obviously, an exciting and dangerous combination, both of which Hendrix indulged in excessively.

Following the Scandinavian tour, the trio headed for America until June 1968, when they started recording with a vengeance. Two singles were issued from the sessions, namely, 'All Along the Watchtower', a Top Five hit during September, and 'Crosstown Traffic', a Top Forty entrant in April 1969. Meantime, the double album titled *Electric Ladyland* became a No. 6 seller. However, with success came disagreements between Hendrix and his manager Chas Chandler. So bitter were they that Chandler sold his stake in the Hendrix organisation to Mike Jeffrey, who had financed the first recording sessions.

Behind scenes, his business interests were in turmoil with contractual problems, internal conflicts and exploitation. His meteoric rise to stardom attracted many forms of unwanted pressure; everyone demanded a slice of his musicianship, his talent. Hendrix's friends glimpsed another, perhaps more sinister side to his persona, as Gary Herman reported: 'Hendrix's close friend Eric Burdon said [in 1976], "Jimi Hendrix was a genius. But one minute he's on stage singing about the mass of underdogs in America and the next he's kicking the hell out of some poor chick in a back alley." ' Suffice to say, the guitarist had several long-term relationships, including one with Kathy Etchingham, who told Herman that following a concert in Manchester, she found Hendrix in a ladies' loo with a girl. This did not particularly bother Etchingham; she was more concerned that Hendrix caught the return train to London. 'He had an incredible sexual appetite and would often sleep with three or four girls in the same night.' However, Etchingham was also seriously injured by his jealous rages. Another close girlfriend was Monika Danneman, who Hendrix met in Dusseldorf during 1969. They were engaged for two years.

A further trip to Europe early in 1969 was followed by a pair of British concerts at the Royal Albert Hall, London, and a North American tour. During this, in May 1969, Hendrix was arrested for possession of heroin at the Toronto International Airport. He denied using the drug but was fined $1,000. This was the start of his drug downfall. Before the year ended, Noel Redding and Mitch Mitchell announced the Experience had disbanded permanently, although the latter would perform again with Hendrix, alongside other musicians, for concert purposes. One such occasion was Hendrix's appearance at the Woodstock Music and Art Fair, staged in Bethal, New York, when the couple were joined by the all-black Gypsy Sons and Rainbows, later known as The Band of Gypsies.

Recording and touring dominated most of 1970. Hendrix's presence was demanded in America until August, when he returned to Britain for his second appearance at the Isle of Wight Festival, held in Godshill. This was destined to be Hendrix's last British concert, while his *Band of Gypsies* album soared into the chart at No. 6. A further European tour followed during which disaster struck in Germany and Denmark; Hendrix was booed off stage. During September, the guitarist jammed with Eric Burdon and others on the stage at Ronnie Scott's, in Soho, London. This was his final London appearance.

It appeared Jimi Hendrix had pressed his self-destruct button when, on 18 September 1970, he died in Monika Danneman's home. During the previous day, Hendrix had finalised his next tour and during the days that followed, intended to fly to New York to complete his next album with Chas Chandler.

According to Danneman, she and Hendrix had taken photographs and shopped for an evening meal she intended to cook. Following dinner, Hendrix went out until 2.30 a.m.; then Danneman had collected him. On the morning of 18 September, she planned to briefly leave the flat. 'I glanced at him, and realised he was ill. I tried to wake him up but I couldn't. Then I saw he had been taking some of my sleeping tablets . . .' She confirmed Hendrix died at 12.45 p.m. prior to being admitted to hospital. Author Charles Shaar Murray reported, 'Early that morning Danneman noticed that Hendrix had been sick during the night but that his breathing was normal . . . She popped out to the corner shop for cigarettes. When she returned, she was unable to wake him. Panicking, she phoned Eric Burdon, who screamed at her to call an ambulance.' It transpired that Hendrix had suffocated on his own vomit. He died without regaining consciousness. However, in her biography of Hendrix published during 1990, Danneman stated that he was alive prior to reaching the hospital and that he had died through the negligence of the ambulance team and doctors.

Noel Redding and Carol Appleby reported, 'The ambulance crew strapped Jimi into a sitting position for the trip to the hospital, though the usual position for a person being sick is lying on the side. He vomited and choked. There was no attempt to use resuscitation equipment.'

Former girlfriend Kathy Etchingham, intent on discovering the truth behind her lover's death, acquired a copy of the surgical registrar's notes. He was on duty at the time Hendrix was admitted to St Mary Abbot's Hospital. The registrar had confirmed the twenty-seven-year-old musician was dead upon arrival, having no pulse or heartbeat. The *Daily Mail* newspaper on 6 April 1996 reported a further version of the events leading to Hendrix's death, this time from a musician who had attended the same party on 17 September. The report stated that Hendrix had taken sleepers instead of drugs known as leapers; an error made due to the loud music being played at the time. He instantly fell asleep; all attempts to wake him failed. Hendrix died at the party.

Kathy Etchingham and Monika Danneman feuded throughout the years, until they met in the High Court during April 1996. Danneman was found guilty of alleging that Etchingham was an 'inveterate liar' regarding her relationship with Hendrix. Two days on, Danneman committed suicide in a fume-filled garage at her East Sussex home.

On 28 September 1970, following an adjournment, the inquest revealed Hendrix had died from an 'inhalation of vomit caused by barbiturate intoxication'. Checks on the musician's urine, blood and liver showed traces of amphetamines and Durophet, known as Black Bomber, traces of Brallobarbitone and Quinalbarbitone. An open verdict was recorded, leaving Hendrix's record company, Warner Brothers, among others, to collect a reputed $1 million, the amount they had insured Hendrix's life for. If the artist had committed suicide, no insurance money would have been forthcoming. Redding and Appleby reported: 'The post mortem showed 400 ml of free fluid in the left chest with the left lung partially collapsed. Both lungs were congested and swollen with vomit even in the smaller bronchi. Contrary to some reports, Jimi was still alive when he reached the hospital. Even as late as 1990, no files had been unearthed regarding the Hendrix tragedy, and more puzzling, the ambulance team, hospital staff and pathologist seem not to exist!'

Jimi Hendrix's funeral was conducted on 1 October at The Dunlap Baptist Church in Renton, Washington. He was buried in Renton's Greenwood Cemetery.

Two months after his death, Jimi Hendrix soared to the top of the British chart with the title 'Voodoo Chile', lifted from the *Electric Ladyland* album. It was his first and only chart-topper. Whether the tragedy inspired the sale was questionable, because the single was one of his most exciting. Whatever the reasoning, the British paid tribute to the guitarist in the best way they could.

Comprising material Hendrix had intended for a future project, the album *The Cry of Love* was issued during March 1971. This release opened the floodgates for a series of titles which, due to his complicated recording deals, were not controlled. Indeed, his talent was positively violated and capitalised upon by companies who probably would never have considered commercial release if Hendrix had been alive.

Ironically, or perhaps mysteriously, Mike Jeffrey died in a plane crash in France during March 1973; jazz master Gil Evans, earmarked to work with Hendrix during the week prior to his death, died in 1974, while Hendrix's manager, Chas Chandler, died in July 1996, the result of living life in the fast lane.

Albums containing Hendrix's performances on stage and jamming in studios were concocted; obscure material was unearthed, including the 1989 release *Radio One* featuring previously unissued BBC radio sessions. Yes, indeed Hendrix lived on.

He even headlined a new decade: 1990 was the twentieth anniversary of his death – Hendrix Year. His 'Crosstown Traffic' was heard across the television advertisement for Wrangler jeans, while the album *If 6 Was 9 – A Tribute to Jimi Hendrix* preceded the *Live at the Isle of Wight* video. On the downside of these and other celebratory releases, Noel Redding revealed he was owed £8 million in royalties from posthumous Hendrix releases and instigated several legal actions to retrieve the amount.

At the close of 1991, Hendrix was inducted into the Hollywood Walk of Fame on Hollywood Boulevard, and early the next year into the Rock and Roll Hall of Fame, before being honoured with a NARAS Lifetime Achievement Award at the Grammy ceremony staged in New York. Before 1992 ended, the guitarist's back catalogue was destined to sell at the rate of several million copies annually, while a year on, Hendrix's father attempted to untangle his son's lost fortune by filing a suit against several business companies, associates and ex-lawyers. It took two years for Hendrix Snr to win the rights to Jimi's catalogue, worth in excess of $65 million, and approve the blueprint for a Jimi Hendrix Museum to be built in Seattle.

Further albums were issued during the early nineties, notably, *The Ultimate Experience,* a Top Thirty entrant; *Blues,* which reached the Top Ten; and *In from the Storm,* a compilation of the musician's tracks recorded by various third parties like Sting and Queen's Brian May.

And so it goes on; the music says it all. Hendrix will live forever . . .

(Quotes: *Rock 'n' Roll Babylon* by Gary Herman; *Crosstown Traffic* by Charles Shaar Murray; *Are You Experienced?* by Noel Redding and Carol Appleby)

December 1970

DAVE EDMUNDS

I Hear You Knockin'

In a year that started with the mindless 'Two Little Boys'; spawned the 'Wand'rin' Star' chart-topper by an actor-turned-singer-and-badly and two soul hits 'Tears of a Clown' and 'Band of Gold'; and practically ended with the brain-blowing 'Voodoo Chile', rock 'n' roll was the last musical style the public expected. But when Dave Edmunds sliced the rock, allegiance was switched once more. Variety certainly was the name of this decade's game.

Born in Cardiff, Wales, on 15 April 1944, Dave Edmunds learned to play the guitar at school, where he later formed his first group, The 99ers. He then switched to The Raiders before moving to London where he joined Image during 1966. After a short spell there, Edmunds and Image's drummer, Tommy Riley, and guitarist John Williams worked as a trio. They were signed to EMI Records' Columbia label where they underwent a name change to The Human Beans. Their first single, 'Morning Dew', was released in June 1967. It bombed. The group then became Love Sculpture; Bob James replaced the departing Tommy Riley, and their first single under this name was 'River to Another Day' issued in February 1968. That also bombed.

In an attempt to infiltrate the emerging blues market in Britain, Love Sculpture recorded and released the *Blues Helping* album. Two singles were swiped from this, namely, 'Wang Dang Doodle' and the album's title. Yep, both bombed! Before 1968 ended, Love Sculpture recorded a frenetic instrumental adaptation of the 'Sabre Dance' for John Peel's Radio 1 *Top Gear* programme. Such was the listeners' response that an edited version of the instrumental was rush-released by EMI Records' Parlophone label to reach No. 5 in Britain during November 1968.

To start the next year, the group toured America and released the album *Forms and Feeling* from which 'Farandole' and 'In the Land of the Few' were lifted as singles. Um, both bombed. As Love Sculpture's future looked decidedly shaky now, they disbanded. Edmunds pursued a solo career and before the end of 1969 had signed a recording contract with Gordon Mills's newly formed MAM label. He then returned to South Wales where he constructed his own recording studios called Rockfield to work on his own material and produce other artists, who included Shakin' Stevens and The Sunsets.

In December 1970 Edmunds established himself as a soloist when he recorded his version of the Smiley Lewis classic 'I Hear You Knockin'' penned by Dave Bartholomew and Pearl King. The track was the first release on the MAM label and shot to No. 1 in Britain during December 1970, where it stayed for six long weeks. 'I Hear You Knockin'' also soared to No. 4 in America early in 1971 and went on to sell in excess of three million copies worldwide. Incredibly, Edmunds was unable to capitalise on his success. It took him three years to return to the British chart. In between time, his *Rockpile* album and 'Down Down Down' single were issued. Due to sluggish sales, Edmunds and EMI Records parted company, leaving Edmunds to work under his own Rockfield label, distributed by RCA Records.

The first title to be issued bearing the new label was his cover version of The Ronettes' classic 'Baby I Love You', written and produced by Phil Spector. Released during February 1973 it soared into the British Top Eight. He had recorded 'Baby I Love You' as a tribute to Spector's 'Wall of Sound', which many had unsuccessfully tried to emulate. The follow-up was a further tribute to an American group, this time The Chordettes. Edmunds's version of their 'Born to Be with You' peaked at No. 5 in the chart during July 1973.

During the next year Edmunds moved into the movie world as actor and composer by starring with David Essex and Keith Moon in the film *Stardust,* for which he also wrote the music. (In the film, his material was performed by The Stray Cats, a non-existent group.) After producing the *New Favourites* album for Brinsley Schwarz, Edmunds released his own album, *Subtle as a Flying Mallet.* When this bombed he switched to the Swan Song label owned by Led Zeppelin. Unfortunately Edmunds carried his bad luck on his sleeve – his first two singles in 1976 'Here Comes the Weekend' and 'Where or When' bombed!

Early in 1977 Edmunds introduced his new group to the British public via an extensive tour. Known as Rockpile, the membership included Brinsley Schwarz's Nick Lowe, among others. As a touring outfit they enjoyed considerable success playing rock 'n' roll, but reaching the charts remained a pipe-dream until July 1977 when 'I Knew the Bride', lifted from the *Get It* album, returned Edmunds to the British Top Thirty.

Prior to Rockpile performing at the Knebworth Festival in September 1978, Edmunds suffered a further setback when his *Tracks on Wax* album bombed. Yet, as a performer, he and his group remained in demand, as was proven in October 1978 when they toured America with Elvis Costello. The Costello magic rubbed off, because 'Girls Talk', which he wrote, re-established Edmunds in the British Top Five during July 1979 and encouraged healthy sales of the following album *Repeat When Necessary.*

Following a late-1979 performance in London as a contributor to the People of Kampuchea benefit concert, Edmunds embarked upon a fully-fledged British tour. Two singles were issued during the year – a cover version of Guy Mitchell's 'Singin' the Blues', a Top Thirty hit; and 'Wrong Way', which . . . bombed.

The eighties saw Rockpile split up, and Edmunds recording further solo outings like 'The Race Is On' and albums which included *Information.* He also wrote and produced for The Everly Brothers and Status Quo, among others. Into the nineties, Edmunds, now resident in Los Angeles, headlined a lengthy American tour before issuing the *Closer to the Flame* album via Capitol Records. In 1994 he released the *Plugged In* album and contributed to a recorded musical project honouring the late Buddy Holly.

Dave Edmunds has never been afraid of failure. He's picked himself up and started again. When his groups disbanded, he worked alone. One gutsy guy!

CLIVE DUNN

Grandad

What a colourful fellow and what pleasure he brought to millions of viewers as 'Jonesy' in the spoof wartime BBC TV series *Dad's Army.* The warm-hearted, often stubborn and scatter-brained member of the Home Guard works as a butcher during the day, and his affection for his fellow comrades and customers is weighed by his generosity with cuts of meat or quality sausages! Certainly a superb ally to Captain Mainwaring and Sergeant Wilson. *Dad's Army* was one of BBC TV's most popular of weekly comedies, as evidenced by the regularity with which the series is re-run. The last was as recent as 1997.

Born on 9 January 1920 in Brixton Road, London, to Connie and Robert, Clive Dunn was thrown into the world of the theatre from an early age. His mother was an actress; his father a comedian, and when the couple were touring, their son would be cared for by relatives.

In 1929, Dunn attended a public school in Sevenoaks, Kent, which was both enjoyable and diabolical due to the class system which prevailed in Britain at the time. During the latter part of his education, in 1935, Dunn's father secured him a bit part in the Will Hay movie *Boys Will Be Boys,* for the princely sum of one guinea a day. During this period, Dunn befriended students from Italia Conti's stage school, thus fuelling his ambition to follow his parents into show business.

Dunn left the Sevenoaks school at the age of sixteen to travel the British summer show circuit with his mother, before enrolling in the Conti stage school, where he became involved in several theatre projects. He worked as an assistant to the assistant stage manager at the Richmond Theatre, the 'try-out' venue for London's West End, before working as stage manager for a touring revue titled *Everybody Cheer,* among others. Dunn's career in theatrics was put on hold when the Second World War was declared, whereupon Dunn first worked as a London ambulance driver before joining the Army. He was captured and was a prisoner of war in Austria until liberated by a handful of American troops with, Dunn wrote in his autobiography, 'tommy guns and cigars bristling from every orifice'!

Upon his return to Britain, Dunn still had two years' Army service to complete; he spent the time as a medical orderly treating troops from the Japanese POW camps. When demobbed, he secured the position of second tenor in The Normandy Singers in the show titled *Goody Two Shoes*.

During 1947, he auditioned for and won a part in the BBC TV television revue titled *Funny Thing This Wireless*. The black and white programmes were broadcast live from a tiny studio with no audience. Dunn: 'I played a few comedy character parts in sketches and learned that acting in front of a television camera is more exacting than on stage.' Nine years on, he performed on the television show *New Faces*, and when his contract expired, did not reappear on the small screen for more than five years. From television Dunn returned to the stage at the Players' Theatre, where he was paid £8 weekly. When he discovered that the washer-up in the theatre's restaurant was earning £12 a week, he almost switched careers. Dunn stayed with the Players' Theatre for almost ten years, during which time he worked with future television stars like Hattie Jacques, Eric Sykes, Tommy Trinder, Frankie Howerd and Tony Hancock.

When Dunn returned to television, it was to participate in the first children's variety programme, titled *Buckets and Spades*. This in turn led to parts in the *Tony Hancock Show*, where he played the role of 'a funny old man' for the first time, and sketches with Jacques and Dick Emery. Further roles followed, including that of Ben Gunn in the children's series *Treasure Island*. He then returned to adult television playing Thora Hird's father, an employment clerk in the *Bootsie and Snudge* series, and Old Johnson in Marty Feldman's weekly programmes.

Through television he moved into the movie world, featuring in *Just Like a Woman*, where he played an eccentric German architect; *The Magic Christian*, playing a wine waiter; *She'll Have to Go* with co-stars Bob Monkhouse and Alfred Marks; and *The Fiendish Plot of Doctor Fu Manchu*, Peter Sellers's final comedy movie.

While he was working with Spike Milligan, Dunn's long-standing friend, David Croft, offered him the role of Lance Corporal Jones in a forthcoming television series *Dad's Army*. Unbeknown to him at this time, the role was the major turning point in his career. Dunn: 'I understood the character. Born in 1870, he had fought at the battle of Omdurman under Lord Kitchener. Thirty-one thousand Africans had been mown down by Kitchener's troops, the bodies being piled high on top of each other as they fell in a fanatical religious fervour. This old soldier was now a butcher, aggressively intent on beating Hitler and very keen to get his lance corporal's stripe back.' Dunn had no hesitation in accepting the role.

In 1968, with a cast that included Arthur Lowe, John Le Mesurier, Ian Lavender and John Laurie, the first on-location shooting began in Thetford. Subsequently, the most famous Home Guard battalion was on the march, and so compulsive was the television series that it ran for a staggering ten years! Dunn: 'It is true to say that the BBC bosses were only half keen on the idea of sending up the Home Guard.' Interestingly, initially the show's opening shots showed newsreel splices of the Nazis invading the Low Countries. Dunn: 'In the name of good taste, the credits were altered to a more symbolic, cartoon-like map with moving arrows which were funny in themselves.'

Two *Dad's Army* characters were publicly loved above the rest of the immediate cast, namely, Clive Dunn's character, and Captain Mainwaring, played by Arthur Lowe. Dunn: 'Physically he was almost perfect; he just added a little henna to his hair, a small moustache and some wartime spectacles . . . People would say, "That Captain Mainwaring," every syllable pronounced separately, exactly as it was spelt, "we've got one down our street." Everybody had a Captain Mainwaring'!

In 1969 *Dad's Army* was successfully transferred to the cinema screen, via United Artists, and later the stage, where the show's highlight was the entire cast singing 'The Floral Dance', which was itself transferred to the Palladium stage for The Royal Variety Show.

As *Dad's Army* catapulted to nationwide popularity, the cast's value escalated at the box office. Offers to appear in pantomimes and summer seasons arrived on their agents' desks by the hundred. Ironically, really, as the majority of the cast had never performed in such shows before. However, Dunn took the series' popularity one step further – he recorded.

At a dinner party following Ronnie Corbett's *This Is your Life* surprise show, which featured Dunn among its guests, he was introduced to singer/musician Herbie Flowers, then currently working in the group Blue Mink, headed by Madeline Bell. Dunn had actually quietly started recording an album with an orchestra at London's Abbey Road studios. The sessions were being financed by EMI Records. Dunn: 'I innocently ploughed ahead, totally unpaid, and recorded a few numbers. I was not too thrilled with what I had done so far.' When Flowers later played him a demo tape of a track titled 'Grandad', using Kenny Pickett's lyrics, Dunn decided to record it. Supported by Flowers playing bass guitar and euphonium and a group of young children, Dunn completed the song in Abbey Road.' "I think we've gotta monster, Clive," Herbie said . . . I didn't know at the time that a monster meant an enormous hit. It was a word I was to hear very often in the next few months.'

'Grandad' was released as a single on EMI Records' Columbia label late in 1970. Dunn supported the title with television guest spots that included Bob Monkhouse's *Golden Shot* show, until it was eligible for BBC TV's weekly music programme *Top of the Pops*. Dunn: 'I found myself rehearsing with Olivia Newton-John, who was beginning to make a name, and a strangely dressed young man called Gilbert O'Sullivan.' Following Dunn's appearance, 'Grandad' shot to No. 9 in the British chart, on its way to the top. Then disaster struck. 'The power workers became totally sick of being underpaid and went on strike. During this absolutely justified action one of the places that ceased production was the EMI factory where the records were made.' Christmas was fast approaching; the public demand for the single was thousand-fold as children queued to buy it for their grandads. 'Suddenly the strike was resolved and the factory re-opened. As the lorries queued up outside the building to take the record all over the British Isles, the machines were set to work exclusively on my little single.'

The singer was holidaying in Tunisia when the sickly, sweet, patronising 'Grandad' completed its trek to the top of the British chart in January 1971. All hopes of it being 1970's Christmas single were dashed when Dave Edmunds's 'I Hear You Knockin' ' would not budge.

The follow-up to the chart-topper was dedicated to grandad's partner, 'My Lady Nana'. Proving grandmothers were less popular with grandchilden, the single bombed. Although this failure marked the end of Dunn's recording career, his acting career continued to flourish. When *Dad's Army* had finally cracked its last joke, Dunn returned to the stage where his appearances were interspersed by television spots, including the starring role in the Yorkshire Television weekly series *My Old Man*.

Rightly or wrongly, whatever role Clive Dunn plays, the viewing public will always have him in their minds as Lance Corporal Jonesy, saying those immortal words 'don't panic'. On the other hand, his single 'Grandad' was one of those singles that collected dust, hidden away in a cupboard to be played on the grandparents' birthday or with a splash of alcohol at Christmastime.

(Quotes: *Permission to Speak – An Autobiography* by Clive Dunn)

GEORGE HARRISON

My Sweet Lord

'I didn't have many tunes on Beatles' records . . . I had been feeling a musical constipation, and *All Things Must Pass* was like going to the bathroom and letting it out.' – George Harrison

The Beatles officially disbanded in December 1970, although they recorded their last work together a year earlier. The probable instigator of the break-up was Allen Klein, a financial advisor/manager hired by John Lennon, George Harrison and Ringo Starr to untangle their business knot. Paul McCartney hired his own representatives, Eastman and Eastman from New York, because he mistrusted Klein. McCartney also had another reason to go solo: he married the boss's daughter, Linda Eastman, in March 1969.

George Harrison, born in Wavertree, Liverpool, on 24 February 1943, was anxious to leave his Beatle connections behind because he had tired of the frictions between Lennon and McCartney, their reluctance to record his compositions and, worst of all, being party to the slow decline of the group's artistic strengths.

While still a member of the Fab Four, Harrison flew to Bombay to record the soundtrack for the *Wonderwall* movie (The Bee Gees were originally earmarked to score the music), which was later premiered at the annual Cannes Film Festival in May 1968, while the soundtrack was released in Britain that November. Before the year was over, Harrison had demonstrated his individuality by opening his own publishing company, Singsong Ltd, and had completed his recording commitments with Apple Records' artist, Jackie Lomax.

In 1969 the ex-Beatle and his wife Patti were found guilty of possessing cannabis and fined £250 each. Despite The Beatles having disbanded and the individual members keeping a relatively low profile, the police continued their vendetta against them. Harrison produced the 'Hare Krishna Mantra' single for the Radha Krishna Temple, released on the Apple label. The single became a Top Twenty British hit. In November that year Harrison's composition 'Something' was issued as a single under The Beatles' name. It peaked at No. 4 in Britain, No. 1 in America, and went on to become a 'standard' song, rerecorded countless times by artists like Shirley Bassey in 1970 when she enjoyed a British Top Five hit. Harrison: 'At the last count there were 140 covers of 'Something', Sinatra, Smokey Robinson, Ray Charles [although] my personal favourite is the version by James Brown.'

Harrison was the last Beatle to release a solo album following the break-up. Titled *All Things Must Pass,* it was released in November 1970 on the Beatles' own Apple label, distributed via EMI Records, the group's record company since 1962. Co-produced by Phil Spector and featuring Ringo Starr, Bob Dylan, Ginger Baker, Billy Preston and Eric Clapton, among others, the album was issued to hit the Christmas market. The lavish box set housed three albums that covered a wide musical spectrum. It peaked at No. 4 in Britain before topping the American chart, giving Harrison the distinction of being the first ex-Beatle to secure a No. 1 position over the Christmas period. *All Things Must Pass* went on to sell in excess of three million copies worldwide. He had proved his point!

A track written by Harrison and originally recorded by Billy Preston on his *Encouraging Word* album, was lifted from *All Things Must Pass* as the first single. Titled 'My Sweet Lord' it soared to the top of the British chart in February 1971 where it stayed for five weeks, following the same success in America four months earlier. The single went on to sell in excess of three million copies worldwide. It was reported that Harrison penned 'My Sweet Lord' after hearing the Edwin Hawkins Singers' version of 'Oh Happy Day', itself a No. 2 British hit during May 1969. Worried at what the public might feel hearing an ex-Beatle lyrically glow with religious expressions, Harrison thought long and hard before recording the track himself, saying 'many people fear the words "Lord" and "God" [it] makes them angry, for some strange reason.'

However, he had more to fear than public criticism: the publishing house, Bright Tunes, filed legal proceedings against him claiming his song plagiarised 'He's So Fine' written by Ronnie Mack, and recorded by The Chiffons, who enjoyed a Top Twenty British hit, with it during April 1963. Subsequently, all royalties earned by 'My Sweet Lord' were frozen until a settlement was reached. Five years later, Harrison was found guilty of copyright infringement in a New York court by US District Court Judge Richard Owen, although the judge insisted he believed Harrison copied 'He's So Fine' unintentionally. Harrison wrote in his autobiography *I Me Mine* that he wasn't aware of any similarity between the two tracks until 'My Sweet Lord' received radio airplay. 'People started talking about it and it was then that I thought, "Why didn't I realise?" It would have been very easy to change a note here or there, and not affect the feeling of the record.'

His error cost him dearly. Bright Tunes was eventually paid in excess of $500,000 in settlement, but the case ran on. Allen Klein purchased the rights to 'He's So Fine', thereby giving him the right to continue suing for damages. Which he did. This exasperated Harrison to the point that he wanted to give 'My Sweet Lord' to Klein to be free of it. 'It's always been in escrow and as far as I'm concerned the effect the song has had far exceeds any bitching that's been going on between copyright people.' Then to add further to Harrison's plight, Jonathan King recorded 'He's So Fine' using the instrumentation from 'My Sweet Lord', while The Chiffons themselves, presumably at Klein's instigation, released 'My Sweet Lord'!

Following a request from Ravi Shankar, Harrison arranged two concerts in New York to help the victims of the war in Bangladesh. Harrison: 'The Concert for Bangladesh was just a moral stance . . . what we did showed that musicians and people are more humane than politicians.' Joining him on the Madison Square Garden stage were Ringo Starr, Bob Dylan, Leon Russell and Eric Clapton. However, despite the best intentions, this effort turned sour. The concert proceeds, estimated to be $250,000 were frozen, leaving Harrison no option but to match the donations with his personal money. The subsequent concert albums and movie raised a further $15 million, but regrettably, due to continuing legal hassles, only part of the money actually fed the starving war victims.

In June 1973 Harrison released his second album proper titled *Living in the Material World*. It was a scorcher and topped the American chart, reaching No. 2 in Britain. 'Give Me Love (Give Me Peace on Earth)' taken from the album as a single soared to No. 1 in America and No. 8 in Britain. Harrison: 'This song [was] a prayer and personal statement between me, the Lord, and whoever likes it.'

A year on, to maintain his continued identity away from The Beatles, he established his own record label, Dark Horse, where apart from himself, Ravi Shankar and Splinter were the first signed acts. In June 1974, Harrison decided to tour America with Shankar and his close friend Billy Preston as support acts. Once more his best intentions fell flat. Audiences slated his performances, claiming he misrepresented The Beatles' material. And before the year of mixed successes had closed, he issued the *Dark Horse* album, his first to bomb in Britain. American sales, though, rewarded him with a No. 4 hit. 'Ding Dong', the track lifted for a single in 1975, stalled in the Top Forty both in Britain and America.

During October 1975 Harrison released his album *Extra Texture (Read All about It)*. This fared better than the last, peaking in the Top Ten in

America and the Top Twenty in Britain and was the last to be released bearing the Apple Records label. 'You' was swiped from the album for single release in October 1975 and stalled in the American Top Twenty, reaching the Top Forty in Britain. Through to the end of the decade, Harrison recorded for his Dark Horse label, distributed by Warner Bros, garnering a string of minor hits, including his eponymous album in 1979 which spawned 'Blow Away', a No. 16 American hit and a Top Sixty British entry.

To start the next decade, the ex-Beatle published his autobiography, titled *I Me Mine,* forcing record buyers to wait until 1981 before releasing his next album, *Somewhere in England,* from which 'All Those Years Ago' was lifted to become a No. 13 British hit, the same position it had previously enjoyed in America. By 1985 his recording career had, to be fair, disintegrated. Warner Bros subsequently dropped Dark Horse from its label roster, leaving Harrison free to concentrate on film production. As an actor he made an appearance in *Water* alongside Ringo Starr and Eric Clapton while on the music front, he guested occasionally on stage and on record. That was all the public were treated to until 1987 when he soared into the British chart to No. 2 with 'Got my Mind Set on You'. The single returned him to the top spot in America during January 1988. The follow-up, though, was a poke at The Beatles' success titled 'When We Was Fab'; a Top Thirty hit in both America and Britain in February 1988. Four months later 'This Is Love' stalled in the British Top Sixty. Behind scenes, meanwhile, Harrison was beavering away on another project.

During August 1988, rumours circulated the media regarding a faceless music group calling themselves The Traveling Wilburys, who would issue an album before the close of the year. All was revealed when *Traveling Wilburys: Volume One* hit the record stores, confirming a superstar group membership of Harrison, Tom Petty, Bob Dylan, Jeff Lynne and Roy Orbison. The album spawned the singles 'Handle with Care' and 'End of the Line' in October 1988 and March 1989 when both became minor British hits. Encouraged by this success, a second album was issued during 1990.

Also in 1990, when most people had rightly forgotten the law suit regarding 'My Sweet Lord', it reared its ugly head again. After twenty years of litigation, Judge Richard Owen's final judgment read that Allen Klein owned the publishing rights to 'He's So Fine' for the world, excluding certain territories which belonged to Harrison. For this, Harrison paid Klein in excess of $250,000!

Really, George, was it all worth it?

(Quotes: *I Me Mine* by George Harrison; *Off the Record* by Joe Smith; *Rock 'n' Roll Babylon* by Gary Herman)

March 1971

MUNGO JERRY

Baby Jump

'I've always had frizzy hair. [My sideburns] developed when I decided to only shave the width of an electric razor up the bottom of my neck and my chin. With that hair and those sideburns, it began to look as if I had a hat on!' – Ray Dorset

As 'In the Summertime' introduced the Mungo Jerry 'sound' to the public, most people believed the follow-up would follow the same pattern. Not so. 'Baby Jump' abandoned jug/blues for what could be described as rockabilly/rock. Like 'In the Summertime', this new single was also a multi-tracked disc, and when first issued it peaked in the chart at No. 32, only to turn itself around to soar to the top of the British chart in March 1971, nearly a year after the group's debut chart-topper. Both singles were included on Mungo Jerry's second album, titled *Electronically Tested,* reputedly so named after the guarantee printed on a packet of Durex. Irrespective of the name's origin, the album reached the Top Twenty, and heralded the start of disharmony between Dorset and fellow group member Paul King, who felt his material was being overlooked. Indeed, none of his compositions were included on the British release of *Electronically Tested,* so he might have had a point.

'Lady Rose' was the group's next maxi-single in May 1971. It stalled in the Top Five due to restricted radio airplay on one of the songs, 'Have a Whiff on Me' (originally intended to follow 'In the Summertime'), which referred to cocaine use. When the Director of Public Prosecutions threatened legal action, Pye Records withdrew the disc, immediately replacing the offending track with the title 'She Rowed'. But valuable selling time had been lost and the disc missed the top spot.

During September 1971, Mungo Jerry took a stab at the Establishment with the multi-tracked single 'You Don't Have to Be in the Army to Fight in the War'. It peaked at No. 13 in the chart. Early the next year, the group toured Australia and the Far East and upon their return to Britain, Ray Dorset told the media he had been sacked from the group. It later transpired that he had wanted to introduce a drummer to the group – previously they had worked without one – but Paul King and Colin Earl disagreed. Their record company then stepped in, claiming Dorset was Mungo Jerry, therefore the two musicians were redundant.

Dorset went on to record his debut solo album, *Cold Blue Excursion*, while Paul King pursued his own career, first as a soloist, then as a member of The King Earl Boogie Band. 'Open Up' was the first outing by Mungo Jerry without King and Earl – but with a drummer. It became a Top Twenty hit in April 1972, but fans mourned the loss of the Mungo Jerry 'sound'. Following the release of the controversial *Boot Power* album, the group underwent several personnel changes before issuing their next single, 'Alright, Alright, Alright', an adaptation of the popular French song 'Et Moi, Et Moi, Et Moi'. This re-established Mungo Jerry in the British Top Three, but was their last runaway hit. 'Wild Love', its follow-up, staggered into the Top Forty in November 1973, while 'Long Legged Woman Dressed in Black' was the group's final serious stab at the big time, peaking in the Top Twenty.

Mungo Jerry switched record companies to Polydor Records before Ray Dorset opened his own label, Satellite. It was mildly successful. Dorset then went on to compose themes for television programmes and other artists, including Kelly Marie's 'Feels Like I'm in Love', a British chart-topper in 1980.

To celebrate Mungo Jerry's twenty-fifth anniversary in the music business in 1995, the group embarked upon an extensive British tour with Marmalade, among others. And there is no reason why Ray Dorset and his musicians should not continue along these lines for years to come.

Also see: 'In the Summertime', July 1970

(Quotes: *Record Collector*, 1995)

April 1971

T REX

Hot Love

'["Hot Love"] was done as a happy record, and I wanted to make a 12-bar record a hit [like] "High Heel Sneakers", though I wasn't sure that it would be a hit.' – Marc Bolan

Marc Bolan was born Mark Feld on 30 September 1947 in Hackney Hospital, London, the second son of Simeon and Phyllis. The family was Jewish and lived in Stoke Newington, a traditional Jewish suburb of the city.

Educated at the Northwood Primary and the William Wordsworth Secondary schools, Bolan was a passionate cinema goer, addicted to horror and science fiction movies. Even at this young age, he preferred his fantasy world to reality. Bolan said, 'I always had trouble at school. I failed my eleven-plus. I was really quite good, except I was hopeless at maths . . . I always hung around with the rough kids. Perhaps it was because I was in the lowest class.'

At eight years old, while he was running with the Sharks gang, wearing his father's Army helmet, Bolan was bought his first drum kit. A year later, he was given a guitar. While still at school, the youngster helped at his mother's fruit stall, situated in the vicinity of the 2I's coffee bar, which in the late fifties was the launching pad for British pop stars like Cliff Richard and Tommy Steele. Some of the coffee bar's magic rubbed off; when Bolan was twelve he joined his first group, Susie and The Hula Hoops, whose membership was guitarist Stephen Gould and vocalist Helen Shapiro, later the child star of the sixties, with huge-selling singles like 'Don't Treat Me Like a Child', 'You Don't Know' and 'Walkin' Back to Happiness'. Shapiro's overnight stardom heavily influenced young Bolan's future.

At this juncture Bolan became interested in clothes; this in turn led to modelling assignments – his classic looks and lithe body attracting fashion photographers' lenses. One of his first sessions was with photographer Don McCullin, and through an agency he became a regular model for mail order catalogues and John Temple stores, where his cardboard cut-out likeness was seen in the store windows. Bolan: 'I didn't like it much, I didn't like the suits . . . But it was worth a grand!'

The youngster was fourteen years old when he and his family moved to a prefabricated house in South London, where he was educated at the Hill Croft School. His stay was short, though; he was expelled. 'I only had about six months to go . . . No one seemed to mind very much.' Subsequently, he concentrated on his modelling career, while his spare time was devoted to mastering the guitar. Working in Edgers, a clothes store in Tooting Broadway, and washing up dishes in the local Wimpey Bar, were his means of earning regular money, until he decided to follow his instincts and join the folk music circuit as a singer/poet/guitarist, Toby Tyler. His act impressed Allan Warren sufficiently for him to become Bolan's manager; Warren believed his new client had a Cliff

Richard quality! With this in mind (or not) Bolan went on to record a version of soul singer Betty Everett's hit 'You're No Good' on acetate for an EMI Records' audition. The company rejected the track, whereupon Warren left Bolan to his own devices.

Diverting from music, Bolan befriended actor Riggs O'Hara, and together they would frequent the National Theatre. In time, Bolan appeared in a bit part in the Sam Kydd television series *Orlando*. Bolan said, 'I did all that because I didn't really know what I wanted to do.' His confusion then took him to France, where he lived in Paris for six months. 'I lived in a forest for a while, and then with this cat who was a magician in a chateau which had about forty rooms.' He called the elderly magician 'The Wizard', and was introduced to the world of mythology, the study of magic, yoga, and the art of thought projection.

Upon his return to Britain and with untold inspiration, Bolan ploughed his energies into composing, using the teachings of the Wizard as his guide. He then trekked record companies until A. & R. executives tired of his presence. Eventually, Decca Records conceded to sign him as an artist; Bolan delivered an acetate of the track 'The Wizard', bearing the name Marc Bowland on the label, as his first release. When the single hit the stores during November 1965, the label read 'Marc Bolan'. The track's lyrical content, based around his French experiences, enthralled critics, who enthused that he was a fantasy poet; a strange young man with a weird background. Despite media interest, and a treasured spot on the Friday night music programme *Ready, Steady, Go!,* the public rejected the magical slice of vinyl.

The title 'The Third Degree' was issued as the follow-up single during June 1966. That likewise bombed, prompting Decca Records to end their business arrangement with the singer. Before 1966 closed, though, Bolan switched to Columbia Records, where he met and worked with producer Simon Napier-Bell. The first result of their union, the 'Hippy Gumbo' single, followed the fate of the previous releases.

Meanwhile, in another section of town, John's Children, possibly the first glam-rock group, who had enjoyed American success with their single 'The Love I Thought I'd Found', and moderate sales with 'Just What You Want, Just What You'll Get', had lost one of their membership. Napier-Bell believed it would be a wise career move for Bolan to fill the vacancy. After a recording session where Bolan immediately took over the writing responsibilities, John's Children released his composition 'Desdemona' midway through 1967. The title never reached its full selling potential; it was banned by BBC Radio because the lyrics included the phrase 'lift up your skirts and fly'. Therefore, a further Bolan track, 'Midsummer Night's Scene', was earmarked as the follow-up single because nobody could object to that. The title was pressed and ready to ship, when, for some reason, it was replaced with the third-party composition 'Come and Play with Me in the Garden'.

After three months in John's Children, Bolan felt creatively strangled, and pined for his freedom. Within months of his departure, the group itself disbanded, but not before releasing the single 'Go Go Girl', a play on Bolan's composition 'Mustang Ford'.

From John's Children, Bolan formed the group Tyrannosaurus Rex, in tribute to the giant of earth creatures. He recruited Steve Peregrine Took, born Stephen Porter, in Eltham, Kent, on 28 July 1949, after he had responded to an advertisement placed by Bolan in the music weekly, *Melody Maker*. Ben Cartland was likewise recruited from the same advertisement.

The group debuted at the Electric Garden in London's Covent Garden during July 1967. A month on, several Bolan compositions were included on *The Perfumed Garden,* John Peel's radio show, transmitted by Radio London. From this airing, Peel and Bolan cemented a lifetime friendship. The DJ was so convinced his friend would become a top-selling act that he insisted any of his bookings, including his weekend stints at London club the Middle Earth, included Tyrannosaurus Rex.

Early in 1968, Bolan met Brooklyn-born record producer, Tony Visconti, following a group performance at the Middle Earth. Visconti shared Peel's enthusiasm for Bolan, negotiated a recording contract with Regal Zonophone, an EMI Records' subsidiary, and with limited resources, recorded an album with the group. Despite Bolan condemning the disc, later titled *My People Were Fair and Had Sky in their Hair, but Now They're Content to Wear Stars on their Brow,* (bring back one-worded album titles!) it was issued during July 1968. Prior to this, Tyrannosaurus Rex released their debut single, 'Debora', recorded in one take, that March. The track peaked in the British Top Forty: at last, Bolan was a charting artist. Following these releases and having tasted success, the group performed, with other acts, at the Woburn Music Festival, staged in Bedfordshire, and the National Jazz and Blues Festival, held in Middlesex. To complete the year, the second single, 'One Inch Rock', stalled in the British Top Thirty. Nonetheless, it was another charting title.

To start 1969, Tyrannosaurus Rex issued the 'Pewter Suitor' single; it bombed. Likewise, their album *Unicorn* released in June. Bolan was devastated; both releases were aimed at the hippie movement who, for the first time, failed to support them, prompting Bolan to rethink their future material. As he thought, his book of poetry, titled *The Warlock of Love,* was published by Lupus via book stores and mail order. It went on to sell 20,000 copies, elevating Bolan to one of Britain's top-selling poets (as remarkable as it now seems).

Like the majority of British acts who have brushed with the mainstream chart, Tyrannosaurus Rex next wanted to crack America. To this end, and following the release of the British Top Fifty entrant 'King of the Rumbling Spires', they visited the USA in mid-1969. The tour was a disaster from start to finish, partly due to Took's increasing acid habit, which would reduce him to nothing more than a vegetable on stage. This forced Bolan to return to Britain without him, vowing at the same time, that he would only return to America when he had a charting single. However, good did come from the visit; he befriended singer/composer/producer Gloria Jones, who would become his future partner and mother of his son.

Obviously Took left the membership, to be replaced by Mickey Finn, born in Thornton Heath, Surrey, on 3 June 1947, whom Bolan had previously met in a Westbourne Grove restaurant. Finn, late of the Hapshash and The Coloured Coat outfit, became Bolan's percussionist, excelling at 'bongos, congas, stomp, atmosphere and dance'. Bolan said of Took's departure: 'We just grew apart. We never were that together. Steve was a really good percussionist, but when it got to expanding, we just couldn't make it work together.'

With new ideas, the duo retired to Wales for rehearsal and recording, with the intention of completing the future album *A Beard of Stars.*

By this stage in his career, Bolan was represented by Blackhill Enterprises, whose other clients included Pink Floyd, and who, apart from representing his business interests, introduced him to his first and only wife June. They went on to share a Notting Hill Gate flat; cold water, no bathroom and a £3.10s a week rent. This was their home for three years; June worked nine-to-five, while Bolan composed and performed, earning up to £10 nightly. To say they survived rather than lived would be a fitting description of their early life together.

And still he recorded. The single 'By the Light of the Magical Moon' saw in the new decade, which inadvertently heralded the turning point in the young poet's career. Hot on the disc's heels, *A Beard of Stars* followed, reaching the British Top Thirty.

Steve Currie, born in Grimsby, Lincolnshire, on 20 May 1947, was recruited to the group as bass player, and, personally-speaking, Bolan married June at the Kensington Registry Office. Bolan said, 'It seemed like a funky thing to do at the time.' Following a composing session locked away in their flat's minute music room, Bolan changed his musical direction to write 'Ride a White Swan'. This title went on to become the debut release on Fly Records by T Rex. As Visconti was responsible for the new recording deal, he insisted the mouthful 'Tyrannosaurus Rex' be abbreviated; radio DJs had always suffered with the pronunciation, newspaper proofreaders with the spelling. Besides, the name looked more compact on record labels.

'Ride a White Swan' shot to No. 2 in Britain during November 1970, pushing the album simply titled *T Rex* into the Top Twenty. When released in America in February 1971, the single peaked at No. 8; nonetheless, Bolan glowed in the success he had craved. 'Ride a White Swan' was his make or break release. 'The success . . . is a gas . . . I know for a fact that "White Swan" is getting to people who have never been interested before and maybe some of them will buy the next album.' Within days of charting, T Rex embarked upon a British tour, with Bolan stipulating that no ticket price should exceed 10 shillings (50p) per ticket, a move that other groups, like The Rolling Stones, would adopt.

With 'Ride a White Swan', Bolan introduced the T Rex sound to the public, a musical style he called 'cosmic rock': uncluttered, uncomplicated, and to the point. And it was with his next single that the singing poet showed his true talent in more ways than one. His cosmic music was matched by his stage presence and aura. To outshine his contemporaries, Bolan used make-up, particularly around his eyes which were, in any event, hidden by a mass of unruly dark curly hair. He often wore women's clothes, usually satin trousers and jackets, showered in sequins and glitter, with his effeminate style drawing attention to his undeclared bisexuality. Unintentionally, he heralded the birth of glam-rock; others followed but never equalled him.

'Hot Love' was the title of the single that shot to the top of the British chart in April 1971, a position it held for six long weeks. It reached No. 72 in America. Bolan modestly claimed it was a pure teenage bopping single, where 'lots of friends joined in on backing vocals and handclaps', written because he wanted to experiment with a rock song: 'I know it's exactly like a million other songs, but I hope it's got a little touch of me in it too.'

More significantly, the single was the first in a series of British chart-toppers, all carrying Bolan's touch of 'cosmic magic' within its simplistic musical grooves.

Also see: 'Get It On', August 1971; 'Telegram Sam', February 1972; 'Metal Guru', June 1972

(Quotes: *Electric Warrior: The Marc Bolan Story* by Paul Sinclair)

May 1971

DAVE AND ANSIL COLLINS

Double Barrel

Squeezed in between a slice of rockabilly rock and an excitable, chirpy pop song, this three minutes-plus of commercial reggae was a bolt of inspiration. At the very least, then, it was another example of the 'anything goes' attitude of the seventies.

Written and produced by Winston Riley, the single titled 'Double Barrel' was issued on the Technique label to top the British chart in May 1971, where it stayed for two weeks.

Dave and Ansil Collins, two Jamaican reggae singers, followed this chart-topper with 'Monkey Spanner' that June. The title peaked at No. 7 in the British chart.

These singles were the duo's only British hits, and were, incidentally, swiped from their debut album, titled *Double Barrel*. Ansil Collins went on to drift through countless reggae labels during the eighties, with little success.

'Double Barrel' was only the second reggae single to become a British chart-topper. Desmond Dekker and The Aces' disc 'The Israelites' was the first in March 1969. By the way, reggae music rarely received the credit due to it; the music appealed to a cult following whose support usually ensured low chart placings, if that. In time, though, British producers introduced their own type of diluted reggae which, of course, was successful.

Ain't nothing like the real thing!

June 1971

DAWN

Knock Three Times

Take a trio whose first single was issued before the membership had actually met, who then reluctantly pursued a recording career, and who by the end of that career had sold in excess of 28 million discs! That's Dawn.

Born Michael Anthony Orlando Cassivitis in Manhattan, New York, on 3 April 1944, to Greek/Puerto Rican parents, Tony Orlando's first singing experience was in 1957 as a member of the doo-wop unit The Five Gents. When not singing with the group, Orlando recorded demo tracks in the hope of securing a recording deal. When The Five Gents disbanded it left the thirteen-year-old no option but to pursue a solo career. From the outset he badgered countless record companies for work until he cut demo recordings for Aldon Music's staff writer Carole King. These included 'Halfway to Paradise', which Epic Records later released as Orlando's debut single during 1961. It reached the American Top Forty, while British singer Billy Fury enjoyed the greater success with a No. 3 hit in May 1961.

Tony Orlando then recorded 'Bless You', composed by Aldon Music's writers Barry Mann and Cynthia Weil. The single swooped into the American Top Twenty, becoming Orlando's debut British hit when it peaked in the Top Five during October 1961. Encouraged by this success, seventeen-year-old Orlando toured the two countries. As he told author Barry Scott, 'Most of the people who were making hit records and travelling around the world were no older than sixteen, seventeen years old. The Paul Ankas and Frankie Avalons [were] all basically kids! It was a great education.'

Following the release of the poor-selling American single 'Happy Times (Are Here to Stay)', Orlando retired from the spotlight to join another music publishing house, Robbins, Feist and Miller. From there he switched to April-Blackwood. Orlando: 'I got my education in music publishing and then I went on to became a general manager at CBS. Some of the people with whom I was working were James Taylor, Laura Nyro, Blood Sweat and Tears and The Grateful Dead. Their music was very much a part of my life then.'

In 1969, Orlando rejoined show business as a singer. His lead vocal was added to a track titled 'Make Believe', later issued by a bunch of studio musicians called Wind. The track reached the American Top Thirty. As Wind did not actually exist, and as the musicians had already been paid a session fee, they received no royalties from the single's sales. So Orlando continued to struggle financially.

A trio of vocalists named Dawn had recorded the track 'Candida' for Bell Records. The company was keen to issue it but disliked the male vocals. Instead of dumping the song, the producers Hank Medress (late of the vocal group The Tokens) and Dave Appell approached Orlando to add his vocals to the backing track featuring the remaining female duo. Once completed, Orlando dismissed 'Candida', believing its destination was the rejection bin. Not so. Two months after his vocals were added, he heard the track being played on the radio in New York. In October 'Candida' stormed into the American Top Three. When released in Britain in January 1971, the title peaked in the Top Ten. Orlando was a recording artist by accident, singing with two girls he didn't know!

The follow-up single was the L. Russell Brown and Irwin Levine composition 'Knock Three Times', which soared to the top of the American chart early in 1971. With this unexpected success, Bell Records were (naturally) anxious to present Dawn to the public and it was at this juncture that Tony Orlando met Joyce Wilson, born in Detroit, Michigan, on 14 December 1946, and Telma Hopkins, born in Louisville, Kentucky, on 28 October 1948. The girls were close friends and studio session singers. They had, for example, provided back-up vocals for Motown chart-toppers, like the Four Tops' 'Reach Out I'll Be There' and Marvin Gaye's 'I Heard It through the Grapevine.' Neither girl was particularly interested in becoming a full-time singer and the thought of performing wasn't part of their future plans either. In fact, Hopkins was due to marry, but such was Orlando's persistence that she cancelled the wedding.

'Knock Three Times' crossed the Atlantic to become a British chart-topper in June 1971, a position it held for five weeks. Orlando: 'I did not think "Knock Three Times" would be a hit. I didn't think anybody would buy a record about a guy knocking once on a ceiling and twice on a pipe!'

Ironically, Dawn was less successful with their next single. Titled 'What Are You Doing Sunday', it stalled at No. 3 in the British chart in July 1971, while abysmal sales in America failed to push it higher than the Top Forty. Their selling power then worsened; during 1972 their success in Britain was negligible, while in America they issued two minor hits, namely 'Runaway' and 'Vaya con Dios'.

Dawn's demise was quickly predicted by the media, but this time the hangmen were wrong. The trio was to rise again with a song that many felt was as irritating as 'Knock Three Times'. It was American tweeness personified.

Also see: 'Tie a Yellow Ribbon round the Old Oak Tree', May 1973

(Quotes: *We Had Joy We Had Fun* by Barry Scott)

MIDDLE OF THE ROAD

Chirpy Chirpy Cheep Cheep

What is it about ridiculous record titles that attracts the public? And one can't always blame Europe because America has produced its fair share – take The Exciters' 1964 release 'Do Wah Diddy Diddy', for example. However, this time the Continent was well and truly responsible.

Formed in Scotland and known originally as Los Caracas, this group comprised lead vocalist Sally Carr, with Ken Andrew, Ian Lewis and Eric Lewis. As Los Caracas, they were unknown in Britain but had built up a healthy following on the Continent. And it was there they first heard Lally Scott's composition 'Chirpy Chirpy Cheep Cheep', a song, many believed, of extremely low esteem. Nonetheless, the group, now known as Middle of the Road, recorded it (as did Mac and Katie Kissoon, who struggled into the Top Fifty during June 1971), RCA Records released it, and it went to No. 1 in the British chart during July 1971. It stayed at the top for five weeks. Could returning Continental holiday-makers take all the blame?

The follow-up single was an equally lightweight slice of nonsense about two Scottish clans, titled 'Tweedle Dee, Tweedle Dum'. Already a European chart-topper, it was issued in Britain during September 1971 to reach No. 2 in the chart.

Before the year was out, Middle of the Road issued their third and last Top Five single titled 'Soley Soley'. Their selling power was maintained for a further year at a reduced level. During March 1972 'Sacramento' first hit the Top Fifty, then upon re-entry peaked in the Top Thirty, while midway through the year, 'Samson and Delilah', a No. 26 placing, ended their chart career.

Aside from this handful of discs, Middle of the Road released two albums, namely *Chirpy Chirpy Cheep Cheep* and *Drive Up*, summing up their British recording career. Like others of that ilk, the group turned to the lucrative cabaret circuit, although it was thought that with such a small repertoire they wouldn't be on stage long!

T REX

Get It On

'I suppose to the average rock 'n' roller I might be considered slightly eccentric . . . I did study magic . . . and I learnt a lot about the other things that go on in the universe.' – Marc Bolan

After four stabs at the British chart, T Rex finally secured the top spot with 'Hot Love' in April 1971. It reached the Top Eighty in America. This title was the first in a run of Top Ten singles which lasted until mid-1973.

With his music, Bolan created a vital yet basic sound which graduated into glam-rock, without thunderous trappings from over-indulgent studio technicians. His lyrics, often confusing, were sharp and spontaneous, and it was this combination and his waif-life appearance in satin and silk androgynous clothes and his man-child persona, that attracted his expanding following. It is true that throughout his career, his public remained loyal, often to the point of obsession. Few artists can attract this kind of adolescent devotion.

Of course, T Rex was now big business. The group now played to capacity audiences, and the rumblings of T Rex fever threatened to explode nationwide. It was no surprise when 'Get It On', the follow-up to 'Hot Love', likewise shot to the top of the British chart, during August 1971, a position it held for four weeks. It became Bolan's biggest-selling single, and the mother album *Electric Warrior,* issued a month later, was another British chart-topper, and reached the Top Forty in America. 'Get It On' featured a backing track of guitar, drums and bass, which was then double tracked. Onto this, sax and strings were added. The song, like the bulk of *Electric Warrior,* was recorded in America and Britain. Of the album, the singer believed it was the 'loosest' he had recorded: 'It was done between gigs in America and I was essentially concerned with putting down rough tracks to establish a sound, but they felt so good that we kept them for the finished tracks. It's a highly communicable album and that's the name of the game as far as I'm concerned.'

To capitalise on this recent success, the album titled *The Best of T Rex,* crammed with Tyrannosaurus Rex material, was released by Fly Records in the knowledge that their recording contract with the group had nearly expired, and Bolan was looking elsewhere. Indeed he was. With a pair of newly-formed companies, Wizard Productions and Warrior Music Projects, he signed a licensing deal with EMI Records during November 1971, the same month as Fly Records issued a title never earmarked for a single, namely 'Jeepster'. The record company's cheek earned them a No. 2 British hit – and a furious artist!

Bolan's T Rex was in constant demand for concert dates. Indeed, the line-up performed at the Weeley Festival, before embarking upon a British tour through to the end of 1971. During this wild trek, Bolan experienced serious fan mania for the first time, both the stripping of headlights, door handles and windscreen wipers from his car, and the clothes from his body, as he attempted to escape clawing hands. Yet he loved it all! 'Isn't it nice that someone can like you enough to put your picture on the bedroom wall? But the frightening thing is the sheer strength of it all. I know they don't want to hurt me.'

Bolan's following would rather sacrifice themselves than see any harm come to their musical elf. 'My fans are the most important thing in my life . . . I owe everything to the kids and for that reason, I always try and please them.'

Also see: 'Hot Love', April 1971; 'Telegram Sam', February 1972; 'Metal Guru', June 1972

(Quotes: *Electric Warrior: The Marc Bolan Story* by Paul Sinclair)

September 1971

DIANA ROSS

I'm Still Waiting

'Starting a career on my own was not as difficult as people might think. Toward the end of my time with The Supremes, I had already been doing lots of performing without them and I had gone into the studio to record a few songs on my own. Once we had become Diana Ross and The Supremes, I was already separated, still a part of the group and, at the same time, not a part of the group.' – Diana Ross

It was with these words that Diana Ross, born on 26 March 1944, in Detroit, Michigan, left The Supremes to embark upon the rocky road to solo stardom, after leading the trio for almost a decade, living the classic rags to riches story so well loved by the American public.

The Supremes' final single, the aptly titled 'Someday We'll Be Together', released in America during October 1969, soared to No. 1. A month later, the title was issued in Britain, where it peaked instead at No. 13 in the chart. The track actually featured Ross only, with two session singers, plus the occasional spoken word from its composer, Johnny Bristol. 'Someday We'll Be Together' marked the end of a musical era; the world's most famous and, of course, successful female trio in history was no more. Public feelings were mixed and, naturally, many blamed Ross's relentless ambition for the group's demise.

However, despite public opinion, all was not lost as The Supremes lived on as a working group with Ross's replacement, Jean Terrell, who had already been rehearsed and groomed as a Supreme. Terrell was later introduced to a star-studded audience during Diana Ross and The Supremes' final highly-charged and emotional concert at the Frontier Hotel, Las Vegas, on 14 January 1970.

Within weeks of her departure and with the words 'Good evening ladies and gentlemen, welcome to the "let's-see-if-Diana-Ross-can-make-it-alone-show," ' the ex-Supreme stepped on the New York stage at the Waldorf Astoria for the start of a three-week season. It was the most terrifying night of her career so far, yet she stunned her capacity audience by working her way through $60,000 worth of dazzling costumes, various comedy routines and twenty songs. Her expensive wardrobe included eight costume changes, casting her in roles from elegant lady to ten-year-old child. However, many believed, the show's high spot was that featuring memories of The Supremes, where Ross sang a medley of their hits while pictures of the group were screened across the back of the stage. For some years, Ross felt obligated to include Supremes' material in her act, despite enjoying a successful career as a soloist.

Although Ross was instantly successful as a performer, she struggled with her debut solo single, the drug-related title 'Reach Out and Touch (Somebody's Hand)' written and produced by Nickolas Ashford and Valerie Simpson. Despite the heavyweight backing, the single struggled to No. 33 in the British chart, making it thirteen rungs higher in America. This failure to sell discs was not in the gameplan devised by Motown founder Berry Gordy. However, the situation reversed when Ashford and Simpson reworked the Marvin Gaye and Tammi Terrell 1967 hit 'Ain't No Mountain High Enough'. Ross's version carried her to the top of the American chart, selling one million copies en route, and reaching No. 6 in Britain.

Following her solo stage debut, Ross celebrated two further major milestones prior to the release of 'I'm Still Waiting' as a single. She married artists' manager, Robert Silberstein, in relative secrecy on 20 January 1971 at the Silver Bells Chapel, Las Vegas. It was generally thought she would marry Berry Gordy; they had been a couple for some considerable time, and he was the father of her first daughter, Rhonda. But not so. On the professional front, she starred in *Diana!*, her first television spectacular shown Stateside in April and five months later in Britain. Guest stars included comedians Bill Cosby and Danny Thomas, while additional music was provided by Motown's newest young signing, The Jackson 5. The hour-long special showcased the star's talent as an all-round entertainer, although the most remarkable sequences were her transformation into Hollywood's greatest – Charlie Chaplin, Harpo Marx and W.C. Fields.

It's fair to say that Ross's first British solo chart-topper, 'I'm Still Waiting', was annoyingly unimaginative, particularly when compared to her emotional 'Remember Me' in May 1971, which soared to No. 7 in the British chart and No. 16 in America; or her second reworking of an established hit, namely the Four Tops' 'Reach Out I'll Be There'. Ross's version bypassed Britain, and faltered in the American Top Thirty. Written by Deke Richards, 'I'm Still Waiting' was hidden on the singer's third solo album, titled *Surrender,* due for American release during July 1971. DJ Tony Blackburn, who hosted Radio 1's Breakfast Show, played an advance copy of the album, selecting 'I'm Still Waiting' as a potential single. To prove his point, and his faith in the title, he played it constantly on air until Motown agreed to release it. Within days, the title raced to the top of the British chart in September 1971, a position it held for four weeks. Ross changed her touring schedule to visit London on a hasty promotional trip. The Americans failed to share the British love of shmaltz; 'I'm Still Waiting' struggled to reach the Top Sixty. Incidentally, the single was rereleased during 1976 to reach the Top Fifty during the November.

While a member of The Supremes, Ross had wanted to prove herself as a serious actress, but to date her roles had been decidedly flimsy due to the nature of the showbiz vehicles open to her. That was to change in 1972 when she undertook a challenging role that most people believed she was incapable of mastering, that of Billie Holiday in the movie *Lady Sings the Blues.* The film was a dramatisation of the life of the legendary jazz/blues singer, in both its glory and despair. Ross gave a spectacular performance which earned her a Grammy Award nomination; she lost to Liza Minelli for her role in *Cabaret.* However, the singer received the Golden Globe Best New Star Award, while the film itself was showered with honours, including three NAACP Image Awards. The *Lady Sings the Blues* soundtrack earned Ross a gold disc, as it topped the American chart for two weeks, becoming Motown's fastest-selling album, shifting 300,000 copies during its first week of release. The movie itself grossed in excess of $6 million during its opening days. Diana Ross must have been doing something right!

From this gruelling yet rewarding role, the singer switched to the lightweight character of a fashion designer in her next movie, *Mahogany*. Ross wrote in her autobiography: 'I really enjoyed doing that movie because it was all about fashion. I love clothes, everyone knows that, and with *Mahogany* I was given the opportunity to design all the clothes and wardrobe for Tracy Chambers, the character I played.' The singer then went on to play in a remake of *The Wizard of Oz*, titled *The Wiz*, with Michael Jackson as her co-star. Turning down the lead role in *Bodyguard*, which catapulted Whitney Houston into movie stardom, Ross intended to star in the life story of Josephine Baker. When plans were shelved, she tackled another serious role, that of a schizophrenic in the highly-disturbing movie titled *Out of Darkness*, released during 1995 on commercial video.

However, back to the music and 1971. As 'I'm Still Waiting' enjoyed such a high profile, Ross was, naturally enough, compelled to include it in her British concert repertoire. Thankfully, her live interpretation of the track was far more emotive than the original on vinyl.

Her record titles turned from bad to worse. Her sixth hit, in May 1972, was 'Doobedood'N Doobedoobedood'N Doobe', presumably composed during a bout of hiccups. The title peaked at No. 12 in the British chart. Following the premiere of *Lady Sings the Blues*, the title 'Good Morning Heartache' was swiped from the soundtrack for single release during March 1973 to stall in the American Top Forty. That August, Ross returned to mainstream music with the Michael Masser and Ron Miller composition 'Touch Me in the Morning', a sweeping tale of love lost and found. The single (rightly) topped the American chart; hitting the Top Ten in Britain. Hot on its heels, the album carrying the chart-topper cracked the Top Ten on both sides of the Atlantic. Ross was pregnant during the album's recording sessions which may, she said, have influenced the baby theme throughout the album: one track titled 'Young Mothers' was edged out and canned, to later be included on her 1983 *Anthology* album.

While this project was being publicly promoted, Ross was in the studio with fellow Motown artist, Marvin Gaye. At least that was what the company's publicity department insisted. In reality, the two singers were rarely in the studio together. According to Gaye, Ross appeared insecure, lacking the confidence she usually exuded, and she was pregnant with her second child.

In 1973, the *Diana and Marvin* album was issued to peak in the American Top Thirty. It reached No. 6 in Britain during February 1984. The first track lifted for single release was 'You're a Special Part of Me', which soared to No. 12 in the American chart, while in Britain it was 'You Are Everything', their version of The Stylistics' 1971 Top Ten American hit, which flew into the Top Five. The next American single, 'My Mistake (Was to Love You)', released in May, reached the Top Twenty. Once again, Britain selected a Stylistics' cover version, 'Stop, Look, Listen (to your Heart)', a Top Thirty hit. As the duet album was rifled, so was the solo Ross release *Last Time I Saw Him,* notably, the album's title track, 'All of my Life', 'Sleepin'' and 'Love Me'.

Most of 1975 was devoted to filming *Mahogany,* although Ross did enjoy a solitary British single hit with 'Sorry Doesn't Always Make It Right' in May. Following the American premiere of *Mahogany,* which grossed $7 million during the first two weeks of its release, the soundtrack album shot into the Top Twenty, while 'Theme from Mahogany (Do You Know Where You're Going To)' topped the American singles chart during January 1976. When issued in Britain, the single, following a hefty promotional push, zoomed into the Top Five. The follow-up single to the American chart-topper, 'I Thought It Took a Little Time (but Today I Fell in Love)', surprisingly faltered in the Top Fifty. That failure was soon overlooked when Motown discovered that The Fifth Dimension intended to release their version of the Ross album track 'Love Hangover'. Having placed great importance on their artist's version, Motown rush-released the title as a single to top the American chart that May, and reach the Top Ten in Britain. 'I Thought It Took a Little Time (but Today I Fell in Love)' followed in Britain, to struggle into the Top Forty during July.

With her movie commitments behind her, Ross was able to plough her energies into her singing career and embarked upon an adventurous series of concerts in 1976 under the banner 'An Evening with Diana Ross'. While touring, Ross divorced her husband, Robert, citing grounds of irreconcilable differences; she was granted custody of her three daughters, Rhonda, Tracee and Chudney. Her petition also stated that property and financial settlements had been reached between herself and her husband. Following the divorce, Ross and her children moved to New York. Meantime, the double album *An Evening with*

85

Diana Ross, recorded at the Los Angeles' Ahmanson Theatre, was issued and reached the American Top Thirty, and the British Top Sixty.

Through to the end of the decade, the singer maintained her chart profile via a pair of albums, namely, *Baby It's Me* and *The Boss;* the latter being the most successful, spawning the title track, 'No One Gets the Prize' and 'It's my House' as hit singles. It was also during this period that Ross was involved in the shooting of *The Wiz,* the black version of the Broadway show and the Judy Garland film. The title 'Ease on down the Road', her duet with Michael Jackson, was lifted from the film's soundtrack for single release to stall in the Top Fifty on both sides of the Atlantic in November 1978. For the follow-up single, 'Pops We Love You', Ross joined Stevie Wonder, Marvin Gaye and Smokey Robinson, singing a birthday tribute to Berry Gordy's father: another staller, in the Top Sixty.

In the eighties, the singer dumped her 'safe' image to join the unpredictable young; she wanted to switch the ballad with beat to revitalise her flagging career. At the time, the top-selling dance outfit Chic was masterminded by Nile Rodgers and Bernard Edwards, and for the first time in her career Ross handed over her next album, *Diana,* to the couple who wrote, arranged and produced the project. Unfortunately, the result sounded too similar to their own releases; it was difficult to distinguish the Motown vocalist from one of Chic's own. Both Berry Gordy and Ross were unhappy with the finished tapes, whereupon she returned to the studio to remix the album with producer Russ Terrana. Ross said: 'When I first listened to the tapes they sounded pretty much like Chic or Sister Sledge . . . both Nile and Bernard have only been in the industry for two or three years and in re-mixing the album I felt I may be able to put a little Diana Ross into [it].' It went without saying that both Rodgers and Edwards were furious that their work had been tampered with, and demanded a public disclaimer be given as they disassociated themselves from the project.

The finished album, packaged in a black and white gatefold sleeve, showing the singer dressed in tattered jeans and T-shirt, relaunched Ross's career overnight. In America, the first lifted title was 'I'm Coming Out', while Britain opted for 'Upside Down' as its debut single, which became a No. 2 hit, earning the singer a silver disc for sales in excess of 400,000 copies. The mother album went on to pass one million sales in Britain alone. 'Upside Down' was the second single released in America, during June 1980; the title soared to No. 1 but was the last to be issued. In Britain, however, the story was much different; her fans devoured the new sound. The next single, 'My Old

Piano', issued during September, soared into the Top Five, while (at last) 'I'm Coming Out' reached No. 13 in November. Ross supported her British success by hosting a press reception at the Inn on the Park hotel, London, breaking a private holiday with Kiss member Gene Simmons.

The next year, 1981, was one of change. 'It's my Turn' was the first single; the theme from the movie of the same name starring Michael Douglas. The track soared into the American Top Ten and the British Top Twenty. A collection of previously recorded and canned songs, produced and co-written by Michael Masser, were issued under the album title *To Love Again*. New material or not, the album was a big seller during April, spawning a pair of British hits, 'One More Chance' and 'Cryin' my Heart Out for You'. These titles led the way for one of the decade's most significant of ballads, namely, 'Endless Love', Ross's duet with Lionel Richie. Once again, it was the theme from a movie of the same name, and was recorded in a whirlwind. Ross was performing in Atlantic City; Richie in New York. They met in Nevada, recorded the track, and went their separate ways. No one would have guessed its hasty birth; 'Endless Love' topped the American chart during August 1981, selling in excess of two million copies and later winning a pair of 1982 music awards: Favourite Single – Soul/R. & B., and Favourite Single – Pop/Rock. In Britain, the title soared to No. 7 two months later. It was Ross's final single for Motown; her recording contract was due to be renegotiated and Gordy was unable to meet her financial demands. The singer moved to RCA Records in March 1981, signing a seven-year contract reputedly worth $20 million. Naturally, Gordy was devastated by Ross's decision. 'Motown was a profound experience. The truth is that I did not leave Motown because I was upset or angry or hurt. I left because I was growing as a person and it was time for me to move on.' Primarily, Ross wanted to control her own career, and to this end opened a series of companies to protect her interests, namely, Ross Records, Ross Publishing Company, Ross Town, RTC Management Corporation and Anaid (Diana spelt backwards) Films. Ross attended night classes in film finance before joining the world of money hands-on. She no longer trusted third parties to handle her cash. 'I won't put my name on a contract unless I understand exactly what I am signing. I sign all my own cheques. I find that to be an area of great importance.' She also added, 'I was pretty vulnerable in the outside world. I had a barrelful of problems, and it took me a long time to get them all sorted out.'

Ross's recording contract with RCA Records afforded her total creative control from a song's concept to the record packaging. In December 1981, her debut single for RCA was issued, amid great speculation. Titled 'Why Do Fools Fall in Love', the track was her version of the Frankie Lymon and The Teenagers' original 1956 hit. Lifted from her album bearing the same name, the single soared into the Top Ten on both sides of the Atlantic.

Before 1982 closed, the singer enjoyed a series of hit singles that included the dance-flavoured 'Work That Body' and 'Muscles', written and produced by her long-standing friend Michael Jackson, accompanied by a promotional video that somehow passed television censorship – just! The latter track was swiped from her second album, *Silk Electric,* itself a Top Thirty hit in both America and Britain.

During 1983, Ross began an annual concert stint in Las Vegas, with a pay cheque reputed to be $2 million per season. The next two years allowed Ross to experiment musically by working with a host of different composers and producers. For instance, late in 1984, she duetted with Julio Iglesias on the ballad 'All of You', much to the annoyance of her staunch followers, but then re-established herself in their favour with her album *Swept Away,* the result of her association with soul masters Arthur Baker, Lionel Richie and Bernard Edwards. The album's title track reached the American Top Twenty during October 1984, while a further swiped track titled 'Missing You' soared into the American Top Ten in April 1985. The song, composed by Lionel Richie, was a loving tribute to the memory of Marvin Gaye who was shot dead by his father on 1 April 1984.

In 1985, Ross took the unprecedented step of working with The Bee Gees to record the album *Eaten Alive,* released in November. The lifted track 'Chain Reaction' shot to the top of the British chart in March 1986, a position it held for three weeks, and her first British chart-topper since 'I'm Still Waiting'. The success of 'Chain Reaction' was aided by an innovative promotional video featuring spoof black and white sixties sequences held together by the singer performing the song in colour. The follow-up single, 'Experience', paled by comparison, faltering in the British Top Fifty during May.

Prior to the release of 'Chain Reaction', Ross married for the second time. Her husband was Arne Naess, a Norwegian shipping magnate and Everest climber who had three children. They first met in May 1984, while holidaying in the Bahamas, and when Naess was to be knighted in Oslo, he invited Ross to be his guest at the ceremony. He then asked her to marry him. Ross said of their relationship, 'We came from completely different worlds. He doesn't know about the show business world . . . I've never had the adventure that he brings into my life.'

Through the remainder of the decade, Ross's recording career declined. America was showing signs of abandoning her, while Britain frantically tried to support her mediocre material. In May 1987 the *Red Hot Rhythm 'n' Blues* album was released to a mixed reception, while her recording of 'If We Could Hold On Together', the theme to the Steven Spielberg movie *The Land Before Time* was reminiscent of her smooth ballad era. The title remained unreleased in Britain until 1993. The singer's worst move at this juncture was the release of the *Workin' Overtime* album during 1989, recorded for her daughters. To support *Workin' Overtime*, Ross embarked upon a lengthy European tour, and as her recording career slumped, her touring commitments heightened.

But her recording career would spiral once more. She released the album *The Force behind the Power* during September 1991, produced by Peter Asher. The first single to be lifted from the strongest album during this part of Ross's career returned her to the big ballad and the world's charts. Titled 'When You Tell Me That You Love Me', the single shot to No. 2 in the British chart in December, while *The Force behind the Power* soared into the Top Twenty. Hence, Ross was in greater demand than ever, particularly in Britain – she opened Harrod's annual New Year sale during January 1992, her reward, a fat cheque and a fried breakfast! A month on, the album's title track reached the British Top Thirty, then 'One Shining Moment' returned her to the British Top Ten in July, whereupon Ross promoted the title by touring Eire and Scotland, and by standing in for BBC Radio 1 DJ Simon Bates to host one of his shows. Before the year closed, Ross abandoned mainstream music to perform jazz and blues material in a New York nightclub setting for American cable television under the title *Diana Ross Live . . . The Lady Sings*. (The programme was later released as a commercial video during April 1993, under the title *Live . . . Stolen Moments – The Lady Sings . . . Jazz and Blues*). She tested her talent further, by performing with Placido Domingo and Jose Carreras in Vienna City Hall for a specially televised festive programme titled . . . naturally . . . *Christmas in Vienna*.

To start 1993, the much-acclaimed movie theme from *Land Before Time* titled 'If We Could Hold On Together' was finally issued as a single to reach No. 11 in the British chart, while in March 'Heart (Don't Change my Mind)' lifted from *The Force behind the Power* reached the British Top Thirty. In between these releases, Ross joined others of her ilk to perform in 'A Call for Reunion – A Musical Celebration' before

President Clinton at the Lincoln Memorial, Washington. Perhaps her performance was better remembered for the label showing on her jacket than the song she sang!

Mid-1993, Ross contributed to the opening ceremony of the famed, and now refurbished, Apollo Theatre in New York, while on the recording front, following months of preparation, she released her *One Woman – The Ultimate Collection,* an offshoot from the lavish *Forever Diana* six-CD box set released to celebrate her thirtieth anniversary in the music business. These issues coincided with the publication of her autobiography, *Secrets of a Sparrow,* and in December she unveiled her star on the pavement outside Radio City Music Hall. Across the ocean in Britain, her next British single, once more lifted from *The Force behind the Power,* titled 'Your Love' peaked in the British Top Twenty.

For some time, Ross had searched for suitable movie scripts to continue her acting career. She remained unimpressed until the script of *Out of Darkness* was given to her, a hard-hitting story of a schizophrenic mother. During the film's early life, viewers were hard pushed to realise it was Ross playing the lead role. Following its American screening, and during February 1994, the singer was honoured at Midem '94 held in France, when she received the Commander in the Order of Arts and Letters from Jacques Toubon, the French minister of culture. She was also given the City of Cannes Gold Medal. Two months on, the next British single, 'The Best Years of my Life', previously previewed on the *Oprey Winfrey Show,* peaked in the Top Thirty. To close the year, the *A Very Special Season* CD was issued, a Top Forty hit.

The only hit single of 1995 was the title track to her next album, *Take Me Higher,* which struggled into the British Top Forty. The album was a poor British seller, likewise the lifted singles. In 1996 Ross paid tribute to her loyal gay following by recording an updated, uptempoed cover version of Gloria Gaynor's 1979 British chart-topper 'I Will Survive'. Unfortunately, Ross's version did not; nonetheless, the impact was remarkable. Produced by Narada Michael Walden, the track was dedicated, she said, to her girls, her gay public. Ross: 'They've always been wonderfully supportive of me, and this is my way of saying thanks for their loyalty. But it isn't just about being gay, it's about being allowed to live your life . . . There's a lot of pain in the world. To me what matters is if you're a good person, that's all that counts. If you're a good person, I'm going to love you, if not, I won't have time for you.' The single's accompanying video was stunning, featuring the singer, the famous drag queen RuPaul, countless Ross lookalikes and 5,000 fans, in a recreation of Los Angeles' annual Gay and Lesbian Pride Celebration.

This release was followed by the CD compilation entitled *Diana Ross – Voice of Love*, conceived by Sharon Davis. Comprising tried and tested material, the release also showcased a trio of new tracks including the powerful 'In the Ones You Love', which reached the British Top Forty singles chart late in 1996. Ross's Voice of Love Tour started with British dates during July 1997.

When Diana Ross celebrated thirty years in the music business, she was listed as the most successful female artist in the British singles chart (to date). This achievement won her a place in the 1994 edition of the *Guinness Book of Records*. The artist was presented with the *Guinness Book of Records* Lifetime Achievement Award to honour this success. There were no direct contenders for the Award, although Madonna and Barbra Streisand both carried criteria necessary for consideration. But not enough!

'I worked hard to make myself a beautiful career. Success is not all that it is cracked up to be. It can be lonely and isolating . . .' – Diana Ross

(Quotes: *Secrets of a Sparrow: Memoirs* by Diana Ross; *Motown: The History* by Sharon Davis)

October 1971

THE TAMS

Hey Girl Don't Bother Me

Although The Tams were not blessed with a lengthy chart career, they fared better than many American soul groups. Indeed, enjoying a British chart-topper for three weeks with a reissued title must break some type of record.

Brothers Charles Pope, born on 7 August 1936, and Joseph Pope, born on 6 November 1933, Robert Lee Smith, born on 18 March 1936, and Horace Kay, born on 13 April 1934, first met in Atlanta, Georgia, where they formed The Four Dots. With Joseph Pope as lead singer, they became a popular vocal outfit on the club circuit, until they boosted their professional reputation by recording for Swan Records in 1960. The product bombed.

The Four Dots renamed themselves The Tams, an abbreviation of Tam O'Shanters, the hats they wore on stage. The name change also marked Floyd Ashton, born on 15 August 1933, joining the membership. The move appeared lucky, as the group secured a deal with the Atlanta entrepreneur Bill Lowery, who represented Ray Whitley and Joe South, among others.

Joe South composed 'Untie Me' for The Tams, which they recorded in the Fame Studios and sold to Arlen Records, based in Philadelphia. The title reached the American Top Sixty and the R. & B. Top Twelve during October 1962. Despite such an encouraging start to their recording career, the title was the group's only hit single until 1963, when they signed a recording contract with ABC Paramount Records. The soul quintet's debut release for the new label, penned by Ray Whitley and titled 'What Kind of Fool (Do You Think I Am)', soared to No. 9 in the R. & B. chart during December 1963, and became a top-selling mainstream single. During the following year, The Tams enjoyed four further hit singles, namely, 'You Lied to your Daddy', 'It's All Right (You're Just in Love)', 'Hey Girl Don't Bother Me' and 'Silly Little Girl'.

At the end of 1964, Floyd Ashton was replaced by Albert Cottle, and the group switched recording studios to the Master Sound Studio in Atlanta. Ironically, the move coincided with The Tams disappearance from the American chart. Indeed, it was not until 1968 that they re-established themselves as a top-selling outfit with the lightweight yet highly tuneful 'Be Young, Be Foolish, Be Happy', released during June. Meanwhile, two albums were issued during 1964, namely, *Presenting The Tams* and *Hey Girl Don't Bother Me*. It was this reissued title track that became the group's debut British single, released on EMI Records' subsidiary Stateside. It entered the Top Forty in February 1970, then disappeared.

A year on, Anchor Records purchased the rights to the entire ABC Paramount catalogue and, realising the wealth of material stored by The Tams, rereleased 'Hey Girl Don't Bother Me' via the Probe label. No one expected the title to grow legs in the manner it did; it shot to the top of the British chart in October 1971, where it stayed for three weeks. Despite the excitement and hype surrounding this single, and The Tams on-hand promotion, the track was their last British hit until 1987. Nonetheless, the group remained popular with soul music followers via performances and albums like *The Best of The Tams* and *Atlanta Soul Collection*, released in 1975 and 1983 respectively.

Thanks to an eighties' dance craze called the Shag (incredible but true!) The Tams returned to the British chart via the Virgin label with

'There Ain't Nothing Like Shaggin''. This dubiously titled single soared into the Top Twenty during November 1987, becoming the group's final British chart entrant. The single was, naturally enough, followed by the appropriately named album *There Ain't Nothing Like . . . The Tams*.

With their charting career behind them, The Tams confine their appearances to the nightclub circuit both in Britain and America. But, given the way British taste changes so frequently, another reissue could well repeat history for the group.

November 1971

ROD STEWART

Maggie May

'[Rod and I] started messing around with a few chords and up came "Maggie May". I thought up the 12-string introduction to the song while I was on the Tube on the way to the studio and I borrowed Rod's 12-string guitar to play it . . .' – Martin Quittenton

Roderick Stewart was born in Highgate, London, on 10 January 1945 to Scottish parents Robert and Elsie who already had two daughters, Mary and Peggy, and two sons, Bob and Don. Stewart's father had retired from the building trade to run a newsagent's shop. Stewart: 'I came from a very poor family but I was extremely well-fed and happy. I was incredibly spoilt as the youngest of five kids.' The Stewart males were football addicts, following the Scottish teams, while Stewart Snr ran the Highgate Redwings Club in his spare time.

Stewart attended the Highgate Primary School, where he failed the eleven-plus examination but where he excelled in sports, before moving to the William Grimshaw Secondary Modern School in Hornsey. There he befriended fellow sports enthusiasts Ray and Dave Davies and Pete Quaife (who later formed The Kinks). His introduction to music came as a fourteen-year-old when his father gave him a guitar. 'I didn't ask for it and I hardly used it . . . I hated music at school.' Eventually, though, he began to show an interest in the instrument, which led to him joining his first school group, The Kool Kats, during 1960. The group comprised eight guitarists (!), their repertoire a cross between rock 'n' roll and skiffle, and somehow they managed to produce listenable music.

At fifteen, Stewart left school to work at the Framery as a silk screen printer, but his obsession with football led to him becoming an apprentice at the Brentford Football Club. His stay was short-lived, as Stewart was physically incapable of coping with the training sessions. Funded by his father, Stewart sailed to France to earn a living but returned home within days to work in the family newsagents, perform with his group and join CND marches. When he outgrew this he befriended the Mods; his long-beatnik styled hair shorn in favour of the spiky style that later became his trademark.

Stewart moved on to play harmonica and sing with The Five Dimensions, an R. & B. outfit from Birmingham. They then backed singer Jimmy Powell before joining The Hoochie Coochie Men, support group for Long John Baldry, who had signed a recording contract with United Artists Records. Stewart's association with Baldry led to Mike Vernon, record producer with Decca Records, signing Stewart as a soloist to record 'Good Morning Little Schoolgirl' in 1964. (The Yardbirds likewise recorded the track to enjoy a No. 44 British hit during November 1964.) Also the same year and with Long John Baldry and The Hoochie Coochie Men, Stewart recorded 'You'll Be Mine' for United Artists, before appearing briefly on the *Long John's Blues* album. However, The Hoochie Coochie Men disbanded, leaving Stewart to pass through The Soul Agents before teaming up with Steampacket in 1965. The membership here was Baldry, Brian Auger and Julie Driscoll, among others, managed by Giorgio Gomelski.

Steampacket were highly popular with north of England audiences, particularly in clubs like The Twisted Wheel, itself the heart of Northern Soul, with a loyal cult following for a particular style of American music. While still a member of Steampacket, Stewart spread his solo wings to record for the Columbia label, a subsidiary of EMI Records. His debut, 'The Day Will Come', bombed.

Early in 1966, Steampacket disbanded, whereupon Stewart joined The Jeff Beck Group whose line-up included Ronnie Wood (a future member of The Faces). Stewart debuted on stage with the group in March 1967 at the Finsbury Park Astoria, before touring America with them a year later. In time, though, the rivalry between Stewart and Beck became openly apparent. Stewart: 'Beck's was a miserable fucking band, horrible. Beck is a miserable old sod, but I do love him as a guitar player.' When Beck refused to perform at Woodstock, the rock festival staged in August 1969, Stewart and the group played alone. This inevitably led to the disintegration of the group which was, ironically, the turning point in Stewart's career – Mercury Records offered him a recording contract. His first album with The Faces as support musicians was titled *An Old Raincoat Won't Ever Let You Down,* issued in February 1970. It bombed in Britain but was a minor American hit. Stewart also signed a recording deal with Phonogram and would from now on run two careers – lead singer with The Faces and solo artist – simultaneously.

The Faces, with the membership of guitarists Ron Wood, born 1 June 1947 in Hillingdon, London, and Ronnie Lane, born 1 April 1946 in Plaistow, London; drummer Kenny Jones, born 16 September 1948 in Stepney, London, and keyboardist Ian McLagan, born 12 May 1945 in Hounslow, Middlesex, were a wild bunch of musicians. Stewart: 'Me and Woody had a lot of fun in The Faces. It was the ultimate heavy drinking band. Not because we had a mission in life to be a load of boozers. We were shit scared, and we didn't think we were very good.' Nonetheless, the group built up a solid following, although Stewart could not understand why: 'We never had the musicianship. Individually, we were good, but we did not come together as a band . . . People must hear something I can't.'

In April 1970 the group's album *First Step* was issued from which the British Top Fifty hit 'Flying' was lifted. It was a minor hit in America, but following an extensive promotional tour there, The Faces gained momentum which stood them in good stead. A year on, the *Long Player* album spawned 'Had Me a Real Good Time', a Top Forty British hit.

Meanwhile, *Gasoline Alley,* released in June 1970, was Rod Stewart's second solo album, but it was the album *Every Picture Tells a Story,* released in October 1971, that launched him as a solo artist, thanks to 'Maggie May'. The track was penned by Stewart and Martin Quittenton, telling the tale of a schoolboy's first sexual encounter. Originally, the title was the B-side to the Tim Hardin composition 'Reason to Believe', which reached No. 19 in the British chart in September 1971. However, when a radio DJ in Cleveland, Ohio, decided to flip the single to air the rock ballad 'Maggie May', the title shot to No. 1 in the American and British charts in November 1971, where it stayed for five weeks. Martin Quittenton told authors Ewbank and Hildred, 'When "Maggie May" became a big hit I couldn't, at the time, see what all the fuss was about. It took me a long while to realise it was actually a very good popular song.'

The runaway success of the single pushed The Faces to the back line. In reality they became Stewart's support group, prompting the future billing of Rod Stewart and the Faces. This was not what the group intended and disagreements inevitably began in earnest. 'Maggie May' also catapulted its mother album *Every Picture Tells a Story* to the top of both the British and American charts, transforming Rod Stewart into a superstar, a position he had craved, to prove to his contemporaries he was more than a hard-drinking lead singer.

Also see: 'You Wear It Well', September 1972; 'Sailing', September 1975; 'Da Ya Think I'm Sexy?', December 1978

(Quotes: *Rod Stewart – The Best Selling Biography* by Tim Ewbank and Stafford Hildred)

December 1971

SLADE

Coz I Luv You

They struggled to the point of desperation; underwent name and image changes. With an untapped composing flair, Slade exploded upon British music like a ten-ton fire cracker, while maintaining their working-class status.

Noddy Holder, born Neville John Holder in Walsall, Warwickshire, on 15 June 1946, was the only son of Leah and Jack. When he was five years old, the local council rehoused the family to an estate near the revolutionary 'spaghetti junction' motorway complex. Holder attended the T.P. Riley comprehensive school, Bloxwich, where he excelled in geology and biology, with ambitions to be a teacher. Before he could progress in this direction, he discovered music, particularly the American heroes like Elvis Presley and Jerry Lee Lewis. However, it was The Beatles who impressed the teenager most. Holder said: 'When the groups started, I began to lose interest in what we were doing at school, and spent as much time as I could listening to the local groups that were starting up.' He frequented local theatres like the Civic Hall in Wolverhampton, where acts like The Who and The Kinks performed.

However, Holder's biggest inspiration came from the example of youngsters who learned their musical art in the Midlands before moving to London to pursue their careers seriously. In particular he cited Denny Laine and the Diplomats, and Roy Wood, who was then guitarist with The Night Riders, back-up group for Mike Sheridan.

While still at school, Holder formed his own group called The

Memphis Cut-Outs, and spent his spare time rehearsing. Predictably, education took second place on his list of priorities until he left school at the age of sixteen. Holder and The Memphis Cut-Outs were relatively successful on the local circuit, but he was the only group member who wanted to risk his future in music. When the remaining membership's enthusiasm turned lukewarm, he moved to another outfit, Steve Brett & The Mavericks. However, he placated his parents by taking a day job in a car dealer showroom.

In 1964, The Mavericks were offered a month-long stint in Frankfurt, Germany; it was this that convinced Holder to become a professional musician. On the boat journey to German territory, Holder befriended members of the group, The 'N' Betweens, who had recently performed in Europe, but who were on the verge of disbanding.

When The Mavericks returned to Wolverhampton, Holder encountered the remaining members of The 'N' Betweens and decided to join them. Thus the line-up of Slade was born – Holder; guitarist Dave Hill, born in Fleet Castle, Devon, on 4 April 1952; drummer Don Powell, born in Bilston, Worcestershire, on 10 September 1950, and bass guitarist Jim Lea, born in Wolverhampton, on 14 June 1952. However, success was a long way in the future; it took five years and a couple of group name changes before they became household names.

As The 'N' Betweens, they recorded demo titles for American producer Kim Fowley, responsible for novelty acts that included B Bumble and The Stingers, and released the solitary single titled 'You Better Run' for the EMI Records' subsidiary Columbia. Holder told *Petticoat* magazine: 'We were just four young kids with a local following in the Black Country. We played dates in the area as the support band to new names like Cream.'

Through the group's American contacts, they performed a season in the Bahamas which was plagued with problems. The hotel responsible for booking them had changed ownership, and when the membership discovered all expenses were not to be settled by the hotel, they were forced to remain in America far longer than intended, 'earning the extra money to pay back the hotel so that we could get our instruments back [to Britain]'. It took six months. Dave Hill told author George Tremlett: 'We had a few arguments over there, but the experience did us good. Musically, it all came together for us.'

Returning to the British club circuit and now known as Ambrose Slade, the group re-established their following, and released their debut album titled *Beginnings* on the Fontana label in May 1969, from which the track 'Genesis' was taken as a single. Meantime, ex-Animal group member and artist manager, Chas Chandler, was looking for another act to represent, having recently parted from Jimi Hendrix, whose career he had successfully launched in Britain. Chandler saw Ambrose Slade perform in the London nighterie, Rasputin, and believed they had hit potential. He told journalist Keith Altham: 'They were just four kids having a ball and their audience were having a great time too. They weren't trying to be the greatest musicians in the world but they were enjoying themselves.' As their manager, Chandler insisted the group start composing their own material, which would generate a greater financial reward for them. He also impressed upon them the need to save money by trimming living and touring expenses – low-priced hotels and roadworthy but non-flashy touring vehicles. Don Powell said: 'Chas told us all about the groups in the sixties who had hit records, toured overseas, broke through in the States and throughout Europe, and came out of it with hardly a penny.'

To capitalise on the current skinhead cult among the British young, Ambrose Slade dressed in the style – short-cropped hair, jeans, bovver boots and braces. And with their new image, they debuted at Walsall Town Hall in April 1969, and that October released their next single for Fontana Records, titled 'Wild Winds Are Blowing'. This time the record label read 'Slade'.

In early 1970, 'The Shape of Things to Come' was issued as their final Fontana single. Like its predecessors, it bombed, despite a press launch in March 1970 held at The Bag O'Nails Club in London. In September 1970, Slade switched to Polydor Records and issued the single 'Know Who You Are', followed a month later by the *Play It Loud* album. Both were poor sellers. However, the struggle was about to end. In June 1971, the group recorded and released a cover version of the Little Richard classic 'Get Down and Get with It'. The title had previously been used on stage by Slade as a five-minute audience warmer, so their fans would recognise the track instantly. Slade took their recorded interpretation one step further by introducing 'boot stomping', inadvertently giving birth to the future Slade sound. 'Get Down and Get with It' became the group's first British hit, peaking at No. 16 in the chart.

Following Chandler's directive, Noddy Holder and Jim Lea collaborated as songwriters, with their first attempt titled 'Coz I Luv You', written overnight. Holder wanted to incorporate Lea's talent for playing the electric violin on the track. 'We thought we'd try to make the most of it . . . [he] said he had a couple of lines and a melody line . . . I took the idea from there . . . thumping away at my old Spanish guitar.'

The loud foot-stomping sound and Holder's roaring vocals almost drowned the simply constructed song. Produced by Chandler, the title was issued as the follow-up to 'Get Down and Get with It'. During December 1971, the title shot to the top of the British chart, a position it held for four weeks. The long wait was over.

'Coz I Luv You' was, by the way, the first record title to carry Slade's customised spelling, which many believed was a sign of ignorance! It was the first of six British chart-toppers during a five-year span.

Also see: 'Take Me Bak 'Ome', July 1972; 'Cum On Feel the Noize', March 1973; 'Skweeze Me Pleeze Me', July 1973; 'Merry Xmas Everybody', January 1974

(Quotes: *The Slade Story* by George Tremlett)

THE NEW SEEKERS

I'd Like to Teach the World to Sing (in Perfect Harmony)

'Doo da da doo . . . lalalalala . . .' Those chirpy voices and acceptable faces of British 'pop' music, whose material was far too cheerful to be true, brought young enthusiasm into the seventies. They performed with gusto, enjoying the accolades that spanned the decade. Indeed, The New Seekers, with two girls – one blonde, one brunette – as vocal attractions, complemented by three guys, were a younger version of The Springfields and the original Seekers, keeping Tom Springfield's sixties dream alive.

When the original Seekers disbanded in 1969, member Keith Potger was reluctant to leave the music business entirely. He had, however, tired of performing, so he did the next best thing by forming and managing a clone group who became The New Seekers. The new line-up included blonde Lyn Paul, born in Manchester on 16 February 1949, and brunette Eve Graham, born in Perth, Scotland, on 19 April 1943 (both former members of the Nocturnes). They were joined by male singers/guitarists Marty Kristian, born in Leipzeig, Germany, on 27 May 1947; Peter Doyle, born in Melbourne, Australia, on 28 July 1949, and Paul Layton, born in Beaconsfield on 4 August 1947.

As Philips Records had released The Springfields' recordings (and was still Dusty's recording outlet) it seemed logical for Keith Potger to approach them. 'Look What They've Done to my Song, Ma', a cover version of Melanie's original, was The New Seekers' first British hit. Released during October 1970, it entered the chart twice but got no further than the Top Fifty.

The group's image was all-smiling and clean cut, while their harmonising was lively as was typified by their next single, a version of Delaney Bramlett's 'Never Ending Song of Love'. This shot to No. 2 in the British chart during July 1971. With a vocal identity established, the group switched record companies from Philips to Polydor to hit gold status with Roger Cook and Roger Greenaway's composition 'I'd Like to Teach the World to Sing (in Perfect Harmony)' when it soared to the top of the British chart in January 1972. (The Hillside Singers had already enjoyed an American hit with it.) Such was the popularity of this happy-go-lucky single that the world did indeed sing, establishing it as an international chart-topper. This runaway success prompted the soft drinks company Coca-Cola to adopt the song as a promotional tool. Not only was an adaptation heard across television advertisements – 'I'd like to buy the world a Coke' – as hundreds of people of all nationalities joined as one to sip a drink, but a flexy-disc of The New Seekers singing the actual advertisement could be obtained from the drinks company. Such promotion was practically unheard of at this time; the scale was enormous and the countries it touched numerous.

It was probably this that resulted in The New Seekers being chosen to represent Britain in the 1972 European Song Contest. The song to be performed by them was another Cook and Greenaway composition, titled 'Beg Steal or Borrow'. It was typical of the group's sound and an ideal contender for Europe. The panel of voters had other ideas, because 'Beg Steal or Borrow' faltered as Luxembourg's entry 'Après Toi (Come What May)' by Vicky Leandros was the winner. Nonetheless, The New Seekers enjoyed British success when the single peaked at No. 2 during March 1972.

Three months on, 'Circles', the title track from their fifth album, was issued and became, rather surprisingly, the group's final Top Ten single, while 'Come Softly to Me' (credited to The New Seekers featuring Marty Kristian) faltered at No. 20 during December 1972. It seemed ironic that following so many accolades, the youngsters should now be faced with a chart struggle. It was a temporary setback, but nonetheless worrying.

During December 1973, the group released the medley 'Pinball Wizard – See Me Feel Me' from the movie *Tommy,* which reached No. 16 two months later. This was followed by two Top Forty titles: 'Nevertheless' (credited to Eve Graham and The New Seekers) and 'Goodbye Is Just Another Word'. The future, once more, appeared dismal.

Not so. Just as it seemed their popularity was waning, The New Seekers recorded and released the Tony Macaulay and Geoff Stephens composition 'You Won't Find Another Fool Like Me'. This immediately reversed the decline to such an extent that the group once more became chart-topping artists in November 1973. The success rubbed off on the follow-up issued four months later. Titled 'I Get a Little Sentimental over You', it reached the Top Five, and was their last major success. For the third time, the group's demise was forecast, but this time they heeded advice to embark upon a farewell tour of Britain before disbanding.

Lyn Paul was the first to strike out as a soloist, although she had a short chart career: one Top Thirty hit single titled 'It Oughta Sell a Million' in June 1975. She then confined her singing to the nightclub circuit. The remaining members dabbled in the music business without making any great inroads.

In 1976 CBS Records enticed the group to return to the music business. The aptly titled 'It's So Nice (to Have You Home)' returned the group to the Top Fifty that August, while two further singles, 'I Wanna Go Back' and 'Anthem (One Day in Every Week)', released during 1977 and 1978 respectively, both reached the Top Thirty. This was their last taste of recorded success. There was no turning back this time. The New Seekers' fatal attraction had worn thin, and with no hits to sustain their career, they disbanded for the second and last time during 1978.

The Springfields/Seekers/New Seekers story was now over. But it really goes without saying that it was great fun while it lasted!

February 1972

T REX

Telegram Sam

'Two years ago I was very into being a poet and I'm not any more, because I am a poet. I don't have to think about it. I've become Marc Bolan.' – Marc Bolan

Early in 1972, Bolan's new recording deal with EMI Records was official, whereupon the next single from T Rex bore the group's label, T Rex Wax Co, and was titled 'Telegram Sam'. Had Fly Records not sneaked out the title 'Jeepster' to peak at No. 2 in 1971, T Rex would have enjoyed two consecutive British chart-toppers. Yes, 'Telegram Sam', recorded at the Honky Chateau in Paris, shot to the top of the British chart during February 1972 within days of its release, thanks to advance orders in excess of 300,000 copies. The title, bearing the hallmarks of its official predecessor, held the top spot for two weeks.

Prior to releasing its follow-up, T Rex, with William Fifield on drums, embarked upon a major American tour, promoting the single 'Bang a Gong (Get It On)', the August 1971 British chart-topper (Bolan was forced to amend the single's title because the American group, Chase, already had released a single under that name), and performed a pair of sell-out concerts at Wembley Stadium before 100,000 people in total. The response was likened to the mass hysteria of The Beatles' heyday – fans rushed the stage, flung themselves against the stage barriers and ran riot as the group performed. The concerts were filmed, following a deal between Bolan and The Beatles' Ringo Starr. To add to the performing footage, the two artists provided ad hoc humour and sequences of a jam session with Elton John, playing 'Children of the Revolution' and 'Tutti Frutti'. Bolan told journalist Anne Nightingale, 'Elton played with us for hours and we did lots of rock 'n' roll . . . We did some filming at Lennon's place where I did a medley of hits with a string quartet. Everyone's eating cream cakes and Mickey's a vampire and there's strawberry jam dripping down his chin . . . disgusting. But basically it's just rock 'n' roll.'

The result was the movie *Born to Boogie*, premiered in London during December 1972. Originally, Bolan had intended to produce a science fiction film, with a cosmic messiah as its main character. Not Jesus as such, but rather a messenger from God, sent to earth to check it remained the Garden of Eden He had created and abandoned centuries earlier. The movie intended to portray the devastation of the Garden and the consequences for mankind. Bolan said of his project, 'We will film his reactions to all the shit we take quite naturally . . . mass murderers and all the rubbish he has never seen before. When they left Earth it was a Garden of Eden with potential gods . . . He expects a race of gods and what he finds is this mess. It was basically about the reactions and disgust that this man feels.' Incidentally, the film ended with the total devastation of the messenger. Bolan was unsure if he wanted to appear in the movie, but certainly, he said, it would involve T Rex. This project never got any further than the storyboard, while *Born to Boogie,* with all the musical ingredients, and released by Apple Films, bombed. Bolan told *Petticoat* magazine that *Born to Boogie* was a gamble for both him and Starr, financially and critically. 'It didn't get good reviews . . . But [the critics] all put it down for the wrong reasons, which is why it didn't bother me. The critics put it down for not being a masterpiece as a film. But it was made for T Rex fans, for no one else. That's what upset the critics.'

Back to the music proper, and the predictable cash-in. Bolan's previously released albums *My People Were Fair and Had Sky in their Hair, but Now They're Content to Wear Stars on their Brow* and *Prophets, Seers and Sages* were coupled for rerelease. Meanwhile, his album for EMI Records was earmarked for mid-1972 issue. Gloria Jones, touring Britain as a member of The Sanctified Sisters, Joe Cocker's back-up group, renewed her friendship with Bolan at this time.

T Rex had rapidly climbed into the megastar status; Bolan's popularity was startling, often frightening to him. Although he had prayed for success and recognition, the impact he and his music made on the public was beyond even his wildest cosmic expectations. His star would rise higher and shine, oh, so brightly for some time yet, only to be tragically burned out on 16 September 1977.

Also see: 'Hot Love', April 1971; 'Get It On', August 1971; 'Metal Guru', June 1972

(Quotes: *Marc Bolan: A Tribute* by various contributors; *The Electric Warrior: The Marc Bolan Story* by Paul Sinclair; author's unpublished interviews)

March 1972

CHICORY TIP

Son of my Father

No, not the salad plant, but a group which was unable to flourish during the heady heights of the decade's glam-rock scene. Nonetheless, Chicory Tip survived for nearly two years following their solitary chart-topper. Today, one would be hard pushed to remember their name – let alone the single. Such is show business!

Peter Hewson, born in Gillingham, Kent, on 1 September 1950, founded Chicory Tip during 1968. He recruited drummer Brian Shearer, born in London on 4 May 1951; guitarists Barry Mayger, born in Maidstone, Kent, on 1 June 1950 and Dick Foster, who was replaced in 1972 by Rod Cloutt, born in Gillingham, Kent, on 26 January 1949.

CBS Records' producer, Roger Easterby, attended one of their performances in Maidstone, Kent, was sufficiently impressed and offered them a recording contract. The annoying yet attractive 'Son of my Father' elevated Chicory Tip to stardom during March 1972. Written primarily by Giorgio Moroder (who went on to become the standard bearer of the European disco movement by launching Donna Summer, among others) the title held the British top position for three weeks.

The single 'What's your Name' followed, to peak at No. 13 in the

British chart during May 1972, while their final hit, 'Good Grief Christina', settled at No. 17 a year later.

And that was that! The disco movement progressed without them!

April 1972

NILSSON

Without You

Although he was one of the most gifted composers of the decade, Nilsson's only British chart-topper was penned by members of a Welsh group. The lyrics of 'WithoutYou' were of particular significance – they represented the death wishes of the writers.

Born Harry Edward Nelson III in Brooklyn, NewYork, on 15 June 1941, he moved with his mother and sister to the San FernandoValley, California, during 1958. Following his graduation from high school Nilsson drifted through a handful of jobs, before becoming a computer supervisor for the Security First National Bank, Van Nuys, by night. During daylight hours he composed and recorded demo tracks of his material, which he tirelessly hawked around record companies and music publishers.

His relentless efforts eventually secured him a recording contract with Mercury Records during the sixties. Using the name Johnny Niles, he recorded and released a single titled 'Donna'; it bombed. Moving on to Capitol Records, he recorded further solo tracks before becoming lead vocalist with The New Salvation Singers; another unsuccessful liaison.

In time, the tall, blue-eyed blond hit the dollar by selling his composition 'Travelin' Man' to The New Christy Minstrels. This injection of confidence led to Phil Spector's female trio, The Ronettes, recording two further tracks, namely 'Here I Sit' and 'Paradise'. These titles were the break Nilsson craved. If his compositions were accepted by the musical genius Phil Spector, they had to have a certain quality other acts could appreciate. Indeed, artists began asking Nilsson for material, ranging from Scottish songstress Lulu and Welsh folk singer Mary Hopkin, to the American-based semi-rock group Blood, Sweat and Tears. When the composer contributed 'Cuddly Toy' to The Monkees' album *Pisces, Aquarius, Capricorn and Jones Ltd,* Nilsson and Van Nuys parted company.

105

Now he was established as a composer, RCA Records quickly secured Nilsson to a $75,000 recording contract during 1968 and his debut album, *Pandemonium Shadow Show,* included a handful of his originals, complemented by cover versions of acts he admired, including The Beatles. When John Lennon heard the album, and his version of 'She's Leaving Home', he dubbed Nilsson his 'favourite American singer', while The Beatles' manager, Brian Epstein, tried unsuccessfully to secure him to the group's Apple label. Lennon's enthusiasm for Nilsson's work led to a friendship which later inspired the Beatle to produce Nilsson's album titled *Pussy Cats* in 1974. The album was a poor seller despite being critically acclaimed: 'His phrasing is perfect, but there is more. He embellishes many of his songs with bits of scat singing, sometimes noodling through an octave or two, sometimes imitating an instrument, sometimes doing things for which there is no adequate description.'

His second album, *Aerial Ballet,* released in 1968 and comprising his original material except one track, 'Everybody's Talkin' ', written by Fred Neil, was completed before he scored the music for the Otto Preminger movie *Skidoo* starring Jackie Gleason, in which he had a cameo role of a security guard. In 1969, the composer scored the music for the American television series *The Courtship of Eddie's Father,* then penned his first million-selling single. Three Dog Night took 'One' (a track lifted from Nilsson's *Aerial Ballet* album) into the American Top Five. Before the year ended, Nilsson recorded and released his third album, *Harry,* while 'Everybody's Talkin' ', swiped from his previous album, was issued as a single. It marked Nilsson's debut Top Ten American hit as a singer, while in Britain it peaked in the Top Thirty upon its second chart entry. Mind you, to be fair, the single had a little help – it was the theme to the block-busting movie *Midnight Cowboy,* starring Dustin Hoffman and Jon Voigt. When the film climbed the ranks, so did the single. 'Everybody's Talkin' ' went on to win a Grammy Award for the Best Contemporary Vocal Performance – Male at the 1970 awards ceremony.

Early in 1970, Nilsson abandoned his own material to record an album celebrating the music of Randy Newman titled *Nilsson Sings Newman,* before composing, singing and narrating the ninety-minute animated children's television movie *The Point.* The soundtrack became his best-selling album to date, peaking in the American Top Forty and the British Top Fifty early in 1972. In 1976, *The Point* was adapted for the stage. Following its American debut in Boston, it was performed at the Mermaid Theatre in London, where starring roles were given to Mickey

Dolenz and Davy Jones, late of the sixties' 'pop' group The Monkees.

'Without You', lifted from the *Nilsson Schmilsson* album, was penned by Pete Ham and Tom Evans, members of the group Badfinger, signed to The Beatles' record label, Apple. Nilsson first heard the group's version during a drinking session at a friend's home whereupon he decided to record it. His version shot to No. 1 in America during February 1972, maintaining that position for four weeks. When released in Britain, that success was repeated during April. Quite possibly, 'Without You' was one of the decade's most stylish of singles; certainly its lyrical content was highly charged and emotionally inclined. In 1973 it, rightly, won a Grammy Award for the Best Male Pop Vocal Performance of 1972. Ironically, the two composers of this musical masterpiece were both suicide victims – Pete Ham died in April 1975, while his partner Tom Evans died in 1983.

Before 1972 ended, two further singles were also lifted from *Nilsson Schmilsson,* namely, 'Jump into the Fire', a Top Thirty American hit, and 'Coconut', a Top Ten American hit and Top Fifty British hit. This pair paved the way for the *Son of Schmilsson* album which earned the artist his second gold record.

Nilsson maintained his selling power through the remainder of the seventies, via albums like *A Little Touch of Schmilsson in the Night* and *Pussy Cats.* His final British hit, 'All I Think About Is You' was released during August 1977 and reached No. 43, following a three-week spell in the chart. It was generally felt that if Nilsson had been more interested in publicly promoting his repertoire, his success rate would have been greater. This belief did not sway the composer, who preferred to spend his time working behind the spotlight.

Midway through the seventies, Nilsson appeared to lose his way. His material lacked the punch and sensitivity of past; he had exhausted his emotional energy to such an extent that he bypassed working on new projects. In 1980 he switched companies to Mercury Records, where in the September, his *Flash Harry* album was issued, following input from John Lennon and Ringo Starr, among others. (His previous working association with Starr had been collaborating on the soundtrack for the *Son of Dracula* movie in 1974).

In the nineties, Nilsson turned his back on recording to concentrate on other business ventures, including the opening of his own movie distribution company in California. He did break his self-imposed retirement to contribute the title 'Blanket for a Sail' to the 1991 *For our Children* album. Proceeds from this charity release went to the AIDS Foundation.

Nilsson's health deteriorated during 1993, culminating in a heart attack that February. He never fully recovered. During January 1994, the singer died in his sleep at his home in California. The world lost a greatly gifted composer. The *Los Angeles Times* said of him, 'His voice has a three-octave range; his imagination a somewhat wider one. He is a vocal chameleon, but, unlike some singers whose lack of limitations robs them of identity, each voice shares a personality common to every Nilsson voice.'

RCA Records celebrated Nilsson's life and his vast contribution to the music industry by releasing the *Personal Best* album during 1995. Featuring his finest work, the compilation was a fitting tribute to a lost talent.

May 1972

THE PIPES AND DRUMS AND MILITARY BAND OF THE ROYAL SCOTS DRAGOON GUARDS

Amazing Grace

One can always rely on the British chart for the unexpected. Novelty discs were invariably throwaway money-spinners; the majority of them were dire, but 'Amazing Grace' recorded by a military unit took everyone by surprise.

'Amazing Grace' was lifted from the album released by RCA Records, *Farewell to the Greys,* the Dragoons' tribute to the Royal Scots Greys. BBC Radio 2 lifted the instrumental for airplay and it caught the public's imagination. So much so, it was swiped from the album to be released as a single, and shot to the top of the British chart during May 1972, where it stayed for a remarkable five weeks. It also earned the distinction of being the first single by a military outfit to reach such a position.

The military band went on to enjoy three further hits – the chart-topper's follow-up 'Heykens Serenade', a Top Thirty hit in August 1972; 'Little Drummer Boy', which made the Top Twenty, and 'Amazing Grace' for the second time, during December 1972. This time, though, it stalled in the Top Fifty.

Several albums were also issued to capitalise on their success, including one (naturally) titled *Amazing Grace,* and, during the eighties,

The Amazing Sound of the Royal Scots Dragoon Guards and *Royal Scots Dragoon Guards.*

In December 1970, Elektra Records had released Judy Collins's version of 'Amazing Grace', which peaked in the Top Five. A year on, the Collins track entered the chart no less than four times: three times in the Top Fifty and once in the Top Forty. In 1972, following the success of the military band, Judy Collins's 'Amazing Grace' charted three times: twice in the Top Forty, once in the Top Twenty. But incredible though it sounds, she never enjoyed a chart-topper.

It must have had something to do with the uniforms!

June 1972

T REX

Metal Guru

'I could retire tomorrow but that's not what it's all about. If I didn't work I'd freak out. I'd OD in two years and be found in the gutter somewhere.' – Marc Bolan

Prior to embarking upon a further British tour, T Rex issued their fourth chart-topper. Titled 'Metal Guru', the single soared to No. 1 during June 1972, where it stayed for four weeks. Despite views that the lyrical content concerned a god of some description, Bolan later confirmed that he wrote the song about a car!

Once again, his previous record company, Fly, capitalised on his success by issuing the *Bolan Boogie* album, which bolted to the top of the chart in May. This unwarranted release was followed by (plans for) another; this time from Polydor Records and Track Records. The companies had coupled to compile an album of incomplete and demo tracks under the title *Hard on Love*. The plan was squashed when Bolan issued a high court writ against both companies to prevent the album reaching the stores. Bolan: 'That court case business really destroyed me. I had two weeks when I was a mess because I'd never felt like that before. I was [also] changing managers at the time and I was very emotional. I'd cut all the tracks for *Slider* [T Rex's new album] and I said, "Fuck the album. Don't wanna put it out!" ' In time he changed his opinion, saying, 'I feel it's the only album in which I've said what I think I am.'

109

Slider, released in July 1972, soared to No. 4 in Britain, selling in excess of 100,000 copies during the first four days; sales were obviously hampered by *Bolan Boogie,* which did not exactly please the singer! When issued Stateside, *Slider* peaked in the Top Twenty.

Before the year ended, T Rex issued a pair of singles, namely 'Children of the Revolution' which, surprisingly, missed the top spot by one place in September, and 'Solid Gold Easy Action', a No. 3 hit during December. Bolan's run of British chart-toppers had ended; his reign as the glam-rock icon was wavering, as artists like David Bowie began digging inroads. In fact, Bolan and Bowie enjoyed a solid friendship. Bowie had contributed to a handful of tracks on the *Slider* album, while Bolan had penned a song for his friend titled 'Lady Stardust' on his 1972 album *Ziggy Stardust.* Interestingly, when Bowie performed his tribute on stage, a backdrop of a white-faced Bolan appeared behind him. Also, before the year ended, T Rex toured the Far East and Australia, and performed a pair of London T Rexmas concert specials, staged in Brixton and Edmonton, which were glittering seasonal successes.

In 1973, Bolan made a surprise appearance on BBC TV's *The Cilla Black Show,* lipsynching to 'Mad Donna', a track extracted from his pending album titled *Tanx,* and duetting on 'Life's a Gas' with his hostess. Bolan had befriended Black and her husband sometime previously, but admitted, 'I took some persuading to do it, but I think she's a good singer and I think it might break some sort of barrier . . . The only thing I didn't like was that I did so much wiggling about that I was out of breath when I did the second song.'

During March 1973, T Rex issued their next single, 'Twentieth Century Boy', a No. 3 British hit, featuring female support vocals and saxophonist Howie Casey. The album *Tanx* hotly followed to reach No. 4. The album cost £12,000 and took seven months to record in Denmark and France. In answer to his critics, Bolan shrugged off rumours of his decline with a mature, fuller sound, in his attempt to switch from flimsy 'pop' to serious music. Bolan: 'I won't be jeered at when I'm doing something that's a craft I've worked at hard for seven years or more. I've never felt so insecure or such pain as I do now because I'm so exposed musically.'

In June 1973 T Rex issued their next single 'The Groover', a No. 4 hit. It was the group's last Top Five entry, but their tenth British hit. Many believed 'The Groover' reverted to Bolan's past style; he agreed, claiming it would be the last, while adding, ' "The Groover" sold a hundred thousand on the first day out. It's my only answer. We still sell the most records in England out of anybody. We sold thirty-nine million records, ten and a half in England in two years.'

It was at this juncture that the singer admitted he was now able to shrug off his image. 'I [don't] want to get sucked into second generation glam-rock. I did that thing for a year and . . . then there was nowhere to go. I felt slightly over-exposed in the papers so I thought I'd back off . . . My next thing won't be glam-rock . . . I don't want to be involved in any of that.' Instead, he turned his mind's eye to the punk movement.

Midway through 1973, the membership of T Rex altered: Paul Fenton, additional drummer, and Jack Green, guitarist, plus a trio of back-up vocalists that included Gloria Jones, now departed from Motown. It was this T Rex line-up that toured America from July to September. In their absence the *T Rex Great Hits* compilation was issued and reached the British Top Forty. For the remainder of the year, Bolan holidayed in the Bahamas, before visiting Australia and later Japan. Following this trek, Bill Legend departed from the group, while the final single of the year, titled 'Truck On (Tyke)', the first to feature Jones on vocals, stalled in the British Top Twenty.

In 1974, T Rex toured Britain for the first time in two years with the line-up of Steve Currie and Mickey Finn, Paul Fenton and Davey Lutton, plus vocalists Pat Hall and Gloria Jones. Under the banner, 'Truck Off', the tour spanned January, before excited, but not hysterical, audiences. During February, the next single, 'Whatever Happened to the Teenage Dream?', bearing the label credit Marc Bolan and T Rex, faltered at No. 13 in the British chart. It proved to be Bolan's final hit for approximately one year. Also in the same month the album *Zinc Alloy and the Hidden Riders of Tomorrow* became a Top Twenty hit. The release, incidentally, marked the end of Bolan's business association with producer Tony Visconti, while the album was critically ravaged, due to its reputed self-indulgence and an expanding production that matched the singer's waistline. Truthfully, Bolan was losing control: his music bored him, he was no longer the teenage megastar. The image he had diligently created for himself was strangling him. By April, in total despair, he left Britain to become a tax exile in Monte Carlo, where he turned to the comfort of alcohol, gaining weight at an alarming rate.

On the music front, the 'Light of Love' single faltered outside the British Top Twenty during July 1974, while Track Records and Polydor Records finally (and legally) released the *Hard on Love* album, under the title *The Beginning of Doves*. Before 1974 closed, T Rex toured

America once more and released the *Zip Gun* album, from which 'Zip Gun Boogie' was swiped as a single, becoming a Top Fifty hit. The album, meantime, bombed; even his loyal following was incapable of making it chart. Bolan claimed he had composed the bulk of the material in the recording studio, not leaving sufficient time to rework the music, yet, declared, 'I haven't slipped, not in my chart. I'm still No. 1 . . . Since the departure of Tony Visconti, my music's been much more heavy and rock and rolly. I've been freer in the studio, the way I was when I first started.' With his music suffering, so did his personal life when his marriage to June ended, although he did have a lifeline – Gloria Jones. Bolan said of his marriage, 'We just grew apart, we couldn't relate to each other any more.'

During the next two years, Bolan's music began to chart again – 'New York City' re-established him as a Top Twenty artist; 'Dreamy Lady' reached the Top Thirty, leaving 'London Boys' to falter in the Top Forty. Then, quite out of the blue, 'I Love to Boogie' zoomed to No. 13, followed quickly by 'Lazer Love' which, ironically, only made the Top Fifty. Nonetheless, Bolan was striding high once again; his career slowly on the upturn, his past glory returning. The album *Futuristic Dragon* reached a healthy Top Fifty position. The T Rex sound was fuller and mature, but tended to lapse into a potpourri of Bolan's musical thoughts. With success came concern for his health; his lifestyle in the fast lane was taking its toll, particularly following a spell of living in America, where, he said, he lived on nervous energy, cocaine and alcohol. When he finally collapsed, doctors told him to reconsider his life's pace. Bolan: 'It had been a warning. If I kept living the way I was I would die . . . It was madness, and it's all finished with now.'

The warning and the prospect of becoming a father changed Bolan for the better. Jones gave birth to his son, Rolan, on 26 September 1975. Bolan: 'I delivered him myself . . . this baby's made all the difference to my life.' So much so, that he announced his intention to marry Jones as soon as the ceremony could be arranged. Sadly, Bolan died before it could.

During the last year of his life Marc Bolan duetted with Jones on 'To Know Him Is to Love Him', their version of The Teddy Bears' classic, while Jones herself issued the *Vixen* album. In March 1977, T Rex toured Britain with support act The Damned. The group's final live performance was staged on 20 March in Portsmouth. A month later, the T Rex single 'The Soul of my Suit' peaked in the British Top Forty, while its follow-up, in August, titled 'Celebrate Summer', bombed. During the same month, Bolan mourned the sudden death of his musical hero, Elvis Presley. This prompted Bolan to confide to close friends that he had now lost his inspiration and felt that he would die before he reached the age of thirty. Many shrugged off his statements. Meanwhile, *Dandy in the Underworld,* the last album to be issued while the singer lived, soared into the Top Thirty. Now sporting a short hairstyle, and wearing designer suits, his new image befitted his changed musical style. The satin and silk was long gone. Bolan said, 'I consider myself to be an elder statesman of punk.' Abandoning his music for the written word, the singer contributed to the weekly music paper *Record Mirror,* but his biggest career break occurred when Granada Television offered him six half-hour shows titled *Marc,* a weekly showcase for him and his guest acts, who included The Boomtown Rats and David Bowie, who appeared on the final programme. Bolan always closed his shows with the words, 'Keep a little Marc in your heart. See you next week, same Marc time, same Marc channel.' Before the last show could be screened, the singer was dead.

During the shooting of his Granada series, Jones was in America, recording tracks for single release in a Los Angeles studio. On 16 September 1977, two days after her return to Britain from Los Angeles, Bolan invited a handful of friends for a reunion dinner, including Jones's musician brother Richard. As night turned into morning, Bolan and Jones left Morton's Restaurant, in Berkeley Square, for their newly-purchased Richmond home. Bolan did not hold a driving licence; Jones drove her purple mini, with Richard and EMI Records' promoter, Eric Hall, following in another vehicle. Turning from the Upper Richmond Road West into Barnes Common, Jones lost control of the mini, swerving off the road into a tree. It was a notorious blackspot. Bolan, who rarely wore a seat belt, was found in the back seat. He had died instantly. Jones, crunched against the dashboard, her left leg and foot in the centre of the mini, was unable to move. Richard Jones, seeing he could do nothing for his sister, pulled Bolan from the vehicle, and attempted mouth-to-mouth resuscitation, tasting the residue of the fish meal on Bolan's lips, before realising he was dead. There were no physical signs of injury on the body, save a solitary spot on the singer's forehead. Jones was rushed to Roehampton Hospital, with injuries diagnosed as a smashed ankle bone, broken jaw, extensive cuts and bruises.

Next morning, media news stories were saturated with Bolan's sudden death; Britain's best loved 'pop' artist was gone at the age of twenty-nine. It was ironic that the singer who never held a driver's licence should die in a car crash.

Jones remained unaware of Bolan's death, despite pleading with the hospital staff for information. As a last resort she asked someone to telephone a close girlfriend so that she could visit. The request was denied. Unbeknown to Jones, EMI Records executives had banned any unauthorised outside contact for fear she would learn of the tragedy, as her extensive injuries excluded any form of sedation. Bolan was cremated at Golders Green Crematorium in London, following a funeral that took on the guise of a circus. Tony Visconti: 'There were genuine fans there, who were crying for Marc, but there were lots of other fans there with cameras and autograph books . . . forgetting this was a funeral, with his family present.' Attending artists included David Bowie, Elton John, Gary Glitter, Cliff Richard and the rest of T Rex. With the funeral over, Jones, with a wired jaw and a leg in plaster, was now told by her brother that Bolan had not survived the accident.

In time she left hospital to recuperate with her brother at Alistair McLean's London apartment, where she attempted to untangle Bolan's numerous business affairs. Although her physical injuries would heal, she was advised that her singing voice would not return. Happily, this was not the case. While grieving over her loss, the police notified her that they intended to charge her with manslaughter. However, before this could be done, further investigation on her Mini revealed that following a service by a Sheen garage three days prior to the crash, a tyre had been replaced. Two nuts on the front off-side wheel were barely tight, while the tyre was at too low a pressure. This caused the vehicle to become uncontrollable; there was nothing Jones could have done to prevent the accident.

The manslaughter charges were subsequently dropped, following a verdict of accidental death at the inquest. Then Jones faced a further trauma. Bolan's parents who, she admitted, felt little for her, intended to raise Rolan claiming, she said, that she was unable to do so. Because of this, and the constant media hounding, much of which was extremely distressing, Jones and her son fled from Britain to Los Angeles, where they reside to this day.

Let's backtrack. Within hours of Marc Bolan's death, his family home was ransacked; music items, in particular, were removed. Further items purchased by Bolan and stored in safe houses, were likewise claimed. Jones had no mementos to remind her of her life with the artist.

Marc Bolan's public life was deliberately outrageous and colourful; he also was extremely talented – the singer who grew from a bopping elf to an electric warrior and, finally, a star. In 1997, twenty years after Bolan's death, fans and the music industry celebrated his life with a major television documentary, a tribute concert and the laying of a memorial stone dedicated by the Performing Rights Society to Bolan's contribution to music. Rolan Bolan, now 22 years old and a Recording Arts graduate, attended these functions and introduced to the British public his own band, Rolan Bolan and the Brothers Bounce.

'I danced myself out of the womb; I danced myself into the tomb.' – Marc Bolan

Also see: 'Hot Love', April 1971; 'Get It On', August 1971; 'Telegram Sam', February 1972

(Quotes: *Marc Bolan: A Tribute* by various contributors; *Electric Warrior: The Marc Bolan Story* by Paul Sinclair)

July 1972

SLADE

Take Me Bak 'Ome

Noddy Holder, the booming voice of Slade, was to be recognised as Britain's most powerful singer since, possibly, John Lennon. Yet he, like the rest of the group, shrugged off the inevitable trappings of stardom to maintain their working-class lifestyle.

With their first British chart-topper, 'Coz I Luv You', behind them, Slade began 1972 with another Holder and Lea composition, 'Look Wot You Dun'. The track soared to No. 4 in the British chart, and was closely followed by their No. 2 album *Slade Alive,* previewed for the media at London's Ronnie Scott's.

While the single lived, Slade played one-nighters around Britain. During March 1972, the group toured Germany before embarking upon their first major British trek in May. Status Quo supported them during the month-long stint.

Everyday life had obviously changed drastically for the quartet; the struggle for recognition was behind them, the future looked positive. For as long as Holder and Lea could compose hard-edged titles, their success was guaranteed. Slade's onstage presence also underwent a vivid transformation. Holder told the weekly music paper the *NME,* 'We used to be right scruffy up to the time of "Get Down and Get With It", but then we had some money in our pockets, and so by the time of

"Coz I Luv You" we were starting to flash out a bit with the clothes.'
Flash out indeed – Holder wore loud coloured shirts and checked pants,
ridiculously balancing a top hat over his unruly hair, and had huge
sideburns that joined under his chin. The rest were subdued by
comparison (or were they?). Jim Lea favoured brightly coloured satins;
Dave Hill overstated his 'yob' image with showy satin colours, while
Don Powell was marginally restrained in striped outfits. All sported
shoulder-length hair and wore platform boots, often of the sparkling
type. Hardly practical, but then this *was* the seventies! Slade's colourful
image worked. While other groups complained of the vast sums spent
on stage clothes, Slade, mindful of their working-class upbringing, did
not. Dave Hill told author George Tremlett: 'It costs nothing . . . to
dress the way we do. I've only ever bought one really expensive outfit
and that was an all-gold leather suit with matching boots which I had
specially made for me for £100.' And, believe it or not, he wore the
outfit more than once.

By now, Holder and Lea had grown into confident composers; the
top-selling singles had proved that. They approached their writing with
the same no-nonsense attitude as they did the music business in general.
One established a chorus, a catchword, then together they built the song.
'Look Wot You Dun' was conceived while Slade was travelling to a concert,
likewise 'Take Me Bak 'Ome'. Lea: 'I just thought of those few words,
sang over the hook to the others, and we knew we'd done it again.'

Indeed they had. 'Take Me Bak 'Ome' shot to the top of the British
chart during July 1972, earning them a silver disc; their second. Three
months later, the title debuted in the American chart, albeit the lower
region. America proved a hard country to crack, but Slade continued
to clutch Britain and Europe in their musical grasp.

Also see: 'Coz I Luv You', December 1971; 'Cum On Feel the Noize',
March 1973; 'Skweeze Me Pleeze Me', July 1973; 'Merry Xmas
Everybody', January 1974

(Quotes: *The Slade Story* by George Tremlett)

DONNY OSMOND

Puppy Love

If in doubt, pluck the youngest brother from a family group, mould him into a solo artist, highlighting a wide-eyed innocence that parents will accept, and a star is born! Donny Osmond fitted the criteria perfectly. Likewise little Michael from the Jackson family group, who rose to Motown's highest ranks to compete against the Osmond creation, or so it seemed.

Born Donald Osmond on 9 December 1957 in Ogden, Utah, the youngster joined his elder brothers' group in 1963. Even at the tender age of six years, he was allowed a solo spot within the group's act, usually singing 'You Are my Sunshine'. Donny Osmond told author Paul H. Dunn, 'I didn't have to be a member of the group. My brothers didn't say, "Donny, get in." I showed an interest in it and I worked hard at it . . . [I] became a fully fledged member when I was seven.'

It soon became apparent that little Donny was the public's favourite brother with his cute, innocent looks and teen charm. So it was to be expected that he would be groomed for a solo career without leaving The Osmonds entirely. It took one hit single from the group, namely 'One Bad Apple', to launch Donny in 1971, the same year as Michael Jackson issued 'Got to Be There', his debut solo single.

Donny Osmond's first outing was the aptly named 'Sweet and Innocent', which climbed the American singles chart to No. 7 in June 1971, selling one million copies en route. Michael Jackson, on the other hand, soared to No. 4 with 'Got to Be There'. The *Donny Osmond Album* followed in August, the same month as the group's *Home Made* album. Both releases passed gold disc status. A month on, Donny issued his next single, 'Go Away Little Girl', penned by Carole King and Gerry Goffin. (Mark Wynter enjoyed a British No. 6 with the title in December 1962.) Donny's version topped the American chart, a position it held for three weeks; again selling in excess of one million copies. Before the end of 1971, his second album, *To You with Love, Donny,* peaked in the American chart at No. 12, earning a gold disc for sales.

'Hey Girl', a cover version of Freddie Scott's original, was Osmond's first single of 1972. Coupled with 'I Knew You When', another cover song, swiped from Billy Joe Royal this time, the disc shot into the American

Top Ten, another million-seller. Midway through the year, the *Portrait of Donny* album became his third to reach gold status, while a further cover version established the young Osmond in the American Top Three. Titled 'Puppy Love' and written by Paul Anka, it was originally recorded by Pat Boone in 1960. The new version became Donny's fourth consecutive American gold disc. When the single was issued in Britain, it reached the top of the chart, a position it held for five weeks.

Osmondmania had firmly gripped Britain, exceeding that raging through America. Fan magazines carried photos of the young teen idol; merchandisers cashed in on the hysteria while record companies counted the cash! Parents despaired; fans ran amok. My, it was exciting!

Prior to Donny's British chart-topper, The Osmonds were an everyday, average-selling American unit, who could travel around, say, Britain, practically unnoticed. Merrill Osmond: 'We were just like tourists . . . If we'd lined up, we couldn't have given our autographs away. Then right after that, Donny's record "Puppy Love" hit. Our records hit. Then we couldn't be seen anywhere in England!' In actual fact, 'Puppy Love' went on to re-enter the British chart three times – October and December 1972, and January 1973 – and each time the single peaked in the Top Fifty.

Donny Osmond would continue as a high-flying teen artist in his own right for some time, and would embark upon another career as duettist with his sister Marie, leaving his elder brothers to contentedly cash in on his success . . .

Also see: 'Young Love', September 1973

(Quotes: *The Osmonds: The Official Story of the Osmond Family* by Paul H. Dunn)

September 1972

ROD STEWART

You Wear It Well

The blond, spiky-haired singer with the gravelly voice and large nose was on his way to solo stardom thanks to the success of the 'Maggie May' single and *Every Picture Tells a Story* album in 1971. Now he had to cement that success.

Still billed as Rod Stewart and The Faces (Ron Wood, Ronnie Lane, Ian McLagan, Kenny Jones) they devoted four months to recording the next album, *Never a Dull Moment,* which soared to the top of the British chart for a two-week stay, peaking a rung lower in America.

The album's lifted single, another rock ballad from the pens of Stewart and Martin Quittenton, titled 'You Wear It Well', became Stewart's second consecutive chart-topper. The Faces, meanwhile, maintained their position as his backing band, letting the singer bask in his glory. The follow-up single was the double-headed 'Angel'/'What Made Milwaukee Famous (Has Made a Fool out of Me)', which peaked in the British Top Five during November 1972.

With Stewart promoting two recording careers – as a solo artist and as lead singer with The Faces – it was not long before a split of loyalties began to show. This was particularly highlighted when The Faces were due to record what would be their last studio album, *Ooh-La-La.* While the group was ensconced in the studio, Stewart failed to join them for two weeks, saying he was uninterested in the project. When the album was finally released, Stewart told the media it was a 'bloody mess'. Ian McLagan: 'He slagged the album off. There was no reason for him to do that . . . he had everything to gain from it being a success.' Their private disagreements were now public and the media waited for more.

Following the release of the Faces' No. 2 single 'Cindy Incidentally' in February 1973, a track recorded while Stewart was a member of the Jeff Beck group was issued by RAK Records. Titled 'I've Been Drinking', it not surprisingly reached the British Top Thirty. Meantime, Stewart's own official single 'Oh No Not my Baby', a cover version of the Maxine Brown 1964 classic, released by Wand Records, peaked at No. 6 during September 1973 and was a Top Sixty American hit. The last charter of the year was The Faces' own 'Pool Hall Richard'/'I Wish It Would Rain'.

Whatever means were tried, nothing could dissipate the animosity which had developed between Ronnie Lane and Rod Stewart. In fact, Lane wanted Stewart to leave the group which would elevate him to leader. The other Faces disagreed. However, following months of arguing and fighting, Ronnie Lane left the group in June 1973. Ian McLagan: 'I didn't speak to him for some years and of course it turned out that around that time he realised he had MS . . . It was very sad that we kicked him out but he never told us.'

During May 1974, Stewart duetted with Denis Law on the Scotland World Cup Football Squad's album, and in the October, the single 'Farewell'/'Bring It on Home to Me'/'You Send Me' (his tribute to the late black singer Sam Cooke) peaked at No. 7 in the British chart.

By the end of the year, Stewart's dispute with his existing record companies reached boiling point. For some time neither had been happy with the recording arrangement afforded them by Stewart, or who chose what material went to which. Instead of bargaining new contracts, Stewart signed a solo recording deal with Warner Bros which, in turn, sealed the fate of his career with The Faces.

Also see: 'Maggie May', November 1971; 'Sailing', September 1975; 'Da Ya Think I'm Sexy?', December 1978

(Quotes: *Rod Stewart: The Best Selling Biography* by Tim Ewbank and Stafford Hildred)

October 1972

DAVID CASSIDY

How Can I Be Sure

'Singing what people coined "bubblegum" teenage stuff was a hard pill to swallow, because it really wasn't the kind of image or music that I wanted to play. But I think The Partridge Family made some really great records.' – David Cassidy

Born on 12 April 1950 in New York, to actor Jack Cassidy and Evelyn Ward, David Cassidy was raised in West Orange, until his parents divorced and he moved to California with his mother. Jack Cassidy then married actress Shirley Jones in 1956, whereupon David moved into their home, where inevitably he was influenced by the entertainment business. While at Redford High School, Cassidy debuted on stage in *The Pyjama Game* during 1960, before joining the Los Angeles Theatre Company, where he performed in several shows. When his family moved to New York, Cassidy worked as a postboy during the day, taking acting lessons in his spare time. He told author Barry Scott, 'My musical roots came from being fortunate enough to be alive and be a reckless teenager in Southern California, hanging around the Strip in the sixties.' He befriended Buffalo Springfield and The Doors in particular and 'got to feel a part of the LA music scene.'

While performing in *The Fig Leaves Are Falling* in 1968, a talent scout from CBS Films arranged for him to be screen tested. The test was a dud, whereupon Universal Films secured him to perform in various low-key productions that included television dramas like *Ironside* and *The FBI*. This acting experience impressed the casters for a new television series, *The Partridge Family*, who auditioned him for the role of Keith Partridge. Unbeknown to the twenty-year-old Cassidy, the part would transform him into an international star. The cast included his stepmother, playing Shirley Partridge. Other members included Susan Dey as Laurie, Danny Bonaduce as Danny, and Suzanne Crough as Tracy.

Based on the story of family entertainers, The Cowsills, *The Partridge Family*, screened by ABC TV after *The Brady Bunch* each Friday night, lasted four seasons. Like The Cowsills, The Partridge Family were a singing unit with a mother who drove her family around the American concert circuit in a vividly coloured bus with the back sign reading 'Caution! Nervous Mother Driving'. The series also heralded the beginning of a successful group recording career, although it transpired that David Cassidy and Shirley Jones were the only cast members to actually sing on the recordings, although Jones admitted, 'I did very little in the recording sessions. I literally was the background vocal for David.' Interestingly, it was Cassidy who first suggested recording the Partridges as a group to the shows' producers, who, in turn, appreciated the viability of the money-spinner.

The suggestion turned to reality when The Partridge Family signed a recording contract with Bell Records, and issued their debut single 'I Think I Love You' in October 1970. Cassidy was, naturally, the featured vocalist on this Tony Romeo composition. 'I got to work with phenomenal musicians. I feel really lucky that I was able to do it.' He cited keyboardist Larry Knechtal; drummer Hal Blaine and guitarist Larry Carlton in particular, who between them had worked with Eric Clapton and Simon & Garfunkel. However, despite The Partridge Family's happy, spontaneous television image of bursting into song at the drop of a note, the recording sessions were quite different. More often than not, Cassidy recorded with the studio musicians; there wasn't another Partridge in sight!

'I Think I Love You' broke into the American chart four weeks after the television debut of *The Partridge Family* before reaching the No. 1 position in November 1970, selling in excess of four million copies. The single held this spot for five weeks.

In March 1971 the chart-topper's follow-up, 'Doesn't Somebody Want to Be Wanted', soared to No. 6 in the American chart, selling one million copies en route. This was one of the few tracks Cassidy regretted

121

recording because the producers wanted him to sound younger than his years. To this end the track was slowed down, Cassidy's vocals were added, then the track was return to normal speed. '[It's] one of the worst vocal performances in the history of recording, in my opinion . . . and they had me do that little talking bit in the middle, which is the most embarrassing moment in my entire career. I have never done the song since it was a hit.' While 'Doesn't Somebody Want to Be Wanted' climbed the American chart, 'I Think I Love You' peaked in the British Top Twenty. A relatively poor showing, by comparison, but the result of the television series not being screened.

By this time, the group had issued a pair of albums, namely *The Partridge Family Album* and *The Partridge Family up to Date;* both Top Five American hits. Meanwhile, a third single was issued. Titled 'I'll Meet You Halfway', it soared into the American Top Ten, followed by 'I Woke Up in Love This Morning', which had a lower placing in the Top Twenty.

Shortly following the release of the third album, *The Partridge Family Sound Magazine,* a Top Ten hit, David Cassidy (predictably) secured a solo recording contract with Bell Records. His debut single, titled 'Cherish', written by Terry Kirkman and a cover version of The Association's 1966 American chart-topper, soared into the American Top Ten, becoming his first million-seller.

During March 1972, following the release of *The Partridge Family up to Date* album and 'It's One of Those Nights (Yes Love)' single, the television series was screened in Britain. Subsequently, the single soared into the Top Twenty, while a month later Cassidy's second solo single, 'Could It Be Forever', faltered in the American Top Forty, although the album *Cherish* peaked in the Top Twenty. In Britain, 'Could It Be Forever', his first solo release, with 'Cherish' featured on its flipside, soared to No. 2 in the chart. In July, Cassidy's next solo single, 'How Can I Be Sure', a revamped version of the 1967 American hit by The Young Rascals and a 1970 British hit for Dusty Springfield, reached the American Top Thirty. Three months later, the single soared to the top of the British chart, a position it maintained for two weeks. This title was the first of two British chart-toppers which would turn the singer into a teen idol, pin-up portrait, sex symbol and the ultimate star who attracted young mob hysteria on a huge scale.

Meanwhile, the 'Rock Me Baby' single followed, marking a distinct change of style. The wispy, pop slant was replaced by a soft R. & B. flavour and the new musical direction affected his selling power. 'Rock Me Baby' struggled into the American Top Forty but reached the Top

Twenty in Britain. While Cassidy began earnestly stealing young girls' hearts and cash, the remaining members of The Partridge Family continued to make their presence felt. Early in 1973, the group issued a cover version of Gene Pitney's 1965 No. 3 British hit, 'Looking through the Eyes of Love'. The group's interpretation struggled into the American Top Forty, while enthusiastic British sales pushed it into the Top Ten. Pitney's deep, intense original won out!

Partridge Family or not, David Cassidy's prime interest was in his own career, and following the release of his *Rock Me Baby* album, he performed before capacity crowds at Wembley, Middlesex, thereby cementing his popularity as a new teen idol. Inevitably, while he was basking in his runaway success, The Partridge Family began their decline. In 1973 they released their second hit of the year. Titled 'Walking in the Rain', it was a version of The Ronettes' classic, and crashed into the British Top Ten. Sadly, it marked the group's last hit. Across the Atlantic, the same fate was sealed with their 'Friend and Lover' single.

With The Partridge Family behind him (although the television series continued until 1974) David Cassidy was able to plough the bulk of his energies into his solo career, particularly in Britain where his status was considerably higher than that in his home country.

Also see: 'Daydreamer'/'Puppy Song', November 1973

(Quotes: *We Had Joy We Had Fun* by Barry Scott)

November 1972

LIEUTENANT PIGEON

Mouldy Old Dough

'Mouldy Old Dough' was yet another seventies title to fall into the category of a novelty single. It was, to be honest, a ridiculous instrumental swiped from the twenties, punctuated by the words of its title. The British record-buying public loved it!

Robert George Woodward was born in 1945 in Coventry, to Hilda and George, both musically inclined. Woodward attended the Caludon Castle Secondary School, while in his spare time he played the ukulele with his parents, performing as The Novelty Trio. In time the youngster learned to play the guitar and piano.

Leaving school, Woodward became a shipping clerk, maintaining his musical interests during the evenings performing 'standard' and current material both as a duettist and soloist. In 1963 he became a professional musician, managed by entrepreneur Larry Page, who nicknamed him Shel Naylor, and who secured him a recording contract with Decca Records under this name. A pair of singles were issued, namely, 'How Deep Is the Ocean' and 'One Fine Day' in 1963 and 1964 respectively. Interestingly, 'One Fine Day' was not a cover version of The Chiffons' 1963 soul classic, but rather a track penned by Dave Davies, a member of The Kinks, whom Page also represented. Following the release of these titles, Shel Naylor supported Brian Poole and The Tremeloes, among others, on a lengthy British tour, but with no hit forthcoming, Decca Records and artist parted company.

Woodward reluctantly returned to the nightclub circuit and joined forces with Nigel Fletcher. They began to compose their own material, and to this end they transformed a room in Woodward's home into a makeshift, yet workable, recording studio, where they experimented with musical ideas. In time, they were sufficiently confident to record a handful of titles to hawk around record companies.

Pyramid Records were interested enough in their music to release 'I Want to Love You Like a Mad Dog' under the name Stavely Makepeace. However, to promote this title the record company needed a group (naturally enough!), so Woodward recruited a membership of three. Then the unthinkable occurred; before a second single could be issued, Pyramid Records went bankrupt. Stavely Makepeace moved on to Concord Records during 1970. With no success, they switched to Spark Records to release a trio of singles. All bombed.

It was during this period that Woodward and Fletcher had, among other titles, produced an instrumental track which they called 'Mouldy Old Dough'. Recorded in Woodward's makeshift home studio with his mother thumping away on the piano, the title carried an unusual keyboard effect. Woodward told journalist Alan Clayson, 'I'd been very impressed with what Sam Phillips did at Sun Records with repeat delay after the vocal. I had the idea of doing the same on speeded-up piano.'

Satisfied with the track, Woodward sent a copy of 'Mouldy Old Dough' to Decca Records, where a company executive rush-released it as the debut single from Lieutenant Pigeon. The title shot to the top of the Belgian chart, prior to being released in Britain, where in November 1972 it likewise topped the chart. It held the position for four weeks, before repeating the success elsewhere in the world. The runaway triumph of what many considered to be a ridiculous three minutes, and which others believed a tribute to Stax Records' mainmen, Booker T and The MGs, caught both Lieutenant Pigeon and Decca Records hopping. This was evidenced by the hastily compiled album titled after the chart-topper, containing a mish-mash of material that included the titles 'Auntie May', 'Scarecrow' and 'Yellow Submarine'.

And yes, there was a soundalike follow-up. Titled 'Desperate Dan', and issued late in the year, it reached the Top Twenty. This single was Lieutenant Pigeon's last British hit. In an attempt to recharge their career, Lieutenant Pigeon recorded a party album titled *Pigeon Party*, from which the lifted track 'I'll Take You Home Again Kathleen' became an Australian chart-topper. However, this success was insufficient to sustain Decca Records' interest in the group; following the release of two further singles, namely, 'Rockabilly Hot Pot' in 1975 and 'Goodbye' a year later, they were dropped from the artist roster. Woodward: 'If we tried to make our records too sophisticated they'd say that it wasn't Lieutenant Pigeon. Yet if we stuck to fun music, they'd moan that it was the same old thing.'

Through the seventies and eighties, Rob Woodward recorded both as a soloist and with Lieutenant Pigeon for various record labels but with little success. During the nineties, however, when the nostalgia tours were in full swing, Lieutenant Pigeon, featuring a solitary original group member, were earning £1,000 per performance! Hardly 'mouldy old dough' by anyone's standards!

(Quotes: *Record Collector* magazine, interview by Alan Clayson, 1996)

Also a No. 1 single in November 1972: 'Clair' by Gilbert O'Sullivan

December 1972

CHUCK BERRY

My Ding-A-Ling

He was hailed as a musical enigma by The Beatles and The Rolling Stones, who not only cited him as their greatest musical influence but who also slavishly emulated him on record. On stage, he gave birth to his famous 'duck walk', while offstage his brushes with the law made headline news. Indeed, Chuck Berry was a complex rock 'n' roller!

Born Charles Edward Anderson Berry in January 1926 or October

1931, in either St Louis, Missouri, or San Jose, California, (the artist offers no confirmation either way!) Berry taught himself to play the guitar as a youngster. However, any ambitions to become a musician proper were blighted when he was arrested for armed robbery and incarcerated for three years in the Algoa Reform School. When released as a teenager, he resumed his interest in music with one-off performances in countless St Louis nightclubs, and by taping his own material in the hope of finding a sympathetic record company.

In October 1948, Berry married Themetta, later joining the St Louis-based Johnnie Johnson Trio as guitarist. He performed with them nightly, while daily he worked as a hairdresser and beautician. The trio's act comprised hillbilly, country and R. & B. material, while Berry perfected his emulation of Nat 'King' Cole's voice. He then moved on to form his own outfit which he called The Chuck Berry Combo, where once again he used the nightclub circuit as his training ground.

During 1955, Berry befriended blues master Muddy Waters after a performance in the Cosmopolitan Club. Another story suggested that Berry moved to Chicago where he heard Waters perform. Either way, Waters asked Berry to play with him and, impressed with the result, arranged for the guitarist to audition for Leonard Chess, who headed Chess Records. Berry played two tracks, one of which Leonard Chess wanted to issue as a single, but with a title change. Berry subsequently restructured the track, using the name 'Maybellene', producing an uptempo country/blues sound which, when modified, became the Chuck Berry trademark, making him the leading innovator of black rock music. His lyrics, on the other hand, were considered dubious, due to their use of sexual innuendo. 'Maybellene' was a good example; it held double-edged lyrics that on the surface related to car racing, but in actuality referred to sexual encounters of the sinister type. Nonetheless, 'Maybellene', released in August 1955 as Berry's debut single, soared to No. 5 in the American chart, while topping the R. & B. chart.

During 1956, Berry's success was limited to the solitary single 'Roll Over Beethoven', which stalled in the American Top Thirty, while an appearance in the music movie *Rock Rock Rock* exposed him to a wide white audience. The following year, the single 'School Day' dominated the R. & B. chart, reaching No. 3 in the mainstream listing, selling one million copies en route. The title also became his British debut, released by the EMI Records' subsidiary label Columbia, and reached the Top Thirty during June 1957. Two further singles reached the American chart before the close of 1957, namely 'Oh Baby Doll', Top Sixty; and 'Rock and Roll Music', Top Ten.

In 1958, Berry's 'Sweet Little Sixteen' single shot to the top of the American R. & B. chart, reaching No. 2 in the mainstream listing, his biggest-selling title to date. In Britain, the disc soared into the Top Twenty that April. The follow-up, 'Johnny B Goode', soared to No. 8 in America, while a further handful of singles kept his name in the American chart. With his newly-found fame and fortune, the singing guitarist purchased his own nightclub in St Louis.

A trio of American singles, namely 'Anthony Boy', 'Almost Grown' and 'Back in the USA', maintained his chart status through to July 1959, while the movie titled *Go Johnny Go* re-established him as a big screen name. However, before 1959 closed, Berry's name was tarnished. He was arrested in Mississippi for allegedly picking up and raping a white girl, in contravention of the Mann Act which was introduced to prevent the transporting of minors across the State line for sexual purposes. In fact, the artist had hired a fourteen-year-old Indian to work as a hat check girl in his nightclub. Berry later learned she was a prostitute, whereupon he dismissed her. She reported him to the police, who arrested him. Berry was convicted, fined $2,000 and sentenced to five years in prison. During the first trial, the judge regularly referred to him as a 'negro'; hence the trial was abandoned because it was considered to be racist. At the second trial in 1962, Berry was convicted and he served sixteen months in prison. During his incarceration, a trio of British singles were issued, namely 'Go Go Go', 'Let It Rock' and 'Run Rudolph Run'; all titles were issued on the Pye International label; all were hits.

By 1964, as The Beatles had immortalised Berry's track 'Roll Over Beethoven' as an album track, the originator was released from prison. He said, 'I made notes of new songs and now think the public will forget and accept me as a performer, not as an ex-jailbird.' Once acclimatised to the outside world, he returned to the Chess recording studio. From those sessions, the title 'Nadine (Is It You)' was the first to be issued as a single and reached the British and American Top Thirty. The public's memory was indeed (tragically) short-lived. Following the single's release, Berry embarked upon his first British tour, supported by The Swinging Blue Jeans, among others. The tour was interspersed with television appearances to promote his new single 'No Particular Place to Go', which in May 1964 soared into the Top Ten on both sides of the Atlantic. Three further titles were issued through the year: 'You Never Can Tell', 'Little Marie' and 'Promised Land'. All were medium sellers, while a handful of albums achieved Top Twenty status.

A further British tour started in 1965; this time with Long John

Baldry as support act. During his stay, Berry recorded titles in London's Pye Studios; those sessions were issued on the *Chuck Berry in London* album.

A change of record company occurred during 1966, when Berry left Chess in favour of Mercury Records, for a reputed advance of $150,000. Despite great expectations with his new record company, his run of hits was exhausted. The reluctant artist had little option but to tour.

Following a performance in the movie *Gather No Moss,* premiered in Britain during August 1966, Berry returned to the country once more to tour. Indeed, hopping from one country to another occupied much of the following two years. With a non-existent recording career with Mercury Records, Berry returned to Chess Records during 1970, where his album *Back Home* was (thankfully) a moderate seller.

Two years on, Berry recorded in Britain once more, this time using The Faces as his back-up group. These tracks and those recorded from one of his concerts were released under the title *The London Chuck Berry Sessions;* a Top Ten American seller. Midway through 1972, Berry performed at the Wembley Stadium in Middlesex, alongside fellow artists who included Little Richard and Bo Diddley. The event was, in actual fact, Britain's first 'Rock 'n' Roll Revival Show'; an instant sell-out.

With such a colourful track record and deep-rooted heritage behind him, it seems ironic – almost pathetic - that Chuck Berry should reach the pinnacle of his career with a novelty song that was childish in conception and simplistic beyond reason. It was a quirk in rock 'n' roll; a blip in black music history. Recorded live in 1972 at the Arts Festival staged in Manchester, and swiped from the album *The London Chuck Berry Sessions,* 'My Ding-A-Ling' catapulted to the top of the American chart during October 1972, earning the distinction of being the artist's most successful single ever (as of 1997), selling in excess of one million copies. Two months on, the single with its double entendres dominated the British chart for four weeks. Due to its content, Mary Whitehouse, Britain's morality 'watch dog', tried unsuccessfully to ban the single from the British airwaves. The public, meanwhile, was undecided whether it was indeed *the* Chuck Berry, or another; it mattered little, the Christmas season was in full swing, and 'My Ding-A-Ling' was ideal for parties and singalongs. On the plus side, Berry's catalogue albums resurfaced, most of them becoming moderate sellers once again.

The follow-up to 'My Ding-A-Ling' was issued in February 1973, with not a penis in sight! Titled 'Reelin' and Rockin' ', this reversion to solid rock music was another live performance, which reached the American Top Thirty, but rose to No. 18 in Britain. Regrettably, it was Berry's last British title. The remainder of the year was dominated by lengthy tours, likewise the start of 1975 when Berry toured Britain once more.

His career jogged along on both sides of the Atlantic for the following four years, until he was imprisoned in July 1979 for non-payment of tax. Apparently, Berry insisted on cash payments for his live performances; eventually this led to his downfall. He served his five-month sentence in Lompoc Prison Farm, California.

To start the new decade, his album *Rock! Rock! Rock 'n' Roll* was issued, while his future career would revolve around worldwide concert dates. During the eighties, Berry received several industry honours, including a Lifetime Achievement Award at the 1985 Grammy ceremony, and performed alongside Etta James and Julian Lennon, among others, at a gala concert organised by The Rolling Stones' guitarist Keith Richard, staged at The Fox Theatre, St Louis, to celebrate Berry's sixtieth birthday.

In 1988, he promoted his autobiography in Britain, while a year on 'Johnny B Goode' was included on *The Voyager Interstellar Record*. At the close of 1989, Berry once more fell foul of the law when he was charged with invasion of privacy by a former cook at his own restaurant, Southern Air. It was alleged in the civil suit that the musician had installed secret video recorders in the ladies' toilets. The secret taping had spanned one year and a total of two hundred women eventually brought a collective action against Berry. It was alleged the tapes were made for the 'improper purpose of entertainment and gratification of the abnormal unrination . . . and sexual predilections of defendant Chuck Berry'. A year on, his troubles worsened. In June, following a lengthy surveillance by the DEA, Berry's Park estate was raided by drug-enforcement agents from St Charles County. They seized a quantity of hashish and marijuana, but more disturbingly, films dealing with bestiality and reputedly pornographic amateur videos were also found.

Berry was subsequently charged with child abuse, possession of a controlled substance, and released on a $20,000 bail. During November 1990, he was cleared of the child abuse charges but pleaded guilty to the possession of marijuana. This time, Berry was given a six-month sentence and ordered to donate an amount of cash to a local charity. In 1991 he toured Britain!

Further wrangles with the law in 1993 occurred when Berry argued that his 'litigious' fights should be moved to the Federal Court from the State, because he believed he had fallen victim to a conspiracy designed to financially destroy him. He lost! And so it went on. From stage to courtroom, from promoter to lawyer. But whatever crime he allegedly commits, nobody will dispute that as an artist Chuck Berry is indeed a rock legend.

LITTLE JIMMY OSMOND

Long Haired Lover from Liverpool

Although he had no idea where Liverpool was, the youngest Osmond brother sang with such gusto that the single sold one million copies in Britain. This was the era of Osmond-mania; his elder brothers, including solo artist Donny, had catapulted into international fame, so why not let the youngest have a go?

Born James Arthur Osmond on 16 April 1963 in Canoga Park, California, to Olive and George, Jimmy was the youngest, and for a time the largest, member of the Osmond family that comprised Virl, Tom, Alan, Wayne, Merrill, Jay, Donny and Marie. He was also known to have the glummest of looks on his face. He told author Paul H. Dunn, 'I was never happy and I always had a big frown on my face . . . Father began spending more time on me – I suppose you could say he disciplined me.'

Joining his brothers' established group meant Jimmy had to work extra hard to master their routines, including song and dance. Jimmy said: 'Whenever I [got] a line wrong when we were rehearsing or recording, they just [had] me do it again. They never jumped on me because I flubbed.'

Like his brothers, Jimmy was taught by tutors between the demands of his professional life. He enjoyed science and geography, while English was, he said, his poorest subject. At the age of nine, cute little Jimmy recorded and released what many believe was the most obnoxious single of the decade. Written by Christopher Dowden, 'Long Haired Lover from Liverpool' topped the British chart in January 1973, a position it held for five long weeks. He was the youngest soloist to achieve this status, and the single won the distinction of being the year's biggest seller. Well, that says a lot for the rest of the tracks released during 1973! In America, record buyers showed more sense, as the single struggled into the Top Forty.

And there was more. Little Jimmy's second hit was 'Tweedle Dee', likewise lifted from his first solo album, titled *Killer Joe,* itself a Top Twenty British hit and an American bomber. The single, a cover version of LaVern Baker's original, peaked at No. 4 in the British chart, while across the Atlantic it shuffled to a Top Sixty placing. Before Osmond could enjoy his third British hit, sister Marie had embarked upon her own solo career with 'Paper Roses', lifted from the album of the same name. Donny, meantime, had sustained his high-selling profile, and The Osmonds continued to cash in where they could.

'I'm Gonna Knock on your Door', another cover version, borrowed this time from Eddie Hodges, became Jimmy's third British Top Twenty hit, peaking at No. 11. The title marked his final British hit, leaving Donny and Marie to fly the Osmond flag, which they did until the eighties.

Due to the exceptional family success throughout the world, which, of course, played a major role in launching Jimmy as a solo artist in the first place, he, like the others, lost much of his normal childhood. Yet, he said, he experienced more than a boy twice his age: 'I've been to the Orient, to Europe, all over the Scandinavian countries . . . Most kids would give their right arm to do what I [did] and I really appreciate it.'

With his solo career behind him, the chubby young superstar performed within the Osmond group until it disbanded in 1980. He then worked on the periphery of show business as an entrepreneur.

(Quotes: *The Osmonds: The Official Story of the Osmond Family* by Paul H. Dunn)

February 1973

SWEET

Blockbuster

With their adventurous use of make-up – eyeshadow, lipstick and beauty spots – the members of Sweet were among the leaders of British glam-rock. The image suited their music; a cacophony of high pitches and straight-forward melodies. Marc Bolan's T Rex had helped spearhead the glam image, prompting other groups to be less inhibited. There were no rules, anything went – and usually did!

Drummer Mick Tucker, born in Harlesden, London, on 17 July 1949, and singer Brian Connolly, born in Hamilton, Scotland, on 5 October 1949, were members of the group Wainwright's Gentlemen before forming Sweetshop. They recruited guitarists Frank Torpey and Steve

Priest, born in Hayes, Middlesex, on 23 February 1950, to play their first date in early 1968.

By July 1968 the group had issued their debut single, titled 'Slow Motion', via Fontana Records. It bombed. Undeterred, they moved to EMI Records' Parlophone offshoot to release a trio of singles, including 'Lollipop Man'. All bombed, whereupon EMI Records dropped them from its artist roster. Sweetshop then underwent a personnel change: Frank Torpey left to be replaced by guitarist Andy Scott, born in Wrexham, Wales, on 30 June 1951. This move coincided with the group name change to Sweet.

Early in 1971, Sweet performed for the first time on British television, which led to a recording deal with RCA Records where they worked with Phil Wainman. That May, Wainman teamed up with producer/composers Nicky Chinn and Mike Chapman (who later worked successfully with RAK Records' artists, among others) to record 'Funny Funny'. The title was Sweet's debut RCA release: it took everyone by surprise when it soared into the British Top Twenty during May 1971. Two months on, 'Co-Co' hotly followed to race to No. 2 in the chart. When issued in America the disc faltered in the lower Top One Hundred. Nonetheless, it was a start. 'Alexander Graham Bell' then became a British Top Forty entrant, ending a remarkable year for a group who had embarked upon a recording career at least twice! However, behind the smiles, there was unrest as Brian Connolly told journalist Jane Kelly in his 1996 *Daily Mail* interview: '[Andy] Scott influenced the others against me. He began stirring and backstabbing behind closed doors.' In turn, the other group members accused their lead singer of drunkenness and unreliability.

To welcome 1972, Sweet threw themselves into the growing lucrative glam-rock scene. They adorned themselves in brightly coloured, sequined stage clothes which they complemented with lavishly applied make-up and (naturally) a smatter of sparkling glitter. To exhibit their new image, Sweet released the first in a serious run of hit singles. 'Poppa Joe' peaked at No. 11 in the British chart during March, while its follow-up, the dubiously titled, but fun single 'Little Willy', soared higher into the Top Five. For television appearances Sweet played down the song's dicey connotations, leaving their saucy exploits for live performances. It was these antics that led to them being banned from the entire Mecca circuit which, during the seventies, was suicidal for a group of their standing. In actual fact, this was the second occasion the group had fallen foul of the obscenity laws; in May 1972 they were taken to court in Belgium for using a 'pornographic' video during their act. 'Little

Willy' refused to lie down; when released in America it sold in excess of one million copies to peak in the Top Three. The Americans obviously enjoyed the double entendre as well!

Leaving their saucy behaviour behind them, Sweet's final single of the year went from the sublime to the ridiculous. Titled 'Wig-Wam Bam', the loud thumper soared to No. 4, helped on its way by the group's accompanying stage clothes – yep, Indian costumes and wild, vivid warpaint – which fans slavishly copied!

After six attempts, Sweet finally enjoyed their first and only British chart-topper during February 1973. Titled 'Blockbuster', it was a full, romping basher and rightly dominated the chart for five weeks. It typified their perfected glam-rock style that had, by now, established them as a serious musical act, despite the glitz. The follow-up single, 'Hellraiser', was another blinding stormer, which shot to No. 2 in Britain; likewise their September 1973 release titled 'Ballroom Blitz'.

The musical storm continued. Sweet's first single of 1974, 'Teenage Rampage', completed their trio of Top Two hits, and marked the start of their first major British tour, which they used to promote their second album, *Sweet Fanny Adams,* ultimately a Top Thirty hit. Incidentally, their debut eponymous album, released during the latter part of 1973, bombed!

Also in 1974 two further titles were issued, 'The Six Teens', a Top Ten success, and 'Turn It Down' which, surprisingly, struggled into the Top Fifty. This low placing prompted the group to relinquish their hit-making relationship with Nicky Chinn and Mike Chapman to embark upon an independent recording career. The move was initially fruitful.

In 1975, 'Fox on the Run', a group composition, soared to . . . No. 2 in the British chart, an encouraging start to their musical independence. The next single, 'Action', reached the Top Twenty. America then called, and before 1975 closed, Sweet toured there, whereupon 'Ballroom Blitz' shot into the Top Five, while its follow-up, 'Fox on the Run', issued early in 1976, repeated the high placing.

Meantime, in Britain, the group began to struggle chartwise. 'The Lies in your Eyes' stalled in the Top Forty, and marked their last hit for two years. However, America supported them; 'Action' became a Top Twenty hit and 'Funk It Up (David's Song)' in 1977 hung around the Top Ninety. Mind you, two albums were Top Twenty sellers, namely, *Desolation Boulevard* and *Give Us a Wink.*

When Sweet reappeared on the recording scene in 1978, they had switched companies from RCA Records to Polydor Records. Their new single was included in the soundtrack from *The Bitch,* a movie starring

Joan Collins and based on her sister Jackie's novel. Titled 'Love Is Like Oxygen', the track returned Sweet to the British Top Ten in January and reached No. 8 in America. It was their final British hit until 1985.

During 1979 Sweet's demise was inevitable and this was, many believed, the probable thinking behind founder member Connolly leaving the group. However, in that same *Daily Mail* interview he insisted he had little choice but to leave, citing the group's last Canadian tour as an example. 'That tour revolved around the three of them . . . they sent me to Coventry. It was quite unbearable.' He claimed the group had resorted to switching off his stage microphone without his knowledge and, when they returned to Britain, deliberately recorded an album in a key they knew was beyond Connolly's capability. This, he said, enabled them to tell him he was finished, whereupon he found solace in alcohol. By 1981, Connolly's drinking was so heavy that he suffered multiple cardiac arrests.

Connolly's retirement in 1979 was short-lived; he formed the new Sweet. Meantime, the remaining members replaced him with Steve Priest as lead singer, whose vacant spot at the keyboard was filled by Gary Moberley. With no single success, the group performed on the concert circuit and tested their strength on the record-buying market by releasing a pair of albums, namely *Water's Edge* and *Identity Crisis* in 1980 and 1981 respectively. Both sold badly, which culminated in Sweet finally disbanding. But the name just would not lie down!

In 1985 BMG Records were keen to sign the group as a recording unit, but Connolly refused to work with Scott. Connolly: 'I don't talk to Scott or see him. I don't talk about him, but he is constantly criticising me, putting me down.' The group may have been non-existent but not so the music. Anagram Records released a compilation titled *Sweet 16 – It's Sweet's Hits,* which surprisingly peaked in the British Top Twenty late in 1984. A year on, 'It's It's the Sweet Mix', a re-vamped, segued twelve-inch single featuring a handful of the group's biggest hits, reached the Top Fifty.

With no new product available, a further compilation of hits titled *Ballroom Blitz* was issued in 1996 and sold a staggering 60,000 copies, earning Sweet a silver disc. To capitalise on this renewed public interest, Connolly re-formed Sweet, whereupon his line-up was reputedly more successful than the group he left behind. Why not? Connolly was 'the voice' on the hit records. Also, if Connolly's comments regarding Scott were true, and he was haunted by the guitarist's jealousy throughout the group's most successful period between 1971 and 1978, he certainly deserved to bask in the credit.

And Brian Connolly did until 1997, when he died at the age of fifty-two on 10 February in a Slough hospital. His kidneys finally gave up, following his fight against alcohol abuse and a muscle wasting disease. He is survived by his ex-wife, his girlfriend and three children.

(Quotes: *Daily Mail,* interview by Jane Kelly, 1996)

March 1973

SLADE

Cum On Feel the Noize

With his Dickensian sideburns and throat-splitting vocals, Noddy Holder led his group from chart-topper to chart-topper. Slade's almost tasteless flair for clothes and boot-stomping music imprinted them in the rock annals as the most popular group since The Beatles. Not bad for a working-class band from Wolverhampton.

During 1972 Slade enjoyed two consecutive British chart-toppers, namely 'Take Me Bak 'Ome' and 'Mama Weer All Crazee Now'. The latter dominated the chart for three weeks and was the second-fastest-selling single of the year after T Rex. The title also became a Top Eighty American hit.

At the close of 1972, and during a performance at the Liverpool Stadium, Dave Hill suffered a broken ankle when fans mobbed the stage. He was unable to work for some time. Meanwhile, with advance orders in excess of 80,000 copies, Slade's album *Slayed* was issued to top the British chart.

Now at the climax of their career, Slade headlined a gala concert at the London Palladium, celebrating Britain's entry into the Common Market, while the readers of the weekly music paper *NME* voted them Top British Band and Top Live Band in their annual poll.

In February 1973, Polydor Records issued the group's seventh hit single. Titled 'Cum On Feel the Noize', the song was dreamed up by Lea one evening at his parents' home, and became a British chart-topper in March. The track dominated the chart for four weeks. Slade had conquered the world, except America where, of course, The Beatles, to whom they were now compared in terms of success, had ruled supreme. They were experiencing the same fan hysteria; riots greeted them at every concert. Their car was chased by fans so often they lost count; audiences threw themselves on stage, oblivious to injury and damage, and the group's hotel stay-overs were besieged. Holder told author George Tremlett, 'I wouldn't dream of trying to walk down a London street now . . . I've even worn dark glasses and a beard!' In July 1973, Slade witnessed fan worship at its extreme, with a concert before a 20,000-strong audience at Earl's Court, London.

Also see: 'Coz I Luv You', December 1971; 'Take Me Bak 'Ome', July 1972; 'Skweeze Me Pleeze Me', July 1973; 'Merry Xmas Everybody', January 1974

(Quotes: *The Slade Story* by George Tremlett)

April 1973

GILBERT O'SULLIVAN

Get Down

Yep, he was the singer who wore strange clothes – flat cap and braces, no less. However, his music represented some of the finest of the decade although he told author Barry Scott, 'When I started writing songs and getting interested in music . . . I had no ambition to make a career out of it.'

Born Raymond O'Sullivan in Waterford, Eire, on 1 December 1946, he moved with his family to Swindon, Wiltshire, when he was thirteen years old. By this time, O'Sullivan had learned to play the drums and piano; indeed, while he was a student at art college his mother gave him a piano, whereupon his creative streak for composing began to emerge. While he was still a student, The Tremeloes recorded a pair of his compositions, namely, 'Come On Home' and 'You'; both titles appearing on their *Here Comes The Tremeloes* album issued during 1967.

Influenced by The Beatles, rock 'n' roll and American R. & B., O'Sullivan played his way through several groups including The Doodles, The Prefects and a group led by Rick Davies called Rick's Blues (Davies went on to become Supertramp's keyboard player). They included several of O'Sullivan's compositions in their stage act. O'Sullivan said: 'As time went by and I finished my college course, I had to think about my future . . . My songs were developing . . . So I had to make a decision whether I'd get a job in the art world . . . or have a crack at music.'

He chose music, and in 1967 signed a recording contract with CBS Records, where he released a couple of singles titled 'Disappear' and 'What Can I Do', using the name Gilbert. They bombed. It was at this juncture that O'Sullivan's brainwave of using a Charlie Chaplin cum Buster Keaton image became reality. In an entertainment world that was neck-deep in denim and long hair, O'Sullivan opted for a flannel suit that fitted too tightly, knee-length trousers and a waistcoat or braces, striped socks and tie, plus a flat cap over a 'pudding basin' haircut. O'Sullivan said, 'I dressed in a way that made me look odd.' And he certainly did.

The artist then signed a short-term recording contract with Major Minor Records, where 'Mr Moody's Garden' was one of two titles released. Still no success, but where to go next? O'Sullivan had heard of Gordon Mills, who went on to build a $40-million empire as manager of two sixties superstars, Tom Jones and Engelbert Humperdinck, and decided to send him a demo recording, together with a photograph emphasising his unusual image. Mills liked what he heard and saw, ultimately adding the young artist to his roster. O'Sullivan said, 'Most people . . . laughed at the way I looked, but he liked my songs enough to put up with the way I looked.'

Manager and artist collaborated for over one year, working on a gameplan, finally going into the studios together to record the O'Sullivan composition 'Nothing Rhymed'. In December 1970, the track became O'Sullivan's debut single on MAM Records, owned by Gordon Mills. The record label bore the artist's new name, 'Gilbert O'Sullivan'. 'Nothing Rhymed' shot into the British Top Ten, peaking at No. 8, while in America it floundered in the Top One Hundred. At this point in the gameplan, O'Sullivan's ambition was to become a respected recording artist in Britain; success elsewhere had not entered the picture – yet.

During April 1971, Major Minor cashed in on the artist's success by releasing the single titled 'Underneath the Blanket Go'/'I Wish I Could Cry'; a fair seller. Four months on, MAM Records issued the 'We Will' single, which peaked at No. 16 in the British chart. Before the close of the year, O'Sullivan had performed on London's Royal Albert Hall stage, contributing to the World Wildlife Fund; had issued his debut album titled *Gilbert O'Sullivan – Himself*, and released his final single of the year, namely, 'No Matter How I Try' which soared into the British Top Five.

The following year, O'Sullivan's career peaked when the single 'Alone Again (Naturally)' shot into the British Top Three. The track was

138

thought to have related to the death of his parents; in actual fact, it had nothing whatsoever to do with the singer's experiences, but, he admitted, it was a serious song that struck a chord with many people. 'Alone Again (Naturally)' also became his first heavyweight American release; cracking the chart to shoot to No. 1 during July 1972, a position it held for six weeks. By now, O'Sullivan's 'Chaplinesque' image had been modified – he wore a college sweater with a large initial 'G' on the front!

The British follow-up single marked a change of musical style, from ballad to beat. 'Ooh-Wakka-Doo-Wakka-Day' (as unlikely as it now seems, considering how serious O'Sullivan was as a composer) reached the British Top Ten in June 1972, while his debut album with 'Alone Again (Naturally)' as an additional track, reached No. 9 in America. By the end of the year, the American chart-topper was the year's biggest-selling single, reputedly with sales of ten million copies.

O'Sullivan's next single, titled 'Clair', was dedicated to Gordon Mills' daughter. '[He] and his wife were extremely good to me . . . [Clair] was the youngest. So I'd be sort of babysitting every now and then, and I kind of got attached to her. As a thank you to her parents for being so good to me, I wrote the song.' The single soared to the top of the British chart during November 1972, reaching No. 2 in America, earning him his second gold disc and multi-million seller.

Early in 1973, the second album, titled *Back to Front,* dominated the chart, while the singer starred in his own BBC TV show. In America, *Back to Front* stalled in the Top Fifty.

In April 1973, the title 'Get Down' became O'Sullivan's second British chart-topper. It held the top spot for two weeks. The lyrical content was based around the singer's unruly dog, whose behaviour left much to be desired, and did not, as people suggested, have any other dubious connotation. O'Sullivan said, 'It was an uptempo song, a complete contrast to a track like "Alone Again". Nothing deep in the lyrics, just a good little rock song. I enjoyed doing it.' The title went on to win the Most Performed British Song Award at the Ivor Novello Awards ceremony held in 1977. O'Sullivan's career had peaked; his selling power was great; a pair of British chart-toppers was heavy business indeed. For as long as O'Sullivan could maintain his creativity, he had little to worry him. When 'Get Down' was released in America, it peaked at No. 7 during August 1973, achieving gold status. 'Out of the Question', a track recorded during the same sessions as 'Alone Again (Naturally)' was released as the follow-up to 'Clair' in America only; it stalled in the Top Twenty.

To capitalise on his British success, the singer embarked upon a lengthy British tour before releasing 'Ooh Baby' as a single; it faltered in the Top Twenty in September 1973. A month later, the album *I'm a Writer Not a Fighter* soared to No. 2, while 'Why Oh Why Oh Why' closed the year in the Top Ten.

The first single of 1974, 'Happiness is Me and You' took O'Sullivan to the Top Twenty in Britain, and the Top Seventy in America. It was his last charter there. 'A Woman's Place' and the obligatory 'A Christmas Song' (which he loathed) were the final titles of the year; Top Fifty and Top Twenty hits in Britain respectively. The album *Stranger in my Own Back Yard* was the year's release, a No. 9 charter in Britain.

During the next three years, O'Sullivan enjoyed a solitary British hit single with 'I Don't Love You but I Think I Like You'; released a *Greatest Hits* package and his last album for MAM Records, *Southpaw*. He admitted to author Barry Scott that by 1976 he was frustrated: Gordon Mills had produced all his recorded work to date, and the singer longed to work with other top producers who were equally sympathetic to his music. In turn that would, he believed, benefit both him and his manager. Mills, however, was not keen to make the move. O'Sullivan said, 'The result was that through 1976 and 1977, I broke up with Gordon. The rot set in. I had to go into litigation.' That litigation included proceedings against Mills and his record company for unpaid royalties. Unbeknown to O'Sullivan at the time, this action would also mark the downfall in his popularity. Before the case could be heard in court, O'Sullivan signed a recording contract with CBS Records to release the single 'What's in a Kiss?', a Top Twenty hit, lifted from the *Off Centre* album. They were the only releases.

Two years on, artist and manager went to court, where the judge ruled in favour of O'Sullivan, declaring his contract with Mills was unrealistic. The judge added that O'Sullivan had not been properly paid for his compositions and record sales, and awarded the singer backdated royalties and full ownership of his master recordings.

Now free to pursue his career, O'Sullivan signed a recording deal with Chrysalis Records, where his album *In the Key of G* was issued during 1989, three years after the death of Gordon Mills. A year on, the re-mixed track 'So What' was lifted from the mother album and faltered in the British Top Eighty. 'At the Very Mention of your Name' followed. It bombed. Also in 1990, O'Sullivan wrote the stage play *Every Song Has its Play,* performed in London. That likewise bombed.

Early in 1991 the singer attempted to restart his career via a series of comeback British concerts. When they failed his career plummeted, although he recorded and released the Top Fifty album *Nothing but the Best* for Castle Communications. Two years later, he was heard once again on the 1993 album *Sounds of the Loop,* critically acclaimed only. Also that year, O'Sullivan prevented rap-artist Biz Markie from sampling 'Alone Again (Naturally)' on his 'Alone Again' single.

Since 1980 the singer has lived with his wife and family in Jersey. Although he has remained absent from the British chart, he continues to compose. Long gone, however, is the era of the 'pudding basin' haircut, flat cap and ill-fitting clothes, but one wonders if without them Gilbert O'Sullivan would have remained a top-selling act for so long. On the other hand, isn't it a fickle public who was initially attracted by an image rather than the music?

(Quotes: *We Had Joy We Had Fun* by Barry Scott)

May 1973

DAWN

Tie a Yellow Ribbon round the Old Oak Tree

'[The song] gently kids the fact that we love stories about turmoil, lyrics with suspense, doubt about a happy ending, as long as we know we are gonna get a happy ending in the last line.' – Tony Orlando

Following the success of 'Knock Three Times', which topped the British chart in June 1971, Dawn – Tony Orlando, Telma Hopkins and Joyce Wilson – scooped a further handful of hit singles until 1972, when their career started to flag. As a touring act they flourished but with no chart singles their bank account was practically empty. Before they were forced to make the decision to disband the trio, Bell Records' producers Hank Medress and Dave Appell chanced upon another song by Irwin Levine and L. Russell Brown (who had previously composed 'Knock Three Times'). The producers believed the song titled 'Tie a Yellow Ribbon round the Old Oak Tree' was a perfect vehicle for Dawn. Hopkins agreed it had hit potential; not so Orlando. 'I thought it was very corny . . . I kept singing it around the house. Against my will because my taste musically has always been what doesn't necessarily do well, rhythm 'n' blues.' He even suggested Bobby Vinton should record it. 'I didn't think at the time, the way the music business was going – we had heavy metal coming – that it would penetrate the radio.'

'Tie a Yellow Ribbon round the Old Oak Tree' was based on a true story. After serving a prison sentence for three years for forging cheques, a man was returning home on a bus to Georgia. Prior to embarking upon the journey he had written to his wife saying he would understand if she hadn't waited for him, but if she had, would she tie a yellow ribbon around the oak tree that stood in their hometown square. As the bus approached White Oak in Georgia, the man spotted the tree draped in a yellow ribbon, whereupon he broke down while his fellow passengers cheered in delight. The story had been publicised by the media to such an extent that it inspired Brown and Levine to compose the track.

The single was issued in America during April 1973 when it shot to No. 1, staying there for four weeks. A month later it became Dawn's second British chart-topper. It dominated the top spot for four weeks, selling in excess of 6.5 million copies worldwide, and was nominated 1973's top-selling single. It went on to become the second most rerecorded song from this era behind Paul McCartney's 'Yesterday'. An estimated one thousand cover versions have been recorded (to date), and when Dawn's original was reissued in January 1974, it peaked in the British Top Forty.

'Tie a Yellow Ribbon round the Old Oak Tree' established more than chart-topping status, it opened other entertainment areas for Dawn. For example, following their performance of the song at the 1974 Grammy Awards ceremony (it lost to Roberta Flack's 'Killing Me Softly with his Song'), the trio was given their own CBS TV show from December 1974 to 1976.

The follow-up single, 'Say, Has Anybody Seen my Sweet Gypsy Rose?', recorded in the same carefree style as their chart-topper, peaked in the British chart at No. 12, while soaring into the American Top Three. Yet, unbelievably this release was to herald the decline of Dawn's recording career. 'Who's in the Strawberry Patch with Sally' faltered in the British Top Forty (in hindsight, with a record title like that, what else could happen?), while 'It Only Hurts When I Try to Smile' stalled in the American Top Ninety. When the 'Strawberry Patch' single was later released Stateside it reached the Top Thirty.

By 1975 Dawn's British recording career was over. Even switching record companies from Bell to Elektra Records was fruitless, although in America they fared much better when 'He Don't Love You (Like I Love You)', a cover version of the Jerry Butler classic, captured the top position. A handful of singles sustained their selling status there, but in mid-1977 Tony Orlando told a Massachusetts audience he was leaving the trio. Telma Hopkins and Joyce Wilson had no prior knowledge of his decision; subsequently his one sentence broke up the trio following seven years of hitmaking. Orlando: 'I went through some personal crisis and decided to take a little time off. I felt that my whole life was just totally confusing to me. I had to put my braking system on. I always had it all on my own shoulders; I didn't know back then how to allocate work to others.'

Two years on Orlando embarked upon a solo career by first signing to Elektra Records, where he recorded a rock 'n' roll album, then by moving to Casablanca Records where he debuted with 'Sweets for my Sweet', a Top Sixty American hit. He then moved to acting. 'I did *Barnham* on Broadway. I got a chance to do *A Star Is Born* with Barbra Streisand. Then, I went on to do two television movies. One was *The Rosemary Clooney Story,* in which I played José Ferrer, the other one was called *Three Hundred Miles for Stephanie*. I continued on for a number of years, working and headlining.'

'Tie a Yellow Ribbon round the Old Oak Tree' was one of those nauseating singles that refused to die. For instance, it was foremost in the American public's mind when in 1981 their hostages were freed following a lengthy captivity in Iran. Yellow ribbons were displayed to welcome them home and the song was, naturally, played constantly. Then during 1991, Orlando composed 'With Every Yellow Ribbon (That's Why We Tie 'Em)' for the American servicemen fighting in the Persian Gulf. The troops returned before the single left the pressing plant! Bad timing or what?

Also see: 'Knock Three Times', June 1971

(Quotes: *Rolling Stone,* date unknown; *We Had Joy We Had Fun* by Barry Scott)

June 1973

WIZZARD

See my Baby Jive

Roy Wood has been remembered for over twenty years, not for his 1973 chart-topper, but for a cheery evergreen Christmas track that's as important as the turkey during the festive season. More importantly, though, he was the master of British 'pop' music, whose talent spanned three groups, starting with The Move.

In 1966 The Move was formed in Birmingham, comprising Roy Wood, born in Birmingham on 8 November 1947; Carl Wayne, Trevor Burton, Bev Bevan and Christopher Kefford. By the end of the year they had attracted a vast following, which in turn led to a recording contract with Deram Records. Early in 1967, The Move debuted with 'Night of Fear', which shot to No. 2 in the British chart, and went on to enjoy two further Top Five singles in 1967, namely 'I Can Hear the Grass Grow' and 'Flowers in the Rain'.

During the next year, the group topped the British chart with 'Blackberry Way' and continued their run of hit singles until 1972 and their final release, 'California Man'. At this juncture, Roy Wood released 'Grandma Plays the Banjo' as a soloist. It bombed, although it was reported that this had nothing to do with the title! The Move then disbanded to make room for The Electric Light Orchestra, although Wood's stay was short, despite his initial enthusiasm and the hit single '10538 Overture'. It was quite simple; he was restless, desperate to try another musical avenue.

He left ELO in August 1972 to form Wizzard with an eight-strong line-up, comprising Rick Price, Mike Burney, Charlie Grima, Keith Smart, Nick Pentelow, Bill Hunt and Hugh McDowell (both ex-Electric Light Orchestra members). Wizzard's debut single, 'Ball Park Incident', charted in the British Top Ten during January 1973. As Wizzard was an extension of The Move, the group's record label Harvest – a subsidiary of EMI Records – automatically issued the single, and continued to do so until The Move's original recording contract expired.

It later transpired that Wood quit The Move and The Electric Light Orchestra because he wanted to experiment with 'pop' material. 'See my Baby Jive' was British music's purest pop – instantly catchy with a full, thundering mid-paced beat. Written and produced by Wood, it soared to the top of the British chart during June 1973, holding the position for four weeks. With 'pop' came the image; Wood took it to the ultimate with an abundance of unruly hair and matching beard. When his face was fully painted, his clothes clashed delightfully. In fact, he was every inch a wizard!

Following 'Dear Elaine', released by Wood as a solo artist, Wizzard issued 'Angel Fingers', their second consecutive chart-topper in September 1973. The busy Wood 'sound' was established, but none so brilliantly as on the group's next single which, despite its immense popularity, never captured the top spot. Titled 'I Wish It Could Be Christmas Every Day', released to celebrate the 1973 festive season, the single soared to No. 4 in the British chart during December. It was such a driving, convincing sound that it continued to sell and rechart – in 1981 it reached the Top Fifty, while three years on it peaked in the Top Thirty. Inevitably, the track was featured on most Christmas compilations and remains among the popular songs cum carols to be played on radio during the seasonal period. While 'I Wish It Could Be Christmas Every Day' climbed the chart, Wood issued his solo single 'Forever', a Top Ten hit.

After a shaky beginning to 1974, partly because of Wood's ill health, Wizzard switched record companies from Harvest to Warner Bros, where in May the group released the No. 6 single 'Rock 'n' Roll Winter (Looney's Tune)'. Two months on Wood issued a further solo outing, 'Going Down the Road', a Top Twenty hit, while Wizzard's next release, 'This Is the Story of my Love (Baby)', was their final single of 1974 and, remarkably, faltered in the British Top Forty.

With the aid of bagpipes, 'Are You Ready to Rock' heralded in the New Year to re-establish the group in the Top Ten, while Wood capitalised on this success by issuing his own single, 'Oh What a Shame', which peaked in the Top Twenty.

Following a disagreement with his management, Wood's career disintegrated and Wizzard met its demise. As a final gesture, he issued his second album, titled *Mustard*, at the end of 1975. (The first had been *Boulders*, in November 1973.) When it bombed, the album was retitled *Roy Wood the Wizzard* but to no avail. It still bombed!

Early in 1976 Wood signed as an artist to a trio of record companies. Jet, (for whom he recorded 'Oh What a Shame'), Warner Bros, then EMI Records' Harvest label. Confusion arose with commitments, and by 1977 the projects Wood was involved with, including the launch of the Wizzo Band and associated recordings, soon failed. From then on, he concentrated on writing and producing for other acts, with an occasional dabble in the singles market.

However, during the eighties, Wizzard rose once more with a compilation titled *The Singles*, comprising Wood's best work with his three groups. Public support pushed the Speed Records' release into the Top Forty. Encouraged by this success, Wood signed an artist contract with Legacy Records to later record and release the album *Starting Up* in 1987, before performing with other Birmingham acts at the 'Heartbeat '80' concert. He then assisted Doctor and The Medics, singing on their cover version of Abba's 'Waterloo'.

Roy Wood will never totally fade from public view, his love of music will ensure that. But if nothing else, he will be seen dressed as Father Christmas, gracing television screens to celebrate the season. Hell, Christmas just wouldn't be the same without him!

July 1973

SLADE

Skweeze Me Pleeze Me

'We're 50 per cent humour and 50 per cent music. Every number we play is a beat number. Not just rock but music you can stomp, clap or just freak out to. It's a violent kind of music, but it provides a release in the form of an escape valve.' – Noddy Holder

With an audience dressed as Slade clones, a stage that boasted a huge back screen to enable the back rows easy sight of the group, and a 13,000 watt sound system that threatened the theatre's very foundations, Slade performed before 20,000 fans, crammed into London's Earl's Court on 1 July 1973. Approximately 200 security men were stationed in and around the stage, although it was left to Noddy Holder to control the audience's over-enthusiasm. The concert was brilliant; a triumph. Critic Chris Charlesworth wrote in the weekly music paper *Melody Maker*, 'It was more of a convention than a concert, a gathering of the converted that rivalled political assemblies, royal weddings and sporting crowds in both size and fervour. It was bluddy wonderful . . .' Indeed, everyone who attended the show hailed it as Slade's finest hour.

Three days after the Earl's Court performance, Don Powell was seriously injured in a car crash which killed his fiancée Angela Morris. The tragic accident occurred after an evening spent at Dix's, a Wolverhampton nightclub. It was believed Powell was driving his white Bentley S3 when he lost control and plunged into a wall. Both were rushed to Wolverhampton Royal Hospital; Morris was dead on arrival, while Powell suffered severe injuries which culminated in memory loss. As Powell was comotose and the group were committed to concerts on the Isle of Man, Powell's brother Frank stepped in as drummer. By August 1973, Don's recovery was sufficient to allow him to rehearse with the group.

A month prior to Powell's return to work, Slade enjoyed their fifth No. 1 single titled 'Skweeze Me Pleeze Me', which shot straight into the chart at the top, selling in excess of 300,000 copies during its first week. The title dominated the chart for three weeks. In the October, the album *Sladest* likewise soared to the top, where it also stayed for three weeks, while the follow-up single to the group's chart-topper was issued. Titled 'My Friend Stan', it peaked at No. 2 in the British chart, and while the single rose, Slade were touring America, playing their way through a month-long stint. They had recently signed a new recording deal with Warner Bros, and wanted to support their new alliance.

During 1973, Slade had sold in excess of 2.5 million singles in Britain alone; they were voted the top band in Britain and Europe, while Noddy Holder secured the top vocalist category. By the close of the year they were, without doubt, one of the world's biggest-selling groups. Only America remained immune. Unfortunately, that position would not change.

Also see: 'Coz I Luv You', December 1971; 'Take Me Bak 'Ome', July 1972; 'Cum On Feel the Noize', March 1973; 'Merry Xmas Everybody', January 1974

(Quotes: *The Slade Story* by George Tremlett)

August 1973

GARY GLITTER

I'm the Leader of the Gang (I Am)

'Although my songs were really nothing more than nursery rhymes, the chants would sometimes take hours to write,' Gary Glitter told author Lloyd Bradley.

He was born Paul Gadd on 8 May 1940 in Banbury, Oxfordshire. His mother was a single parent and they spent the early part of his life in the county's workhouse/maternity home. When Gadd was two-and-a-half years old, his brother Tony was born; he also had a half-brother David, who lived with his grandmother. Tony and Paul had the same father, who was the manager of a local aluminium factory and married with six daughters.

When he grew older, Paul, his brother Tony and their mother went to live with his grandmother at her bed and breakfast hotel and tea room, located on the outskirts of Stratford-Upon-Avon. In time, mother and sons moved into their own home. Despite being a Protestant, Gadd attended a Catholic primary school. It was at this juncture in his life that he was influenced by the varying styles of music and fascinated by the theatre, although in truth, his only experience to date was performing at the annual Scout Club Gang Show. Gadd and his family moved house so frequently that his education suffered; likewise his ability to cement lasting friendships.

When his mother moved to London to secure a home and job, her sons were placed in care in the Banbury area for a year. In time, Gadd and his brother joined her to live with Alan Prince Russell, and although the couple never married, Gadd adopted Russell's surname.

A year on, Paul Russell purchased his first guitar; he desperately wanted to be party to the rock 'n' roll craze that was gripping Britain, and London was the place to be. However, his guitar became redundant when he opted to be a singer. Like all ambitious rock 'n' rollers he headed for the 2I's coffee bar in London's Soho, where he was enthralled to watch acts like Cliff Richard and The Drifters (later re-named The Shadows) and the regular coffee bar group Vince Taylor and The Playboys. Russell was thirteen years old! Eventually, the youngster plucked up the courage to ask Tom Littlewood, owner of the coffee bar, if he too could perform for the drinkers. With an act that comprised Buddy Holly and Elvis Presley material, Russell built up a regular audience.

During 1958, the youngster took one step further by forming his first group to perform at nighteries like the Overseas Visitor's Club and the Safari Club. Known as Paul Russell and The Rebels, they later played dates outside the London circuit. Music was in Paul's blood; it was an ambition he was determined to pursue. To enable him to concentrate full-time on his chosen career, Russell, then fifteen years old, left school and home to rent a bedsit in London's Clapham area. He was now on hand for any last-minute bookings.

While performing at the Safari Club, he befriended a small-time movie producer, Robert Hartford, whose knowledge of the music business was sadly zero. Nonetheless, he became Russell's manager and secured him a recording session with Decca Records, where he was supported by an orchestra instead of The Rebels. Glitter said: 'I was given a song called "Alone in the Night", and I didn't object because I was desperate to get my name on a record . . . We were given two hours to finish both sides [of the single]. I didn't enjoy it too much, but at least I learned about different keys.' The single, issued during January 1960, bore yet another name – Paul Raven! The release bombed, despite a performance on the television music show *Cool for Cats*. Nonetheless, this television debut led to a British tour with The Rebels, as support act to comedian Bernard Bresslaw and entertainer Anthony Newley. As the stint was a financial disaster, Paul Raven and The Rebels earned not a penny!

Russell and Robert Hartford subsequently ended their relationship, whereupon the singer joined the theatrical agency, Fosters Talent, who arranged for him to support singer Vince Taylor on a forthcoming British tour. Russell moved through various managers before settling with Vic Billings during 1961, who secured his most adventurous stint to date, a tour of Norway, before netting a recording deal with the EMI Records' subsidiary, Parlophone Records. The result was the single 'Walk On Boy', released during August 1961. Glitter: 'It was more like a sweaty nightclub jam than a staid recording session and the record, a cover of the bluesy American number . . . had a wonderful raw excitement to it.' The title sold in excess of 25,000 copies and, like most of EMI Records' recording contracts at the time, the singer earned one penny per single sold – and that final figure had to be halved with Vic Billings! Based on this success, a second single titled 'Tower of Strength', originally recorded by American soulster Eugene McDaniels, was Paul Raven's next release during November 1961. The version bombed; popular British vocalist Frankie Vaughan recorded and released the hit version which soared to the top of the British chart. As was to be expected, Parlophone Records dropped Raven/Russell from its artist roster. Undeterred, the singer returned to the touring circuit, before being the voice-over on the soft drink television commercial advertising, of all things, Cherry B!

Life in 1963 was a struggle. Vic Billings became Dusty Springfield's manager; she had left The Springfields to pursue a solo career and much of Billings's time was devoted to her. However, Springfield shared her growing popularity with Raven: via her involvement with the cult Friday night music programme *Ready, Steady, Go!* he was hired as the show's warm-up act. The programme not only provided viewers with the best British and American acts, but afforded Raven a new social life, although he was engaged to be married. His fiancée, Ann, worked in the box office at the London Palladium. The marriage took place during 1964, lasted three years and produced two children, Paul and Sarah.

Following the *Ready, Steady, Go!* spot, Paul Raven and The Rebels disbanded to give birth to Paul Raven and Boston International, later The Bostons. As such, they took up residency in Germany; primarily in Hamburg. Glitter: 'If my first six years had been an apprenticeship,

Germany was my finishing school.' The group's music spanned pop, soul and rock 'n' roll, while Raven discovered the joys of drug taking, alcohol and groupies – not necessarily in that order. The outfit remained in Germany until 1968, when they returned to Britain to re-establish themselves on the constantly changing concert circuit.

One of the first people Raven contacted was his long-standing music associate, Mike Leander, who was now head of A. & R. at MCA Records. Almost immediately, Leander secured a recording contract for Raven; his debut single, titled 'Musical Man', was released under yet another pseudonym, Paul Monday. The name change couldn't save it; the disc bombed. The follow-up, 'Soul Thing', a dance track, was likewise lost; MCA Records failed to grasp the disc's potential.

And so the singer moved on. Following a stint as a DJ in a German club, Raven and Leander returned to the recording studio during September 1969 to experiment with the classic track 'Amazing Grace'. The result was actually titled 'We're All Living in One Place', released under a further pseudonym, Rubber Bucket. That too bombed! The follow-up single, a cover version of George Harrison's 'Here Comes the Sun', bore the name Paul Monday, while a further cover version, this time of Sly and The Family Stone's 'Stand', carried Paul Raven on the record label. Nothing worked; both titles disappeared without a trace. The latter marked Raven's final release for MGM Records.

Sheer determination alone should have guaranteed Paul Raven, er, Monday, success; the will power to continue in the cut-throat business of music should have, by now, given the young man a taste of the big time. But no; the national spotlight was still way out of reach.

At the close of 1970, following a further German trek and a series of demo recording sessions, which included one for Tim Rice and Andrew Lloyd Webber, Raven was offered the singing role of the priest on the soundtrack album of *Jesus Christ Superstar*. Glitter: 'I had a choice of payment – £40 or 1 per cent of the album royalties. I was so skint that I jumped at the cash. If I'd taken the other option, I'd still be getting an income from it today.'

One unwise decision led to a positive step. Glam-rock was making its presence felt in British music, with Marc Bolan spearheading the movement. Acts like The Bay City Rollers, Sweet and David Bowie were, though, strong contenders for his crown. Raven was worried about this unexpected musical changeover, and seriously considered abandoning his ambitions, afraid he was no match for the glamour and glitz. Within weeks, he and Mike Leander recorded 'Rock 'n' Roll, Parts 1 and 2'.

The recording session for his debut Glitter outing happened by accident. Leander had studio time booked for David Essex, who failed to keep the appointment. So Leander and Raven used the time. The song's title was, in actual fact, swiped from the weekly music paper *Melody Maker,* which was carrying a series of articles under the heading 'Rock 'n' Roll Parts 1 and 2'. Glitter: 'Recording [the track] was probably more haphazard than the way we'd written the song, so it was by a series of completely unplanned events that we ended up with what came to be known as the Glitter Sound.' Recorded on an outdated eight-track tape machine which constantly broke down, the tape subsequently jammed and the outcome was a series of unwanted 'clips'. Rather than editing these, Leander utilised them, by adding guitar, drum, among other instruments, handclaps and nameless musical improvisations. Yes indeed, there was little about the Glitter Sound that was hi-tech or sophisticated!

Bell Records were sufficiently interested in the final project to issue 'Rock 'n' Roll' across both sides of one single. Released in March 1972, with the record label bearing the name Gary Glitter, it soon became obvious that 'Rock 'n' Roll Part 2' was attracting most attention, mainly from the dancefloor crowd. This interest crossed over into mainstream music, to push the single to No. 2 in the British chart, whereupon Glitter realised he had no group to promote the single: 'The very first Glitterband was literally bodies filling in the space behind me. Nobody was actually playing – a few of them couldn't play at all.' The Glitter name befitted the Glitter image and, in time, that image, by intention, would become more preposterous by the month. Following David Bowie's advice, Glitter shopped for stage clothes at Alkusura, in the Kings Road, London, which specialised in velvets, sequins and glitter, plus exaggerated clothes, like shirts with huge collars and triple-thick platform shoes. Before long, singer and group glittered from head to toe. Glitter: 'Marc Bolan had at the time been wearing more and more glitter, as had Sweet, and we simply had to wear more than anybody else.'

By the time Glitter was ready to tour in August 1972, the Glitterband more or less comprised members from The Bostons. They had sufficiently rehearsed to join Emile Ford, Bo Diddley, and others, at the London Rock 'n' Roll Festival staged at the Wembley Stadium, Middlesex. A month later, Glitter's 'Rock 'n' Roll' single peaked at No. 7 in the American chart.

'I Didn't Know I Loved You (Till I Saw You Rock 'n' Roll)' followed, peaking at No. 4 in the British chart, and No. 35 in America. As the single lived, Glitter equalled Slade as the biggest touring group in Britain; a feat which boosted his first album, titled *Glitter*, into the Top Ten.

During January 1973, Glitter decided to bury his varied past – Paul Monday-Russell-Raven-Rubber Bucket – with a reception on HMS *Belfast*, moored on the River Thames. All memorabilia connected with these names was ceremonially piled into a coffin and lowered into the river. Unfortunately, it refused to sink; preferring to float out to sea.

A month later, 'Do You Wanna Touch Me (Oh Yeah)', another example of Glitter's hit style, shot to No. 2 in the British chart. The single was born, in actual fact, from Glitter shouting the phrase to his audiences – members of which willingly accepted his offer. 'Hello Hello, I'm Back Again', released during April 1973, soared to No. 2 (again!) in the British chart, proving the public had taken Gary Glitter, his outrageous persona and exaggerated stage presence, to heart. He was larger than real life, which enabled him to easily take his audiences into his fantasy world. A fact that remained true for two decades.

His public's loyalty was proven when, in August 1973, they put the next single 'I'm the Leader of the Gang (I Am)' on the top of the British chart, a position it held for four weeks. Glitter and Leander who, to date, had penned all the singles, wrote the track primarily for the stage, as singer and group started their act with their backs towards the audience, posing like a gang. Therefore, because of the nature of the lyrics, Glitter abandoned his camp sparkles for a leather jacket with protruding shoulder chains, with, of course, just the required amount of glitter. 'I'm the Leader of the Gang (I Am)' was the first of three British chart-toppers. Incidentally, the title was recorded by the American outfit, Brownsville Station, thereby denying the originator an American hit.

Yes, Glittermania had dazzled the British public into submission. They loved the manner in which he was able to laugh at himself, while acknowledging that he took his music seriously. Although the Glitter Sound was not one he had intended to pursue, preferring the raw side of R. & B., he and Leander realised a musical monster had been created from which there was no escape. Public loyalty, record sales and capacity audiences confirmed Gary Glitter was a winner. His star was destined to shine for a while yet!

Also see: 'I Love You Love Me Love', December 1973; 'Always Yours', June 1974

(Quotes: *Leader – The Autobiography of Gary Glitter* by Gary Glitter with Lloyd Bradley)

September 1973

DONNY OSMOND

Young Love

During the two years that Donny Osmond reigned as a superstar solo artist, his hit singles were all cover versions of other artists' work. This tried and tested material presented him with three British chart-toppers and four Top Twenty entrants, earning the composers pocket money for doing absolutely nothing except listen to their tracks being Osmondised!

Donny Osmond's first British No. 1, 'Puppy Love', in August 1972 opened the floodgates to an unprecedented wave of Osmond-mania. Young Donny was, of course, the fans' prime pin-up with his angelic looks, wide-eyed smile, clean-cut appearance and faultless manners. Also, the fact that he had been raised within a strict Mormon household held him in high esteem with parents. Yes, The Osmonds had covered every angle!

A version of the Nat 'King' Cole original 'Too Young' was the follow-up to 'Puppy Love' in September 1972. Swiped from Donny's album bearing its title, the single shot into the American Top Twenty and reached the Top Five in Britain. Before 1972 closed, the group issued the *Osmonds Live* album, and made a guest appearance on Steve Lawrence and Eydie Gorme's single titled 'We Can Make It Together'.

Jimmy Osmond, on the other hand, had other ideas and followed Donny's lead by reaching the top of the British chart with 'Long Haired Lover from Liverpool', while Donny himself issued the single 'Why', a No. 3 British hit. Albums from the group and Donny could be sighted in the charts on both sides of the Atlantic, although, inevitably, the British placings were higher.

Yet another non-original composition was recorded and released by Donny. The choice this time was 'The Twelfth of Never', composed by Jay Livingston and Paul F. Webster, previously a hit for American singer Johnny Mathis and British star Cliff Richard. Donny's interpretation swept to the top of the British chart during March 1973, with brother Jimmy hot on its heels with 'Tweedle Dee'.

Speculation was rife: if Donny Osmond had recorded an original composition instead of tried and tested cover versions, would he have scaled such heady heights? It is common knowledge that the public tend to buy tracks that are familiar and it was probably with this in mind that Donny Osmond recorded a song by yet another artist. This time he borrowed 'Young Love' from Tab Hunter. Written by Carole Joyner and Ric Cartey, Donny's single shuffled into the American Top Forty during August 1973, but soared to the top of the British chart a month later, a position it held for four weeks. The follow-up, 'When I Fall in Love', rose to No. 4 in Britain during December and, yes, it was a non-original, and another swiped from Nat 'King' Cole.

By this time, Donny's sister Marie had embarked upon a solo career, debuting with 'Paper Roses', first released by Anita Bryant, and a Top Twenty British hit for The Kaye Sisters in 1960. By the close of 1974, Donny and Marie released their first duet 'I'm Leaving It (All up to You)', swiped from Dale and Grace. The single sold in excess of one million copies in America and peaked in Top Five, while in Britain it soared to No. 2. An album bearing the single's name rounded off the year, together with Donny's solo outing 'Where Did All the Good Times Go', a Top Twenty British hit, and his last for MGM Records.

The first Donny and Marie duet of 1975, 'Morning Side of the Mountain', a cover version of the Tommy Edwards' original dating back to the fifties, peaked in the Top Ten on both sides of the Atlantic. In between Marie's solo outings, she continued her duetting career, which in turn led to ABC TV offering the Osmond couple their own series, *Donny and Marie*. The shows (naturally) included other members of the Osmond family, lasted three years, and won a handful of entertainment awards. Incidentally, on the personal front, while the television series was in its prime, Donny Osmond married Debra Glenn.

In July 1975, Donny and Marie issued the Eddy Arnold track 'Make the World Go Away', a Top Twenty British hit, which reached the Top Fifty in America, followed by 'Deep Purple', a reworking of the Nino Tempo and April Stevens' track which had been a Top Twenty British hit during 1963. This was the Osmond duettists last British hit, and it would take Donny Osmond eleven years to re-establish himself as a charting artist.

During 1977, though, Donny and Marie's singing relationship continued with a version of Marvin Gaye and Tammi Terrell's 1968 Top Forty British hit titled 'Ain't Nothing Like the Real Thing', while Marie solo released 'This Is the Way that I Feel', her final American hit. At

Christmas 1977, the young couple joined the Osmond family for a festive television special.

Through the next year, Donny and Marie released two further duets; a version of The Righteous Brothers' 1966 classic '(You're my) Soul and Inspiration', and 'On the Shelf', their final American hit.

During the eighties, the entire Osmond family maintained a low profile; the heights of their fame were long forgotten, replaced by new pin-ups and star idols. As was to be expected, Donny was the first brother to re-establish himself as a recording artist when in 1987 he secured a contract with Virgin Records. His debut British hit 'I'm in It for Love' struggled into the Top Eighty that September. A year later, supported by an American tour, Donny enjoyed a No. 2 hit with 'Soldier of Love', which reached No. 30 in Britain. This was followed by 'If It's Love that You Want', another minor British hit, while 'My Love Is a Fire', released via EMI Records' Capitol label in 1991, faltered in the British Top Seventy.

The American media may have cruelly dubbed Donny Osmond's as the Most Unwelcomed Comeback during 1989 but facts speak for themselves. Whether the media liked it or not, the Osmond family's contribution to seventies' music was vast, and although today they are viewed with some ridicule, they were no better or worse than Britain's more eccentrically inclined music makers.

Also see: 'Puppy Love', August 1972

(Quotes: *The Osmonds: The Official Story of the Osmond Family* by Paul H. Dunn)

October 1973

THE SIMON PARK ORCHESTRA

Eye Level

This instrumental oddity became a chart-topper thanks to the popularity of the detective thriller *Van Der Valk,* a weekly television series based on the novels of Nicholas Freeling. It was Simon Park's only No. 1 single; in fact, it was the only television theme (to date) to become a chart-topper.

Born in March 1946 in Market Harborough, Leicestershire, Simon

Park mastered the piano at five years old. He graduated from Winchester College in Oxford with music honours. His first professional break actually came when he, with Jack Trombey, composed the theme to *Van Der Valk* which was later credited to the Simon Park Orchestra which, of course, did not actually exist.

Interestingly, 'Eye Level' was first issued on EMI Records' Columbia label during November 1972, when it struggled into the British Top Fifty. The release coincided with the screening of the first series of *Van Der Valk* by ITV. The title was then reissued when the second television series was screened, and this time soared to the top of the British chart in October 1973, where it remained for four weeks. An album carrying the chart-topper's title hotly followed.

Simon Park's later success was confined to albums that included *Venus Fly Trap* and *Danger UXB* during the remainder of the seventies. *Van Der Valk* has subsequently been rescreened but unlike its theme music did not grow old gracefully.

November 1973

DAVID CASSIDY

Daydreamer/Puppy Song

'That people respond to my work for me is the greatest compliment, and the way people reached and responded from the very beginning was a bit overwhelming.' – David Cassidy

The double A-sided single 'I Am a Clown'/'Some Kind of a Summer' was David Cassidy's first single of 1973, and when it raced into the British Top Three it further established him as a major artist. The follow-up was likewise a double-headed release, namely Terry Dempsey's composition 'Daydreamer' and 'Puppy Song', penned by Harry Nilsson. Due to the singer's on-hand television promotion in Britain, the disc became Cassidy's second chart-topper, in November 1973. It dominated the chart for three weeks. Before the year ended, the album *Dreams Are Nothin' More Than Wishes* likewise topped the British chart, while in America it bombed, much to the embarrassment of both singer and record company.

However, Cassidy still had Britain within his grasp, where mania for him prevailed; it was nightmare city on a large scale for a singer who, on the one hand wanted to be considered a serious purveyor of music and on the other, languished in the teenage adulation. On occasion, the hapless enthusiasm of his fans went drastically and tragically haywire. For example, in 1974 when Cassidy appeared at London's White City Stadium, a young fan died from heart failure, while one thousand more were given First Aid treatment during his performance. And with such heady hysteria came the inevitable queue of groupies vying for the singer's body. They burst through stage doors, sneaked undetected into hotel rooms, as Cassidy, who had taken advantage of these willing 'star fuckers', told author Gary Herman: 'On the road there was always this one room where we'd corral a handpicked dozen of the most beautiful . . . After the show, I'd go up to this room, pick the one I wanted, and let the band divvy up the rest. I was an animal.' Eventually, he said, he outgrew this backstage decadence, tired of strangers in his bed.

In June 1974, Cassidy's next single 'If I Didn't Care' swept to No. 9 in Britain, while an adventurous (stupid?) version of The Beatles' 'Please Please Me' stalled in the Top Twenty.

After a successful four years *The Partridge Family* television series with David Cassidy and Shirley Jones at the helm was screened for the last time in 1974. In fact, the series was cancelled when viewers switched channels and, of course, when the group was no longer a recording unit. Interestingly, Cassidy's contract was renegotiated after the first year of being associated with the series and included a departure date in 1974. Coincidence or what? However, prior to the cancellation, new young characters were introduced into the series to replace Cassidy's role of Keith Partridge, but when the programme was switched from its prime time Friday night slot to a spot opposite a top programme, there was no way it could survive. Cassidy: 'I really felt the show could have gone on easily without me . . . At the time, I couldn't wait to be done with it. I was planning a world tour.' However, it was not until four years afterwards that he realised the ramifications that his decision had on so many people's lives. 'I'm thinking specifically about all the people who worked on [the programme] . . . In a way I feel a little remorseful that I didn't stick around for at least another year, so that they could make a lot more money.'

The following year Cassidy switched record companies from Bell to RCA Records. The relationship was ineffectual in America but maintained his superstar status elsewhere. Cassidy: 'Part of the problem I had with the middle seventies is that I [was] no longer going on tour and I was no longer really working.' He was tucked away in the recording studio experimenting with musical ideas. Not the right attitude, of course, when keeping a career on an even keel and certainly not an approach accepted in America where artists are expected to be seen to be airplayed. 'In Europe the structure is a lot different; so that if they are fans of yours, they continue to play your records when they come out. So I continued to have hits there without a whole lot of effort. I didn't have to go over there and promote them.'

His debut single for RCA Records, written by Bruce Johnston (a leading member of The Beach Boys), was 'I Write the Songs', released during August 1975. The title peaked at No. 11 in the British chart, while its mother album, *The Higher They Climb,* peaked in the Top Thirty. It was his final charting album. It transpired that Cassidy had heard Johnston's composition prior to its completion. 'He told me what it was and I said we've got to cut it . . . I had a No. 2 record in about seven or eight countries with [it] before the single came out in America.' Captain & Tennille and Barry Manilow also recorded the track; the latter enjoyed an American chart-topper with it in 1976. Before 1975 closed, Cassidy paid further homage to The Beach Boys by recording their 1968 Top Twenty British hit, 'Darlin' '. His version likewise faltered in the Top Twenty, and was his last British charter for ten years.

The bubble had dramatically, and presumably unexpectedly, burst. The superstar had fallen, the clawing fans had moved elsewhere. David Cassidy was forced to rethink his career. Following a three-year hiatus, he appeared before the public once more on the New York stage, with his wife Kay Lenz, playing the starring role in *Voice of the Turtle.* Following this stint, he returned to the small screen as a policeman in the NBC TV series *David Cassidy – Man Undercover.*

Early in the eighties, Cassidy returned to the stage to perform in *Little Johnny Jones,* before replacing Andy Gibb in the Broadway production of *Joseph and his Amazing Technicolor Dream Coat.* This was followed by a role in *Jesus Christ Superstar.* On the personal front, he divorced Kay Lenz to marry Meryl Tanz, and for approximately four years retired from the entertainment business.

The performing spotlight beckoned once more in 1985 when Cassidy signed a recording deal with Arista Records. In actual fact, he had little choice – Arista had purchased Bell Records with whom he remained a signed artist. His first release was 'The Last Kiss' single in March. George Michael assisted on vocals and together they enjoyed a Top Ten British hit. The follow-up single, 'Romance (Let your Heart Go)', faltered in the Top Sixty, resulting in a shattered recording comeback.

In 1987 he replaced Cliff Richard in the London stage production of *Time* before starring in the movie *Instant Karma,* but singing beckoned once more. During the next year he attempted a further comeback; that failed, but Cassidy was to be given another chance. When a Los Angeles radio DJ speculated on air about the whereabouts of the singer, he contacted the station to appear live on air. This led to another stab at a recording career with Enigma Records, and a one-off American Top Thirty hit titled 'Lyin' to Myself' in 1990.

Early in 1991, Cassidy and his third wife, Sue Schrifin, became parents; on the professional front he joined other artists to record a charity track to raise funds for the American Red Cross Gulf Crisis Fund, before dabbling in the movie sector and embarking upon an extensive American tour where he included The Partridge Family material in his performances, a move he vowed he'd never make. However, by reworking some of the tracks, he said, he realised they had a rightful place in his stage act. A further association with Scotti Brothers Records proved hitless, so with his wife he concentrated on composing material for third-party artists who included Cher, notably 'I'll Never Stop Loving You', a track included on her *Love Hurts* CD.

During the nineties, rumours circulated the industry that The Partridge Family would regroup. Nothing materialised (to date), so fans (are there any left who would admit to being fans?) had to content themselves with television reruns of the series and spin dusty vinyl. As for David Cassidy, he seems content to remain behind the scenes, using other artists as his vocal mouthpiece. 'I started playing and writing music because I loved it and I still do it for that reason. My work and the people who have been there and have cared about what I do [make] it all worthwhile.'

Also see: 'How Can I Be Sure', October 1972

(Quotes: *We Had Joy We Had Fun* by Barry Scott; *Rock 'n' Roll Babylon* by Gary Herman)

December 1973

GARY GLITTER

I Love You Love Me Love

'Instead of doing an interview with the *NME,* I'd choose to be on the cover of *Woman's Own* – their readers liked me, and it had a bigger circulation.' – Gary Glitter

One of Gary Glitter's first tours of 1973 was a financial flop. Introducing the Glitter Sound to Australia was, many believed, a natural progression, and as British artists rarely took the gigantic step of crossing the world, Glitter felt the time was ripe to head the new wave of seventies acts that included Elton John, David Bowie and, of course, Marc Bolan. Glitter: 'The Australians weren't quite sure what to make of [me]. I think most of them took one look and decided I must be some sort of Pommie poofter!' In retrospect, part of the tour's failure was the size of the venues, some holding as many as ten thousand people. At this juncture in his career, Glitter was not able to command such audiences. Of course, this would come – at the end of 1973 where, for example, he performed before five full houses at the Melbourne Festival, and later headlined a free concert in Moore Park, Sydney, before 150,000 people!

With Australia and Europe now under the Glitter spell, the singer wanted to crack the American market. In 1972 his 'Rock 'n' Roll' single had peaked at No. 7, while 'I Didn't Know I Loved You (Till I Saw You Rock 'n' Roll)' faltered in the Top Forty. However, Glitter believed there was an interest in his music; after all, Brownsville Station had confirmed that. The American arm of Bell Records, who released his recorded work in Britain, had likewise issued his product in America but, from December 1972, it had failed abysmally.

Before Glitter set foot on American soil, he enjoyed his second consecutive British chart-topper. Titled 'I Love You Love Me Love', the slower-paced, three-minute chant, entered the chart at No. 1 during December 1973, where it stayed for four weeks, selling in excess of one million copies. The single was a play on words, dreamed up by Glitter when Bell Records had pestered him for the title of the single to follow 'I'm the Leader of the Gang (I Am)'. Mike Leander and the singer had then built the song around the ambiguous title, in much the same fashion as they had previous singles.

Incidentally, with each single release, Glitter devised a new stage costume and stage set. For the 'I Love You Love Me Love' title, he performed lounging over a large glittering half-moon!

Glitter-mania was at its peak; Gary's impact on the music business was so phenomenal that he starred in his own movie titled *Remember Me This Way* late in 1973. To capitalise on his long-awaited success, The Glitter Band recorded as a separate unit. Signed to a recording deal with Bell Records, the group – Tony Leonard, John Springate, Harvey Ellison, Pete Phipps and Gerry Shephard – debuted with 'Angel Face', a No. 4 British hit. Six further singles charted in Britain: 'Just for You' and 'Let's Get Together Again', both Top Ten hits in 1974; while the following year 'Goodbye my Love', 'The Tears I Cried' and 'Love in the Sun', all reached the Top Twenty. In 1976, 'People Like You and People Like Me' peaked at No. 5, their final British hit. While enjoying a career of their own, The Glitter Band continued to record and tour with their leader.

In between the group releases, Glitter finally visited America, not as a performer though, but rather as headliner of an expensive promotional trip. Plans went astray from the moment Glitter landed in Los Angeles. Dressed in full 'Glitter style', the US Customs whisked him behind scenes to body search him for drugs. Glitter: 'Only a complete idiot would [take] illegal substances into Los Angeles, because everything you could want is available there twenty-four hours a day.' Even his platform-soled boots were X-rayed! During the entire visit, the singer crammed in media interviews between drinking binges with American acts he had befriended. The visit was Glitter's last for one year, when Arista Records purchased Bell Records, a company that did less for his career than its predecessor.

However, back in his home country, Glitter's single titled 'Remember Me This Way', taken from the movie of the same name, shot to No. 3 in the chart during March 1974. Before the year closed, Gary Glitter celebrated his third chart-topper.

Also see: I'm the Leader of the Gang (I Am)', August 1973; 'Always Yours', June 1974

(Quotes: *Leader – The Autobiography of Gary Glitter* by Gary Glitter with Lloyd Bradley)

SLADE

Merry Xmas Everybody

'The groups that stick together are the ones that make it.' – Noddy Holder

For many acts who are successful, recording a Christmas single appears to be mandatory. And Slade were no exception. Recorded during their American tour, the title 'Merry Xmas Everybody' soared to the top of the British chart in December 1973, a position it held for a remarkable five weeks. The title sold a staggering 310,000 copies during its first day of sale, and within one month had notched up sales in excess of one million. Needless to say, it became Slade's biggest-selling single of all time.

Jim Lea told author George Tremlett that Noddy Holder had actually written the track four years prior to its release but not as a Christmas tune. It was during the group's second American tour when they were exposed to Bob Dylan's material, and became influenced by his writing. 'Every time I hear that single I can hear Dylan's influence on me because we took Nod's chorus, I wrote a melody as a Christmas song, and then Nod added the lyrics, which seemed to fit it perfectly.'

When 'Merry Xmas Everybody' was completed, the group felt it was too twee; maybe a more gritty sound should be added, but when the title sold in such alarming proportions, they realised their thinking had been misplaced. However, with success came criticism – Holder was reprehended for emulating John Lennon's vocals. Lea: 'Of course we're all Beatles-influenced, everybody is in the music business because they were the ones who started it all for the British groups.' He then added that Holder's biggest musical influences were Motown's roster of artists, Joe Cocker and Aretha Franklin.

'Merry Xmas Everybody' grew legs. The title re-entered the British chart in the Top Seventy during Christmas 1980 as a reworking by Slade and the Reading Choir; a year on, the group's original version returned to the British Top Forty; in 1982 it peaked at No. 67; in 1983 at No. 20; in 1984 it reached the Top Fifty; in 1985 No. 48, and in 1986, the Top Eighty. The single, like Wizzard's 1973 hit 'I Wish It Could Be

Christmas Everyday' remained synonymous with the festive season through to the mid-nineties.

Early in 1974, Slade enjoyed their third consecutive chart-topping album, titled *Old, New, Borrowed and Blue,* while in April, 'Everyday' became a Top Three British single. Two further singles likewise reached the Top Three before the year was out, namely, 'Bangin' Man' and 'Far Far Away', the latter lifted from the movie *Flame* featuring the group, Tom Conti, and radio DJs Emperor Rosko and Tommy Vance. *Flame* (directed by Richard Concraine and produced by Goodtime Enterprises, known for the pair of David Essex movies, *That'll Be the Day* and *Stardust*) was the story of an unsuccessful sixties group, portrayed by Slade, whose management deceived them during their early career, yet they survived to succeed. The soundtrack album, *Slade in Flame,* peaked at No. 6 in the British chart and made the Top One Hundred in America.

In March 1975, as remarkable as it seems, Slade-power began to weaken when their single 'How Does It Feel' marked the end of their run of Top Five British hits. The title reached No. 15 in the chart. Two months on, 'Thanks for the Memory (Wham Bam Thank You Mam)' peaked in the Top Ten, while 'In for a Penny' reached No. 11 that November. Early the next year, 'Let's Call It Quits' climbed into the Top Twenty; the group's final hit with Polydor Records. A significant title under the circumstances! But one that also predicted the downward slide of a successful career.

In the eighties, Slade continued to record, first for the Barn label, then for Cheapskate Records. All releases were moderate sellers, certainly none reached the Top Ten, except the outstanding title 'We'll Bring the House Down' in January 1981, their first major hit for six long years.

During September 1981, the group signed a recording contract with RCA Records, where their first single, titled 'Lock Up your Daughters', reached No. 29 in the British chart. This title was the start of a new chart career, although the group would never have the sales potential of previous years. Before the year ended, though, their album *Till Deaf Us Do Part* faltered in the Top Seventy. It was a healthy enough result, sufficiently encouraging to enable the group to tour Britain once again. This 1982 trek also boosted the sales of the 'Ruby Red' single, which climbed into the Top Sixty that March. A year later, in November, Slade made great strides by reaching No. 2 with the single 'My Oh My'. In early 1984, their newly-found success continued with the No. 7 hit 'Run Run Away', which also, ironically, became their biggest-selling American hit at No. 20! Before the year was out, Slade returned to the British

Top Fifteen with the single 'All Join Hands'.

Slade's public profile was maintained via further minor British hits until 1988, when the group disbanded. Noddy Holder turned to radio, to present a rock 'n' roll revival show on Piccadilly Radio, a position he held through to the nineties. Don Powell left the music business to concentrate on the antique trade, while Dave Hill embarked upon a solo career, leaving Jim Lea to produce third-party acts that included Chrome Molly.

However, the group break-up was relatively short-lived; Slade reformed in 1991 to release the single 'Radio Wall of Sound' via Polydor Records. The title peaked at No. 21 in the British chart during October. A month on, their first CD compilation was issued under the title *Wall of Hits;* a Top Forty British hit. In 1993, Slade issued the single 'Hold on to Love', swiped from the album *Emergency;* both sold badly.

The vividly coloured clothes, the silks and satins, platform boots and striped suits may be faded, but the group, now known as Slade II with a new lead singer, remain popular with nineties' nightclub audiences. Fans have grown up with them, and like the group, have survived the heady days of the seventies to do it all again. Slade without Noddy Holder though? Doesn't sound right somehow!

Also see: 'Coz I Luv You', December 1971; 'Take Me Bak 'Ome', July 1972; 'Cum On Feel the Noize', March 1973; 'Skweeze Me Pleeze Me', July 1973

(Quotes: *The Slade Story* by George Tremlett)

February 1974

MUD

Tiger Feet

New bands introduced a certain 'fun' element into the music of the seventies – Mud were no exception. Their blatant approach to pop music with repetitive lyrics and easy-to-learn choruses ensured their chart presence for three years.

This Surrey quartet of youngsters was formed during 1966 from members of different groups. After working his way through jazz units, vocalist Les Gray, born in Carshalton on 9 April 1946, befriended drummer Dave Mount, likewise born in Carshalton on 3 March 1947, to plan the formation of Mud. They recruited a pair of experienced musicians to complete their line-up, namely bass guitarist Ray Stiles, born on 20 November 1946, and lead guitarist Rob Davis, born on 1 October 1947, both in . . . Carshalton.

In their year of formation Mud debuted at South London's Streatham Ice Rink. The success at this venue secured the group a recording deal with CBS Records, where their first single, 'Flower Power', was issued in April. Six months on they debuted on BBC Radio 1's *Monday Monday*.

Fame and fortune passed them by as there then followed a two-year recording gap. However, instead of abandoning their music, they concentrated on establishing a healthy fan following on the concert circuit, usually through a series of one-nighters. Encouraged by the response, they became a professional group during 1968 and released their second single for CBS Records, titled 'Up the Airy Mountain'; it followed the fate of its predecessor.

All was not lost because after an appearance on the BBC TV children's programme *The Basil Brush Show,* Mud switched record companies to Philips to release 'Shangri La' during May 1969. Despite all indications of becoming a hit, it bombed.

Still they plodded on. Early in 1973 they were given the chance of supporting American love crooner Jack Jones on tour. It was their luckiest break yet, resulting in an introduction to Mickie Most, ex-rock singer, composer/producer and now founder of his own company, RAK Records, licensed via EMI Records.

Mud joined forces with Most to work with composer/producers Mike Chapman and Nicky Chinn (who become known as Chinnichap). 'Crazy' was their first collaboration and the group's debut single which, in April 1973, peaked at No. 12 in the British chart. Three months on, 'Hypnosis' reached the Top Twenty, and before the end of the year the group's 'Dyna-Mite' soared to No. 4. Their success was simple; the music was fast-lane material, plenty of zing, almost pop rockabilly, combined with a lively stage presentation of young men enjoying themselves. In other words, an image the young audiences could associate with and who, if the chance arose, were allowed to join on stage.

Early in 1974, Mud recorded and released the Chapman and Chinn composition, 'Tiger Feet'. It was another fast mover and typified the duo's ability to produce frenetic pop tunes. 'Tiger Feet' became a British chart-topper in February 1974, a position it held for four weeks, presenting Mickie Most with his second No. 1 single (Suzi Quatro's 'Can the Can' was the first in 1973).

When performing 'Tiger Feet' Mud developed a simple dance routine – knees and arms bent, while jerking the body from side to side. Not really suitable for the over forties! But, it was quite a spectacle – and rather alarmingly can still be seen today at high-spirited dances and the like . . . and during Mud's oldies but goldies tours.

Mud, like the majority of Mickie Most's acts, who included Hot Chocolate and the aforementioned Quatro, had staying power, and went on to prove their stability by enjoying a second chart-topper during 1975.

Also see: 'Oh Boy', May 1975

March 1974

SUZI QUATRO

Devil Gate Drive

Leather and rock – that was Suzi Q! Slight in build, with a twangy accent and a belting voice, she was the raunchy white messenger for Nicky Chinn and Mike Chapman, the decade's musical gurus.

Born Suzi Quatrocchio in Detroit, Michigan, on 3 June 1950, she was one of four daughters and a son born to Art Quatro, a popular jazz musician during the fifties. In fact, as an eight-year-old, Suzi joined his group, the Art Quatro Trio, playing the bongos. With music instead of blood in her veins, as a schoolgirl she spearheaded her own outfit, in 1958. When she left school, she used the name Suzi Soul and joined her sisters, Nancy, Arlene, and Patti (who went on to form another all-female group called Fanny) in The Pleasure Seekers.

For at least five years the sisters' rock group was a local favourite, particularly at The Hideout Club, Detroit's infamous venue for amateur acts. Shortly after a stint there, The Pleasure Seekers recorded their first single for the Hideout label. Titled 'Never Thought You'd Leave Me', it was a best-seller in Michigan. Another single followed, 'Light of Life', via Mercury Records, before the group performed a series of concerts for wounded military personnel in Vietnam.

During 1968, young Suzi, who by now sang and played bass guitar, and her sister Nancy left The Pleasure Seekers to form Cradle, a more seriously slanted rock band. A year later, RAK Records' founder, Mickie Most, chanced to be in Detroit, recording sessions with Jeff Beck. During a leisure period he saw the Quatrocchio sisters perform, and was sufficiently impressed by Suzi to invite her to Britain to record for his London-based company.

Quatro disbanded Cradle in 1970 to move to London, and two years later her debut single for RAK Records was issued. Titled 'Rolling Stone', it bombed. Her second single, written by the record company's in-house composing/producing duo Nicky Chinn and Mike Chapman, didn't. The razor-sharp, chugging rock track 'Can the Can' soared to the top of the British chart during June 1973. Quatro was on her way. The single was also released in America during 1976 and became a Top Sixty hit.

It wasn't only her deep voice that attracted public attention, but her performance. On stage, with her androgynous image, black leather cat suits or biker's leathers, she stalked the stage with her guitar slung over her shoulder. A true rocker indeed. And female!

With the chart-topper descending, Quatro embarked upon a British tour with Slade, supported by her back-up band comprising Dave Neal, drummer; Alastair McKenzie, keyboardist; and Len Tuckey, guitarist and her future husband.

The chart-topper's follow-up in August 1973 was '48 Crash' which peaked at No. 3, while her debut album, *Suzi Quatro*, became a Top Forty hit. Before the year ended, her third single, 'Daytona Demo' stalled in the Top Twenty. Nonetheless, Ms Q was 'hot property'; had established herself as a serious threat to British acts, but next was America, her home country.

Maintaining the hard-edged rock approach, Quatro's first 1974 single was a further Chinnichap composition titled 'Devil Gate Drive'. High on chorus lines, hard as nails, the single topped the British chart during March 1974, a position it held for two weeks. It was Quatro's second chart-topper in as many years.

The follow-up, 'Too Big' was issued six months later, and reached the Top Twenty. Meanwhile, she cracked the American chart with a daring cover version of Elvis Presley's 'All Shook Up', via a recording deal with Bell Records. In 1974, two of her albums charted there, namely her first eponymous release, and its follow-up, *Quatro*, albeit in low positions. Her next British Top Ten entry 'The Wild One', was her last of the year.

Early in 1975, Quatro changed direction to record the mellow 'Your Mama Won't Like Me' single. This faltered at No. 31 in the British chart, before her next release bombed altogether. The public had rejected 'I Bit Off More Than I Could Chew', taking the leather-clad singer along with it. This was a remarkable turn of events; quite inexplicable, particularly as Quatro was such a vibrant singer, backed with singles that had sold by the million. Indeed, 'I Bit Off More Than I Could Chew' turned out to be her last charting single in Britain for two years. Perhaps the disc's title was correct – maybe she had. Across the Atlantic, meantime, her final album, titled *Your Mama Won't Like Me* was a semi-hit, but sold sufficiently to enable her to tour coast-to-coast with Alice Cooper.

Suzi Quatro made her presence felt once again on the British public early in 1977 when she toured the country to re-establish, if possible, her past status, or, at the very least, make a tentative stab at success. To coincide with this, she issued the single 'Tear Me Apart', which happily returned her to the British Top Thirty. More than that, it afforded her a career diversion.

The producers of *Happy Days*, a highly successful ABC TV American series based around the lives of a group of teenagers, offered the singer the role of Leather Tuscadero, a lady rocker. So impressed were the producers with the role that Quatro was included in further programmes, but when she was offered a series of her own based around her character, she declined, preferring to stay in Britain with her husband.

During 1978, the singer returned to her recording career with gusto thanks to the Chinnichap Midas touch. Three singles became British hits, namely, 'If You Can't Give Me Love', the biggest seller at No. 4; 'The Race Is On' and 'Stumblin' In' (a duet with Chris Norman, lead vocalist with the hitmaking group Smokie, also signed to RAK Records). Both were Top Fifty entrants. In actual fact, the duet was her biggest-selling American single, soaring into the Top Ten. Midway through 1979 she re-established her Stateside footing with the album *If You Knew Suzie* and a trio of singles, while in Britain she enjoyed a late-year Top Twenty hit with 'She's in Love with You'.

'Mama's Boy' was the first single of 1980, a Top Forty British hit, not a bad start to the new decade. Alas, its follow-up, 'I've Never Been in Love', struggled into the Top Sixty. During October, she switched companies from RAK Records to join Nicky Chinn and Mike Chapman's new label Dreamland. Her debut release there, 'Rock Hard', taken from the *Times Square* movie, was a poor seller and her last. Not a wise company change, it would seem.

Suzi Quatro settled into family life, away from the public spotlight, until 1982 when, after securing a recording contract with Polydor Records, she issued the single 'Heart of Stone', lifted from the album *Main Attraction*. Both were semi-hits. A year on, she underwent a career change – she returned to television, this time, though, hosting the popular daytime programme *Gas,* which in turn led to other more lucrative small screen spots. Her new career sustained her for the next nine years.

To start the new decade, Quatro performed in the London stage production of *Annie Get your Gun* before playing Tallulah Bankhead in the musical *Tallulah Who?* which she wrote with Willy Russell. Her most recent television appearance was as a rocker in a dream sequence sketch in *Absolutely Fabulous,* screened by BBC 1 and written by Jennifer Saunders, who also had a starring role, with Joanna Lumley as support.

Needless to say, the Suzi Quatro of the eighties and nineties was no longer a wild woman of rock. Her leather garb was exchanged for everyday clothes as she attracted an adult audience rather than one of the reckless young. She may have mellowed with age, but Ms Quatro will always be remembered for her hard-edged contribution to British rock. And, of course, for her leathers.

Also No. 1 in March 1974: 'Jealous Mind' by Alvin Stardust; 'Billy Don't Be a Hero' by Paper Lace

April 1974

TERRY JACKS

Seasons in the Sun

This wasn't the most cheerful of seventies' songs but it captured the hearts of the British public.

Born in Winnipeg, Manitoba, Canada, Terry Jacks and his family moved to Vancouver while he was a youngster. He spent his adolescence listening to rock 'n' roll, and cited Buddy Holly as his musical hero. When he graduated from high school, his family hoped he would become an architect. However, while studying for this goal and at the age of sixteen, he formed his first group, The Chessmen. Jacks told author Barry Scott, 'They liked this song I wrote, "The Way You Feel", and we didn't know who was going to sing it. I ended up singing it and that's how I became a singer. We made a record of it and it became No. 2 in Vancouver.'

While The Chessmen were performing on a local television programme, Jacks met Susan Pesklevits. 'I wasn't really a singer. I was more of a producer and writer. I wanted to find a singer with a unique voice, who could express what I wanted to say better. That's when I met Susan . . . she had a very natural voice. We got together and recorded some songs and things just clicked.' So much so, that Jacks married her during 1967, before turning his back on The Chessman to form a new group, The Poppy Family, with his wife. They recruited Satwan Singh, percussionist, and Craig MacCaw, guitarist, to complete the line-up. The name 'Poppy Family' was chosen from the Webster dictionary – 'a varied species of flowering plants'. Jacks: 'At the time we were in the flower-child era and everyone was smoking dope. Susan and I had just gotten married. It could be taken either way. We liked the intimacy of the word "family".'

Released by Decca Records, 'Which Way You Goin' Billy', penned by Jacks, was intended to be the flipside of 'Endless Sleep'. The public thought otherwise, flipped the disc, and when released in Britain during August 1970, it soared into the Top Ten, marking their only British hit but winning the distinction of being one of 1970's top-selling singles. Following a handful of American hits, in 1973 The Poppy Family disbanded and Jacks's marriage ended in divorce.

Susan Jacks pursued an unsuccessful solo career, while Terry worked with The Beach Boys before recording 'The Dying Man', an adaptation of 'Le Moribond', composed by Jacques Brel, with lyrics written by British poet Rod McEwan. The finished track, with Jacks's own modifications, remained unreleased until, much later, he played it to friends. Such was their enthusiasm that he decided to release it on his own Goldfish record label. Now known as 'Seasons in the Sun', it sold sufficiently for Bell Records to distribute it on a national basis. The single literally shot to the top of the American chart in March 1974, and a month later became a British chart-topper, holding that position for four weeks. Worldwide sales were in excess of six million copies.

'If You Go Away', a brilliant slice of Brel's sophisticated magic, was issued as the follow-up, reaching the British Top Ten during June 1974.

Both singles were emotionally draining, highly charged with doom and gloom, and typical of Jacques Brel's work. They also comprised the total of Terry Jacks's British success. Dry eyes returned!

ABBA

Waterloo

Bjorn Ulvaeus – the cheeky-faced one with a fringe
Benny Andersson – the cuddly, bearded one
Anni-Frid Lyngstad – the red head
Agnetha Faltskog – the blonde one

'Coming from Sweden, the [Eurovision] contest was the only way of promoting ourselves in other countries. We knew that nobody would really listen to us otherwise . . . We decided to take a chance.' – Bjorn Ulvaeus

Bjorn Ulvaeus, born in Gothenburg, Sweden, on 25 April 1945, was introduced to music at an early age. At eleven years old, his family moved to Vastervik, where he purchased an acoustic guitar and joined his first skiffle group. With school friends from Vastervik High, and with the encouragement from their art teacher, Ulvaeus pursued Dixieland jazz, building up a solid local following.

After graduating in 1963, it was intended that Ulvaeus would progress to law college. But music pulled. Taking a few months off, Ulvaeus and his group travelled to Europe, busking and performing to cover their daily expenses that included the upkeep of their travel-weary Volvo. During their absence, Ulvaeus's mother entered them in a national talent contest, sponsored by Swedish radio. Using the name the West Bay Singers, the group lost the contest, but won the attention of Stig Anderson and his business partner Bengt Bernhag, owners of the newly-formed publishing house and record label, Polar Music.

Following lengthy discussions, including should Ulvaeus resume his education, the group with a membership of Hansi Schwarz, Tony Roth, Johan Karlberg and Ulvaeus were contracted as Polar Music's first act. With a name change from the West Bay Singers to The Hootenanny Singers, they released their debut single, 'Jag Vantar Vid Min Milla', in 1964. It was the track they had performed in the talent contest. The title became a Swedish hit, whereupon the group turned professional, although Ulvaeus took a break in 1965 to study economics and law at the University of Stockholm, before being called, with the other group members, into national service. During their lifetime, The Hootenanny

Singers recorded in excess of twenty hit singles and nine albums, and became a top touring name in Europe.

With encouragement from Stig Anderson, Ulvaeus embarked upon a solo career in 1968. His singles included 'Honey', a cover version of the Bobby Goldsboro 1968 hit. Ulvaeus may have shrugged off the confines of a group for the immediate future, but he was soon to join another unit when he met The Hep Stars, fronted by Benny Andersson.

Born Goran Bror Benny Andersson in Stockholm on 16 December 1946, he, like Ulvaeus, lived in a musical household. His father and grandfather, both accomplished musicians, taught Andersson to play the accordion and piano by the time he was ten years old. But it was his later awareness of The Beatles that persuaded him that his career would be in music. Meantime, on the personal front, Andersson became engaged to his school 'sweetheart' Christina: both were fifteen years old. They never married, but had two children. As much as Andersson was devoted to his family, the pull of music was stronger. Subsequently, when he was offered the keyboardist vacancy in The Hep Stars, he didn't hesitate. With vocalist Svenne Hedlund, the group quickly became dominant in Swedish music. The first track to actually feature Andersson was 'Tribute to Buddy Holly', released as a single during 1964.

By the next year, Andersson began composing for the group. His first track, titled 'No Response', was included on The Hep Stars' album *We and our Cadillac*. The title was later lifted as a single to become their biggest European hit. Encouraged by this success, Andersson wrote further tracks for the unit, notably, 'Sunny Girl', 'Wedding', 'It's Nice to Be Back' and 'Consolation'; all titles which helped The Hep Stars grow in status to become Sweden's biggest-selling group. Their success was instant; the group had little time to consider business dealings that included The Hep House production company, originally opened by the group for their use only. Following a series of failed business ventures, including the costly movie titled *Habari Safari,* which was ultimately shelved, Hep House faced the bankruptcy court in 1968. The Hep Stars also owed the Inland Revenue a fortune in back taxes. Andersson's personal debt totalled in excess of 174,000 kronor plus a further 83,000 kronor for 1969. It took him four years to clear it.

During 1969, The Hep Stars split. A trio from the membership, namely, Christer Petterson, Janne Frisk and Lennart Hegland, continued using the group name, while Svenne Hedlund and Andersson joined vocalist Charlotte Walker.

Benny Andersson and Bjorn Ulvaeus had met occasionally while each was a member of his respective band. Yet it was 1969 before the two actually collaborated as songwriters, when their first composition was titled 'Isn't It Easy'.

Anni-Frid Lyngstad, born in Bjorkasen, Norway, on 15 November 1945, was the fruit of a love affair between her mother Synni and a German officer, Alfred Haase. Mother, daughter and grandmother were subsequently outcasts in their small community, and when Norway was liberated in 1945, Haase was reported lost at sea. Devastated, Synni Lyngstad sunk into a deep depression which ultimately killed her. She was twenty-one years old. In fact, Haase was very much alive; he had returned to Germany at the end of the war, and was married with two children.

Unable to live among their fellows, Anni-Frid and her grandmother crossed the border into Sweden. With no money and desperate, Mrs Lyngstad worked her way through a series of low-paid jobs before securing a regular sewing position in a factory in Eskilstuna. Anni-Frid's early life, therefore, was poverty-stricken and insecure, yet she was educated and cared for by her devoted grandmother. During the evenings, the pair listened to their battered gramophone scratch its way through the grooves on 78 rpm jazz records. Anni-Frid was smitten: she too wanted to sing. Her first performance as a singer was as an eleven-year-old; two years later, looking older than her years, she sang professionally as part of the Ewaldek Jazz Group. At sixteen, now street-wise and ambitious, Lyngstad switched jazz outfits to the Bengt Sandlund Band. In time, she befriended the band's bass player, Ragner Frederickson, and eventually left the line-up to form, with two others, The Anni-Frid Four. Frederickson went on to marry Lyngstad; they had two children.

Her career began to drift, until Lyngstad returned to the spotlight with the occasional nightclub appearance. In 1967 she won first prize in Sweden's famed talent contest singing 'A Day Off', whereupon she instantly sang the song on national television, joining a gala of Scandinavian stars. Such was her subsequent popularity that she was offered a recording contract with EMI Records. She accepted, knowing that embarking upon a solo career meant sacrificing her husband and children, to move to Stockholm. Lyngstad's debut single in 1967, titled 'En Ledit Dag', was quickly followed by 'Din'; neither were big-selling titles, but sufficiently successful to launch her as a leading Swedish performer. From EMI Records, she switched to Columbia Records where, from 1968, she enjoyed a handful of minor selling singles including the titles 'Simsalabim' and 'Mycket Kar'. However, her destiny was set when, in 1969, she chanced to appear in the same Malmo nightclub as The Hep Stars. She befriended Benny Andersson and within weeks of that meeting the two were lovers. In August 1969 they were engaged to be married.

Agnetha Ase Faltskog, born in Jonkoping, Southern Sweden, on 5 April 1950, debuted on stage at the age of fifteen in a Christmas pantomime. The performance had been encouraged by her father, Ingvar, an enthusiastic member of his local amateur dramatic society. However, all did not go according to plan; while the youngster recited 'Billy Boy', her pants fell down! However, this incident failed to dampen her ambitions; two years later she was a proficient pianist and a regular stage performer.

Faltskog left school at fifteen, whereupon she became a telephonist in a local car showroom, pursuing her first love at the weekends, singing with The Bengt Enghardt Orchestra. This association led to Enghardt recording a handful of demo tracks with his vocalist, the most notable being 'Folj Med Min' and 'Jag Var Sa Kar'. In turn, these tracks were given to a talent scout for the CBS Records' subsidiary, Cupol Records. Greatly impressed, he offered Faltskog a recording contract that did not include the orchestra. Like any ambitious young singer in her position, Faltskog signed on the dotted line. Her debut Cupol single titled 'I Was So in Love' topped the Swedish chart during 1968, the same year as her self-penned eponymous album was issued. By 1969, she was a top-selling artist across Scandinavia thanks to her second album, *Agnetha Faltskog Vol 2,* and a series of hit singles that included 'En Gang Fannsbara Vi Tva' and 'Zigenarvan'.

Following a failed attempt to launch a career in Germany instigated by composer Dieter Zimmerman, Faltskog returned to her home country. She was initially unsuccessful, but thankfully this was a short-lived situation, helped by singles like 'Ta Det Bara Med Ro' and a duet with Jorgen Edman titled 'Sjung Denna Sang'.

Unwittingly, Faltskog had often appeared on the same bill as The Hootenanny Singers, but it was on a television show in Stockholm that they first met. That meeting led to a relationship with Bjorn Ulvaeus.

During 1969, both The Hep Stars and The Hootenanny Singers disbanded, whereupon Benny Andersson and Bjorn Ulvaeus joined forces as composers and producers. Both Faltskog and Lyngstad continued their respective solo careers, but they became friends via their partners. Or did they? Years later, they admitted their friendship was hardly the perfect working relationship. Nonetheless, they socialised and holidayed together.

After stockpiling compositions, Andersson and Ulvaeus decided they would record as a unit. Their debut album titled *Lycka* was completed in Stockholm's Metronome Studios, and featured the uncredited Lyngstad and Faltskog on one track, 'Hej Gamle Man'. This title was the first to contain all four members of the future Abba.

Released during 1970, *Lycka* soared into Sweden's album chart; in turn, Andersson and Ulvaeus embarked upon a tour of selected venues until 1 November 1970, when they were joined on stage by Lyngstad and Faltskog, using the name The Festfolk Quartet ('The Engaged Couples Quartet').

Early in 1971, Andersson and Ulvaeus entered their composition 'Livet Gar Sin Gang' in the Malago Melody Festival. Although it faltered at position 6, the track was widely sold to other countries, including France, where it was recorded by Françoise Hardy. Meantime, Faltskog secured the starring role in the Swedish production of *Jesus Christ Superstar*, written by Tim Rice and Andrew Lloyd Webber, subsequently enjoying a Swedish hit single with 'I Don't Know How to Love Him' swiped from the musical's soundtrack. Lyngstad, on the other hand, having failed an audition to represent her country in the 1971 Eurovision Song Contest, recorded her second solo album, titled *Frida*, with her partner Andersson producing.

On the personal front, Bjorn Ulvaeus and Agnetha Faltskog married on 7 July 1971 in the village of Verum in South Sweden. The occasion was marred when, the following day, Stig Anderson informed them that his business partner, Bengt Bernhag, had committed suicide, and asked Andersson and Ulvaeus to replace him at Polar Music. Before the year closed, they became the company's in-house producers, where their first project was to work with The Hootenanny Singers!

A year later, Andersson, Ulvaeus, Faltskog and Lyngstad recorded in English together at the Metronome Studios. The result was a handful of titles that included 'People Need Love', 'She's my Kinda Girl' and 'Santa Rosa'. 'People Need Love' was the first single to be released in Sweden, in June 1972, using the credit Bjorn, Benny, Agnetha and Anni-Frid. The title peaked at No 2 in the Swedish charts, and was issued in America by Playboy Records to falter outside the Top One Hundred chart. 'She's my Kinda Girl' was issued in Japan only, using only Andersson and Ulvaeus's names, and sold 500,000 copies, while 'Santa Rosa' was entered in the 1972 Japanese Song Festival, requiring all four to perform. The single bombed.

Following the chart success of 'People Need Love', a second title was issued featuring the quartet. Titled 'He Is your Brother', it likewise shot up their home chart before achieving equal success in France and Germany. It was at this juncture that the decision was made to record as a group.

Late in 1972, Andersson and Ulvaeus were requested by the Swedish Broadcasting Corporation to compose an entry for the 1973 Swedish heat of the Eurovision Song Contest. In January 1973, their composition, 'Ring Ring', with lyrics by Stig Anderson, was recorded in Swedish, French, German and English; for the latter version, the partnership of Neil Sedaka and Phil Cody provided the lyrics. 'Ring Ring' stalled at third position in the Swedish heat, but went on to soar into countless European charts. While the single lived, Agnetha Faltskog gave birth to a daughter, Linda, on 23 February 1973.

Following the unexpected initial failure and later success of 'Ring Ring', the four recorded their debut album using the single's name as its title. Upon its release, the group entered the Swedish music history book – the single 'Ring Ring' was at Nos. 1 and 2 in the Swedish chart. The first version was sung in Swedish, the second in English, while the album peaked at No. 3. To take advantage of this unusual success, the four toured Europe, promoting themselves as a serious, full-time group, creating maximum media attention. Stig Anderson, now the group's official manager, likewise conducted his equal share of press interviews. Tired of constantly using the group's individual names, he decided to lift the initial from each first name. Abba was born.

In October 1973, Abba began recording in earnest for a new album, before realising that entries for the Swedish heat for the 1974 Eurovision Song Contest were due. Following historical research, Abba's manager believed 'Waterloo' to be an ideal song title, and wrote lyrics relating to the famous battle, omitting the glaring fact that 40,000 men died during it, whereupon Andersson and Ulvaeus composed the melody. However, before 'Waterloo' was completed, Anderson had composed a second possible entrant titled 'Hasta Manana'. Both tracks were equally strong; 'Waterloo' was finally chosen because it featured both female vocalists instead of one.

In February 1974, Abba performed 'Waterloo' before the Swedish nation, and won. This would now represent their country in the Eurovision Song Contest proper. However, prior to the actual contest, Stig Anderson spearheaded a mammoth advertising campaign to promote the group and title; he saturated European record companies with Abba promotional packs and generally hyped them up. Subsequently, when Abba arrived in Britain, they were guests at a party hosted by their new music publishing house, United Artists.

Staged at the beautifully-renovated Dome Theatre, situated in the heart of Brighton on the Sussex coastline, the 1974 Eurovision Song Contest got underway in April. Abba was the seventh act to appear. Dressed in skin-tight pant suits of pseudo-Napoleonic style, with high boots and dangling braid, the group sang and smiled their way through the track, before an estimated five hundred million viewers, despite looking ridiculous and feeling extremely uncomfortable in their second-skin clothing. Their jaunty song won the contest with a clear twenty-four points, pushing Italy into second place.

When the champagne had run dry, Abba were guests at the obligatory party hosted by BBC TV, who televised the contest. The following day, the group was besieged by the media – interviews naturally were stilted due to the group's limited command of the English language – before being rescued by their British record company, CBS, who feted them with a further champagne reception. The afternoon was spent on Brighton beach for an unofficial photo shoot. Unlike other artists who won the Eurovision Contest, in whom British interest was practically non-existent due to the low calibre of the contest's music, Abba were swamped with television guest spots, international interviews and record company offers. Two decades later, the Eurovision winner could walk home alone. However, Stig Anderson, confident Abba would win, had secured record company deals throughout Europe and had further arranged an extended stay in London to exploit the demand for the single. First was the imperative performance on BBC TV's premier music show *Top of the Pops,* followed by an endless round of radio interviews and official photograph sessions. No one in Britain could escape the Abba hype!

Returning to Sweden via Holland to appear on selected television shows, Abba spent the Easter weekend together on their island in the Archipelago, Stockholm, away from the public spotlight, deliberating the fate of 'Waterloo' now that the Eurovision Contest was over. They didn't wait long.

In May 1974, the winning song, released via CBS Records' subsidiary Epic, soared to the top of the British chart, a position it held for two weeks. 'Waterloo' repeated its British success across Europe, while in America it peaked at No. 6, and, regrettably, inspired a run of soundalike Eurovision Song Contest entries for years to come. That chirpy, happy-go-lucky, smiley sound with short, sharp lyrics would eventually drive the voters to distraction. Hardly a fitting memorial for the 40,000 lost lives – but then that's show business!

Also see: 'Mamma Mia', January 1976; 'Dancing Queen', September 1976; 'Knowing Me Knowing You', April 1977; 'The Name of the Game', November 1977; 'Take a Chance on Me', March 1978

(Quotes: *Abba: The Name of the Game* by Andrew Oldham, Tony Calder and Colin Irwin)

June 1974

GARY GLITTER

Always Yours

'I was living the way I believed a successful pop star should . . . I drank a great deal during 1975 and 1976, but my drug dependency over that period is something that has been continually overstated.' – Gary Glitter

The more successful Gary Glitter was, the more reclusive he became. Not one to socialise at record company binges or West End nighteries, he spent much of his leisure time in his flat in Kensington High Street, London. The Who's drummer, Keith Moon, befriended him, and convinced him to do 'showbusiness things' by visiting the top nightly haunts. Glitter: 'He introduced me to a circuit of places where having a famous face would get you in and then made sure you had a good time, usually with somebody else footing the bill.' In time, Glitter noticed, it was he who paid!

On the other hand, the singer was introduced to the rural way of life by Rod Stewart who, at the time, lived outside the London perimeter. In time, Glitter would act on Stewart's advice and purchase Mizzards Farm, situated in twelve acres of prime Hampshire land. He paid £70,000 for the house and another £100,000 on renovations, transforming his new home into a luxurious abode – at least those rooms he used! He then hired a housekeeper and groundsmen to maintain the place inside and out; played cricket at weekends on the village green as part of a star-studded team, and opened his home to all participants, when it took on the appearance of a hippie commune rather than a desirable residence. All in all, Glitter believed he was living in a style 'pop stars' should, and how the public envisaged they lived when not on stage.

On top of this expenditure, Glitter had his professional props to finance. For instance, his stage suits cost approximately £3,000 each;

shoes averaged £50 a pair, his office costs included a handful of staff, while tour bills, from limousines to room service, were eventually debited from his future record royalties. It was this lifestyle that eventually led to his financial ruin. On the personal front, Glitter had no permanent partner, preferring to avoid serious relationships by entertaining countless ladies who usually visited his Hampshire home.

Glitter enjoyed his third British chart-topper during June 1974. Titled 'Always Yours', it was another Glitter/Leander composition but it lacked the obvious punch of previous work. The single was also of a slower pace, enabling listeners to actually hear the singer's powerful voice.

One further single was issued before 1974 closed, namely 'Oh Yes! You're Beautiful', dedicated to his fans (now known as his 'gang') for their constant support. The title soared to No. 2 in the British chart. However, as remarkable as it seems, the Glitter decline was ready to begin.

During 1975, he released a trio of singles – 'Love Like You and Me', which made the Top Ten; 'Doing Alright with the Boys', which hit No. 6, and the weakest of all, a cover version of The Rivingtons' original 'Papa Oom Mow Mow', which faltered in the Top Forty, his poorest selling single to date. This year of 1975 was also personally traumatic for the singer, as he existed in a drug- and alcohol-induced haze. Previously Glitter admitted to dabbling with speed to assist his demanding and exhausting career. Glitter: 'The only problem [was] that once I started I became reliant on it. It happened very quickly, and I had to start taking other stuff to counterbalance it when I wasn't working.' He was on a drug cocktail merry-go-round. Also worrying him at this time was his escalating weight, which prompted visits to a Harley Street doctor. Slimming tablets, including more amphetamines, subsequently joined his staple drug diet.

By the close of 1976, the singer's finances were quivering on the zero mark. He needed a means to boost the bank balance, and was persuaded to perform a 'farewell' series of concerts early the following year. Glitter: 'The announcement of my retirement was purely a scam to sell tickets, and I went along with it because I couldn't be bothered to argue.' Needless to say, venues filled to capacity greeted him. To coincide with this British trek, the title 'You Belong to Me' was issued and reached No. 40 in the British chart; his only release of the year. Obviously, Glitter's retirement was short-lived. In December 1976, he performed without The Glitter Band on the televised *Supersonic Royal Christmas Party*, staged at London's Theatre Royal.

The first single of 1977, titled 'It Takes All Night Long' reached the

British Top Thirty during February, while the last single of the decade, 'A Little Boogie Woogie in the Back of my Mind' struggled into the Top Forty. As the single gasped for life, so did Glitter; the bank foreclosed on Mizzards Farm and the Inland Revenue was hounding him. He felt he had little option but to join other high-bracket earners by leaving Britain. Following an Irish concert for a fee of £20,000, he took the cash and flew to Paris.

While living on French soil, he was offered the role of Frank-N-Furter in the New Zealand production of *The Rocky Horror Show*. Almost fundless, he played the part of the transvestite count to more than sixty thousand people. Once again, he lived on amphetamines to ensure he sustained the fast-lane pace of theatrical schedules. When the tour ended, Glitter holidayed in Australia, before returning to Britain in 1979, on the promise of a British tour. It was a low-key series of dates which he loathed, and the singer tried to boost his intensely low self-esteem with alcohol and drugs, the only crutch he could rely on to ensure his performances were watchable. He was backed on stage by a mature group of musicians, and they helped alleviate the boredom of performing to audiences who were more interested in their food in a basket.

In 1980, Glitter was declared bankrupt. He had no choice now but to continue his cabaret dates. In time, these expanded to the university campus and punk/rock clubs. By concentrating on these venues, Glitter slowly built up a new and loyal following, until his audiences followed him from date to date. What he now needed was the faith of a record company to back his popularity as a performer.

Following an introduction to multi-millionaire Baron Stephen Bentinck, Glitter was signed to the Baron's record label, Eagle Records. While there, the singer was reunited with his composing/producing partner, Mike Leander, to release a pair of singles, namely 'What your Momma Don't See (your Momma Don't Know)' and 'When I'm On'. Both bombed in 1980. A year on, his version of The Crystals' 1963 classic, 'And Then She Kissed Me', issued by Bell Records, peaked in the British Top Forty. To end 1981, *All that Glitters*, a disco mix of his biggest-selling singles, was issued to stall in the Top Fifty.

The only single of note during 1982 was his contribution of 'Suspicious Minds' to Heaven 17's compilation album, *Music of Quality and Distinction*, which featured a host of acts including Tina Turner. It took two years before Glitter's name appeared in the British chart once more.

Reverting to his seventies hit formula, 'Dance Me Up' returned him to the Top Thirty; while its follow-up, titled 'Another Rock 'n' Roll

Christmas' elevated him to No. 7 in the British chart during 1984. This title marked his last charting single until 1992.

Glitter refused to concede defeat. During 1984 he became the uncrowned king of the universities and was now able to expand to theatre bookings. When he was offered the chance to star in a Heinz soup television advertisement, the fee from that and his concert dates settled his receiver's bill, which in turn encouraged the Inland Revenue to settle. Whatever he earned in the future went into his bank account.

During 1988, Glitter appeared on vinyl at the request of KLF, calling themselves The Timelords, and released the single 'Doctorin' the Tardis'. Then in his own right during 1991 he recorded and released the album *Leader* via his own label, Attitude Records, and in 1992 recorded *And the Leader Rocks On* and *Through the Years,* both Top Fifty hit albums released via EMI Records.

Gary Glitter's recording career may now be sporadic, but his performances have grown by spectacular proportions, particularly his annual Christmas extravaganzas, which play before capacity audiences dressed in their glitter finery. The tours include selected venues nationwide, ending at the Wembley Arena, Middlesex, where performances have ranged from two to five nights. Glitter is luckier than most British seventies acts. He has survived even though the odds were, on occasion, stacked high against him.

In the nineties, he boasts a loyal cult following now spanning three generations, who travel Britain to watch their leader perform. Still referred to as his 'gang', the Glitter clones become an integral part of Glitter's shows, which are loud and vividly colourful, with several costume changes during the performance, flashing white house lights, fireworks and the flamboyant presentation that befits the leader of his people.

As recently as 1996, Glitter was asked to perform in the largest concert to be staged in Britain since Live Aid, eleven years previously. The Who planned to perform their rock musical *Quadrophenia* in London's Hyde Park before an audience of 150,000 people. At the request of The Who's Pete Townsend, Glitter played the role of the Punk Godfather in the musical, which included Bob Dylan and Eric Clapton among others, and which was transmitted to forty countries reaching an audience of 120 million, to raise £500,000 for the Prince's Trust. However, all did not go according to plan. During the final rehearsal on the Hyde Park stage, Glitter spun the microphone stand and accidentally hit Roger Daltrey in the left eye. He was taken to hospital but recovered sufficiently to perform the next day, where his black eye was covered by an eye patch bearing the mod target symbol. Daltry told a worried Glitter, 'It could have been worse, I could have swallowed your quiff and choked on it!'

Quadrophenia in Hyde Park was a massive success, whereupon Glitter was asked to join the group for the New York production that July. Such was its American success, that he also joined in the touring company, playing at major venues in both America and Canada throughout the autumn of 1996. Glitter then returned to Britain to prepare for his now obligatory Christmas concerts.

'Gary Glitter is still larger than life, and everything he does has to be an event.' – Gary Glitter

May his glitter never tarnish!

Also see: 'I'm the Leader of the Gang (I Am)', August 1973; 'I Love You Love Me Love', December 1973

(Quotes: *Leader – The Autobiography of Gary Glitter* by Gary Glitter with Lloyd Bradley)

July 1974

GEORGE McCRAE

Rock your Baby

'Woooman, take me in your arms and rock your baaaby . . .' Yep, once that long musical introduction was over, the power of the dance took a grip. And from 'Rock your Baby' other hits were born, using the same formula but without being repetitive. 'Everybody is dancing and my aim is to keep it that way,' George McCrae said.

Born in West Palm Beach, Florida, on 19 October 1944, George McCrae formed The Fabulous Stepbrothers and later The Jiving Jets while at high school. From college he was drafted into the Navy where, in his spare time, he masterminded a further group called The Atsugi Express.

During the sixties he married singer Gwen and both signed a recording contract with Alston Records, owned by Henry Stone. The couple recorded material as a duo, but the public's interest was negligible. It was at this point that George opted to concentrate on his wife's solo career by taking a step back to manage her. For two years he devoted himself to Gwen's career and raising their family of two children. Eventually, though, the pull of the centre stage proved irresistible, and he contacted Steve Alaimo, A. & R. executive at TK Records in Florida.

Already working at TK Records was a pair of writer/producers, Richard Finch and Harry Wayne Casey, who recorded demo tracks for signed acts like Betty Wright. It happened that the couple had been experimenting with a new song but decided they needed a vocalist who was capable of reaching falsetto notes. To preserve the song, they recorded it on a reel of spare tape in less than an hour at a cost of $15. Alaimo and Stone believed the track would suit a duo but when George McCrae chanced to hear it, he felt he could do it justice.

'Rock your Baby' was the result and in one swoop added another dimension to disco music, that of a lightweight, less cumbersome and cluttered sound which would typify the music which later emanated from TK Records. The single shot to the top of the American chart in July 1974 where it stayed for two weeks. British release on the Jayboy label also led to a chart-topper during the same month. The track held that position for three weeks, and was, incidentally, the first No. 1 by a black act since 1972 and Chuck Berry with 'My Ding-A-Ling'. It became 1974's biggest-selling single.

Ironically, McCrae never intended to become so seriously involved in the recording side of the business, even though he had signed a recording contract with TK Records. 'I really wanted to concentrate on helping Gwen to make it. Then when "Rock your Baby" made it, I had to go through a period of adjustment and that was perhaps the most trying time of all in some ways.'

Gwen's music was, by the way, far removed from her husband's style; she aimed her talents at the R. & B. market with her relaxed, funky vocals. Perhaps some of her husband's luck rubbed off, because within a year of 'Rock your Baby' she enjoyed a major R. & B. hit with 'Rockin' Chair'. However, with this success came family heartache. Previously, George and Gwen had toured together, but with separate careers to now promote, their home life was placed on hold; one child went to live with Gwen's sister, while the other stayed with George's mother. George: 'I found myself away from home for weeks at a time and then Gwen had a couple of other hits and we found that when one of us was at home, the other was away and we were just never together.'

Following the unexpected success of 'Rock your Baby' George McCrae realised he had no choice but to make a commitment to his career. To this end he recorded the obligatory album bearing the single's title, which also spawned the follow-up single. Titled 'I Can't Leave You Alone' it was a lukewarm version of the chart-topper, yet held a charming distinctive chorus that attracted record buyers. It soared into the British Top Ten during December 1974, establishing McCrae as a major contributor to the booming disco era.

To capitalise on his newfound British fame, McCrae hastily toured Britain while conceding he wasn't ready to hold a show together. His second tour was therefore carefully planned and rehearsed. 'Last time I didn't know what to expect . . . everything about the second show [is] better. I've got my own band and that makes the world of difference to my show.' Through 1975, McCrae was a regular visitor to Britain and its chart. Following a sluggish start with 'Sing a Happy Song', a Top Forty hit, the spontaneous 'It's Been So Long' burst with that McCrae sound to soar to No. 4 while its soundalike 'I Ain't Lyin'' peaked in the Top Twenty. All singles possessed a compelling beat which did not, like so many other dance records at this time, swamp McCrae's falsetto vocals.

However, like all things good, perhaps the singer overdosed on that TK Records' sound because in 1976 his selling power faltered as he struggled into the British Top Forty with 'Honey I', which was his last significant hit. His British nosedive coincided with his divorce, inevitable in the opinion of many, yet it was a move that neither George nor his wife planned. George said at the time, 'From a career point of view, it probably hasn't hurt or helped either one of us because we have always been two different entities. We are still good friends and we have just to accept it as part of show business.'

During the next two years, the singer decided to change his musical direction; it had served its purpose but dance music was altering and he refused to be left behind. To this end, he moved to New York to work with Greg Diamond, who replaced the hitmaking duo Casey and Finch. McCrae: 'After the success of "Rock your Baby" I felt that we needed something a little more sophisticated, away from the usual TK sound.' The result was the album *That Diamond Ring,* critically acclaimed but a poor seller. Maybe that 'usual TK sound' wasn't so bad after all!

Despite the lack of record sales, McCrae remained a touring act of note, backed by his multi-racial group. As his home country failed to support his career as avidly as his European fans, it was logical he should concentrate on the overseas territories. McCrae: 'The whole disco thing is bigger in Europe than in America. In fact, I have spent so much time outside America that I feel almost as much at home in London as I do in Miami.'

Although he continued to record, McCrae only managed one further British hit. Ten years on from his chart-topping 'Rock your Baby', 'One Step Closer (to Love)', released via President Records, peaked in the Top Sixty. An album bearing the same name followed, plus a cash-in compilation titled *The Best of George McCrae*.

Twelve years later, in 1996, McCrae appeared again with a CD release on Koch International. Titled *Do Something*, it swept the singer into the nineties and included remixed versions of three of his seventies classics as a medley, namely, 'Rock your Baby', 'I Can't Leave You Alone' and 'It's Been So Long'. The CD's release coincided with his sell-out British tour, which attracted both young and not-so-young, with an ageless McCrae performing like a true trooper who refused to hang up his microphone.

Oh! The shivers when he sang '. . . sexy mama . . .'

(Quotes: *Blues and Soul* magazine, 1979)

August 1974

THE THREE DEGREES

When Will I See You Again?

Many considered they were The Supremes' most dangerous of rivals; they were glorified by the British media as Prince Charles' favourite trio, when he requested the ladies perform at a private function, but when all is said and done, they will probably be remembered for a handful of hits, the most notable being their 1974 chart-topper.

'We were all born and grew up in Philadelphia. The original Three Degrees were Linda Turner, Shirley Porter and me. One day I was playing around the piano at one of the girls' houses and I'm just singing at the top of my lungs not knowing that it's a producer sitting there, on the couch. After we'd finished messing around, he got up and said, "I'm Richard Barrett, I'm gonna make you into stars." ' – Fayette Pinkney

During the fifties, Richard Barrett had been a successful recording act as a soloist and as a member of the group The Valentines. He also produced material for The Imperials, Frankie Lymon, and The Chantels, whom he discovered during 1957. Barrett then went on to discover a female vocalist named Sheila Ferguson, who recorded with The Royalettes in Baltimore for Chancellor Records during 1964. Barrett then groomed her as a soloist.

When Barrett first met Turner, Porter and Pinkney, he had recently moved from New York to Philadelphia to work for Swan Records, formed in 1957 by Bernie Bennick. He had signed Ferguson to this label, and intended to secure the new trio also. Known as The 3 Degrees, they released their debut single titled 'Gee Baby (I'm Sorry)' in March 1965. Pinkney: 'We had some quite successful records with Swan. After "Gee Baby", we had "I'm Gonna Need You", "Close your Eyes" – that's an old Five Keys song – and "Look in my Eyes", a number Richard originally wrote for The Chantels. We also did our first version of The Chantels' "Maybe" for Swan in '66.'

Meanwhile, fourteen-year-old Sheila Ferguson embarked upon a singing career. Her father was a professional golfer and her mother was, sadly, a schizophrenic; she spent much of her childhood alone. Her father was absent from the household for long spells at a time, and it was this and her mother's illness that forced a divorce when Ferguson was young. From the age of ten she moved from one relative to another, attending numerous schools, which prevented her from forming lasting friendships. However, she believed her childhood gave her the confidence to succeed.

Ferguson was recording as a solo artist, namely 'Little Red Riding Hood (That's What They Call Me)' and 'How Did That Happen', in 1965. On her recording sessions, Ferguson was supported by The 3 Degrees and the trio's recordings would, in turn, be 'padded' by Ferguson! She was also a regular nightclub performer, following her debut at the Apollo Theatre during 1965, where her regular back-up vocalists were . . . The 3 Degrees!

Pinkney: 'I guess the company was getting into difficulties after losing The Beatles, 'cause the last couple of Swan records, "Tales Are True" and "Love of my Life", didn't sell too well. But then we were doing some pretty good nightclub work.' Richard Barrett: 'Bernie Bennick [of] Swan was just calling all the wrong shots . . . after I'd cut [Sheila Ferguson] as a solo, I put her with The Three Degrees, but all Bernie wanted me to do was copy the Motown Sound. And people weren't buying copies . . . who needed 'em? Bernie had over-extended himself, and the company just folded up. That was that, Swan was finished.'

To salvage the group's career, Barrett moved from Philadelphia to Boston, to perfect their stage act, among other things. 'Because a lot of groups get a hit and they don't know the front from the back of stage. We thought it would really be a feather in our cap to be able to perform and entertain people as well as just singing the records. So that's how we got out on the road, working and working, and in a year or so, we had gained popularity and worked our way up to the largest nightclub in Boston.'

In 1965, the trio underwent a membership change to now include Pinkney, Helen Scott and Janet Jones, later replaced by Valerie Holiday. Scott had been educated at the same school as Ferguson, who also introduced her to the trio and Barrett. After a year with the line-up, Scott left in 1966, to marry and raise a family. Ferguson, then nineteen years old, replaced her on a temporary basis – and stayed for twenty-two years, leaving in 1986.

After signing with a major booking agency, the trio were in demand as performers, which stood them in good stead in the future. The girls went on to record several titles that included the single 'The Feeling of Love' for the Metromedia label, and the one-off single 'Contact' for Warner Brothers. They next moved to Roulette Records, where they rerecorded their Swan track 'Maybe'. The single was their first major American hit, when it soared to No. 29 during June 1970. Pinkney: 'It was our biggest hit and a lot of people say our best record. It was the first time we'd ever done a wailing kind of thing. Valerie did the lead and that big monologue got to all the girls.'

Barrett: 'I wasn't happy with the way record companies were handling the group. The sessions I was producing weren't very satisfying . . . By '69 Gamble and Huff had really blown the Philly thing [Philadelphia Records] wide open. Everyone was interested in them. It was like my vision of what Philly could become was really coming true. So I thought it'd be nice if we teamed up.'

Pinkney: 'We had met Kenny [Gamble] and Leon [Huff] when we were with Swan. They weren't into producing then, though they were writing songs all the time. They saw us at the Latin Casino in New Jersey and said they'd like to record us. We did one track, "What I See" . . . They released it and we didn't even know they were going to put it out. A deal was going to be negotiated but, by the time it came out, we had already signed with Roulette.' The trio's stay with Roulette Records was lucrative. The title 'I Do Take You' was released as the follow-up to their debut hit to falter in the Top Fifty. During 1971, two further singles became minor American hits, namely 'You're the One' and 'There's So Much Love all around Me'. However, when The 3 Degrees' contract expired, they cared little. Pinkney: 'We worked in *The French Connection* movie, did some television commercials and toured with Engelbert Humperdinck. Backing him was a new experience.' The trio was pleased to leave Roulette Records; the move meant they were free to sign a recording contract with Kenny Gamble and Leon Huff to release product via the Philly International label. Having the opportunity at last to be members of the Philadelphia family was a godsend to the trio. Pinkney: 'We did an album at Sigma Sound and as soon as we heard the musicians there, we knew we were going to get with the younger fans who buy records. That had been our problem. We would play shows to an adult audience but it's the teenagers who buy the records.' The album *Three Degrees* (the figure '3' had been dropped) spawned the single 'Dirty Ol' Man' in October 1973. The title bypassed the mainstream listing but scored as an American R. & B. hit. The trio then charted a second time with 'MFSB' (Mother, Father, Sister, Brother, or as some preferred, Mother Fuckin' Son of a Bitch), Philly's in-house group of musicians and singers with a forty-plus membership, under the title 'TSOP (The Sound of Philadelphia)'. Don Cornelius, producer of the American television music show *Soul Train,* asked Gamble and Huff to compose a new theme for the show: 'TSOP' was the result. The single shot to the top of the American chart during April 1974, a position it held for two weeks. 'TSOP' would, in time, be the title of Gamble and Huff's second record label.

At this juncture in the trio's rise to fame, author Tony Cummings observed, 'Barrett had skilfully taken this raw trio from the Swan Records' era and rehearsed and instructed them until they emerged as something quite unlike any other act in popular entertainment . . . They were black but their three-part harmony style was fairly far removed from black "soul" acts, with only Sheila's theatrical lead occasionally showing through . . . They were outrageously sexy, always dressed in slinky dresses clinging to voluptuous bodies in a dazzle of sequins, but their hip-thrusting stage movements had a kind of antiseptic obviousness too deliberate for real sexual allure or suggestiveness.' Slinky dresses or not, rock journalists loathed the sequined-trio. 'They are like black Barbi dolls. Posturing and wriggling . . . they are a hypnotic tribute to all that is tasteless, the ultimate plastic performers for a plastic world.' Strong or what?

'TSOP (The Sound of Philadelphia)' was released in British and reached No. 22, while The Three Degrees themselves debuted in the chart with 'Year of Decision', a No. 13 hit, but a poor seller in America, as was MFSB's second single to feature the trio. Titled 'Love Is the Message', it stalled in the American Top Ninety during July 1974. A month later, The Three Degrees released the haunting, highly-melodic 'When Will I See You Again?', penned and produced by Gamble and Huff. The title, not surprisingly, shot to the top of the British chart, a position it held for two weeks. Stateside, the track stalled one position lower in September. 'When Will I See You Again?' was the trio's top-selling single (to date), and went on to sweep across Europe, earning in excess of twelve gold discs, and prompting a Continent-wide visit. However, one of the trio's biggest markets was Japan, a country where they would tour often. Ferguson told journalist John Abbey, 'We have even recorded in Japan, we cut a Japanese version of "When Will I See You Again?" and we did a Japanese rock song . . . We were pleasantly surprised with the reaction our show got there. They really love soul music and especially Philly.'

During November 1974, the single 'Get your Love Back' faltered in the British Top Forty, while the next, 'Take Good Care of Yourself' returned The Three Degrees to the Top Ten during April 1975, but was a poor-selling American release. 'Long Lost Lover' followed to stall in the British Top Forty in July, and became the trio's final hit to be issued by Philadelphia International Records. However, prior to their departure, the girls' second album, *Three Degrees International,* was issued. Ferguson: 'There's more on it than the first album, which was basically a mood album. You'll see and hear more sides of the group and our ability.'

The Three Degrees moved to the Epic label, a subsidiary of CBS Records, to release the single 'Toast of Love', a British Top Forty hit during May 1976, before joining Ariola Records, with the intention of concentrating on the European market because their home country had failed dismally to support their art. A year later Ferguson's long-standing relationship with manager/mentor Richard Barrett ended. Unable to cope with his mental abuse, she attempted suicide. Two years later, she met Chris Robinson, owner of a nightclub on the holiday island of Jersey; within six months they were married. They moved to Philadelphia where, she told journalist Lester Middlehurst, they encountered racism for the first time: 'They burned a cross on our lawn when we first moved in . . . Eventually we got our own group of friends in Philadelphia, but knew that when the twins were born we would have to move to Britain.'

In 1978, after working with producer Giorgio Moroder, Ariola released the disco-slanted 'Givin' Up Givin' In', which, thanks to the dancefloor support, soared into the British Top Twenty. The marked musical change had been a gamble; from ballad to dance was not an ideal move to make. 'Givin' Up Givin' In' was swiped from the trio's album on Ariola Records, *3D.*

Reverting almost to the style of the early, sweeping melodies, The Three Degrees' next single, 'Woman in Love', reached No. 3 in Britain early in 1979, while the follow-up singles, namely, 'The Runner', 'The Golden Lady' and 'Jump the Gun', reached the Top Ten, Top Sixty and Top Fifty respectively. Before the year ended, The Three Degrees strode back into the Top Ten with 'My Simple Heart', a jerky type of track that was instantly forgettable.

It would take The Three Degrees six long years to re-establish themselves in the British chart with a recording liaison with Stock, Aitken and Waterman, titled 'The Heaven I Need', on the composer/producers' Supreme label in October 1985. Soul fans had for some time despaired at the girls' recordings, and to record with the British trio, responsible for the likes of Kylie Minogue, following a relationship with the masters Gamble and Huff, was the final insult. The soul market and The Three Degrees parted company. The 1985 single titled 'The Heaven I Need' marked the girls' final British hit.

In June 1986 Ferguson left the group to pursue a solo career. 'We haven't spoken since. I cried for months afterwards. I suppose from their point of view it was as if I had committed a crime because I was, theoretically, putting them out of work . . . I enjoyed my time with the group but there were bad times to.' While the trio, with the additional member Victoria Wallace, switched record labels to Ichiban, Ferguson performed as a solo artist without recorded success, before establishing herself as a television attraction and publishing the book *Soul Food* during 1989.

In the nineties, The Three Degrees confined their touring schedules to cabaret venues on both sides of the Atlantic. In Britain, the holiday camp circuit provides a lucrative career, although confusion does arise between the two touring entities. In 1997 Ferguson had a role in the West End musical *Always,* based on the life Edward VIII and Wallis Simpson.

For a female trio born from such established soul roots, and who enjoyed international status thanks to Gamble and Huff, two of the most innovative composer/producers in the history of music, The Three Degrees have lasted longer than most, despite falling into the commercial trap of white music.

(Quotes: *The Sound of Philadelphia* by Tony Cummings; *Blues and Soul* magazine, interview by John Abbey, 1975; *Daily Mail,* interview by Lester Middlehurst, May 1997)

THE OSMONDS

Love Me for a Reason

When the Osmond seniors were asked to identify the prime factor behind their children's success they answered, 'Apart from their obvious talent, undoubtedly it was our emphasis on the family. Even their talents would not have been so continually developed and encouraged but for this strong family relationship.' In other words, many believed, the youngsters lost their childhood to become what their parents had not, and this was true for many, if not all, family groups. Nonetheless, The Osmonds took on the world and won.

The foundation of the family group comprised Alan Osmond, born on 22 June 1949; Wayne, born on 28 August 1951; Merrill, born on 30 April 1953, and Jay, born on 2 March 1955, all in Ogden, Utah, to Olive and George. Their first two sons Virl and Tom were both born deaf and were unable to join the family singing group as permanent members.

After school, the brothers would rehearse under their parents' guidance, singing and dancing until a particular song sequence was perfected. Wayne Osmond told author Paul H. Dunn, 'Every Friday we had what we called a family night and it was on those evenings that we actually began to sing separately and together. We just sang for fun, to entertain the family really. As soon as one of us was big enough to stand there and carry some sort of tune, he would take part.'

In 1961 the family group entered the annual International Barbershop Quartet Convention held in Kansas City, Missouri. Although they lost to The Night Hawks, they secured one-night performances in local clubs. Merrill Osmond: 'When people found out we could sing, we got to sing in church socials. From there it spread to the Kiwanis Club, Lions Club and other places. Eventually we were taking our group to Salt Lake City. On some nights we made sixty dollars – just for singing.'

The brothers – Virl, Tom, Alan, Wayne, Merrill, Jay and Donny (born on 9 December 1957 in Ogden) – were signed by Disneyland's entertainment manager, Tommy Walker, for a three-month contract as a barbershop act during the summer of 1962. Olive Osmond: 'They could all carry a tune quite easily . . . In those days Virl and Tom took part with the others . . . though of course they haven't been able to

191

make it their career as the others have.' Among their regular audience members was Walt Disney himself, founder of the entire empire, who sufficiently believed in the boys' potential to include them in a handful of his television shows.

When the Disney contract expired, The Osmonds had little choice but to return to Ogden and school, believing their brush with show business had ended. Nonetheless, evenings remained rehearsal times. Quite unexpectedly, crooner Andy Williams's brother, Tommy, contacted the Osmond home. He had seen the Walt Disney television shows, was impressed by the brothers' act, and as Andy Williams was embarking upon a series of his own shows for NBC TV, he wanted The Osmonds to join him. Eventually, they were offered a five-year contract, forcing the family to move to Los Angeles. However, what the family had not planned on were the expenses involved – fees for a manager and agent, costume designer and choreographer, which naturally ate up most of the brothers' five-figure pay cheque. Thankfully, the money that the Osmond seniors had invested helped sustain them during this period.

The downside to the brothers appearing with Williams for so long meant the viewing public believed them to be his protégés, his 'boys'. Of course, that was not so; they were a performing vocal act before he gave them their first national break. When in 1964 *The Andy Williams Show* finished, the brothers switched to *The Jerry Lewis Show*, screened by ABC TV, until that too ended in 1969. By the time they left the two television series behind them, The Osmonds were on the verge of stardom.

In mid-1968 the group signed to the Barnaby label, owned by Andy Williams, before switching to Uni Records. With no success with either, The Osmonds moved to MGM Records in 1971, at the invitation of the company's president, who believed they could be marketed as a white version of The Jackson 5. Like The Osmonds, Motown's young family group was nurtured and encouraged by their parents until that relationship disintegrated under the glare of the public spotlight.

The Osmonds' debut single was in fact a number rejected by The Jackson 5 titled 'One Bad Apple'. It was released in February 1971. The two family groups would now be in direct competition, even to the extent of their youngest members embarking upon solo careers. Of course, the media didn't help, as stories of intense competition made good copy, but were largely the result of journalists' imagination rather than fact. 'One Bad Apple' gave The Osmonds their first American chart-topper, selling one million copies on the way, while their first eponymous album soared into the Top Twenty. To capitalise upon this remarkable success, Uni Records rereleased the single 'I Can't Stop'.

This was the era of teen acts, screaming female fans and youthful hysteria. The girls demanded pin-ups and usually nominated group lead singers to be their trophies. It was no surprise, then, when following the American success of 'One Bad Apple' MGM Records swiped little Donny from the group to record him as a soloist and, they hoped, a new teenage million-selling idol. The aptly titled 'Sweet and Innocent' was Donny's debut solo outing in June 1971. It shot into the American Top Ten, notching up sales of one million copies. 'Double Lovin'' quickly followed, likewise his first eponymous album, which went on to pass gold status. Despite media interference, Donny had not left his brothers for a solo career; it would run parallel to that of the group until the late eighties.

In March 1972 The Osmonds (now with little Jimmy, born on 16 April 1963 in Canoga Park, California, in the line-up) issued 'Down by the Lazy River' penned by Alan and Merrill. The single crashed into the American chart to peak at No. 4; another million-seller to their credit, while a month later, the title became the group's debut British hit, albeit in the Top Forty.

Jimmy became the second Osmond brother to record and release a solo single. Titled 'Long Haired Lover from Liverpool', it climbed into the American Top Forty, but for some inexplicable reason topped the British chart during January 1973.

Osmond-mania was peaking in Britain; it far outweighed the American hysteria (naturally!) and when the 'Crazy Horses' single was released in December 1972 amidst the frenzied fan worship showered on Donny and Jimmy, the title shot to No. 2 in the British chart. Ironically, the high-pitched single faltered in the American Top Twenty. To this day, fans recall with humour the frenetic dance routine the brothers performed, encompassing bent knees and criss-cross arm movements. Wayne: 'So long as it's all clean and in fun there's nothing wrong with dancing.'

'Goin' Home' followed in August 1973 and returned the brothers to the British chart's higher placings (a month after its American release when it struggled into the Top Forty). Then their next album, *The Plan*, publicly confirmed their Mormon faith (daily prayer meetings, abstinence from coffee, tea, alcohol and tobacco), which was both ridiculed and respected. In any event, it was their most ambitious project to date and reached the Top Ten.

The Osmonds were now, of course, world tourers, but before 'One

Bad Apple' launched them as headliners, the brothers had included stipulations in their concert agreements. For instance, they refused to support what they believed to be unsuitable acts. Wayne: 'When we were second acts, we always had clauses in our contracts specifying that we didn't have to work on the same programme with someone who was using dirty material . . . What another performer presents on his own is his business and not ours, but if we work with someone it looks as if we agree with the tone of his act.' He admitted, though, that the group lost out financially, particularly as they also refused to work on Sundays in any capacity relating to entertainment. 'We need to rest one day in seven, as everyone else does. And we need to go to church and recharge our spiritual batteries. That's what the Lord's day is all about.'

Back to the music, 'Let Me In' was their last single of 1973. Penned by Wayne, Merrill and Alan, the title peaked in the American Top Forty, while once again, British sales catapulted it to No. 2. Between group releases, the family soloists continued their run of hits – in fact, any note connected with The Osmonds sold in vast quantities. While Donny and now sister Marie (born on 13 October 1959 in Ogden, and who began her solo career in 1973, following a probationary period as a group member) fed public demand for Osmond material, The Osmonds' first British hit of 1974 was 'I Can't Stop', a No. 12 hit in May. Three months on, their album *Our Best to You* was issued. In August, The Osmonds secured six consecutive evenings of live performances to be screened by BBC TV. It was probably due to this daily peak viewing that their next single, 'Love Me for a Reason', became their first and only British chart-topper as a group. The ballad, penned and recorded by soul artist/composer/producer Johnny Bristol, soared to the top in Britain in September 1974, a position it maintained for three weeks. In America, the title faltered in the Top Ten.

Incidentally, the group rejected more songs than it recorded because of lyrical content. If they felt lyrics were double-edged, they refused to consider the song. Alan: 'In many of the lyrics you could interpret meanings two ways, so we had to rewrite quite a few lyrics. But where that wasn't possible we just had to turn the songs down altogether . . . We probably lost a lot of money that way, but we didn't care.'

Following a lengthy tour of Australia and the release of a duet by Donny and Marie early in 1975, The Osmonds released 'Having a Party', which surprisingly stalled in the British Top Thirty in March. Four months on, they released a version of the Frankie Valli hit 'The Proud One', which re-established them in the British Top Five and reached the Top Thirty in America during September. An album of the same name followed. The last single of the year, 'I'm Still Gonna Need You', struggled into the British Top Forty, and represented the start of the group's decline.

Once more it was left to the young Osmond soloists to maintain chart status until the group issued their last charting title, 'I Can't Live a Dream', a Top Forty British and American chart entrant. And while Donny and Marie Osmond continued to fly the family flag during 1977, The Osmonds toured America for the last time. By 1980 the group disbanded altogether; the magical era had gone, The Osmonds were yesterday's news.

However, the name would not die. Two years later Alan, Wayne, Merrill and Jay re-formed the group and signed a recording contract with Elektra Records to release country and western material. In 1984 they switched to Warner Bros and promoted their new music in Britain via a short tour. A year later, now signed to EMI America Records and known as The Osmond Brothers, they performed at the Country Music Festival staged at Wembley, Middlesex.

With The Osmonds now a blip in the public's memory, it seemed appropriate that the new decade should see the birth of a new family line-up. As all the elder brothers married early in their career, their children were now able to continue the Osmond tradition. Alan's sons, Nathan, Douglas, Michael and David, recorded 'Hey Girl' under the name The Osmond Boys, while in 1992, their father and his brothers reformed to contribute to soul artist Jeffrey Osborne's 'The Heart of a Hero' single. The profits from this release went to AIDS research.

The following year, the Osmond family appeared to retire from the music business altogether. This move was partly due to ill health – Merrill had diabetes and a heart condition; Alan was battling against multiple sclerosis, while Wayne underwent surgery to remove a malignant brain tumour. Merrill: 'If I didn't know better, I'd swear it was a family curse. Whatever has befallen my brothers and me seems to be working its way down the family tree. I don't believe in curses, but what else can you call it?'

(Quotes: *The Osmonds: The Official Story of the Osmond Family* by Paul H. Dunn)

CARL DOUGLAS

Kung Fu Fighting

Most subjects can be adapted to music, so why not Kung Fu? Rather off-beam, perhaps, but nonetheless, the record-buying public had a mad few moments to elevate Carl Douglas to the top of the British chart.

Biddu, born in India, a British record producer who had previously scored the soundtrack to the movie *Embassy* starring Richard Rowntree, using Carl Douglas as his vocalist, was searching for a singer to record the Larry Weiss composition 'I Want to Give You Everything'. Searching for suitable vocalists, Biddu remembered Douglas, offered him the track and requested that he provide the proposed single's flipside.

After suggesting at least six songs, Douglas recited the lyrics to 'Kung Fu Fighting', not believing Biddu would take the title seriously. As it was to be tucked away as a B-side, Biddu agreed to work on 'Kung Fu Fighting' with the singer, stipulating it was 'a fun thing to do'. Due to lack of studio time, ten minutes was allocated to recording the slice of nonsense. Biddu told *Billboard* magazine, 'We did a lot of "hoos" and "haas", like someone giving somebody a karate chop.'

With both 'I Want to Give You Everything' and 'Kung Fu Fighting' completed, Biddu took the tape to Pye Records, where an A. & R. executive, fascinated by the B-side's title, insisted on hearing it in its entirety. Yep, he went for it! 'Kung Fu Fighting' became the single's topside, leaving Biddu flabbergasted, insisting the title would only sell 20,000 at best. The executive thought otherwise, particularly as karate was fashionable at the time and Bruce Lee had regained his crown as a fighting icon. Biddu: 'The first five weeks, we didn't get one play on radio. It didn't sell one copy. And then suddenly, it just took off.' Disco promotion had secured a minor chart position which, in turn, had encouraged national airplay, a pattern followed by so many questionable hits of the seventies.

In October 1974, the relatively unknown Jamaican singer, who was studying as an engineering student, dominated the British chart for three long weeks. 'Kung Fu Fighting' went on to become one of the biggest international hits of the decade, including in America where, via 20th Century Records, it topped the chart during December 1974, a position it held for two weeks. Biddu: 'If I had a theory why the record was a hit, I'd have more hits! It was a bit of a novelty . . . Maybe it was just a good pop record without us knowing about it.'

The single was Carl Douglas's only big-selling title, although he issued the soundalike 'Dance the Kung Fu', which peaked at No. 35 in the British chart in November 1974. Quite rightly so; the song was identical to the chart-topper – only the lyrics had altered. Three years on, Douglas released his final British charting title, namely, 'Run Back', which reached the Top Thirty during December. And that was that!

Biddu, on the other hand, went on to enjoy further chart-topping success with another dancefloor single, 'I Love to Love', recorded by Tina Charles in March 1976. As an artist, he charted with a trio of titles, namely, 'Summer of '42' (1975), 'Rain Forest' (1976) and 'Journey to the Moon' (1978). Among other projects, the producer worked with ex-Supreme member Mary Wilson and British singer Dotty Green (the featured vocalist on Mark Fisher's 1985 British Top Sixty hit titled 'Love Situation') on 'My Love Life Is a Disaster'. The track remains un-released at the time of writing but is heavily bootlegged on tape and video.

The whereabouts of Carl Douglas, though, remain a mystery. Bruce Lee, on the other hand, still graces posters and videos.

November 1974

DAVID ESSEX

Gonna Make You a Star

Singer/actor David Essex, with his cheeky grin, curly hair and Cockney accent, was more fortunate than most – he was successful in two fields of entertainment. And it was this talent that ensured his thirty-year stay in show business, an achievement not too many of his ilk can boast.

Born David Cook in Plaistow, London, on 23 July 1947, David Essex left school at the age of sixteen to join the local group called The Evertons as a drummer. During a performance at a Walthamstow public house, Derek Bowman, journalist for the *Daily Express* newspaper, was sufficiently impressed to become the group's manager. Bowman arranged for Essex to record his debut single titled 'And the Tears Come Tumbling Down' in 1965 on the Fontana label. Indeed, Essex went on to record a handful of titles during the next two years, but all bombed. Disappointed, he abandoned recording for acting, to appear in the 1967 movie *Smashing Time* with Lynn Redgrave and Rita Tushingham.

A year later, his disappointment forgotten, Essex returned to recording to release a pair of one-off singles titled 'Love Story' and 'Just for Tonight' on Uni Records and Pye Records respectively. In 1969, 'That Takes Me Back' was issued by Decca Records, but that followed the fate of the other titles. Once again, Essex turned to acting. He became Tommy Steele's understudy, before appearing on the London stage in *Godspell*, Jean Michael Tebelak's religious musical. Starring Jeremy Irons in the lead role of Judas Iscariot, the show started its life at London's Roundhouse, before being staged at the Wyndham Theatre. Essex played a popular Jesus – indeed audiences believed he was the son of God or at the very least a distant relative – and he stayed in the role for more than two years, taking leave of absence to perform in his first significant film role. With producer David Puttnam at the helm, Essex played rock star Jim Maclaine in *That'll Be the Day,* alongside pop music luminaries like Ringo Starr, Keith Moon and Billy Fury, whom he said was unassuming yet a proficient actor. With this group of life-loving characters, filming was, predictably, one huge laugh from the opening scenes. When premiered in London during April 1973, the movie received critical praise, and became a box office record breaker. Essex went on to receive the Variety Club of Great Britain Award for the Most Promising Newcomer of 1972.

On the strength of his performance, CBS Records secured him as a recording artist proper. His debut single, 'Rock On', issued during September 1973, was penned by Essex and was in tune with the fifties feel of *That'll Be the Day.* The title shot to No. 3 in the British chart; in America during March 1974 it sold in excess of one million copies. Essex-mania was simmering; all the signs were there. Before the close of 1973, his second single, 'Lamplight', and his debut album *Rock On* both peaked at No. 7 in their respective charts. 'Lamplight' failed abysmally across the Atlantic, struggling into the Top Eighty, while the album did better, reaching the Top Thirty.

Early in 1974, the singer fulfilled his two-film contract by playing Jim Maclaine in *Stardust,* the sequel to *That'll Be the Day.* This time, Adam Faith co-starred, as Maclaine rose and fell as a recording artist. Essex said *Stardust* was hard to film; the situations portrayed on film were similar to those experienced in his own life, creating an unwanted identity crisis for him to work through. Playing Maclaine for a second time led to public confusion; cinema-goers believed he was the character while Essex conceded he could easily have suffered the same disasters as Maclaine but for the support of his wife and the birth of his baby daughter. He told journalist Peter Doggett, 'I had a tiny little baby girl, and at the back of my mind whatever situation I was in, I always wanted her to be able to respect me, so I didn't want to end up . . . on the front of the *News of the World.*' The movie was premiered in London during October, with all indications that it would repeat its predecessor's success. While Essex was involved in the film's shooting, his recording career continued with the 'America' single, although it only managed the British Top Forty. But in November 1974 Essex enjoyed his first British chart-topper with 'Gonna Make You a Star'. Again the title was his own composition, produced by Jeff Wayne, and was an outright pop song, which dominated the chart for three weeks. Hot on the chart-topper's heels, Essex released his eponymous album, also a huge best seller.

The follow-up to his No. 1 single was the title track from the *Stardust* movie released early in 1975. It reached the British Top Ten, as did his second single of the year, 'Rollin' Stone'.

Following the release of his third album, *All the Fun of the Fair,* Essex struck gold with his second British chart-topper, 'Hold Me Close, in October 1975. The title dominated British sales for three weeks. Unfortunately Essex was unable to join in the celebrations; he was touring the world, fuelling Essex-mania in every country he visited. His escalating popularity eventually led to the breakdown of his marriage and by mutual consent the couple separated. His young fans were totally and unashamedly besotted by their handsome idol, who, in turn, attempted to live a disciplined lifestyle, unlike others in his privileged position. Essex: 'I was always locked away in the hotel suite while the roadies and the band were running riot. I was smuggled out of the theatre and thrown in my room and kept behind lock and key. So I don't think I went nuts in that way. Maybe I would have enjoyed it a bit more if I had . . .'

Alarmingly, his immense popularity was destined to plummet as quickly has it had risen, beginning with his lack of chart success. 'If I Could', the follow-up single to the British chart-topper, marked the start of the decline by stalling in the Top Twenty early in 1976. A pair of singles, 'City Lights' and 'Coming Home' (lifted from the album *Out on the Street,* itself a Top Forty title), struggled into the Top Thirty during 1976, while one single, 'Cool Out Tonight', reached No. 23 in the chart the following year. It was astonishing how Essex fell from stardom so quickly.

As he fell, so he eventually rose. In March 1978, he released a cover version of the Lorraine Ellison soul classic 'Stay with Me Baby'. It was an unusual move for him, and a song of considerable vocal range which, thankfully, he did not attempt. His interpretation stalled at No. 45 in the British chart, leading to CBS Records dropping him. Undeterred, Essex joined Phonogram Records, though his British releases would be via the Mercury subsidiary. Practically overnight, Essex was re-established as a top-selling vocalist thanks to 'Oh What a Circus' which shot to No. 3 in Britain during September 1978. The title had help; it was swiped from *Evita,* the stage musical composed by Tim Rice and Andrew Lloyd Webber, in which Essex had secured the role of Che Guevara. The singer recreated Guevara's image of student militant in battle fatigues, whose role was to destroy the Perons' fantasy world. Essex was also earmarked to play the role in the movie version, but when directors changed, so did the politics, and Antonio Banederas secured the part, studying Essex's recordings to do so. To capitalise on the Mercury hit single, CBS Records did what any record company would, and released an album of their ex-artist's greatest hits. The move presented them with a Top Thirty hit, while Essex recouped the composer's royalties.

Towards the close of 1978, the artist embarked upon a nationwide tour, coinciding with the release of the poor-selling single 'Brave New World' on the CBS label. Mercury Records retaliated the following year by issuing Essex's new album *Imperial Wizard,* a No. 12 seller, and the single of the same name, which faltered in the Top Forty.

To greet the new decade, Essex shrugged off his teen-idol image, to return to the film world as actor, composer and vocalist by co-starring with Beau Bridges in *Silver Dream Racer,* a film devoted to motorcycle racing. The project bombed but afforded Essex the chance to race around Brands Hatch at 160 mph, although, for insurance purposes, the more dangerous stunts were executed by experts. Essex penned the soundtrack from which his next single, 'Silver Dream Machine', was lifted. Released amidst the movie's hype, the title soared to No. 4 in the British chart during May 1980. A year later, he returned to the London stage, playing Lord Byron in *Childe Byron,* staged at the Young Vic. This time he did not abandon his recording commitments: 'Hot Love', the title track from the album issued in 1980, faltered in the Top Sixty, while during 1982 a pair of singles, 'Me and My Girl (Nightclubbing)' and the seasonal 'A Winter's Tale' reached Nos. 13 and 2 respectively. Two further albums were also issued, *Be-Bop the Future* and *Stage-Struck;* neither reached the Top Thirty. Essex could sell singles; albums were a different story.

The stage beckoned once more. In October 1983 he played Fletcher Christian in his self-penned musical *Mutiny on the Bounty.* Co-starring with him were his (then) girlfriend, disco singer Sinitta, and Frank Finlay. The soundtrack album *Mutiny* peaked in the British Top Fifty, while the lifted single, 'Tahiti', soared to No. 8. To close 1983, the single You're in my Heart' struggled into the Top Sixty, while its mother album, *The Whisper*, floundered around the Top Seventy.

The following two years were painfully abysmal for Essex as his recording career practically hit a standstill. Even the television-advertised album *Centre Stage* featuring tracks from both stage and screen, only reached the Top Ninety late in 1986.

One final single charted before the decade was out, 'Myfanwy', a Top Fifty hit, taken from the Mike Read project titled *Betjeman*, a musical based on the poems of the late Sir John Betjeman. Nevertheless, Essex worried not – he returned to acting, this time on the small screen. In 1988 he played a lock-keeper in the BBC-TV series *The River*, a highly successful project where he played his character as a cheeky Cockney charmer, the lovable rogue.

While Essex recorded his album *Touching the Ghost*, to be released on his own newly-opened Lamplight label, Michael Damian took his version of Essex's debut single 'Rock On' to the top of the American chart. The American actor was only eleven years old when the original single was issued. Essex: 'Michael's version is a lot more poppy than the way I originally recorded it . . . but once he realised I liked the way he did the song, we got on fine.'

In the nineties, Essex became president of the Voluntary Service Overseas organisation, while his recorded work comprised a trio of compilations, supported by a lengthy British tour. In 1993 he released a collection of pop standards *Cover Shot;* a No. 3 album. A year later, he recorded a further musical potpourri album, *Back to Back,* a Top Forty British hit. Meanwhile, his duet with Catherine Zeta Jones, 'True Love Ways', likewise struggled into the Top Forty.

David Essex is now considered to be one of Britain's foremost entertainers; indeed he spends most of his time acting and touring Britain. In 1996, he embarked upon an extensive tour, where the majority of venues were sold out. He also released the album *Missing You,* a Top Thirty entrant. A year later, he recorded a further concept album, titled *A Night at the Movies,* for Polygram Records. Although Essex wanted to record his own material no record company would support him. *A Night at the Movies* appealed to him because the project allowed him to record with the Royal Philharmonic Orchestra, and was the perfect sister album to *Cover Shot.* Essex supported the release by touring Britain.

Yes, an all-rounder who now appeals to all ages. A far cry from a rampant teen-idol, eh?

(Quotes: *Record Collector,* interview by Peter Doggett, 1997)

December 1974

BARRY WHITE

You're the First, the Last, my Everything

'I never wanted to sing. My career that I was reaching for was writer, composer, arranger and producer.' – Barry White

Born on 12 September 1944, in Galveston, Texas, White and his family moved to Los Angeles, where his childhood was spent running against the law, with his younger brother Darry. Barry White, expelled from high school following an incident with a teacher, led his lawless existence until he and Darry were incarcerated in juvenile hall for crimes that included robbery and car theft. This humiliation taught Barry determination; his life would no longer be spent on the wrong side of the legal system. Pursuing music was his only ambition now. White: 'My mom did a bit of acting, she was in a movie *Trader Horn.* When I was ten she took me to church and I sang in the choir . . . We never had any money . . . and I didn't get new clothes every year. But we had love. We would watch television together and my mother used to read to us a lot . . . maybe we weren't like other folks but we loved each other. Other families may have had fathers, but often they were alcoholics, gamblers, or they would beat up on their wives. So maybe it was good that my father wasn't there.'

As a sixteen-year-old, White composed tracks for a number of R. & B. groups, including The Upfronts, during 1960. From the start, it had been his intention to create music as writer and producer; he never intended to stand before a microphone. At seventeen years old, White secured an arranger's position for Rampart Records, where 'I had lots of starving cold days but I really believed in my ability which kept me going. I worked free for a year and a half with a guy called Jack Stern who taught me how to produce sounds in the studio.' At Rampart Records, White tasted success for the first time with 'Harlem Shuffle', recorded and released by Bob and Earl on the Marc label during 1963. White: 'I knew Bob Relf and Earl Nelson and I played keyboards on and helped produce the single. And I did a thing with a guy named Leon Rene. And when Earl, he was Jackie Lee then, cut "The Duck" and it was a big hit, I went as his road manager. I gained a lot of experience.' White also duetted with Jackie Lee, as Smoke, to record 'Love We Finally Made It', a future Love Unlimited track.

In 1966 White, now married with four children, joined Mustang/ Bronco Records as a producer, then A. & R. manager. During his stay he worked with Viola Wills to release the title 'Lost Without the Love of my Guy', and with Felice Taylor on 'It May Be Winter Outside', a Top Fifty American hit during 1967. White: ' "I Feel Love Comin' On" was a bigger success in Britain for Felice [No. 11 in October 1967] than America. She went to Britain but soon lost out. She was a very mechanical singer, and she had a very bad attitude to the business so she blew the whole thing.' He then went on to record his own single titled 'All in the Run of a Day'; it bombed.

White: 'I left Mustang when it folded. What I had enjoyed most there was working with unknowns. I wasn't much interested in established artists. I just wanted to raise artists from the living dead. I knew that if I could find the right artist or group who'd allow me to implement the ideas in my head, I could really set the world alight.' In 1969, he very nearly did: he discovered Love Unlimited, a female trio comprising Diane Taylor and sisters Linda and Glodean James. In time, White became their record producer: 'I met Love Unlimited in a studio. I was producing a record for a friend of theirs and they were background singers for her. They asked me would I produce them as a group . . . and we came together.'

White negotiated a recording contract for the trio with Uni Records during 1971. 'I'd worked out this concept which involved a very complex production with rain effects, footsteps, a story in sound.' That was, of course, 'Walkin' in the Rain with the One I Love' and it was very big. The single (which featured White's spoken word – a booming bass voice) peaked at No. 14 in both the British and American charts during 1972.

In many ways, Love Unlimited's debut outing was White's tribute to the Motown sound that emanated from Detroit, Michigan, particularly the company's female groups, like The Supremes. In 1973, following a switch to 20th Century Records when Uni Records folded, Love Unlimited enjoyed two further American hits, namely, 'Yes, We Finally Made It' and 'It May Be Winter Outside (but in my Heart It's Spring)'. The latter title was also the trio's last British hit, in February 1975, when it peaked at No. 11 in the chart. This year of 1973 also marked

Barry White's first single as a soloist. Titled 'I'm Gonna Love You Just a Little Bit More Baby', it shot to No. 3 in America, while in Britain it reached the Top Thirty. Its follow-up, 'I've Got So Much to Give', faltered in the American Top Forty in mid-1973, and bypassed Britain. White: 'I'd never honestly thought too much about recording myself, I really lived for Love Unlimited. But when I cut "I'm Gonna Love You Just a Little Bit More Baby", I realised the public was willing to accept me as an artist.' The tracks were, incidentally, lifted from White's first album, *I've Got So Much to Give*, a Top Twenty American hit.

It was thanks to Love Unlimited's second album that the Love Unlimited Orchestra was born. Included in the track listing was an instrumental piece which preceded the albums's title track, 'Under the Influence of Love'. The two tracks were played as one by nightclub DJs, prompting a demand for the song's instrumental section. Whether he wanted it or not, White now had another musical mouthpiece for his work, and formed the 41-piece Love Unlimited Orchestra, who, led by its creator, recorded in its own right titles that included 'Love's Theme' in 1973, their first and last British hit when it soared to No. 10 in the chart during 1974; 'Rhapsody in White', 1974; 'Satin Soul', 'Share a Little Love in your Heart' and 'Forever in Love', 1975; 'Midnight Groove' and 'My Sweet Summer Suite', 1976, and 'Theme from King Kong (Pt 1)' in 1977. All titles were released via 20th Century Records. White: 'Love Unlimited Orchestra was my opportunity to create an orchestra of enormous size and play beautiful music – and that's what I did.'

By the close of 1973, Barry White and his Love Unlimited family had sold a staggering sixteen million dollars' worth of records. Not bad going for a man who never wanted to be a singer and whose ambition was to earn a gold disc for his record sales. He received that for 'Walkin' in the Rain with the One I Love' and by 1979 had seventy more.

During 1974, Love Unlimited issued a pair of poor-selling American singles, namely, 'Under the Influence of Love' and 'I Belong to You'; the outfit would not chart again until 1977. However, the trio was the first female act in history to enter the Top Five album chart published by the American music trade magazine, *Billboard*. Also the same year, White himself issued singles like 'Never, Never Gonna Give You Up' and 'Can't Get Enough of your Love Babe' (the titles practically as long as the songs themselves!). Both were American and British charters, with the latter track topping the American chart in September 1974. Meantime, the Love Unlimited Orchestra issued their *Rhapsody in White* album, and the soundtrack to the *Together Brothers* movie, which also included a pair of Love Unlimited tracks.

White's British career peaked in December 1974, when his single 'You're the First, the Last, my Everything' topped the chart, where it stayed for two weeks. A month later, the title catapulted to No. 2 in America, earning the artist his fourth solo gold disc.

Indeed, the luxurious Barry White 'love' sound was truly established, and like the Motown sound before it, his was impossible to dissect, although many tried. The ingredients used to build his unique style were many as its originator once said: 'The Barry White Sound is rhythm and melody. I use violins differently . . . People were used to violins as a swaying, flowing sound, but I use them as a rhythm instrument.' More than that, he did not divulge.

By the close of 1974, White had also issued the albums titled *Stone Gon'* and *Can't Get Enough,* both big sellers, while on the personal front, he married Love Unlimited member Glodean James – the lady with the talon-long nails! The couple lived in a mansion overlooking the San Fernando Valley, where White oversaw his expanding business interests and recorded in his own state-of-the-art studio.

For the following two years, 'Big Bad Baz' sustained his high-selling profile via the singles 'What Am I Gonna Do with You?', '(For You) I'll Do Anything You Want Me To', 'Let the Music Play', 'You See the Trouble with Me', 'Baby, We Better Try to Get It Together' and 'Don't Make Me Wait Too Long'. He released albums that included, *Just Another Way to Say I Love You, Let the Music Play,* and the inevitable *Greatest Hits* package.

To capitalise on his continuing British success, White and his family of singers and musicians performed at the Royal Albert Hall in London before a capacity audience. White, looking every inch the star, strutted and growled his way through the evening, oozing immeasurable amounts of love and sweat, necessitating regular dabs with his silk handkerchief. Most certainly, a 'love-in' on a sophisticated, mature level!

Despite his international stardom and the lifestyle that it now afforded him, White believed his record company had failed him. To confirm this, he cited the *Let the Music Play* project which fell short of his expectations. 'There were a lot of things happening. Twentieth Century became so big in three years, there was a lot of internal fighting.' In fact, Russ Regan, who had originally signed White and his family as artists, had departed to open his own record label. Hence White was left to flounder. So precarious was his position that within a year, Barry White would chart for the last time.

Meantime, the singer's 'I'm Qualified to Satisfy' opened 1977; the title bombed in America, but struggled into the British Top Forty. The follow-up, 'It's Ecstasy When You Lay Down Next to Me', likewise reached the Top Forty in November. Some believed the single's theme was 'persuasive love-making', which led to countless American radio stations banning the title. White defended his work as 'an honest song . . . it's a song that people do when they go out on the dance floor. It's things that they go through when they see somebody they like. It's things they feel when they're with somebody they are interested in.' British sales reflected the public's feeling; the title was confined to the Top Forty.

In between releases, White issued the second volume of his *Greatest Hits,* an immediate Top Twenty hit in Britain, and *Barry White Sings for Someone You Love,* a platinum seller across the Atlantic.

Following the release of 'Oh What a Night for Dancing' midway through 1978, a Top Thirty American hit, and the album *Barry White the Man,* 'Your Sweetness Is my Weakness' marked his final American hit single; his last for 20th Century Records, where he had stayed for five years, selling in excess of 100 million discs. Thankfully, Britain was kinder: early in 1979, his version of Billy Joel's 1978 hit 'Just the Way You Are' peaked in the Top Twenty. It was lifted from *Barry White the Man,* as was its follow-up, 'Sha La La Means I Love You'; a British Top Sixty struggler. Neither single was released in American. White: 'We made a deal with CBS Records in 1979 and the first album *The Message Is Love* was platinum. Then the industry crashed.' For an artist who had maintained a regular high chart profile between 1972 and 1978 this downfall was a major disappointment. Obviously, the disco whirlwind was partly to blame, and, in all honesty, it was not until this had blown itself out towards the end of the decade, that artists like White were able to re-establish themselves. In fact, it took him until 1987 to enjoy his next British hit.

However, during the lean years White was far from idle. He continued to record and released nine albums, that included work with his Love Unlimited Orchestra, a duet collection with his wife Glodean and his own work, like *Barry White's Sheet Music* and *Change.*

By 1987, White was free of CBS Records to sign with A&M Records, where his career began again. The album *The Right Night and Barry White* spawned the hit titled 'Sho' You Right', a British Top Twenty entrant. As is inevitable when an artist enjoys success with a new record outlet, a previous company will cash in; 20th Century Records was no exception and issued a remixed version of 'Never Never Gonna Give You Up', a Top Seventy British hit. The next 'official' charting title was

'Secret Garden' during 1990, released on Quincy Jones's Qwest label and recorded with James Ingram, Al Be Sure and El DeBarge. Despite its low placing in the Top Seventy, White embarked upon a world tour with the Love Unlimited Orchestra. Dates included ten sell-out concerts in Britain.

In the nineties, Barry White worked on with *The Man Is Back* album, followed by *Put Me in your Mix,* and a compilation, originally issued in 1988, titled *The Collection,* which peaked in the British Top Forty. In 1992, he diversified slightly, to duet with British vocalist Lisa Stansfield on the title 'All around the World', the B-side to her solo 'Time to Make You Mine'; and with Isaac Hayes on 'Dark and Lovely (You Over There)'. Two years on, 'Baz' returned to both the American and British Top Twenty singles charts with 'Practise What You Preach', and his version of Dusty Springfield's 1963 international hit 'I Only Want to Be with You', which peaked in the British Top Forty in April 1995, the same month that his album *The Icon Is Love* achieved sales of two million.

The man of love continued to tour spasmodically both in America and Europe during this decade, and as recently as 1996 performed at Madison Square Garden in New York. Barry White – 'The Maestro', 'The Love Man', 'Big Bad Baz' – was the artist who made love possible for everyone: all races and all sizes. And it is for this alone that his music will be remembered in future years. Modestly, he once said, 'I think my size and my stature, mixed with my voice, have given me an identity.'

Huh! What about your talent, Mr Big Man?

(Quotes: *We Had Joy We Had Fun* by Barry Scott; *Black Music* by Gavin Petrie)

STATUS QUO

Down Down

'I always thought I'd be dead at forty-five, but now I want to make it to eighty. I don't drink any more and I don't eat meat . . . [I] do three hundred sit-ups a day.' – Francis Rossi

Two school friends, Alan Lancaster, born in Peckham, London, on 7 February 1949, and Alan Key formed their first group at the Beckenham Comprehensive School in Kent. Initially playing jazz, they switched to contemporary material, recruiting new members Francis Rossi, born in Forest Hill, London, on 29 April 1949, and Jess Jaworski. A further membership change led to Key departing and John Coghlan, born in Dulwich, London, on 19 September 1946, replacing him. It was this line-up which formed the nucleus of the future Status Quo, but in 1962 they were known as The Spectres, and worked the local club circuit.

With amateur managerial guidance from a local gas fitter (yes, tis true), The Spectres moved up-market to perform in a Brompton Road nightspot, before securing a four-month summer season contract at a Butlin's holiday camp. At this juncture Jaworski left, to be replaced by Roy Lynes, while the group befriended future Status Quo member Rick Parfitt, born Richard Harrison in Woking, Surrey, on 12 October 1948, who was also performing at the Butlin's camp.

During 1967, following an introduction to a Pye Records A. & R. executive, The Spectres recorded a trio of singles, namely, 'I (Who Have Nothing)', 'Hurdy Gurdy Man' and 'We Ain't Got Nothin' Yet'. All titles bombed. With a name change to Traffic Jam and later Status Quo, the group signed a recording contract proper with Pye Records during the same year. Status Quo's debut release, the first to feature Parfitt, titled 'Pictures of Matchstick Men', was issued in February 1968 to soar to No. 7 in the British chart; and reach No. 12 in America. With the release of their second single, 'Black Veils of Melancholy', that April, the group embarked upon their first full-length tour of Britain, with Gene Pitney, among others. Before 1968 ended, Status Quo had also issued their first album, titled *Picturesque Matchstickable Messages;* visited America on a promotional trip and released their next single, the Marty

Wilde composition 'Ice in the Sun'; a Top Ten British hit which reached the Top Seventy in America.

In 1969 Status Quo toured America and Britain, once more with Gene Pitney. The group's only hit single of the year was 'Are You Growing Tired of my Love', which struggled into the British Top Fifty, while their second album, *Spare Parts,* bombed. It was obvious a rethink was needed; perhaps an image change and a new musical direction. This was just about apparent in their 1970 single titled 'Down the Dustpipe' which re-established the group, now minus Roy Lynes, in the Top Twenty. That December, a further single, 'In my Chair', likewise hit the Top Twenty, although 'Tune to the Music' represented the group's last charting title until 1973.

After the release of their album *Dog of Two Heads,* Pye Records dropped the ailing group. Undeterred, although privately worried for their future, the group switched to Vertigo Records, an offshoot of Phonogram Records where, in 1973, the album *Piledriver* soared into the British Top Five.

The new Status Quo had arrived. Discarded were the matching stage suits, short hair and mid-paced music; instead, they had long hair, and wore Levi jeans and T-shirts, and were playing British heavy metal. Status Quo never looked back!

Three singles sustained the group during 1973, namely 'Paper Plane' and 'Caroline', issued by Vertigo Records and both Top Ten hits, and 'Mean Girl', a left-over track from Pye Records which became a Top Twenty hit. To close the year on a spectacular footing, their album *Hello,* produced by the group, shot to the top of the British chart.

During 1974, the solitary single 'Break the Rules' and album *Quo* became Top Ten hits in their respective charts, paving the way for the British rocking chart-topper 'Down Down' during January 1975. The title was the group's only No. 1 single. Two months later, their album *On the Level* topped the British chart for two weeks.

Their moderate success in America needed supporting, so Status Quo toured the country for a staggering eight weeks. In their absence, a live EP featuring tracks 'Roll Over Lay Down', 'Junior's Wailing' and 'Gerdundula' was released in Britain to reach the Top Ten during June 1975. The next year, a pair of singles – 'Rain' and 'Mystery Song' – soared into the Top Ten while the album *Blue for You* shot to No. 1.

Three members of Status Quo were arrested following an altercation at Vienna Airport. Lancaster was charged with attacking an airport official, while Parfitt and Rossi were arrested for resisting arrest. All were released on bail, but later pleaded guilty and were fined £1,000 each. The growing notoriety of Status Quo, rock group, established them alongside other hardened bands like The Rolling Stones, whose private antics hit the headlines more frequently than their professional activities. With the rock 'n' roll came its trappings: drugs and women, though why the three should always go hand in hand remains something of a mystery. Nonetheless, Status Quo lived up to the fans' expectations. Rossi told Ruth Brotherhood, 'After a show, I'd be at a club and there'd be girls fighting to get to the band. I'd think, "Great, I've pulled." Then I'd get to my hotel room and think, "Why did I do this? I could have lain down and relaxed." I had no great feelings for the women. I only did it to prove I could.' And later on, 'There were a lot of nights of sitting alone just waiting to come down off cocaine, taking downers to get to sleep, and putting Vitamin E up my nose to try to heal the bleeding so I could do more cocaine the next day.'

To start 1977, 'Wild Side of Life' peaked in the British Top Ten, while to close the year, 'Rockin' All over the World' shot into the Top Three. The latter title went on to become the public's evergreen favourite, a concert highlight. The album of the same name became a Top Five British hit. Most of the following year was spent touring Australia to avoid the British tax system. In their absence, two singles kept the group in the charts, namely, 'Again and Again' and 'Accident Prone', while the album *If You Can't Stand the Heat,* recorded in Holland, soared into the British Top Three.

In 1979, Status Quo maintained their high profile of Britain's top rock group, although the media attacked them for musical repetitiousness, claiming they were restricted to the same, safe chords. There was an element of truth in this, but why change a winning formula? The single and album titled *Whatever You Want* typified the formula; both were Top Five hits in their respective charts.

A pair of albums, *12 Gold Bars* and *Just Supposin',* were issued during 1980; again Top Five titles. And the single 'What You're Proposing' shot to No. 2 in the British chart.

During the eighties, at the peak of their career, Status Quo were rock 'n' roll rebels. Their hair grew longer; their attitude wilder. It was during this decade that Rossi divorced his first wife, Jean whom he married as a teenager and with whom he had three children. A later relationship produced his fourth, a daughter.

Three singles were issued in 1981: 'Lies', 'Something 'bout You Baby I Like' and 'Rock 'n' Roll'; all were Top Twenty hits. Accompanying these titles, two albums were issued, namely, *Never Too Late* and *Fresh Quota.* These releases were backed by a lengthy British tour.

The group membership underwent an upheaval during 1982, when John Coghlan left to be replaced by ex-Honeybus member, Pete Kircher, born in Folkestone, Kent, on 21 January 1948. Coghlan pursued his interests in his new group called Diesel.

Status Quo's first hit of 1982, titled 'Dear John', soared into the Top Ten, whereupon the group undertook a further British tour. They were affectionately known by their fans as 'Quo', their album simply titled *1982* topped the British chart, their fourth to do so, while they performed at a charity concert for The Prince's Trust at the NEC Birmingham. Both the Prince and Princess of Wales were in attendance; the concert was taped for release as a triple-record package alongside previously released material and titled *From the Makers of.* The track 'Caroline' was lifted for single release, and reached the British Top Twenty.

Through 1984 and 1985, after Lancaster moved to Australia and became a part-time touring group member, Quo treked Britain once more, and participated in Bob Geldof's Band Aid project for the starving Ethiopian nation, and the later Live Aid gala spectacular. Their act was one of the gala's recognised highlights, particularly their 1977 hit single 'Rockin' All over the World'.

Behind scenes, the group suffered upheaval when Lancaster took out an injunction to prevent the remaining group members recording as Status Quo without him. The presiding judge ruled in favour of Parfitt and Rossi, whereupon Kircher, the last to join the line-up, departed. However, the membership settled down during 1986 to include Parfitt, Rossi, Jeff Rich and John Edwards to release the British Top Ten single 'Rollin' Home' in May. The changed line-up had further success as participants in the Knebworth Festival before an estimated audience of 210,000. The group shot to No. 2 with the stomping single 'In the Army Now' in November, the follow-up single to the Top Twenty entrant 'Red Sky'. Before the eighties closed and on the personal front, Rossi re-met his future wife, Eileen, whom he first befriended during 1973.

In 1987, Quo headlined the Reading Festival, and released 'Burning Bridges (On and Off and On Again)', a Top Five hit, which earned them the distinction of being Britain's most successful singles group with thirty-nine consecutive charters. Yes, they beat The Rolling Stones, with thirty-four titles, into second place.

In 1990, Quo climbed to No. 2 with the unlikely-titled single 'Anniversary Waltz Part I', followed by the compilation *Rockin' All over the Years*, likewise a No. 2 seller. The next year, 1991, representing the group's twenty-fifth anniversary, was one of honours. Firstly, Quo received an award for their Outstanding Contribution to the British Music Industry at the BRITS award ceremony; secondly, they were included in the *Guinness Book of Records* after playing at four venues in one day – Sheffield, Glasgow, Birmingham and London – as part of their 'Rockin' All over the UK' tour.

During the next two years, Quo spent much time touring, notably on their 'Rock till You Drop' trek. On the recording front, they switched companies from Vertigo to Polydor Records, where their first hit, 'Roadhouse Medley (Anniversary Waltz Part 25)' reached the Top Thirty. In 1993, Parfitt and Rossi published the group's autobiography.

In May 1994, a reworking of 'Burning Bridges (On and Off and On Again)', titled 'Come On You Reds', was recorded by the Manchester United Football Club, and topped the British chart, while the group itself struggled into the Top Thirty and Forty with 'I Didn't Mean It', 'Sherri Don't Fail Me Now' and 'Restless'.

The nineties saw founder members Rossi and Parfitt settled into family life, respectable and quiet living; their wild, hell-raising image confined to the stage. Rossi, now a drug-free person and occasional drinker, is the father of seven children at the time of writing, three by his wife Eileen. Rossi told journalist Lester Middlehurst, 'I wasn't really enjoying my life until Eileen came to live with me. I genuinely believed I would be dead by the time I was forty-five because of my lifestyle, and it didn't bother me much because I wasn't very happy.' He further told Ruth Brotherhood, 'Before I met Eileen I was just after women for sex. But with Eileen sex isn't the most important thing.'

Parfitt broke up his second marriage, to Patti, with whom he had one son, to return to his first wife and childhood girlfriend, Marietta, who had divorced him for adultery, following twelve years of marriage. Parfitt told journalist Lina Das, 'I loved Marietta when we married, but the drink and drugs obliterated all that. I don't blame her for divorcing me and to be honest, it didn't bother me at all at the time.' Like Rossi, Parfitt's hell-raising days are behind him, particularly the fast lane which (literally) practically killed him. In an attempt to obliterate his failed second marriage, he had spent the night drinking and snorting cocaine with a friend, before swallowing sleeping tablets, and driving back to his home. Parfitt: 'I can't remember a thing after that. My first recollection is of being questioned in the police station.' He was told he had driven his Porsche at 100 mph down a motorway, spun off the central reservation and across the road before dropping down a bank into a field. He should have been killed. Parfitt said, 'I figure that's my last warning.' He was banned from driving for eighteen months, while his divorce from Patti reputedly cost him £500,000 to settle.

The year 1996 saw Status Quo clash with BBC Radio 1. Despite the group celebrating their thirtieth anniversary, the radio station refused to air their fiftieth single, a revamped version of 'Fun Fun Fun' with the single's originators The Beach Boys, claiming the group was 'somewhat conservative and old hat'. Rossi and Parfitt instigated legal action against the station contending it banned singles by 'unfashionable' artists, despite a remit to play Top Forty records. In response, Radio 1, which has taken over a decade to die slowly, denied the ban, insisting each record was judged on its merits. Status Quo alleged they would suffer commercially, and intended to prove Radio 1 had acted unlawfully. Needless to say, Quo lost the case, with a BBC Radio 1 representative's words ringing in their ears: 'A record will not be played purely because it is a commercial success. The station has lost audiences because of this policy but they are targeting younger listeners with more radical music.' Quo were not the only act to fall foul of Radio 1; Edwin Starr likewise was told he was too old to be featured on the station's airplay listing. And it was this same radio station that was dumped in 1997 by DJ Chris Evans, who commands a multi-million listening audience.

Irrespective of BBC Radio 1, Status Quo's pulling power on the concert circuit and television has never been stronger. Indeed, the group's series of Christmas dates are now a part of British life, while their recorded success continues.

The two founder members, Francis Rossi and Rick Parfitt, may have mellowed with age, but the rock remains as vitally loud and brash as ever. Thank God for that!

(Quotes: *Daily Mail,* interview by Lina Das, 1996; *Daily Mail Weekend* magazine, interview by Lester Middlehurst, 1996; *Woman's Own,* interview by Ruth Brotherhood, 1996)

February 1975

THE TYMES

Ms Grace

This black American group had to discard their easy-flowing melodies and tight harmonies, inspired by the Mills Brothers, to gain seventies chart success. Albeit reluctantly, they switched from the smooth to the dance groove, and when the beat died, they, like so many, became redundant.

Norman Burnett and George Hilliard first met at a summer camp in Philadelphia, and in 1956 recruited Donald Banks and Albert Berry to form The Latineers. They perfected a tight harmonising vocal act and won audience support at local talent shows and nightclub dates. In 1960 George Williams joined them to become lead singer, whereupon the group became The Tymes.

During April 1963 the group entered a talent show sponsored by the radio station WDAS. A representative from Cameo Parkway Records heard them, was impressed and signed them to the Parkway label. George Williams felt his composition titled 'The Stroll' would be an ideal choice as a debut single. He worked on the track with arranger Roy Straigis and producer Billy Jackson until 'So Much in Love' was born. The Tymes recorded it and when it was released in Britain in July 1963, the public's enthusiasm pushed it into the Top Thirty. A month later, it sold one million copies to top the American chart. The title was a wonderful sound for summer listening, bringing alive scenes of glorious sun-kissed beaches and the sweet cacophony of birds singing. An album titled after the single was swiftly issued and spawned 'Wonderful Wonderful', an equally smooth and sophisticated three minutes.

In 1964 The Tymes' British success plummeted to zero, while in their home country they survived by issuing four singles – 'Somewhere', from the musical *West Side Story*, a Top Twenty hit; and a trio of minor hits, namely, 'To Each his Own', 'The Magic of our Summer Love' and 'Here She Comes'. The beauty of the group's vocals was then forced into the background to make way for the beat boom, instigated by British groups. So, by early 1965 not only had the quintet's single 'The Twelfth of Never' bombed, but their career with Cameo Parkway had ended. Unswayed, The Tymes opened their own label, Winchester Records, but within a year that too had folded.

Moving on to MGM Records in 1966, The Tymes were reunited with producer Billy Jackson, whereupon future success was happily predicted. In reality, though, the prediction was wrong; the group bombed. It became obvious a drastic rethink was needed if they were to continue. The first to change was their image. Shrugging off their comfortable middle-of-the-road attitude and material, they spruced up, seventies-style, with an injection of musical ideas to attract a younger audience.

Again with Billy Jackson on board, The Tymes signed a recording contract with CBS Records, where their version of Barbra Streisand's 'People' re-established them as Top Forty American sellers in 1968. In

Britain, the hard-paced single fared much better. When issued by Direction Records, it climbed into the Top Twenty; it was perfect for the dance boom then gripping the music scene. Remarkably, despite this success, CBS Records dropped The Tymes and Billy Jackson, whereupon they floundered, with no means of releasing a follow-up to maintain a chart profile. Instead, the group concentrated on performing, mostly on the cabaret circuit.

By the early seventies, frustrated with major record companies' lack of interest, and after Charles Nixon had replaced George Hilliard in the group line-up, Billy Jackson financed his own recording sessions for The Tymes at the Sigma Sound Studios in Philadelphia, with a view to leasing the finished product to a record company. With a tape of listenable tracks, Jackson first played them to producer/composers Kenny Gamble and Leon Huff, who passed on them but who recommended RCA Records. That company signed The Tymes to a recording contract where one of the provisos was financing the completion of the project Jackson had started.

The group's debut RCA single, 'You Little Trustmaker', in October !974, heralded the start of a new, lucrative career, by peaking at No. 18 in the British chart and No. 12 in America. The album *Trustmaker* quickly followed but inexplicably bombed. Yet the next lifted track, 'Miss Grace', penned by John and Johanna Hall and renamed 'Ms Grace', shot to the top of the British chart during February 1975. It was The Tymes' best-selling single ever, yet mysteriously it bombed in America! Oh, the peculiarities of musical taste.

But the saga didn't end there. As no one within The Tymes' camp was prepared for such a runaway success, a suitable follow-up single was not recorded. A wasted golden opportunity indeed, with the predictable consequence of the group falling into the category of 'one-hit wonders' almost overnight.

It took two years for The Tymes to return to the British chart with a single titled 'God's Gonna Punish You' (certainly He should have punished someone for short-sightedness in 1975!). Although the title was an immensely popular nightclub single, it crawled into the British Top Fifty mainstream chart, signifying the group's final hit on both sides of the Atlantic.

Although The Tymes disappeared from pop music, they continued to enjoy the support of the soul sector, who appreciated their non-commercial albums that included *Digging their Roots* in 1977.

Like most groups of their ilk, The Tymes continue to milk the nostalgia concert circuit.

STEVE HARLEY AND COCKNEY REBEL

Make Me Smile (Come Up and See Me)

'I set out to be a winner, I [didn't] want to lose . . . nice guys don't make it.' – Steve Harley

Born Steven Nice on 27 February 1951 in London, Harley worked as a journalist for the *Colchester Gazette,* although his ambitions were music-orientated. In fact, he often told his fellow hacks that he was destined for musical stardom.

In time, Harley pursued his ambitions to sing in countless folk clubs on the London circuit before securing a residency at the Beckenham Arts Lab in Kent, owned by David Bowie's wife, Angie. It was at this juncture that Steve, now using the surname Harley, met violinist Jean Paul Crocker and drummer Stuart Elliott. Together they formed the nucleus of Cockney Rebel. After experimenting with different types of music, they recruited bassist Paul Jeffries and keyboardist Milton Reame-James. Rehearsing and performing on a regular basis won them a loyal following and media interest. So much so that following their debut performance at London's Speakeasy Club during mid-1973, they were offered a recording contract with EMI Records. In August of that year Cockney Rebel issued their debut single, composed by Harley, titled 'Sebastian'. It bombed in Britain, but grew legs in Europe to become a widespread hit. The title was swiped from the group's first album, *The Human Menagerie,* issued in November 1973 and a reasonable seller.

Early in 1974, success was waiting in the wings with 'Judy Teen', another Harley composition, which shot into the British Top Five in May 1974. To cash in on this unexpected high placing, the group issued their second album, *Psychomodo,* and embarked upon a lengthy British tour to promote it. Audiences saw first hand Harley's love of the theatre, from costume to make-up, permeate through the group's stage act. Despite public enthusiasm, the tour ended in disaster with internal group disagreements caused, many believed, by Harley's aggressive attitude towards the music media and his own self-importance. With no compromise in sight, the group disbanded.

When 'Mr Soft', Cockney Rebel's third single, soared to No. 8 in the British chart during August 1974 there was no one except Harley to promote it. For television promotion, he recruited stand-in Cockney Rebels Stuart Elliott (an original group member), B.A. Robertson and Francis Monkman. When Harley and Cockney Rebel appeared at the Reading Festival, guitarist Jim Cregan from the group Family, keyboardist Duncan MacKay, and bassist George Ford became the new, permanent line-up. However, when they toured Britain, the reaction was mixed; many fans believed Cockney Rebel's original membership to be the better of the two. This prompted Harley to say, 'This band is not stage two . . . Cockney Rebel was a thing in itself, but it was phase one of a masterplan. It succeeded and now I've got a new masterplan.'

Indeed he had. Renaming the group Steve Harley and Cockney Rebel, their first single of 1975, 'Make Me Smile (Come Up and See Me)' shot to the top of the British chart in March, where it stayed for two weeks. EMI Records' executives were so convinced the title was a million-seller they instructed the company's pressing plant to work non-stop to ensure sufficient copies were available for shop re-orders. Harley told journalist Andy Davis in 1992, 'If you listen to "Make Me Smile", there's a dichotomy between the music and the words. The words are actually scathingly cynical. They're bitter. It's an attack on people whom I owed one to at that time. It was very personal. If you actually see the words without the music, you'd see what I meant.'

The single also became a minor American hit; the group's only one. Yet by 1992 it had been rerecorded twenty-four times. 'Make Me Smile (Come Up and See Me)' was lifted from the blinding album *The Best Years of our Lives*, written by Harley, who co-produced it with Alan Parsons. This capitalised on the single's premier status in April 1975 to reach No. 4 in Britain. With this success came, many believed, a downside, namely, Steve Harley's attitude to the media. His interviews were outspoken; often controversial; indeed he always provided good copy! Harley: 'I'd been trained as a reporter. Very well trained. I'd worked on weekly papers under two news editors who were very hot, really top-line stuff. So when I found myself suddenly being interviewed by these sort of guys, I knew how to make a headline. Also, I found it was partly their fault because I got loads of front pages out of it . . .'

'Mr Raffles (Man It Was Mean)', the chart-topper's follow-up, was likewise swiped from *The Best Years of our Lives*. It failed to repeat the chart success, stalling at No. 13 in June 1975. The next single, 'Black and White', bombed, likewise 'White White Dove' lifted from *Timeless Flight*, the Top Twenty hit album, released early in 1976. A change of direction was needed.

Harley returned to the studios to record his fifth album, *Love's a Prima Donna,* from which a cover version of George Harrison's 'Here Comes the Sun' was lifted as the first single. The title returned Steve Harley (now credited as a soloist on the record sleeve) to the British Top Ten during July 1976. The album's title track, 'Love's a Prima Donna', quickly followed, but struggled into the Top Fifty during November. By the end of 1976, Cockney Rebel was dissolved; Harley moved to America two years later.

During 1977 and 1978, *Face to Face – A Live Recording,* featuring members of Cockney Rebel's second membership became a Top Forty album in Britain, proving public interest and support remained. Meantime, 'Hobo with a Grin', Harley's solo effort recorded Stateside, bombed miserably. An album titled *The Candidate* followed, another failure, yet it did spawn Harley's only 1979 British hit and last EMI Records' single. Titled 'Freedom's Prisoner', it reached the Top Sixty in October, his last entrant for four years. During this hiatus Harley returned to Britain to live and signed a short-term recording contract with Chrysalis Records in 1981. The single 'I Can't Even Touch You', featuring Midge Ure, bombed. Two years later, he joined Stiletto Records where 'Ballerina (Prima Donna)' re-established him in the British chart, albeit the Top Sixty.

A further period of inactivity followed until the artist took the unlikely step of duetting with Sarah Brightman on 'The Phantom of the Opera', the title of Andrew Lloyd Webber's hit musical. Released by Polydor Records, the single crashed into the British Top Ten to peak at No. 7 in January 1986; yet Harley, inexplicably, lost the leading role in the Webber musical to Michael Crawford. Back on the recording front, Mickie Most, owner of RAK Records, rescued Harley with a recording deal. While signed, he recorded the album *El Grande Señor* and a handful of singles including 'Heartbeat Like Thunder'. Despite Most's recording expertise, Harley remained a hitless artist.

Nonetheless, the singer moved on when, in 1988, he recorded a further duet titled 'Whatever You Believe' with Jon Anderson. Released by Epic Records in November, it was a poor seller. Likewise 'When I'm with You', issued by Vital Vinyl Records. However, Harley's dismal selling power did not dissuade him from embarking upon an exhaustive British tour, titled 'All Is Forgiven', which reunited him with Stuart Elliott, among others. During December 1988 Cockney Rebel hit the tabloid headlines once more. Not due to Harley's tongue, but sadly when Paul Jeffreys, an original group member, was one of many killed in the tragic Lockerbie plane disaster.

Also in 1988, the single 'Mr Soft' was used in a TV advert, prompting EMI Records to capitalise on the exposure by re-releasing the single and a compilation of the group's best-loved material. Steve Harley, meantime, continued to tour through to the nineties. When 'Make Me Smile (Come Up and See Me)' was reissued to reach the British Top Fifty in 1992, his touring schedules increased. Harley: 'I'm happy knowing in my heart of hearts that I've learned how to play a live performance and that I get respect for it . . .'

His major touring commitments, however, were in Europe, where his high profile had been maintained since his seventies' peak. Of his British presence he said, 'Since I started touring in March 1989, I've done three hundred shows to over one and a quarter million people! 1989 was a comeback in a way, but the little tours I've done have been very low-key because I had no product to promote.'

During 1996, with the promise of a new album, Steve Harley and Cockney Rebel took to the British concert circuit once more. When radio stations advertised forthcoming dates what record was played? 'You've done it all, you've broken every code . . .' No prizes!

(Quotes: *Record Collector*, interview by Andy Davis, 1992)

April 1975

BAY CITY ROLLERS

Bye Bye Baby

When Osmond-mania began subsiding, parents sighed in relief, while the music industry pined for another young group to whip up the fan hysteria again that would, in turn, generate money. Almost on cue, along came five teenage lads who caused alarm among the adults, but who restored confidence into the music business. The teeny-bop quintet also introduced a fashion craze with the lavish use of tartan in their stage clothes. The fresh young image flourished until they broke the rules.

Formed at Tynecastle School in Edinburgh by the Longmuir brothers, the group known as The Saxons combined their musical training with their studies. Derek Longmuir, born in Edinburgh on 19 March 1955, and his brother Alan, also born in Edinburgh, on 20 June 1953, spearheaded the first line-up of the future Bay City Rollers. The brothers, with four school friends, came to the attention of Tom Paton, bandleader at the Edinburgh Palais, who also reputedly chose the name The Bay City Rollers. However, Eric Faulkner, born in Edinburgh on 21 October 1955, who joined the group in 1971 believed Derek Longmuir was responsible. He told author Barry Scott, 'The famous story is that Derek stuck a pin in a map of America and it landed on Bay City [Michigan]. He sticks with that one . . . it was a time [in Britain] when they wanted American-sounding names of bands.'

Tom Paton left his bandleading residency to manage the group on a full-time basis, and during 1969, secured them a year's booking at the Top Storey Club in their home city, and two years' worth of local gigging. In 1970, while performing at the Caves Club, they were seen by Bell Records' president Dick Leahy. Apparently, he had missed his American flight and was killing time, which was fortunate for the youngsters because midway through 1971 they were signed to a recording contract with Bell Records to work with Tony Calder.

'Keep On Dancing' was The Bay City Rollers' debut single in June 1971. Produced by Jonathan King, it soared into the British Top Ten. 'We Can Make Music', issued in March 1972, bombed, throwing the group into a dilemma, prompting a personnel change. Eric Faulkner joined the line-up, whereupon his first single with the group was another bomber titled 'Mañana', although it was a big European hit and chart-topper in Israel, of all places. The title also won Radio Luxembourg's Grand Prix Song Contest. A further membership change occurred early in 1973 when Leslie McKeown, born in Edinburgh on 12 November 1955, and Stuart Wood, also born in Edinburgh, on 25 February 1957, replaced the unit's original members Nobby Clarke and John Devine. Faulkner also introduced the group to a new, cheap wardrobe, one he'd swiped from the successful British group Slade. 'They had the striped socks . . . I kind of copied them, as you do when you're young. Then we started adding the tartan plaid and it developed from there. It was all we could afford at the time.'

The clothes' change was an omen as their next single 'Remember (Sha La La)' re-established them as a Top Ten act, during February 1974. Two further singles penned by Phil Coulter and Bill Martin, titled 'Shang-A-Lang' and 'Summerlove Sensation', both soared into the British Top Three. It was these tracks that heralded the initial signs of Rollermania, whether parents liked it or not. By the time their debut album *Rollin'* charted at No.1 in October 1974, scenes of hysterical, screaming fans were commonplace. Their lengthy end-of-year tour of Britain was marked by the tabloids lavishly chronicling Bay City Roller mayhem at the extreme, while predicting that tartan accessories like trousers and scarves, would be the new fashion fad. Indeed, Bay City Roller clones paraded their wares with pride! Faulkner: 'What was hard was the fans screaming all the time. It was really hard to hear yourself playing on stage.' He felt too much media attention was given to these hysterical scenes, without any consideration given to the group's music. Like other groups who attracted this type of worship, the Rollers could do nothing but accept it as part of their career. Eventually they were banned from touring Britain following incidents like BBC Radio 1's Fun Day which attracted in excess of 45,000 people. It was held at Mallory Park, Leicestershire, in 1975, and four fans were hospitalised, nearly forty required First Aid treatment, and another forty were rescued from a lake. They had been swimming across it to meet the group.

For their second album, The Bay City Rollers switched producers to Phil Wainman, who had worked with Sweet. Titled *Once upon a Star,* the album spawned 'Bye Bye Baby', the group's first British chart-topper, in April 1975. Originally penned and recorded by Frankie Valli and The Four Seasons in 1965, it became a Top Twenty American hit for them. The Bay City Rollers remained at the top of the British chart with their interpretation for a staggering six weeks, while the mother album swept into its chart at No. 1.

The follow-up single, 'Give a Little Love', written by Johnny Goodison and Phil Wainman, likewise shot to No. 1 in July 1975. Yep, Rollermania had well and truly established itself as sales of vinyl and tartan material rose alarmingly!

By a remarkable stroke of luck, the youngsters' American debut was via ABC TV's new programme *Saturday Night Variety Show,* hosted by Howard Cosell. The track they chose to perform was the aptly titled 'Saturday Night' which had bombed when released in Britain in January 1973. The Americans, on the other hand, purchased two million copies to push the title to No. 1 during the first week of 1976. Faulkner: 'It was a big baseball chant. I understood it used to get played in the ball games . . . I think that the natural energy of the band came through there. It was raw and it was naive . . .' Like most of the group's singles, he said, 'Saturday Night' was recorded in five hours without a great deal of thought. 'We used to just walk into the studio and throw them down.'

Meanwhile, in Britain the next single, 'Money Honey', penned by the group's Eric Faulkner and Stuart Wood, reached the Top Three in November 1975, likewise their third album, *Wouldn't You Like It.* 'Money Honey' then followed the American chart-topper but stalled in the Top Twenty, while their first British hit of 1976, 'Love Me Like I

Love You' peaked at No. 4 in April. Personal turmoil hit The Bay City Rollers when Faulkner took a near fatal overdose at Tom Paton's home. Subsequent reports indicated that he had taken the dose while suffering from exhaustion, although a handful of journalists suggested a more sinister motive.

The year of 1976 saw The Bay City Rollers conquering America with scenes comparable to Beatlemania during the sixties. As the group were now prevented from touring Britain due to uncontrollable fan hysteria, they had to move elsewhere. Touring generated extra finance and as the group could not be sustained on record sales income alone, the Rollers had little choice but to leave their home country. Their Stateside following donned the tartan clothes with pride. Faulkner: 'It was like a gang. The fans dressed up the same as us. It was more than just a show . . . it was just good fun.'

In 1976 the group's membership changed. One of the founder members, Alan Longmuir, retired to handle the group's business affairs which by now included running their own publishing company. Ian Mitchell, born in Scotland on 22 August 1958, replaced him, and within a year, Pat McGlynn, born in Edinburgh on 31 March 1958, took his place.

As the album *Dedication* shot to No. 4 in Britain and into the American Top Thirty, the group issued a cover version of Dusty Springfield's 'I Only Want to Be with You' in September 1976. It also soared to No. 4 in Britain and into the American Top Twenty. It was the group's last single of the year.

By 1977, the decline of The Bay City Rollers became evident. The first single of the year, 'It's a Game', stalled in the British Top Twenty, while the second, 'You Made Me Believe in Magic', faltered in the Top Forty. The single was to be their final hit. In America, though, the track stormed into the Top Ten. The next, a stylish ballad titled 'The Way I Feel Tonight' bombed in Britain, yet managed to peak in the American Top Thirty, due to its appeal among the older record-buying public.

Strangers in the Wild, issued during 1978, was hailed by critics as The Bay City Rollers' best album to date, consisting of their own original material. The singles lifted were, the group claimed, insufficiently promoted. Faulkner: 'There were serious business problems between our manager and a lot of the record and publishing deals. That really stopped the product from coming out because all these deals went into dispute.' It was a dire situation; seemingly The Bay City Rollers were now at the point of no return. Other events would indeed nail down their coffin.

Tom Paton, their original manager, was sentenced to three years in prison, guilty of gross indecency with teenage boys. Although The Bay City Rollers were not involved in this matter, the media attempted to forge a connection, and destroy any public standing they had. The ploy failed. Nonetheless, the group was fighting with its own problems. Les McKeown was charged with reckless driving after fatally injuring an elderly widow, while Ian Mitchell played a starring role in a pornographic movie. The group's precious image was smashed to pieces.

It took several years for The Bay City Rollers to unravel all their problems, legal and otherwise, but they survived. During the hiatus, they continued to work behind scenes until 1983, when the five remaining members recorded the album *Live in Japan*, with Billy Lyall, Pat McGlynn and Ian Mitchell. Apart from this release, The Bay City Rollers relied heavily on their back catalogue to attract audiences rather than attempting to realise new ideas. Faulkner: 'There really wasn't much interest in getting new stuff done. Woody and I couldn't hack the attitude.'

Touring became more regular midway through the eighties; the public's memory was short and their music still created a demand. The line-up now comprised Stuart Wood, Alan Longmuir, Eric Faulkner and a female vocalist Kass; together they toured Japan, Australia and Europe.

In 1993 the group returned to America for a lengthy tour, their first visit since the mid-seventies. The theatres may have been smaller, but the audience reactions were extremely positive. The Bay City Rollers remain a working band today, drawing support on the nostalgia circuit. Whether they have resurrected their tartan scarves and other rigmarole for the nineties stage, I can't say.

(Quotes: *We Had Joy We Had Fun* by Barry Scott)

MUD

Oh Boy

Following the young quartet's British chart-topper 'Tiger Feet' in February 1974, a similar-sounding single 'The Cat Crept in' soared to No. 2. Before 1974 was out, 'Rocket' reached the Top Ten, and with Les Gray vocally emulating his musical hero, Elvis Presley, 'Lonely This Christmas' dominated the British singles chart during the festive season, bringing to an end a spectacular year for the group, RAK Records and their composing/producing duo Nicky Chinn and Mike Chapman.

At this juncture, Mud decided to switch labels and composers to sign a new recording contract with Private Stock Records. However, before any new material could be issued, RAK Records released the first of several canned tracks. Titled 'The Secrets that You Keep', it soared into the British Top Three during March 1975. But it was to be the next that re-established the group as chart-toppers.

In December 1957 Buddy Holly's backing group The Crickets recorded and released 'Oh Boy', which shot to No. 3 in the British chart. In 1975 RAK Records released Mud's version of the West, Petty and Tilghman composition, produced by Chinn and Chapman, to give them their third No. 1 in two years. 'Oh Boy' topped the chart for two weeks, and represented the first Chinnichap production on a third-party composition.

RAK Records went on to issue a further pair of singles, namely, 'Moonshine Sally' and 'One Night', Top Ten and Top Forty hits respectively, plus the album *Mud Rock Volume 2*, indicating that most of their canned material had been issued.

It was now time for Private Stock Records to take over. In October 1975 Mud's debut single for the new company was 'L-L-Lucy', followed by 'Show Me You're a Woman', both British Top Ten entrants. The first Private Stock album, *Use your Imagination*, was also a big seller, reaching the Top Forty. A change of record company appeared not to have affected their career, although they would not enjoy further chart-toppers.

Midway through 1976, Mud released 'Shake It Down', a No. 12 hit in Britain, and followed it with their version of Bill Withers's 1972 British Top Twenty hit 'Lean on Me'; a Top Ten title for them.

Then quite inexplicably Mud's rising star tarnished as their selling power dropped. To help alleviate falling sales, they moved to RCA Records and released the poor-selling album *It's Better Than Working,* while lead vocalist Les Gray secured a solo recording contract with Warner Brothers. He enjoyed one minor hit during 1977 with 'A Groovy Kind of Love', previously a British hit for The Mindbenders in 1966.

The recording situation was precarious; nonetheless RCA Records hosted a media party to celebrate Mud's tenth anniversary in the music business and to launch their new album, *Mudpack.* The investment was futile, although other albums followed like *Rock On* in 1979 and *Mud* during 1983.

By the early eighties, the group's recording career was over, so they turned to the lucrative cabaret circuit where audiences flocked to hear and participate in their seventies favourites. Well, it was fun!

Also see: 'Tiger Feet', February 1974

Also No. 1 in May 1975: 'Stand by your Man' by Tammy Wynette

June 1975

10CC

I'm Not in Love

Their material was a combination of wit, and anti-establishment satire, using a subtle play on words. As musicians they were second to none, yet most people remember 10cc for the bitter-sweet 'I'm Not in Love'. That track was just one example of their exemplary talent.

Graham Gouldman, born in Manchester on 10 May 1946, played his way through a variety of groups before joining forces with Whirlwind. In time, he crossed paths with The Sabres, whose membership included Kevin Godley, born in Manchester on 7 October 1945, and Lol Creme, born Lawrence Creme, also in Manchester, on 19 September 1947, who both attended art college.

In 1964, Gouldman disbanded Whirlwind who had, incidentally, recorded the Buddy Holly title 'Look at Me' as a single, with Lol Creme's composition 'Baby Not Like Me' on the flipside, for EMI Records' HMV label. He later formed another group called The

Mockingbirds, comprising two Whirlwind members and ex-Sabres' drummer Kevin Godley.

Meanwhile, Eric Stewart, another Mancunian, born on 20 January 1945, an ex-member of Jerry Lee and The Staggerlees, joined Wayne Fontana and The Mindbenders in 1964. The group went on to enjoy British Top Twenty hits with 'Um Um Um Um Um Um' in 1964, and a pair in 1965 titled 'Game of Love' and 'Just a Little Bit Too Late'.

The Mockingbirds signed a recording contract with EMI Records' Columbia label, whose A. & R. executive rejected Graham Gouldman's composition titled 'For your Love', earmarked as the group's debut single. However, the track wasn't entirely lost because The Yardbirds took their version to No. 3 in the British chart during March 1965. In its place, 'That's the Way It's Gonna Stay' was issued to mark the start of a recording career that would span several recording labels during the next two years.

The Yardbirds also recorded further Gouldman compositions (including 'Evil Hearted You), as did other acts like Herman's Hermits and The Hollies. Godley and Creme went on to record a handful of demo tracks for Gouldman who, in turn, signed them to Marmalade Records, owned by Giorgio Gomelsky. Several tracks were recorded, most notably a single by Frabjoy and the Runcibie Spoon (named from a line in Edward Lear's poem 'The Owl and the Pussycat'.)

Graham Gouldman joined Robbins Music, the American publishing house, before working as a composer for Kasenatz-Katz, a production outfit based in New York.

Meantime, Eric Stewart and partner, Peter Tattersall, purchased a record studio in Manchester which they named Strawberry. In November 1969, Kasenatz-Katz booked Strawberry, and it was at this juncture that the nucleus of 10cc was born. Stewart and Gouldman hired Lol Creme and Kevin Godley to work on the various musical projects required, including releasing material under different pseudonyms like 'There Ain't No Umbopo' by The Crazy Elephants.

In 1970 when the Kasenatz-Katz projects were completed, the group penned 'Neanderthal Man'. A representative from Philips Records purchased the finished track for £500 and, when released under the name Hotlegs in July 1970, it sold in excess of two million copies, peaking at No. 2 in the British chart. Follow-up sales bombed.

Through 1971, the quartet concentrated on writing and producing for other artists, including re-establishing American singer Neil Sedaka as a charting name. The following year, the group decided to test their own talent as a recording entity by signing to Jonathan King's label,

UK Records. King christened them 10cc, and released their debut single titled 'Donna', penned by Godley and Creme. Much to everyone's surprise the track soared to No. 2 in the British chart during September 1972, while its follow-up, 'Johnny Don't Do It', another reminder of fifties' American pop, bombed.

Another direction was tried. 10cc changed track to record 'Rubber Bullets', a particularly sensitive issue in the seventies because the British Army had introduced these bullets in their continuing bloody battle in Northern Ireland. Radio airplay was subsequently spasmodic, yet that didn't prevent the single soaring to No. 1 in Britain during June 1973. To capitalise on this success, 10cc debuted on stage during August in the Isle of Man before embarking upon a lengthy British tour.

As their next single, 'The Dean and I', peaked in the British Top Ten, 10cc issued their eponymous debut album, and enjoyed their first minor American hit with 'Rubber Bullets'. The group then boosted their popularity by touring America early in 1974, but midway through the trek, Kevin Godley became ill, forcing the remaining dates to be cancelled. The tour was subsequently rescheduled for May.

Following the release of their second album, *Sheet Music,* the group's fourth Top Ten single was issued, 'Wall Street Shuffle'. Its follow-up, 'Silly Love', stalled at No. 24 in September. Early in 1975, 10cc switched record companies from UK Records to the major Phonogram, enticed by a $1 million pay cheque. *The Original Soundtrack* album was the debut release under the new deal, issued via Phonogram's Mercury label. 'Life Is a Minestrone' was the first lifted single to become a Top Ten British hit in April 1975. But the best was yet to come.

When radio DJs began playing *The Original Soundtrack,* one track in particular was a favourite – 'I'm Not in Love'. So much so, that Phonogram had no option but to rush-release the title as 'Life Is a Minestrone' left the chart. 10cc, however, were unsure of its viability as a forty-five; live performances would be nigh impossible because it was a multi-tracked song with lavish vocal over-dubs. Problems could be overcome, said Phonogram, who insisted they bow down to public demand. 'I'm Not in Love' took four weeks to reach the top of the British chart in June 1975, where it stayed for two weeks. The public loved the track, although many believed it to be a sugary, sweet love song, with lyrics that held a double-edged meaning. Despite the downside, 'I'm Not in Love' was classed as one of the finest pop songs of the decade, and went on to win Ivor Novello Awards for the Best Pop Song, the Most-Performed British Work and International Hit of 1975. However, it was also a single 10cc could not follow, so they didn't try.

Early in 1976, 'Art for Arts Sake' was released to reach the British Top Five, followed by the album *How Dare You?*, which also became a Top Five seller. Both discs became minor American hits. As 10cc were partway through an exhausting British tour, they issued the cheeky 'I'm Mandy Fly Me', a Top Ten single and a Top Sixty American hit.

Instead of seeing 10cc through to its natural conclusion, Kevin Godley and Lol Creme decided to leave the group to experiment with new musical ideas using state-of-the-art instruments. Their planned single grew into the triple album *Consequences,* while the remaining members of 10cc (Graham Gouldman and Eric Stewart) recruited drummer Paul Burgess, to continue as a trio. As such they went on to enjoy two Top Ten singles during 1977, namely, 'The Things We Do for Love' and 'Good Morning Judge'. For touring purposes, keyboardist Tony O'Malley and guitarist Rick Fenn joined the line-up. However, by 1978, Duncan MacKay had been recruited as a permanent keyboard player.

'Dreadlock Holiday', written by Stewart and Gouldman in the pop/reggae vein, was the group's final British charting single during September 1978. But what a way to leave; it topped the British chart for one week!

For the rest of the decade 10cc and Godley and Creme beavered away behind the scenes, providing material for other acts, as well as themselves. In 1981, Godley and Creme re-established themselves in the British chart with 'Under your Thumb' via a recording deal with Polydor Records. The follow-up in November, titled 'Wedding Bells', reached the Top Ten.

Diversification was the name of the game, or rather survival. By 1984, the enterprising duo had made their mark as promotional video producers. In fact, they won a handful of MTV Music Video Awards for 'Rockit', while receiving high acclaim for their adventurous videos promoting singles by Duran Duran and Toyah. Godley and Creme next produced television advertisements, where their greatest success was Stateside.

In 1985, though, they returned as recording artists on the Trevor Horn production 'Cry', which reached the British Top Twenty in March, and upon re-entry five months later, the Top Seventy.

Most certainly, Kevin Godley and Lol Creme changed British music with their innovative compositions, and by introducing a new dimension to music videos, transforming those three-plus minutes into a storyboard mini-film.

Both 10cc and the duo are still actively involved in music at the time of writing, whether it be recording, scoring movie themes or promoting artists into top-selling stars.

Also No. 1 in June 1975: 'Whispering Grass' by Windsor Davies and Don Estelle

July 1975

JOHNNY NASH

Tears on my Pillow

He was an easy-listening artist whose smooth sounds were often confined to background listening: soft reggae and a mellow voice. Indeed, Johnny Nash was categorised as a crooner before he wore long trousers!

Born in Houston, Texas, on 19 August 1940, Nash first sang as a choir member at his local Baptist church. From there he entered a talent contest where the winner performed at Harlem's Apollo Theatre. Nash lost to Joe Tex, who went on to become a soul singer of considerable note. Undeterred, the youngster pursued his musical ambitions until he secured a position in the entertainment show *Matinee*.

This led to a guest spot on *Arthur Godfrey's Talent Scouts*, where Nash, then sixteen years old, stayed for several years before securing a recording deal with ABC Paramount Records. Nash's style was immediately categorised as middle-of-the-road, his mature vocalising outweighing his young years. In 1958 he released 'A Very Special Love' which became a Top Thirty American hit, followed by 'As Time Goes By', a Top Fifty entrant a year later.

Nash maintained his career on an even keel until the early seventies via recording contracts with a handful of companies like Warner Bros and MGM Records. Towards the end of the decade, though, he opened his own label, JoDa, with musical and business partner Danny Simms. Based in New York, Nash produced a pair of minor R. & B. hits for Sam and Bill, namely 'For your Love" and 'Fly Me to the Moon' in 1965 and 1966 respectively. During that same period, Nash also recorded his own pair of poor-selling mainstream singles for the label – 'Let's Move and Groove (Together)' and 'Somewhere'.

When JoDa became JAD, Nash flew to Kingston, Jamaica, to record further titles including 'Hold Me Tight', a Top Five American pop hit, and 'You Got Soul', a Top Sixty entrant during 1968. Both titles were released in Britain: 'Hold Me Tight' on the Regal Zonophone label, and 'You Got Soul' by Major Minor Records. Both soared into the Top Ten and reflected a sound that would be dubbed 'soul/reggae' because the music fell into neither category totally.

'Cupid' was the next single in April 1969, reaching No. 6 in the British chart. It was at this juncture that Nash moved to Britain. He desperately wanted to sustain his top-selling status and felt he could not achieve this unless he switched countries. With a new lucrative recording deal with CBS Records he worked with an unknown reggae artist, Bob Marley. Together they produced Nash's next British hit 'Stir It Up', his debut for his new record company. It faltered in the Top Twenty during April 1972. Also this year, Nash returned to Jamaica to record. One result was 'I Can See Clearly Now', issued in June to become a Top Five British hit. The title fared better in America where it shot to No. 1, a position it held for four weeks. Its follow-up four months later, 'There Are More Questions Than Answers', raced to No. 9 in the British chart.

The mellow Nash approach to music was a winner; its reggae flavour was more commercially slanted than ethnic. However, the best was yet to come. Written by Ernie Smith and produced by the singer, 'Tears on my Pillow' shot to the top of the British chart in July 1975. It was Nash's first and only chart-topper, and remarkably was his final high-ranking single. The follow-up was 'Let's Be Friends', a Top Fifty struggler, while '(What a) Wonderful World', a year later, released via CBS Records' Epic label, climbed marginally higher into the Top Thirty.

Johnny Nash sank from sight until the mid-eighties when he issued 'Rock Me Baby' on the FED label, while his last British hit appeared four years later on Epic. Like many artists, he enjoyed (or fell foul of) the remixing studio engineers who worked on 'I Can See Clearly Now' to push an in-vogue version into the British Top Sixty.

To date, Johnny Nash is the top-selling reggae artist in Britain and was, many believe, the force behind Bob Marley's later success. Where is he now?

THE STYLISTICS

Can't Give You Anything (but my Love)

'We have always been a working band, singing is our trade . . . we are far from over the hill because we were so young when we first started.' – Russell Thompkins Jr

Airrion Love, born in Philadelphia, Pennsylvania, on 8 August 1949; James Smith, born in New York on 16 June 1950, and Russell Thompkins Jr, born in Philadelphia on 21 March 1951, were all members of a group called The Monarchs. Meantime, James Dunn, born in Philadelphia on 4 February 1950, and Herb Murrell, born in Lane, South Carolina, on 27 April 1949, were members of another unit called The Percussions.

The five decided to form their own group during 1968. They called themselves The Stylistics and secured a recording contract with Sebring Records, an independent Philadelphian label. That same year, the group recorded the single 'You're a Big Girl Now', penned by Robert Douglas and Marty Bryant, the group's road manager. The single was leased to Avco Embassy Records, predecessor to H&L Records. Murrell told journalist John Abbey, 'At the time we were all working day jobs and working the clubs at night. And when the record first started hitting, we took two weeks off to tour.' 'You're a Big Girl Now' eventually peaked in the American Top Eighty during January 1971 thanks to Avco Embassy distributing it. Murrell: 'My ambition was to play the Uptown Theatre in Philly. That was our first real achievement . . . and as hard work as that gig was, it was exciting. It's like the old Apollo in New York, three or four shows a day but a hive of excitement and activity.'

Midway through 1971, The Stylistics joined creative forces with Thom Bell and Linda Creed to record at Philadelphia's Sigma Sound Studios. The result catapulted the group into the American Top Forty. Titled 'Stop, Look, Listen (to your Heart)', the single peaked during May 1971, giving birth to what would become The Stylistics' sound – a soft, warm fusion of richly-honed ballads, highlighted by the group's lead falsetto voice. 'Stop, Look, Listen (to your Heart)' went on to be re-recorded countless times but perhaps the most notable was the duet between Diana Ross and Marvin Gaye, a track on their eponymous album issued in 1973.

Early in 1972, The Stylistics followed their version with 'You Are Everything'. The title soared into the American Top Ten, selling one million copies en route, to pass gold status, the first in a series of singles to do so. 'You Are Everything' was likewise reworked by other artists including Ross and Gaye.

Bell and Creed's working relationship with The Stylistics was proving bankable, and the two would continue to collaborate for a further eighteen months. The title 'Betcha By Golly Wow' was the next hit during May 1972, when it flew to No. 3 in America, passing gold on its way to one million sales plus. As the single (not recorded by Ross and Gaye!) climbed, The Stylistics' eponymous album was finally released, and reached the Top Thirty. 'Betcha By Golly Wow' was also the group's debut British hit. Released via the Avco label, the title peaked at No. 13 in the chart during June 1972, heralding a successful career.

The title 'People Make the World Go Round' was the follow-up to the American release of 'Betcha By Golly Wow'. It surprisingly stalled at No. 25 in the chart in July 1972. Following their debut British tour, The Stylistics' next single, 'I'm Stone in Love with You', raced to No. 9 in the British chart late in 1972. British audiences had welcomed the slick, precise stage presence which accompanied the warm, rich vocals, and this response was to endure for some years to come. When 'I'm Stone in Love with You' was released in America, it shot into the Top Ten; the group's third consecutive million-seller. The single was, incidentally, swiped from their second album, unimaginatively titled *Stylistics: Round 2,* itself a big seller early the next year. In 1973 four singles shot into the high regions of the American chart, namely 'Break Up to Make Up', 'You'll Never Get to Heaven' (a cover version of Dionne Warwick's 1964 classic), 'Peek-A-Boo' and 'Rockin' Roll Baby', the first mid-paced track from the Bell/Creed composing partnership. All titles were likewise big British sellers. Dunn: 'We had become labelled as a soft group so we needed the change. We like to always adapt to the market. We were fortunate enough to have a few uptempo hits [but] we always revert to the ballads.'

Midway through 1974, The Stylistics began to work with the composing/producing duo Hugo Peretti and Luigi Creatore (H&L Records), who worked with arranger Van McCoy (himself a recording artist of note, particularly his 1975 chart-topper titled 'The Hustle'). With the change in musical mentors, the group enjoyed their final American million-selling title, 'You Make Me Feel Brand New'. When the single was released in British, it soared to No. 2 during August. Thompkins: 'The company never even believed in [the song] and we had to force them to release it as a single. We were on the road with James Brown at the time and that song was getting such a great reaction everywhere we played . . . the thing was Hugo and Luigi were not young men and they came from a different era.'

The album *Let's Put It All Together* followed, recorded in the Media Sound Studios, New York, instead of the group's usual Philadelphia studio. The album's title track was issued as a single during September 1974 to reach the American Top Twenty and the British Top Ten.

The first single of the new year heralded the decline of the group. Titled 'Star on a TV Show', it stalled in the American Top Fifty, while in Britain it climbed into the Top Twenty. Meanwhile, the American album *Heavy* was retitled *From the Mountain* in Britain, and became a Top Forty hit. This was hotly followed by the compilation *The Best of The Stylistics,* which faltered in the American Top Fifty but which topped the British chart for two weeks in April 1975. The release earned the distinction of being the biggest-selling album by a black group. The follow-up album, *Thank You Baby,* issued in May, spawned The Stylistics' first and only British chart-topper (as well as two previous singles, 'Thank You Baby' and 'Sing Baby Sing'). Titled 'Can't Give You Anything (but my Love)', and penned by Hugo, Luigi and George David Weiss, it sped to the top of the British chart during August 1975, where it stayed for three weeks. The single was the group's contribution to the growing disco boom on both sides of the Atlantic, although in essence they were not a dance band. In America, the title stalled in the Top Sixty as the group's career began its rapid decline. Love: 'We had one of the first disco records with [that single] but we never followed through on it. We just didn't make disco records and we ended up hurting because of it . . . the record company we were with didn't concentrate their efforts on us in the States. Instead, because we were so big overseas, they did all of their promoting there. It was a real pity because . . . we felt [we] could have made it if they had tried for us at home.' Once again, when America tired of its soul acts, it was left to Britain to sustain them; The Stylistics lived through to the next year.

The follow-up single titled 'Na Na Is the Saddest Word' was lifted from the group's pending album, *You Are Beautiful,* and reached the British Top Five. As the album climbed into the American Top One Hundred and British Top Thirty, the next single to be swiped, 'Funky Weekend', was issued. The title crawled into the American Top Eighty but made the British Top Ten. When the album's title track was issued in April 1976, it marked the group's final American charter. The Stylistics had risen so high, and now were dropping like a stone down a well. Nonetheless, there remained the loyal British. Thompkins: 'It got to the point where London was like a second home. We first went there in 1976, and we have been back every year since . . . They just want to hear us sing our hits . . . the fans are so loyal. In some cases, we've seen them grow from being kids into adults and that's a nice feeling for us.'

Midway through 1976, the group issued their version of Elvis Presley's 1962 hit 'Can't Help Falling in Love', which shot to No. 4 in Britain. Following this release, The Stylistics moved with Hugo and Luigi to record proper on their H&L Records. The switch marked a musical change for the group – for the worse! The Stylistics' debuted on H&L Records with '16 Bars', a No. 7 British hit in August, followed by the EP titled *You'll Never Get to Heaven*, a Top Thirty entrant. Four months later, the group's British hit run ended with '7000 Dollars and You', which stalled at No. 24 in the chart. The magic that was The Stylistics had worn thin; one wondered if their chart presence would have lasted longer if they had remained with Thom Bell and Linda Creed. Thompkins: 'I feel our best work was done with Thom Bell, because, even with the Van McCoy material, he was only the arranger, not the producer. Hugo and Luigi are our producers.' He added that, although the group was happy with the arrangement, 'We don't have any control over what we record and that is one stipulation that we will have in any future agreement. We simply do not want to record what we cannot feel ourselves.'

In the eighties, The Stylistics moved to Phonogram's Mercury Records, where the album *Love Spell* was their solitary release. Thompkins: 'We really enjoyed doing that album for Mercury with Teddy Randazzo and we felt good about that one. But the company never seemed to get behind it properly and it never really surfaced. Our fans enjoyed the album but it was never promoted further and once the product has been created it's nearly all down to the company's efforts.'

From Mercury, the group switched to TSOP Records, a subsidiary of Philadelphia Records owned by Kenny Gamble and Leon Huff. Thompkins: 'We [were] actually signed to TSOP Records since June 1979. Our deal with Phonogram had expired and Philadelphia International made us an offer. It was as easy as that . . . We recorded our first three albums in Philadelphia . . . and it felt good to be back . . . My dream is that we could record with Thom Bell again. Thom and Linda Creed were like magic. Perhaps we had a better dialogue with Van McCoy, because when we worked with Thom Bell we were young and didn't have the experience we have now. The dialogue tended to be one way. We have learned a lot, though, from everyone we have worked with.'

Despite the high profile of the TSOP label and the other acts on the company's roster who promoted the Sound of Philadelphia until it became an international success, The Stylistics struggled to reach the charts. It was only the loyalty of soul fans that sustained the group's career via albums like *Closer Than Close* in 1981. During 1984, they switched record companies once more to sign to Arthur Brown's Streetwise label, based in New York; leased to Virgin Records in Britain. The album *Some Things Never Change* spawned the single 'Love Is Not the Answer' during 1985. A year on, the album *A Special Style* was released.

In the nineties, a series of CD compilations kept the group in the public eye, while in 1996, James Smith and James Dunn left and the group continued as a trio, to earn a living on the oldies but goldies club circuit on both sides of the Atlantic. Murrell: 'Most of the [British] clubs we appear at have been booking us for years and know we always put on a good show, and pull a good crowd.'

Style on, guys!

(Quotes: *Blues and Soul* magazine, interviews by John Abbey, 1977–80)

September 1975

ROD STEWART

Sailing

'I'm a changed man . . . I just don't fancy other birds anymore. Britt's everything I want.' – Rod Stewart

Apart from their recording achievements together Rod Stewart and The Faces were huge as performing artists. Their dates would be sold out as audiences were treated to both the group's repertoire and Stewart's solo material, and by 1974 they were the biggest-grossing working band in Britain.

However, it was clear the public flocked to these concerts to see the lead singer – a fact even The Faces could not dispute. So, following an extended American tour in 1975 which was far from placid, the group realised Stewart's departure was imminent. Stewart: 'The friction came when promoters started putting up signs "Rod Stewart and the Faces".'

In fact, he admitted, Billy Gaff (their manager) used to travel to a town early to ensure he could remove the signs advertising their concert before the group arrived. One night, however, Gaff flunked – and the atmosphere on stage was fractious to say the least.

Behind the performances, Stewart had another, more pressing matter on his mind – romance. In March 1975 in Los Angeles he met Britt Ekland, a Swedish actress mourning a loveless marriage to actor Peter Sellers which produced a daughter, Victoria. This was the start of a well-documented relationship, despite the fact that Stewart already had a partner, Dee Harrington, tucked away in Britain. His reputation as a womaniser was widely known. Stewart's (then) publicist Sally Croft: 'Rod had an amazing effect on women. He oozes charm. If he wanted a girl he could be so charming he was irresistible.' However, with women traipsing through his life, Stewart needed the stability of male companionship, and none more so than Elton John. The friendship they built up during the years was solid and humorous, and was both personal and professional. Few can have escaped their concert appearances as 'Phyllis' and 'Sharon', usually in drag!

After meeting Britt Ekland, and owing British taxes in excess of £700,000, the singer applied for American citizenship. Stewart: 'I left Britain because I was paying 83 per cent of everything I was earning to the taxman . . . I was in a position to move and I fell in love with the place.' The move to America had a remarkable effect on his music, and he produced his finest album to date. The aptly titled *Atlantic Crossing,* produced by Tom Dowd, and recorded with the Muscle Shoals Rhythm Section in Alabama, spawned Stewart's next international chart-topper, 'Sailing'. Written by Gavin Sutherland, and originally recorded as an album track by The Sutherland Brothers, 'Sailing' soared to the top of the British chart in September 1975, a position it held for four weeks. The track had the distinction of being the longest-running chart single of the year, was adopted as an anthem by football fans and was the theme music to the BBC TV series *HMS Ark Royal.* This latter exposure in 1976 returned the single to the British chart during September when it peaked in the Top Three. Ten years later, 'Sailing' reappeared; all royalties this time went to the survivors and families of the Zeebrugge ferry disaster.

When the single was first released, Stewart was still working with The Faces and to this end was committed to an American tour with them. It was an abysmal trek but was nonetheless completed because the concerts were sold out and they refused to disappoint their public. Ian McLagan: 'Each of us was feeling insecure because everything was different to how it usually was.' In their absence, 'This Old Heart of Mine', a cover version of The Isley Brothers' 1966 and 1969 Motown hit, was issued in Britain as the follow-up to 'Sailing'. It reached No. 4 in November 1975 and represented the debut release on Riva Records, a company owned by Billy Gaff.

As was to be expected, Rod Stewart announced to the media that he was leaving The Faces to concentrate on his solo career. Not because he wanted to, as he explained: 'Woody went with the Stones, then we lost Ronnie Lane. For me, Lanie was The Faces. He was to The Faces what Keith Richard is to the Stones. Once Lanie left it took the ass out of it for me.'

'Tonight's the Night', swiped from his next album, *A Night on the Town*, followed in June 1976 to reach the Top Five, while the mother album easily secured the No. 1 position, reaching No. 2 in America. The single's lyrical content caused controversy Stateside because it told of a virgin's 'deflowering'. Radio airplay was subsequently restricted. Not so in Britain, BBC Radio 1 turned an unusually deaf ear, yet its weekly television music show *Top of the Pops* banned it, claiming it unfit for family viewing. 'The Killing of Georgie (Parts I and II)' also attracted media controversy. Released as a single in August 1976, the disc told of the murder of a young gay man in New York. The single reached No. 2 in Britain.

The start of 1977 saw Stewart touring Britain, following a lengthy Norwegian hike. This was the singer's debut tour with his new backing group comprising guitarists Phil Chen, Jim Cregan, Billy Peek and Gary Grainger, and drummer Carmine Appice. All concerts were sold out. Two further singles became British hits during the year, namely the double A-sider 'I Don't Want to Talk about It'/'The First Cut Is the Deepest', which topped the British chart for four weeks, his fourth single to do so, and 'You're in my Heart', which peaked at No. 3 during October.

On the personal front the singer's relationship with Britt Ekland deteriorated, his womanising proving too difficult for her to accept. At the time of their separation Ekland claimed she and Stewart had had a verbal agreement to pool their financial resources. She now wanted recompense. Author Gary Herman reported, 'Everything, she said, should have been split down the middle and, considering how she had sacrificed her acting career to help Rod, she felt she deserved £6,000,000 – especially, she said, since Rod was about to sign a £13,000,000 deal when he left her. As an interim award, Britt asked for £2,750 a month while her claim was being assessed.' No matter how strongly Ekland believed her case was, the judge rejected it. Rod Stewart was free to pursue his future wife.

Also see: 'Maggie May', November 1971; 'You Wear It Well', September 1972; 'Da Ya Think I'm Sexy?', December 1978

(Quotes: *Rod Stewart: The Best Selling Biography* by Tim Ewbank and Stafford Hildred ; *Rock 'n' Roll Babylon* by Gary Herman)

October 1975

ART GARFUNKEL

I Only Have Eyes for You

Born in Forest Hills, New York, on 5 November 1941, Art Garfunkel, the curly-haired blond, enjoyed a remarkably successful composing/ singing career with Paul Simon. To all intents and purposes, that career ended with their milestone album *Bridge over Troubled Water* in 1970. It was ironic that while the duo had reached its peak, receiving the highest accolades known to the music business, plans were in the offing for individual careers.

Still maintaining their friendship and the occasional reunion performance, Paul Simon continued his solo musical career with CBS Records, leaving Garfunkel to test his acting abilities after his work for the Mike Nichols movie *The Graduate*. Subsequently, his singing career as a CBS Records' artist was put on hold. Simon told authors Joseph Morella and Patricia Barey: 'I think . . . Arthur would have preferred to maintain two careers. He would like to have done films and Simon and Garfunkel. However, that wasn't to be.'

Garfunkel's acting debut was as Lieutenant Nately in another Nichols film, the screen version of Joseph Heller's *Catch 22* in 1970. He then co-starred with Jack Nicholson in the 1971 movie *Carnal Knowledge*, where the couple played two old college friends whose sex lives had developed into middle-aged discontentment. Garfunkel said at the time, 'I'm pleased with my role. I don't mind saying I would like an Academy Award for it.' However, a critic wrote in the *New Republican* newspaper, 'Arthur Garfunkel . . . is not an actor at all. Nichols evidently thought his personality [which is apt enough] was worth the risk, and he has helped Garfunkel at least to behave credibly. I'd be perfectly willing never to see Garfunkel again . . .'

The singer's next significant role was nine years later, when he played an American psychoanalyst in Nicholas Roeg's *Bad Timing*.

Late in 1973 Art Garfunkel recommenced his recording career by releasing 'All I Know', written by Jimmy Webb and lifted from the *Angel Clare* album, a name, incidentally, borrowed from the Thomas Hardy book *Tess of the D'Urbervilles*. Garfunkel: 'I didn't know if I was going to do it [the solo album]. I had shaky confidence about my ability now . . . Didn't know what my own thing was.' The single peaked in the American Top Ten; reaching No. 14 in Britain. During the next year, Garfunkel's recorded success was confined to America with a pair of Top Forty hits, namely, 'I Shall Sing' and 'Second Avenue'.

However, that situation was to alter when late in 1975 and following his reunion with Paul Simon on the American television show *Saturday Night Live*, Garfunkel recorded and released 'I Only Have Eyes for You', written by Harry Warren and Al Dubin during the thirties, and previously recorded by The Flamingos two decades later. Garfunkel's updated, transparent version soared to the top of the British chart in October 1975, where it stayed for two weeks. In America, it stalled in the Top Twenty.

'I Only Have Eyes for You' was the first of a trio of singles to be culled from the *Breakaway* album. The second, 'My Little Town', featuring Paul Simon, soared into the American Top Ten, while the third, the album's title cut, faltered in the Top Forty. Both bombed in Britain.

Late in 1976 Garfunkel began working on his next album and, as on *Breakaway* before it, he worked with top-ranking session musicians. Recording began at the Muscle Shoals Sound Studios, moving to countless American states before the closing touches were laid in Dublin. Once again, Garfunkel relied on others' compositions for the project, with Jimmy Webb the prominent contributor. Titled *Watermark*, the album took a year to complete, and was released early in 1978. 'Crying in my Sleep' was the first track to be lifted as a single, followed by '(What) A Wonderful World' in March 1978. Both were American hits, but not so in Britain.

Art Garfunkel's British career was slipping, but, unknown to him, it was destined to turn around . . . thanks to a family of rabbits!

Also see: 'Bright Eyes', May 1979

(Quotes: *Simon and Garfunkel: Old Friends* by Joseph Morella and Patricia Barey)

DAVID BOWIE

Space Oddity

'Ground control to Major Tom . . .' Oh, those immortal, quirky, spaced-out sounds from a song that has haunted Bowie throughout his career. Funny how some things just stick!

Bowie was born David Robert Jones in Brixton, London, on 8 January 1947, to Peggy and John. John had been previously married to an Irish singer, with whom he had a daughter. Peggy had a son before her marriage, Terry, born during 1937, who would, in later years, play a significant role in the singer's life. Bowie was raised in a middle-class environment, and by the age of three he was, he said, fascinated by his mother's make-up.

The youngster developed an interest in music by listening to his father's records, before learning the saxophone following lessons from Ronnie Ross. Bowie told author Joe Smith, 'I had a very reserved, respectable childhood. Nothing really happened to me that one would consider freaky. I went to one of the first art-orientated high schools in England, where one could take an art course from the age of twelve.' This, in turn, led to him attending the Bromley Technical High School, Kent, where he studied with Peter Frampton, whose father was the tutor. Bowie: 'Some of us went straight into street jobs because we didn't really believe in ourselves as painters . . . I went into the visual side of an advertising agency.' Unbeknown to him at this time, there sadly was a hint of mental illness on his mother's side of the family. When he was older, Bowie believed that insanity would be manifested in himself. His half-brother Terry showed schizophrenic tendencies and lived with various members of the family, including Bowie's parents. And it was during these stays that he and Bowie bonded.

Musically-speaking, Bowie played his way through The Kon-Rads, The Underwood, and The King Bees; the last group issued the solitary single titled 'Liza Jane' via the Vocalion label, a Decca Records' offshoot. The single bombed in 1964. Before the year closed, Bowie switched to The Manish Boys to record the title 'I Pity the Fool', issued via EMI Records' Parlophone label during March 1965. Three months on, The Manish Boys disbanded, whereupon Bowie created The Lower Third, who likewise recorded for the Parlophone subsidiary. Their single titled 'You've Got a Habit of Leaving' bombed.

Early in 1966, the group moved to Pye Records, hired a manager, Ken Pitt, and Davy Jones became David Bowie because future confusion would, he felt, arise with The Monkees' member of the same name. With the details finalised, David Bowie and The Lower Third released the single 'Can't Help Thinking About Me'. When that title . . . er . . . bombed, the group disbanded, leaving Bowie to pursue a solo career with his single 'Do Anything You Say' issued during April 1966. Following the release of 'I Dig Everything' and no success, Bowie and Pye Records parted company.

Undeterred, the singer returned to Decca Records; not the company proper, but rather its subsidiary, Deram, where 'Rubber Band', late in 1966, was his debut outing. In 1967, Bowie, now experimenting with face make-up, strode in an obscure musical direction by recording 'The Laughing Gnome' as a single. Although the title was innovative for its time, it bombed, but went on to cause Bowie considerable embarrassment in future years. Despite the title meaning little in 1967, Bowie issued his eponymous album that June, from which the title 'Love You till Tuesday' was swiped for single release. Yep, it bombed! During this period, Bowie developed an interest in dance and mime technique, studying under Lindsay Kemp, a theatrical artist of considerable note. To learn the art, Bowie appeared in one of Kemp's mime productions. With no further solo releases in the offing, he formed Feathers, a trio comprising John Hutchinson and Hermoine Farthingale.

Before the sixties ended, Bowie repromoted his first album, with the addition of one new track, 'Space Oddity', via a short movie. On the strength of the new title, the singer signed a recording deal with Mercury, part of the Philips Records cluster of labels. A reworked version of 'Space Oddity' was subsequently issued as a single, coinciding with the recent Apollo landing. Yep, the marketing ploy worked when, after several stabs at becoming a charting name, Bowie's 'Space Oddity' fired itself into the British Top Five in September 1969.

Following this long-overdue success, Bowie temporarily retired from the music business to run the Arts Lab in Beckenham, a club operating from the rear room of a South London public house. He met Angela Barnett, with whom he lived in Haddon Hall, Beckenham. They married in March 1970 in Bromley Registry Office. The media soon reported on the couple's 'open' marriage when they professed to being bisexual, while allowing Bowie to publicly distinguish himself as a child of the future, although few understood what he really meant!

On the strength of 'Space Oddity', Bowie signed a lucrative recording contract with Philips Records, and it was under this deal that his album *David Bowie* was issued late in 1969.

In 1970 he formed his first support group, called Hype, whose membership included his record producer Tony Visconti as guitarist. During the year, Bowie recorded the single 'Memory of a Free Festival' and issued *The Man Who Sold the World* album. The release raised eyebrows; the packaging showed the singer wearing a dress. Public outrage resulted in the album sleeves being withdrawn and replaced.

America beckoned at the start of 1971. Following the short promotional trip there and working on material for a future album tentatively titled *Hunky Dory,* Bowie's son Zowie was born in May 1971. An RCA Records' executive, excited at Bowie's demo album tapes, signed the singer to a recording contract, whereupon *Hunky Dory* proper was issued. The title bombed in Britain, but when released in April 1972 in America, it slightly dented the Top One Hundred listing. The debut single of 1972, 'Changes', charted in the American Top Seventy as Bowie was trapped in a lengthy British tour, during which, incidentally, he introduced his alter-ego, Ziggy Stardust, to audiences. In fact, Stardust was derived from Japanese theatre mixed with sci-fi, with clothes designed by Kansai Yamamoto. From Britain, Bowie and friends switched to the American circuit, promoting on the way their new album, *The Rise and Fall of Ziggy Stardust and the Spiders from Mars*. The album marked Bowie's British chart debut, zooming to the Top Five, while in America, it sauntered around the Top Seventy.

A further British and American trek; the release of the hit single 'John I'm Only Dancing'; the reissued album *The Man Who Sold the World* via RCA Records, and a further British hit and American bomber titled 'The Jean Genie' signified an extremely successful year for the singer.

In 1973 Bowie hit the American circuit once again on the strength of his debut Top Twenty hit there, the rereleased 'Space Oddity'. It may have taken a little while, but the Americans finally got there! Then, with an eye on a quick buck, Bowie's previous record label, Deram, issued the album *Images 1966–1967*. By April and when Bowie's world tour had reached Japan, his album *Aladdin Sane* dominated the British chart, entered the Top Twenty in America, and the single 'Drive-in Saturday' soared to No. 3 in Britain. During May, he closed his world tour at London's Earls Court before an estimated 18,000 fans, and with a sell-out concert at Hammersmith Odeon. Coinciding with these final dates, the single 'Life on Mars' shot to No. 3 in Britain, which to all intents and purposes buried his musical obsession with space-orientated material. Indeed, following the Hammersmith Odeon concert, he stunned his band by announcing to his audience that it marked the end of his career as a live performer. He later told an *NME* journalist, 'Those were my final gigs. I don't want to do any more . . . all my forthcoming American dates have been cancelled. From now on, I'll be concentrating on various activities that have very little to do with rock and pop.' He also told Joe Smith, 'I moved out of Ziggy fast enough so as not to get caught up by it . . . The Ziggy thing was worth one or two albums, so after *Aladdin Sane* I had to start thinking quickly what I wanted to write.' It transpired that Bowie was working on the *Diamond Dogs* project, which began its life as *1984*.

Meanwhile, like a recurring nightmare, 'The Laughing Gnome' was reissued by Deram and, incredibly, shot into the British Top Ten, while *Pin Ups*, an album containing the singer's favourite sixties' titles, raced to the top of the British chart, selling in excess of 200,000 copies en route. The spawned single, titled 'Sorrow', a cover version of The Merseys' solitary British hit in 1966, became a No. 3 hit for Bowie. Interestingly, before the year closed, it was reported that the singer had sold 1,056,400 albums and approximately 1,000,000 singles for RCA Records alone. Yes, indeed, David Bowie was extremely big business, both as an artist and composer.

Early in 1974, Lulu joined the queue of artists to record his material, to release a version of his 'The Man Who Sold the World'; quite possibly her best single (to date), highlighted by the composer's vocals. Meantime, Bowie himself released 'Rebel Rebel'; a Top Five British single, followed by 'Rock and Roll Suicide', a Top Thirty struggler. That year, he moved to America, staying for approximately two years. *Diamond Dogs* then returned him to the top of the British album chart during May 1974, and hit the American Top Five. The album's title track was later released to flounder in the British Top Thirty. Probably the most interesting tracks on the mother album were 'Big Brother' and '1984' taken from the stage musical *1984* but which George Orwell's widow refused to acknowledge, thereby preventing any authenticity being attached to the titles.

As happened after most of his album releases, Bowie once more toured; this time he embarked upon a two-month 'Diamond Dogs' American stint, where the theme was the breakdown of modern-day society following the devastation of a holocaust, and the subsequent deformation of the human race. Then to close 1975, the singer took an unprecedented move by issuing a cover version of 'Knock on Wood', a British Top Ten entry, previously associated with soul man Eddie Floyd.

The following year was devoted to the *Young Americans* album (and single), Bowie's musical exercise in what he called 'plastic soul' – his view of American music at the time. The project marked a complete musical diversion into the funk/soul area. *Young Americans* soared to No. 2 in Britain, while the single peaked in the Top Twenty. Recorded in Philadelphia, with Luther Vandross contributing to the star-laced line-up of musicians, the album went on to peak in the American Top Ten in April 1975, and the single in the Top Thirty. The follow-up, 'Fame', was likewise lifted from the album to reach the British Top Twenty in September, while in America the title shot to the top, where it stayed for two weeks, passing gold status.

Then, for some reason, the 1969 track 'Space Oddity', together with 'Changes' and 'Velvet Goldmine' as the B-side, was issued to soar to the top of the British chart during November 1975. As Bowie progressed, so this release back-tracked. Did record buyers really prefer this music to that he was now recording? The singer was in turmoil. Perhaps influenced by the oddness of the oddity, Bowie retired for the second time. 'I've rocked my roll . . . The last thing I want to be is some useless fucking rock singer.' However, on the upside, *The Man Who Fell to Earth,* in which he played his first serious movie role, was premiered in London during March 1976.

It was during this period that Bowie admitted his life was dominated by a serious drug habit. He told author Gary Herman, 'I used to try a new drug every time one came onto the market . . . I guess I've been near death a lot.' Retired or not, Bowie tucked into a 1976 world tour, when audiences saw him dropping his theatrical costumes and elaborate stage props, to return to the basics of rock 'n' roll, as his single 'Golden Years', swiped from the British Top Five album *Station to Station,* set the pace. All was well until the singer and musical cohort Iggy Pop were arrested in Massachusetts for alleged marijuana possession. The case would eventually be dismissed. Then, following a stint in Moscow, Bowie was held at the Russian/Polish border for secreting Nazi literature in his luggage, intended, the singer said, for a proposed movie project. Ironically, both singer and Iggy Pop would move to West Berlin to wean themselves off drugs, while soaking up the immense history of the city. They stayed in their self-imposed semi-exile for approximately three years.

In 1976, with six sell-out performances at Wembley Arena, Middlesex, behind him, Bowie issued the *Changesonebowie* compilation, while a year later, his album *Low,* co-produced by Tony Visconti and inspired by his Berlin stay, was issued. Bowie: 'The first side of [the album] was all about me; "Always Crashing in the Same Car" and all that self-pitying crap. But side two was more of a musical observation – my reaction to seeing the Eastern bloc, how West Berlin survives in the middle of it, which is something I couldn't express in words. It required textures instead.'

Bowie and his wife Angie separated early in 1978, finally divorcing two years later, whereupon Angie was said to have received £30,000 in settlement and custody of their son. Midway through 1980, he topped the British chart for a second time with 'Ashes to Ashes', and appeared on the Broadway stage, playing John Merrick in *The Elephant Man.*

Now living in Montreux, Switzerland, the artist recorded the theme for the movie *Cat People,* and teamed with Queen in a chance recording session which resulted in 'Under Pressure' being issued to later soar to the top of the British chart in November 1981. A year later, the second compilation album, *Changestwobowie,* peaked in the British Top Thirty, reaching the Top Seventy in America, followed by the *Christiane F* soundtrack album and the 'Cat People (Putting Out Fire)' single.

Returning easily into the film world, Bowie began location shooting in the Pacific for *Merry Christmas Mr Lawrence* with co-star Tom Conti. Before 1982 closed, he took the unusual step of releasing the title 'Peace on Earth – The Little Drummer Boy', his duet with Bing Crosby, actually recorded in 1977.

With a switch of record companies to EMI America Records, following a reputed $10 million incentive, Bowie recorded and released his most exciting single for some time. With the pulsating disco boom prevalent, he aimed 'Let's Dance' at the feet. The track was swiped from the album of the same name, produced primarily by Chic mentors, Nile Rodgers and Bernard Edwards, with others. Both titles topped their respective British charts, while Stateside, the single became a chart-topper during May, leaving the album to peak at No. 4. Nonetheless, it passed platinum sales status.

During June, Bowie embarked upon the 'Serious Moonlight 83' tour, with London concerts as the opening dates. Meanwhile, his single titled 'China Girl' soared to No. 2 in Britain, hitting the Top Ten in America. The tour finally ended in December 1983 in Thailand.

A series of singles – including 'Blue Jean' and 'Tonight' – and albums – *Fame and Fashion* and *Tonight* – during the next two years sustained Bowie's high profile, until in 1985 he duetted with Mick Jagger as part of the Live Aid fundraising project, instigated by Bob Geldof. The Bowie/Jagger duet was a version of Martha and the Vandellas' timeless classic 'Dancing in the Street', which entered the British chart at the top during September 1985, reaching the Top Ten in America.

Bowie's acting roles included *Absolute Beginners* and *The Last Temptation of Christ*, while his recordings included the album *Never Let Me Down* during 1987. Two years later, he formed a new group, Tin Machine, to debut at the International Music Awards ceremony staged in New York, and to release their eponymous album in June 1989.

With the new decade came the new world tour, 'The Sound and Vision World Tour 1990', which began in Canada and took in Britain and America. Used to promote Bowie's current album *Sound and Vision*, the trek pushed the album sufficiently for it to win a 1990 Grammy Award for Best Album Package. In March, *Changesbowie*, unrelated to the previous similarly titled albums, shot to the top of the British chart, as the soundtrack of the movie *Pretty Woman* carried a re-vamped version of Bowie's 'Fame'.

During 1992, the artist's public profile was higher than ever. For instance, he attended Elizabeth Taylor's extravagant party to celebrate her sixtieth birthday; appeared at the AIDS fundraising gala 'A Concert for Life: Freddie Mercury Tribute' staged at Wembley Stadium, and attended Bill Clinton's Presidential Rally in New Jersey. The following year, the much-awaited Bowie album, *Black Tie White Noise*, released by Savage Records, topped the chart in April. Three months on from the release, the record company fell into liquidation, leaving Bowie and album to flounder.

Bowie signed a worldwide recording deal with Virgin Records midway through 1995. His debut album, titled *Outside*, soared into the British Top Ten, hitting the Top Thirty in America that October. Hot on the heels of this release, Bowie returned to the British touring stage with 'The Outsiders' trek. Then in 1996, following his induction into the Rock 'n' Roll Hall of Fame, during a ceremony held in New York, Bowie was honoured by his home country when he received the BRIT Award for his Outstanding Contribution to British Music. During the gala evening, he performed his current single 'Hello Spaceboy' with the Pet Shop Boys. The single peaked in the British Top Twenty, while his performance was (possibly) remembered more for his one dangling earring and stiletto shoes worn with a designer suit, than for its musical content.

That's David Bowie; the man and artist who scratched his way into British music. The ever-unpredictable Bowie, who began his career with a slow transformation from the straight singer to the sexual ambiguity of Ziggy Stardust, which persona, many believe, was the escape mechanism needed to protect the shy young man.

The talent still shines: in 1997, Bowie released his twenty-first studio album, titled *Earthling*. He also sold himself on the stock market via the Bowie Bond issue scheme. Shares were reputedly worth £50 million in total. And, of course, it was the year Bowie reached fifty years old! An achievement he never believed would happen.

'It's only in the last few years that I've resigned myself into believing that I'm a moderately good singer.' – David Bowie

(Quotes: *Off the Record* by Joe Smith; *Rock 'n' Roll Babylon* by Gary Herman)

December 1975

QUEEN

Bohemian Rhapsody

' "Bohemian Rhapsody" took bloody ages to record but we've had all the freedom we wanted and we've been able to go to greater extremes.' – Freddie Mercury

Queen did not start its life with lead singer Freddie Mercury, but with Brian May. Born in Twickenham, Surrey, on 19 July 1947, May used a section from a nineteenth century fireplace to carve his first guitar. It was on this instrument that he perfected his art that would form the basis of Queen's musical trademark.

With a handful of A-level and O-level examination passes, May attended London's Imperial College as a student of physics and astronomy. While there, he followed his musical ambitions by joining a group called The Others, who went on to record one single for Fontana Records titled 'Oh Yeah'.

In 1966, May was offered a position at Jodrell Bank, but declined, preferring to pursue a musical career. He formed his first group, Smile, and recruited guitarist Tim Staffell, a fellow student at Imperial College, and drummer Roger Taylor, born Roger Meddows-Taylor in King's Lynn, Norfolk, on 26 July 1949. During 1969, Smile recorded and released the Staffell composition 'Earth' for Mercury Records in America. When it bombed (there was no British release), Staffell left the group to join Humpy Bong, recommending his friend as his replacement.

His friend, Freddie Mercury, born Frederick Bulsara in Zanzibar, Tanzania, on 5 September 1946, joined May and Taylor to form Queen.

Mercury had moved to Britain with his family during 1959 and, ironically, was Brian May's neighbour although the two had never previously met. With a diploma in graphic art and design, Mercury had graduated from the Ealing College of Art, to open a fashion stall in Kensington Market, London. Musically, he had passed through groups like Sour Milk Sea and Wreckage, as a vocalist.

The three Queen members and a succession of bass players secured regular local gigs, specifically one at Ballspark College, Hertford. However, the group could not develop musically without a regular bass player so, to this end, placed an advertisement in a local newspaper. John Deacon was the final Queen member to be recruited, during February 1971. Born in Leicester on 19 August 1951, Deacon was an ex-science student who had majored in electronics and was now teaching.

Queen's first official performance was at Hornsey Town Hall, London, followed by college dates and club gigs. Midway through 1971, the group embarked upon their debut British tour, ending with performances at the Imperial College. Early in 1972, the group tested new recording equipment at De Lane Lea Studios in return for free recording time. Working with engineer/producers John Anthony and Roy Thomas Baker, Queen recorded a series of demo tracks which, when played to the owners of the recording studio, Trident Audio Productions, led to a three-pronged contract covering management, publishing and production. Now contracted, Queen began experimenting with tracks for a debut album, while Trident negotiated a recording deal with EMI Records. Prior to the release of their debut single, Queen performed for the media at the Marquee in London, and Freddie Mercury, using the pseudonym Larry Lurex, issued a cover version of The Beach Boys' 1969 classic 'I Can Hear Music'.

During July 1973, the single 'Keep Yourself Alive' and album *Queen* were released. The short-sighted BBC Radio 1 banned the single, claiming it was the subject of an industry hype. The title subsequently bombed. To promote the album, Queen embarked upon a cross-country tour with Mott The Hoople, before headlining their own trek during the early part of 1974. In April, the group's album *Queen II* was issued to soar to No. 5 in the British chart, while, following the release of their debut album in America, the quartet toured there, once again as support act to Mott The Hoople.

For their second single, the group decided to remix a track from their first album. Titled 'Seven Seas of Rhye', it captured the public's imagination and BBC Radio 1's support, to peak in the British Top Ten during April 1974. This chart position was the result of the group's appearance on BBC TV's music programme *Top of the Pops,* an appearance that was by default. A planned video by another act was not forthcoming at the eleventh hour, whereupon Queen filled the vacancy to enjoy their debut British hit.

A second tour of America, this time as headliners, followed. Midway through the tour Brian May developed hepatitis, which in turn led to a duodenal ulcer. Working around May's incapacity, the group postponed the remainder of the tour to return to the recording studio to work on their third album, to be titled *Sheer Heart Attack.* The dynamic 'Killer Queen' was lifted as the first single and shot to No. 2 in the British chart during November 1974; the same position as the album. 'Killer Queen' also became the group's debut American Top Twenty entrant.

Queen fulfilled their American commitments early in 1975, again as headliners. As the demand for concert tickets was extraordinarily high, they added shows to the itinerary, often performing a pair of concerts in one day. Fate struck once more, when Mercury developed a throat virus which led to the dates being cancelled. While in America, Queen instructed Jim Beach, a music business lawyer, to negotiate the expiry of their Trident agreements due to a waning interest on the company's part. Meanwhile, the music played on. 'Now I'm Here' was issued as the follow-up single to 'Killer Queen' in February 1975. The title peaked in the British Top Twenty as the group paid their first visit to Japan. When they arrived at the airport, in excess of three thousand fans greeted them. It was, many said, Beatlemania over again. By the time of their departure, *Sheer Heart Attack* topped the Japanese chart.

Not a group to be idle, Queen began recording tracks for their new album, titled *A Night at the Opera.* Having purchased the Mountain Studios in Montreaux, Switzerland, they used this and, reputedly, five other studios to complete the album, which included their most innovative slice of sheer brilliance, titled 'Bohemian Rhapsody', which was to have the same effect on the music industry in the seventies as The Beatles' *Sergeant Pepper's Lonely Hearts Club Band* had done a decade earlier. The single highlighted Mercury's passion for opera and Roy Thomas Baker's adeptness for fully-blown productions. It was intended as a seven-minute glimpse of Queen's ability to create a dramatic rock-opera, but EMI Records dealt them a death blow when the decision was taken to edit the track to the acceptable three-minutes-plus befitting a 45 rpm single. What the record company failed to take into account was Kenny Everett's pig-headed determination to convert the world. Everett, zany and unconventional, was an established and popular radio DJ for London's Capital Radio, whose on-air opinions had led to several conflicts. The more he ridiculed the Establishment, the larger his listening audience grew. Mercury respected Everett, and sent him a 5 minute 55 second copy of 'Bohemian Rhapsody', insisting it was for his personal use and not for airplay. Such was the impact it had on him, that he publicly played it fourteen times in two days. Calls swamped Capital Radio's switchboard to such an extent that EMI Records were forced to issue the single in its full-length glory.

As 'Bohemian Rhapsody' climbed the British chart, Queen went one step further and, with director Bruce Gower utilising ideas from the group, produced a promotional video that marked a revolution in the genre. Mercury: 'That was our first lavish production even though we didn't have much money to spend and had to do everything ourselves . . . Queen are capable of great things but sometimes great things take great courage.' It was the first of a series of extraordinary promotional videos that were to be as entertaining and larger than life as their future concerts, because Mercury could gorge himself in a fantasy world of fun.

'Bohemian Rhapsody' shot to the top of the British chart in December 1975, where it stayed for a remarkable nine weeks, while the album *A Night at the Opera* dominated the chart, to remain on the listing for over one year in total, passing platinum status; Queen's first. The album's packaging, incidentally, featured a reworked Queen crest which Mercury had originally designed for their first album, comprising the group's star signs – two Leo lions, two Virgo fairies and a Cancer crab. *A Night at the Opera* also became a No. 4 American hit, but, surprisingly, 'Bohemian Rhapsody' stalled in the Top Ten.

For the first three months of 1976 Queen toured America and then Japan, where, once again, riotous scenes greeted them. In their absence, all four Queen albums were positioned in the British Top Twenty, while the single 'Bohemian Rhapsody' won an Ivor Novello Award for the Best Selling British Single of 1975. From Japan, the group flew to Australia, leaving a second single to be swiped from the platinum album, namely 'You're my Best Friend'. The track peaked in the British Top Ten in July 1976; reaching No. 16 in America. During September, Queen returned to British soil to headline a free concert in Hyde Park, London, before an audience estimated at 150,000–200,000 people; the highest-ever attendance record for a Hyde Park concert (to date). At the close of the year, 'Somebody to Love' soared to No. 2 in the British chart.

The group's next album, *A Day at the Races,* was issued upon their return from the Australian trek. To promote its release, the group entertained the media at Kempton Park where EMI Records sponsored a special race titled 'A Day at the Races Stake'. Queen's membership backed the same horse without telling each other – and won! Five days prior to the album's release, advance orders were in excess of 500,000.

Once more, the group embarked upon an American trek, where Mercury exaggerated his passion for theatrical costumes, much to the delight of the audiences. The tour went on to push the single 'Somebody to Love' into the Top Twenty. Queen continued to tour outside Britain until the end of March when the track 'Tie your Mother Down' was issued to stall in the British Top Forty and the Top Fifty in America. It was at this juncture that Roger Taylor financed his first solo single, titled 'I Wanna Testify', before joining the rest of the group for a lengthy European tour. When it was completed, they returned to the recording studio to concentrate on their next project, and performed a concert at Earl's Court, London, which introduced the £50,000 'Crown' lighting rig, weighing five thousand pounds and standing twenty-six feet tall and fifty-four feet wide.

During October 1977 Queen fan club members were invited to appear in the promotional video for their next single titled 'We Are the Champions'. It was filmed at the New London Theatre, and the group remained on stage following the video shoot to perform an impromptu concert for their loyal audience. Also in October, 'Bohemian Rhapsody' tied with Procol Harum's single 'A Whiter Shade of Pale' as the Best British Pop Single 1952–1977 at the British Record Industry Britannia Awards ceremony celebrating the Queen's (the ruling monarch's, not the group's!) Silver Jubilee.

The heavy chant of 'We Are the Champions' was teamed with 'We Will Rock You' for a double A-sided single, whereupon the disc shot to No. 2 in the British chart. Both titles were swiped from the *News of the World* album, also issued during October 1977, which reached No. 4 in Britain; and No. 3 in America. However, despite the public success, it was apparent there was conflict between the group members. Taylor said at the time, 'Our rows are partially a conflict of musical ideas and partially ego problems.' Deacon went one step further by telling *Rolling Stone* magazine that he was annoyed at Mercury's flamboyant and often vulgar image. 'Some of us hate it, but that's Freddie and you can't stop it.' Also at this juncture, Mercury stated that rumours regarding the group disbanding regularly cropped up because certain people actually wanted it to happen. 'There are a lot of tensions and stresses in the band and sometimes we have the most almighty rows, but they just clear the air.'

Irrespective of personal feelings, Queen was big business. During February 1978, they opened their own management company, severing their past relationship with John Reid (Elton John's manager), who had stepped in following their break-up with Trident. Now on their own, Queen started recording once more. Prior to the release of their seventh album, *Jazz,* the tracks 'Bicycle Race' and 'Fat Bottomed Girls' were lifted for single release. Issued during November, the single reached No. 11 in the British chart. As a publicity stunt to help the disc's ascent, the group hired fifty naked girls to race around Wimbledon Stadium, with the intention of using a picture of the naked girls' bums as the single's front cover. Such was the public outcry that certain countries insisted the bare bums were covered by superimposed panties. The album launch party was held, appropriately enough, in New Orleans. With Queen hosting, American record company personnel were invited to share a stunning affair – with topless waitresses, midgets and mud wrestlers among the guests. While on American soil, Queen performed at New York's Madison Square Garden where the audience was treated to semi-naked lady cyclists riding on stage during 'Fat Bottomed Girls', and where the group earned the prestigious Gold Ticket for an audience numbering in excess of 100,000 people.

During 1979 and between sell-out concerts, the quartet was invited to compose the soundtrack for the science fiction movie *Flash Gordon.* Before the album could be issued they embarked upon 'The Crazy Tour' of Britain and performed with other groups at London's Hammersmith Odeon to raise funds for the starving people of Kampuchea. In November, the track 'Crazy Little Thing Called Love' was issued as a single to peak at No. 2 in the British chart. Mercury had composed the title in the bath, and it marked the first time he played rhythm guitar on record.

To start the next decade, *The Game* spawned the singles 'Play the Game' and 'Another One Bites the Dust'. Both reached the British Top Twenty, while the album topped its chart. At the close of 1980, the *Flash Gordon* soundtrack was finally issued, contributing to Queen's 45 million album sales registered worldwide. Queen then embarked upon their first tour of South America, giving them the distinction of being the first group to perform in stadiums instead of theatres. Their debut concert staged in Buenos Aires during February 1981, was followed by five sell-out stadium performances in eight days. On the first two dates at Sao Paulo's Morumbi Stadium in excess of 130,000 people attended: it was the largest paying audience for a band anywhere in the world (to date).

Through the eighties, the quartet continued their high profile on record and stage. The ambitious project of *Greatest Hits* (the album), *Greatest Pix* (the book) and *Greatest Flix* (the video), paved the way for their twelfth album, *Hot Space*. While the group was experimenting in their Montreaux studio, David Bowie arrived unexpectedly. The track 'Under Pressure' resulted from the visit, and when issued as a single during 1981, became a British chart-topper. Mercury: 'That record came about by pure chance . . . We began to dabble on something together. It happened very spontaneously . . . and we were both overjoyed by the result.' So were Queen's record company who had initially insisted it be issued. As there was, obviously, no flipside available, the group's 'Soul Brother' was hastily nominated. Interestingly, Mercury went on to record a trio of tracks with Michael Jackson which remain unreleased (to date). Also during the year, Queen entered the *Guinness Book of Records* as Britain's highest-paid executives. Mercury then started recording a solo album, while Taylor began his second.

In 1984 'Radio Ga Ga', swiped from *The Works* album, was promoted by one of the group's most exciting of videos, directed by David Mallett. While Queen performed the title, members of their fan club acted as the audience, whose raised arms and chanting went on to become an integral form of audience participation in future live concerts. Scenes from the movie *Metropolis* were interspliced with the band's performance. The single became a No. 2 British hit. A £100,000 video accompanying the single 'I Want to Break Free', again swiped from *The Works*, likewise featured fan club members. Queen dressed as characters from ITV's top soap series *Coronation Street:* Mercury wore a tight black mini-skirt and outsized false breasts, brandishing a vacuum around a living room. May, on the other hand, donned curlers in his mass of hair and lolled across a sofa. Taylor said that the video was shot to prove to the public the group could still laugh at itself. It was a British hit.

In 1984, Taylor's solo album, *Strange Frontier,* was issued. A year on, Mercury's debut as a soloist, titled *Mr Bad Guy,* spawned a handful of singles including 'Foolin' Around', 'Living on my Own' and 'Made in Heaven'; the latter pair went on to become runaway hits following his death in 1991. With these projects, rumours of the group disbanding surfaced once more. Mercury: 'There were still lots of styles I wanted to do with Queen but I wasn't able to. This album gave me the chance to use a live orchestra, which I always wanted to do with Queen but never succeeded because Brian does an orchestra with his guitar.' Also during 1985, the group participated in Bob Geldof's Live Aid gala, and following a short hiatus returned to the spotlight with the album *One Vision.*

Queen's next release of note was the album *A Kind of Magic,* which shot straight to the top of the British chart, later remaining in the Top Five for thirteen consecutive weeks. The album's title was lifted for a single to soar to No. 3 in Britain during April 1986, thanks, once again, to an ingenious video. Mercury was portrayed as a magician who, with a sweeping of his black cloak, conjured up animated dancers as quickly as he made them disappear again. The group supported the releases with 'The Magic Tour of Europe', starting at Newcastle's St James' Park football stadium (where all the proceeds were donated to the International Save the Children Fund), and including two sell-out performances at Wembley Stadium where four huge inflatables, identical to the characters on the album artwork, were released into the audience. The concert later became the first simulcast between the British independent radio network and Channel Four television. The final date of the tour was at Knebworth Park, Hertfordshire, during August 1986. Queen arrived at the park in a repainted helicopter featuring the cover of *A Kind of Magic,* to play before an estimated 120,000 fans, bringing the British audience total to approximately 400,000 people. This was to be Queen's last tour. Mercury: 'I don't think a forty-two-year-old man should be running around in his leotard any more. It's not very becoming.' In truth, the singer knew he no longer had the strength to fulfil the gruelling commitments of stage presentation.

To close the decade and despite his failing health, Mercury satisfied a personal ambition by recording with his musical heroine, the opera star Montserrat Caballe. Following their initial meeting in March 1986, Mercury composed 'Barcelona' for her; when recorded as a duet and released as a British single during November 1987, the title peaked at No. 8 in the chart. When released in Spain, 10,000 copies were sold in less than three hours. During October 1988, Mercury and Caballe performed the single at a star-studded concert to launch the city's bid for the 1992 Olympic Games at the Avinguda De Maria Cristina stadium. Unbeknown to the audience, Mercury was suffering from a throat infection and was forced to lipsynch. It was at this point that concern escalated regarding his health; rumours began to grow within the music industry that he was an extremely sick man. Only his close friends new the truth: he had AIDS.

An album titled after the hit single became a British Top Thirty entrant late in 1988, following an extravagant launch party at London's Covent Garden Opera House. Mercury: 'It was fantastic singing with her . . . I have never written anything for opera or the operatic voice before. This really was a dream come true.'

Early in 1991, Queen issued the six-and-a-half-minute single 'Innuendo', followed by the album of the same name. Both discs became British chart-toppers. Shortly after this success, Mercury appeared in what was to be his last promotional video for a future single titled 'These Are the Days of our Lives'. Shot in black and white, the film portrayed a desperately ill lead singer, and was the group's most moving video.

On 23 November 1991, Freddie Mercury announced to the world in a personally written statement that he had AIDS. He died, aged forty-five, the next day at his Kensington home. Mercury's close friend Dave Clark said, 'Freddie felt the time was right to put out the statement because of increasing speculation about his health. It was untrue of people to say he did it then because he expected to die the next day.' Prior to his sudden death, Mercury suffered great pain and had battled against severe pneumonia and blindness as his closest friends, including the Queen membership, Elton John and Kenny Everett (himself later an AIDS victim) paid their last respects. Mercury's long-standing girlfriend Mary Austin was a daily visitor, while his boyfriend of several years standing, Jim Hutton, was by his side constantly. Clark: 'Freddie was very brave and he was determined not to be a burden on anyone . . . [He] fought against his illness with such strength, and he never gave up, hoping and praying that he would be OK.'

When his death was announced, flowers and condolences flooded to his Kensington door from colleagues, friends and fans the world over. Many travelled to Kensington to sit outside Mercury's home, almost disbelieving the news. In a statement, the Queen membership paid their own tribute. 'We have lost the greatest and most beloved member of our family. We feel overwhelming grief that he has gone; sadness that he should be cut down at the height of his creativity, but above all, great pride in the courageous way he lived and died.'

Mercury's funeral, conducted in the Zoroastrian faith, which his parents strictly followed, was held privately at the West London crematorium, in Harrow Road. Following this, Queen announced Mercury had donated all rights to 'Bohemian Rhapsody' to the Terrence Higgins Trust, an AIDS charity that he had supported. EMI Records honoured his wish that the title, with 'These Are the Days of our Lives' as the flipside, should be issued almost immediately. In December 1991, 'Bohemian Rhapsody' once more dominated the British chart, where it stayed for five weeks; the title went on to receive the Best British

Single Award at the Brits Awards ceremony staged at the Hammersmith Odeon, London, while Freddie Mercury posthumously received the Outstanding Contribution to British Music special award. In April 1992, when the title's sales had passed their peak, Queen donated $1.76 million to the Terrence Higgins Trust in accordance with Mercury's wishes.

Prior to Mercury's death, Brian May had been commissioned by a London advertising agency to compose music for a forthcoming campaign for Ford cars. 'Driven by You' was the result, and when released as a single, the title peaked at No. 6 in the British chart during December 1991, while 'Bohemian Rhapsody' sat five places higher. 'Driven by You' went on to win an Ivor Novello Award for the Best Theme from a TV/Radio Commercial. May and Roger Taylor attended the Novello ceremony held at the Grosvenor House Hotel, London, and announced plans for an open-air concert to be held at Wembley Stadium as a celebration of Mercury's life, with all the proceeds going to AIDS Awareness. It was intended that some participating artists would perform Queen material: the response was overwhelming. Elizabeth Taylor, undaunted by the musical mayhem around her, pleaded for AIDS awareness; Liza Minnelli led an all-star choir for 'We Are the Champions'; David Bowie and Annie Lennox sang 'Under Pressure'; Elton John chose 'Bohemian Rhapsody', while George Michael duetted with Lisa Stansfield before singing 'Somebody to Love', backed by the London Community Gospel Choir. In 1993, this latter performance would be released as part of Queen's *Five Live* EP, with proceeds going to Mercury's Trust. Michael's version of 'Somebody to Love' entered the British chart at No. 1 in May, where it stayed for three weeks before becoming a Top Ten hit in over thirty countries.

Titled 'A Concert for Life', the gala was watched by a 72,000-strong audience at Wembley Stadium on 20 April 1992; all tickets had sold within six hours, although no participating artists except for May, Taylor and Deacon had been announced. The concert was broadcast to seventy countries and ultimately watched by over one billion people.

Midway through 1992, the registered charity, the Mercury Phoenix Trust, was founded to distribute the money raised by the concert. A notable American contributors was Fox Television, who broadcast the concert at prime time in America. Together with the royalties from the American reissue of 'Bohemian Rhapsody', in excess of $1 million was raised, which was distributed among American AIDS charities. To date (1997) a further £2.2 million has been raised and distributed to 100 established charities and self-help groups in Britain, Europe and Africa. Further funds were generated from the Christmas release of *The Freddie Mercury Tribute Concert* video.

Naturally, in death Freddie Mercury became a big-selling record name. By demand (or to cash in?), the album *Freddie Mercury* was reissued in November 1992. The track, 'In my Defence', was lifted as the first single, followed by 'The Great Pretender' two months later, while 'Living on my Own' soared to the top of the British chart in spring 1993. The accompanying promotional video was originally banned on the single's first outing; it was filmed at one of the singer's more flamboyant parties, showing numerous music industry figures dressed in drag. It really was a 'spot the boss' exercise! 'Living on my Own' went on to win a posthumous Ivor Novello Award for 1993's International Hit of the Year.

It was estimated that following Mercury's death, Queen albums sold in excess of 20 million copies in Britain, while in America it was one quarter of that figure. Today, the catalogue remains a regular seller for EMI Records.

However, there was one project to come. During November 1995, after four years in the making, Queen's twentieth and last album was issued. Titled *Made in Heaven*, it featured the last material to be recorded by Mercury and the group. When the singer realised his time was short, he requested that the trio give him as many songs as they could for him to record. It was then left to the three members to complete the tracks. The title 'Mother Love' was the very last vocal track to be recorded, while 'A Winter's Tale', a British No. 6 single in December 1995, was Mercury's final composition. Prior to the release of this single, the first title swiped from *Made in Heaven* was 'Heaven for Everyone', a No. 2 British hit. In March 1996, a further track was lifted, titled 'Too Much Love Will Kill You'. The title, probably summing up Mercury's lifestyle, reached the British Top Twenty. A large proportion of the album was recorded in the Montreux studio, where Mercury owned property. The artwork of *Made in Heaven* was the breathtaking view across the lake which Mercury's house overlooked, while the darkened backs of Taylor, May and Deacon stood on one side, with the statue of Mercury with arm raised in the opposite corner. The project was 'Dedicated to the immortal spirit of Freddie Mercury', and was considered by many to be their finest work ever.

In November 1996 the commercial video *Made in Heaven: The Films* was released by Wienerworld. This was the visual companion to the album which, without Mercury, could not be promoted by the traditional video. Instead of relying on dated group footage or computer generated imagery, May and Taylor approached the British Film Institute who, in turn contacted producers Hot Property, to commission new young film directors to demonstrate their skills on the individual album tracks. May said, 'Freddie loved film, and we've no doubt that he would definitely have approved.'

The evolution of *Made in Heaven: The Films* was another notable chapter in the history of Queen. There will be more . . .

'We [agreed] if any of us disappeared, that would be the end of it . . . I don't have any inclination to try to be Queen without Freddie.' – Brian May

'I think the reason [Queen] stayed together so long is that none of us wants to leave . . . As long as people keep buying the music that's OK.' – Freddie Mercury

(Quotes: *Queen Biography* by Jacky Smith; *The Show Must Go On – The Life of Freddie Mercury* by Rick Sky)

ABBA

Mamma Mia

'What is important is that people sit and listen to the music that we play and like what they hear . . . England has been a most difficult market for us.' – Benny Andersson

Prior to winning the 1974 Eurovision Song Contest with 'Waterloo', their first British chart-topper that May, Abba had agreed to tour Sweden's 'folk parks' in July. Of necessity, however, all future schedules had to be reorganised and as the 'folk park' project would take a month to prepare, and a further month to honour, Abba had little choice but to cancel the tour. At once, the quartet was publicly attacked by the organisers and subsequently the media, exemplified by statements like, 'This is, without question, the ugliest betrayal I have experienced in my many years in this business . . . and now I am ridiculed by a group of Swedish amateurs, assuredly forgotten within one year,' and 'Abba's decision is terribly immoral. Abba has won an important international music competition with the support of the Swedish people. Now they abandon their home audience completely to concentrate on the foreign markets.' To placate fiery tempers, the group hastily announced details of their debut European tour which included dates in Sweden.

Hot on the heels of the 'Waterloo' single the group's album bearing the single's name was issued, and Abba embarked upon a further British promotional trip. The single 'Honey Honey' was released as the chart-topper's follow-up single to become a European hit only. The title by-passed Britain, much to the dismay of their record company, CBS Records.

However, the hiccup was quickly quelled, when, during June, a re-mixed version of 'Ring Ring' was released in Britain. The single's chart progress, however, was severely hampered by an industrial action at BBC TV which included the music show *Top of the Pops* and Abba's subsequent performance of the single. Eventually, 'Ring Ring' moved slowly to stall in the British Top Forty, leaving the group fair game for the media, who spared no punches in predicting their immediate downfall as 'one-hit wonders'. Indeed, at the time, this possibility was likely.

Abba next visited America for the first time, again as a promotional ploy. The general media consensus appeared to be that predicated by their British counterparts – 'one-hit wonders'. Upon their return to Sweden, Agnetha Faltskog and Anni-Frid Lyngstad attended vocal and dance lessons to tighten their stage routines, which to date were pretty disorganised, leaving Bjorn Ulvaeus and Benny Andersson to produce a pair of albums for Polar Music acts.

With the 1974 European tour looming, Abba recruited tried and tested musicians to support them on stage; the Abba sound had to be recreated if the tour was to be successful. The group next chose their costumes – vividly coloured or sparkling skin-tight suits of varying styles. Let's face it, Abba would never win any awards for stage clothes!

The tour was to cover Denmark, West Germany, Austria, Switzerland and Britain. However, the final stage of the tour was cancelled; Britain did not consider Abba to be a musical force of longevity and promoters were dubious whether to chance financing a week's trek. Instead, the quartet moved the dates to Norway, finishing in Sweden. The entire tour was an unequalled success, inspiring Andersson and Ulvaeus to prepare for their next album. Meanwhile, Faltskog recorded her sixth and last solo album, *Elva Kninnor I Ett Has,* which included her version of the future Abba track 'SOS'; and Lyngstad completed her album *Ensam,* featuring the track 'Fernando', a further Abba single.

The group's eponymous album was issued first in their home country, where advance orders were in excess of 100,000 copies, with future sales passing the 450,000 mark, earning Abba the distinction of being Sweden's biggest-selling unit ever. Prior to the album's British release, the single 'I Do, I Do, I Do, I Do, I Do' struggled for life. CBS Records' promotional budget remained unimpressive when compared to other chart-topping acts – perhaps the record company needed assurance that Abba was worth further investment. Whatever the reason, 'I Do, I Do, I Do, I Do, I Do' was afforded relatively low-key promotion that included record company personnel, dressed in the wedding attire of top hat and tails, delivering the singles to radio stations. Rather passé, even for the seventies! Like 'Ring Ring' a year earlier, the title floundered in the Top Forty during July 1975. Elsewhere, the disc topped charts!

Despite the group nursing further blows, the poor-selling album *Abba* received several excellent media reviews. Indeed, this project was stylishly presented and produced, although one critic felt otherwise: 'Stick to singles, Abba, you are just a mediocre album band.'

By now, Abba's popularity in Europe had catapulted beyond the expectations of their manager, Stig Anderson, particularly when a massive interest was noted from Eastern Europe, where record companies were government-owned, which meant each company had a yearly budget to pay for Western music imports. In 1975, Poland's entire import budget was spent on Abba albums, while Russia imported 25,000 albums, which was a figure much below public demand. Hence, Abba albums were costly purchases on both countries' black markets.

Then there was Britain. During September 1975, the group issued the 'SOS' single, which to all intents and purposes would be a lifeline if they were to succeed. Thankfully the title dissipated any fears of a jinx by soaring to No. 6 in the chart. Ulvaeus: 'We thought "SOS" would make a very good single . . . would give our fans some sort of clue as to what musical direction we're heading for.' Correct. The single topped most European charts, and reached No. 10 in America, prompting a further promotional visit by the group. During their stay, they appeared on several television shows, including the *Mike Douglas Show*, the *Merv Griffin Show* and the *Dinah Shore Show*, when the hostess asked if Andersson and Lyngstad would like to get married on her show. The response was short: 'We'll get married when we have the time and in a place we want to!'

Touring took its toll on Faltskog, who openly admitted she pined for her home life, and was not a champagne party goer like the rest of the group, preferring to return to the seclusion of her hotel room when a day's work was completed. The blonde singer also detested flying and this dislike would get worse, instead of better, the more the group had to travel.

To capitalise on the British success of 'SOS', its follow-up single was hastily issued to soar to the top of the chart during January 1976. Titled 'Mamma Mia', it held the top spot for two weeks. One-hit wonders no more!

Once again, the group and the British media clashed. Ulvaeus, in particular, felt the press remained uncertain and somewhat negative regarding their ability as musicians, but it was Andersson who said, 'We didn't get the image we deserved. Because we won Eurovision we got the image that goes with [that] and it's not really correct . . . We thought that it was extremely difficult to reach the English but we believe so much in ourselves, we have so much self-confidence, that we agreed sooner or later it was bound to happen in England.' It must have been Andersson's modesty that appealed to the British journalists! And there was more to come, much more.

Also see: 'Waterloo', May 1974; 'Dancing Queen', September 1976; 'Knowing Me Knowing You,' April 1977; 'The Name of the Game', November 1977; 'Take a Chance on Me', March 1978

(Quotes: Abba – *The Music Still Goes On: The Complete Story* by Paul Snaith)

<hr>

February 1976

THE FOUR SEASONS

December '63 (Oh What a Night)

'The most important thing we wanted to establish was a sound that would be uniquely ours, and as soon as you heard the radio, you would know who you were listening to,' Frankie Valli told author Joe Smith. The Four Seasons went on to sell approximately 86 million discs during their career. So, I guess the sound was unique enough.

Born Francis Castelluccio in Newark, New Jersey, on 3 May 1937, Frankie Valli first started singing at school. During this period he was spotted by Texas Jean Valley, a noted country singer, who oversaw the recording of the youngster's first disc, 'My Mother's Eyes', released by the Corona label, a subsidiary of Mercury Records. The title was credited to Frank Valley and The Travellers, while the publicity handouts wrongly enthused that Frank was Texas's younger brother. The follow-up single titled 'Somebody Else Took Her Home' marked the last from 'the group'.

Valli joined The Variety Trio, befriending Nick DeVito and his brother Tommy, who was born in Montclair, New Jersey on 19 June 1936. In time, the unit became The Variatones, a draw on the New Jersey club circuit. In 1956, prior to releasing their debut single titled '(You're the) Apple of my Eye' via RCA Records, the group was renamed The Four Lovers. Like their recording career, The Four Lovers were short-lived.

In 1958 Valli, using the pseudonym Frank Tyler, issued the 'I Go Ape' single on Okeh Records as a solo artist, before returning to The Four Lovers, now known as Frank Valle and The Romans. As such they went on to record the single 'Come St Bella' for the Cindy record label. Also in 1959, another group from New Jersey, called The Royal Teens, had recently enjoyed a No. 3 American hit with the single 'Short Shorts'. The membership of that group included Bob Gaudio, born in the

Bronx on 17 November 1942, and when they were booked to appear on a Baltimore television programme, their co-stars were Frank Valle and The Romans. This marked the first meeting of Valli and Gaudio; a significant step for the future, although it would be a further two years before their careers crossed once more, when Gaudio auditioned for the vacant keyboardist position in The Romans.

A further line-up change in The Romans led to the membership of the group that was to become The Four Seasons, namely, Frankie Valli, Bob Gaudio, Tommy DeVito and Nick Massi, born Nicholas Macioci in Newark, on 19 September 1935. This group became back-up vocalists for numerous acts who worked with record producer Bob Crewe, including Bobby Darin and Freddy Cannon. In between studio sessions for others, the quartet performed in local nightclubs, building up an audience following. They later auditioned for a permanent singing spot in the cocktail lounge of a bowling alley in New Jersey, but were rejected. Gaudio told *Billboard* magazine, 'We figured we'll come out of this with something, so we took the name of the bowling alley. It was called The Four Seasons.'

Using their new name, the group recorded 'Bermuda', a title associated with The Bell Sisters. Bob Crewe licensed the track to Gone Records, owned by George Goldner, and in 1961 it was issued as The Four Seasons' debut single. It bombed. Crewe then took five new Four Seasons' tracks to the NARM Convention in Miami, where he played them to selected record company executives. He told Joe Smith, 'The bidding started, and we wound up making a deal with Ewart Abner at Vee Jay. On paper, it was one of the largest deals that had ever been made on a record, sixteen cents a record.' The deal eventually turned sour, but in 1962, Crewe was delighted. This recording contract was the turning point for The Four Seasons who, by now, were a self-contained unit, encompassing their own composers and producer. Gaudio: 'Some songs come quickly and some songs take forever. "Sherry" was a quickie. It took fifteen minutes.' Penned by him, produced by Bob Crewe, 'Sherry', which began its life as 'Terry', was issued as a single during September 1962 to storm up the American chart to the top. The most endearing feature of this track was Frankie Valli's distinctive falsetto voice, part of his three-octave tenor range. Sales were boosted when the group performed on *American Bandstand,* the most illustrious of music shows, hosted by Dick Clark. That solitary appearance reputedly generated in excess of 170,000 sales in advance orders. Sales eventually soared beyond two million. When issued in Britain, 'Sherry' became The Four Seasons' debut hit in October 1962, via the Stateside label, when it peaked in the Top Ten.

The follow-up to the American chart-topper was once again from the same writer/producer couple; titled 'Big Girls Don't Cry', it took five weeks for the new single to replace 'Sherry' at the top of the chart. Incidentally, both titles were recorded at the same session; the group simply tossed a coin to determine which track was issued first. The title of the song was, apparently, taken from the lips of Clark Gable in an obscure movie which both Crewe and Gaudio are now hard-pushed to remember. When released in Britain, 'Big Girls Don't Cry' peaked at No. 13 during February 1963. Gaudio: 'I didn't feel it was the freshest follow-up. After the success of "Sherry", we had to follow it with something vaguely similar. The harmonies were structured differently, a little bigger.' Prior to their second British hit, The Four Seasons released their first album, *Sherry and 11 Others* (!), together with a Christmas album, *The Four Seasons Greetings*.

In America, the quartet was constantly in demand; their popularity stunned them and their record company. Touring was a priority, leaving little time for Crewe and Gaudio to collaborate. The Four Seasons' third consecutive American chart-topper was written and recorded prior to their big success. Titled 'Walk Like a Man', the single dominated the chart during March 1963; in Britain, the title faltered in the Top Twenty. This single made The Four Seasons the most successful recording unit in America in 1962–63.

Finding the appropriate follow-up was difficult; the group had too many commitments. Eventually, a cover version of Fats Domino's 1955 classic 'Ain't that a Shame' was issued in America in May 1963. The title climbed to No. 22, ending The Four Seasons' chart-topping run. It struggled to No. 38 in Britain in July. A month on, the imaginatively titled album *Ain't that a Shame and 11 Others* was issued, from which the track 'Candy Girl' was swiped for single release. Written by Larry Santos this time, it fared much better than its predecessor to peak at No. 3 in America.

As so often happens when a recording act immediately produces mega-million sales, their record company adopts a greedy attitude, and this, reputedly, was the case with Vee Jay and The Four Seasons. A dispute over unpaid royalties led to contractual difficulties, resulting in the group withholding new material. It later transpired that Vee Jay had cash flow problems. The legal wrangle was not helped when the executive responsible for signing them, Ewart Abner, left the company; instead, the move added impetus to the dispute that went on until December 1963. Frankie Valli told Joe Smith that despite the trio of

American chart-toppers with Vee Jay, 'there was very little money. Maybe an accumulation of $30,000. Later on, we found out that there was a lot more money, but we never saw any of it.' And further: 'It's frustrating knowing you had earned a certain amount of money, sold a certain amount of records, and now you're not going to get paid for it. Someone was cheating us . . .'

Despite the hassles, The Four Seasons recorded 'Dawn (Go Away)', which they released via their new recording deal with Mercury Records, based in Chicago. The group's product was issued on the Philips label in Britain. The title was another American million-seller, reaching No. 3 in February 1964, while British sales were negligible. The remainder of the year saw Mercury Records and Vee Jay Records fighting for chart positions, while The Four Seasons returned to the recording studio to recharge their musical batteries. Amidst the battle of the record companies, Mercury released the Crewe/Gaudio composition 'Rag Doll'. The title soared to the top of the American chart during the July, reaching No. 2 in Britain, the group's highest placing to date. Gaudio was inspired to pen this track when a young girl cleaned his car windows as he stopped for a red light. At first he thought she was a boy because of the clothes she wore, then when he wanted to pay her he had no cash, only a $5 bill. Gaudio told *Billboard* magazine, 'She just stood there with the bill in her hand . . . standing in disbelief in the middle of the street with the five dollars. And that whole image stayed with me, a rag doll was what she looked like.'

Through the remainder of 1964 and into 1965, The Four Seasons continued to enjoy American success, although no singles hit the Top Ten. 'Bye Bye Baby (Baby Goodbye)' peaked the highest at No. 12. The title went on to become a British chart-topper, not for The Four Seasons, but for the young Bay City Rollers during March 1975.

Following the release of the 'Girl Come Running' single during August 1965, Nick Massi departed from the group to work full-time behind scenes. His temporary replacement was Charles Callelo, before Joe Long joined permanently. Before the year closed, The Four Seasons re-established themselves as Top Three American sellers with the vibrant 'Let's Hang On', which reached No. 4 in Britain. Chasing this track up the American listing was an obscure disc credited to Wonder Who. Titled 'Don't Think Twice, It's Alright', it was a cover version of the Bob Dylan classic. Wonder Who were The Four Seasons. 'Don't Think Twice, It's Alright' was intended for an album track, but as the result held such a commercial slant, the group decided to release it immediately. A pseudonym was used to avoid a conflict of sales with

'Let's Hang On'. With renewed success came the downside. The group was plagued by backstage arguments. Valli: 'It's strange, but when people are struggling for success together, it's amazing how close you become . . . And then, as soon as success comes, everybody needs his own limousine, everybody wants his own suite in a different hotel. I think it's sad that people drift away from each other.'

Early in 1966, Frankie Valli took the (natural) step and released his debut solo single, titled '(You're Gonna) Hurt Yourself', which only reached the Top Forty. During March, the group issued 'Working my Way Back to You', a Top Ten American hit, which made the Top Fifty in Britain. In 1980, incidentally, The Detroit Spinners took their version to the top of the British chart. Four further singles were issued before 1966 closed, namely 'Opus 17 (Don't You Worry 'bout Me)' and 'I've Got You under my Skin' from The Four Seasons; 'On the Good Ship Lollipop' by Wonder Who; and the second Valli solo outing, titled 'The Proud One'.

For the remainder of the decade, the group and Frankie Valli were regular American chart names. Indeed, Valli enjoyed his first million-seller with 'Can't Take my Eyes off You', which soared to No. 2. Meantime, the group members became involved in individual projects; for instance, Gaudio opened his own Gazette label with distribution via CBS Records.

Early in the seventies, Tommy DeVito left the line-up through illness, to be replaced by Bob Grimm. With the addition of a drummer, The Four Seasons embarked upon a British tour. To coincide with the visit, the 1966 title 'You're Ready Now' was issued. This disc had for some time been adopted by followers of the Northern Soul circuit, having the sharp-edged, booty sound, typical of the genre. When the single was officially issued, it shot to No. 11 in the British chart during February 1971. But then the title no longer held that valuable credibility to warrant the cult following. The Four Seasons enjoyed commercial success; 'You're Ready Now' lost its home.

In 1972 The Four Seasons switched record companies once more to Motown, on the understanding that the company founder Berry Gordy would work with them. It transpired he was too involved with Diana Ross's movie *Lady Sings the Blues* to do this. Nonetheless, the group recorded their solitary album *Chameleon* on Motown's newly formed Mowest label. Sales were poor, but critics glowed in praise. The Four Seasons then moved to the Motown label proper, where once again American success eluded them. Not so in Britain. Motown/EMI Records rereleased 'The Night' in response to pressure from nightclub punters. The title soared to No. 7 in the chart in 1975; whereupon Valli capitalised on the success by releasing 'Swearin' to God': a Top Forty hit, reaching No. 6 in America.

Prior to this release, Valli had recorded the Bob Crewe/Kenny Nolan composition 'My Eyes Adored You' for Motown. Unsure how to promote the title, Motown canned it for approximately two years. When The Four Seasons' recording contract with the company expired, Valli purchased 'My Eyes Adored You' for a reputed $4,000. The singer recouped that figure and more when the single became an American chart-topper in March 1975 via Private Stock Records, heralding both artist and company's first No. 1.

With the start of 1976, The Four Seasons' membership read Don Ciccone and John Paiva, guitarists; Gerry Polci, drummer; Lee Shapiro, keyboardist, and the fifth member Frankie Valli! It was this line-up that recorded 'December '63 (Oh What a Night)', originally titled 'December '33', telling the tale of prohibition thirty years earlier. Written by Bob Gaudio and his future wife, Judy Parker, they admitted the track's lyrics were 'pretty bizarre'. Gaudio told *Billboard* magazine, 'Judy was never too happy with the lyric and Frankie was not overwhelmed. We cut the track, but we were planning on dropping it.' Luckily, the couple reworked the song with superb results. 'December '63 (Oh What a Night)' topped the British chart for two weeks during February 1976. In March 1976, the single also dominated the American chart, holding the top spot for three weeks.

Two months after their British success, The Four (Five) Seasons toured Britain, to pave the way for Valli's solo release 'Fallen Angel' and the group's magnificent 'Silver Star'. Before 1976 closed, 'We Can Work It Out', recorded for the movie soundtrack *All This and World War II*, faltered in the British Top Forty.

The following year, the group enjoyed a pair of semi-hits with 'Rhapsody' and 'Down the Hall'; whereupon Valli announced his departure from the group to concentrate fully on his solo career. It was a wise move. In August 1978, he scooped the American No. 1 spot with 'Grease', swiped from the soundtrack of the movie starring John Travolta and Olivia Newton-John. The soundtrack itself went on to sell an estimated 24 million copies, establishing it as runner-up to *Saturday Night Fever*, the top-selling soundtrack album, also featuring Travolta.

To start the new decade, The Four Seasons regrouped without Valli to tour America. Valli had, by this time, secured a recording contract with Warner Brothers, where his recordings were spasmodic because for some years he had suffered from otosclerosis, a rare disease that causes deafness. To enable him to perform, Valli had memorised the group's act sufficiently to enable him to sing without actually hearing the music. And nobody was the wiser. Early in the eighties, the singer underwent the last of three ear operations to regain his hearing. For the first time in a long, silent age, Valli could hear the group performing and his own voice! His wife Mary-Ann told *Billboard* magazine, 'Those years were a terrible strain for Frankie. For so long he missed all the little sounds we take for granted . . . When fans would come up to him, he wouldn't even know they were there.'

In the late eighties and early nineties, countless compilations were issued. *The 20 Greatest Hits* released by Telstar, and *25th Anniversary Collection* via Rhino Records are good examples. Frankie Valli, supported by The Four Seasons of varying memberships, continued touring America, while in 1991, the dance single 'Grease Megamix' featuring John Travolta, Olivia Newton-John and Valli soared to No. 3 in Britain. A year on, the group embarked upon a lengthy British tour, while in 1993 Valli was presented with a gold disc for British sales of *The Very Best of Frankie Valli and The Four Seasons*.

A further remix of the 1973 chart-topper 'December '63 (Oh What a Night)' soared into the American Top Twenty during 1994, following The Four Seasons' induction into the Rock 'n' Roll Hall of Fame; while, a year on, Gaudio and Crewe were honoured by the Songwriters Hall of Fame. There's probably more to come . . .

(Quotes: *Off the Record* by Joe Smith)

March 1976

TINA CHARLES

I Love to Love (but my Baby Loves to Dance)

She may have stood on the small side but Tina Charles could pack a vocal punch along with the best of 'em. British dance music was more exact than the sound emanating from America. It went straight to the point; the beat tended to be sharper, the lyrics, well, who listened to them anyway? For heaven's sake, this was music for dancing.

Miss Charles started her professional career as a member of the vocal instrumental group 5000 Volts, who enjoyed a Top Five British hit with 'I'm on Fire' in September 1975. Charles then moved on to work with

Indian record producer Biddu, who had recently brushed with chart success with his orchestra and the theme from the movie *Summer of '42*.

'I Love to Love (but my Baby Loves to Dance)', written by James Bolden and Jack Robinson, and issued by CBS Records, was the result of her first collaboration with Biddu. A blinding, high-speed dance track, typical of British disco, it soared to the top of the chart in March 1976, a position it held for three weeks. It was Charles's first and Biddu's second chart-topper (his first was Carl Douglas's 'Kung Fu Fighting' in October 1974). A month after Charles's No. 1 achievement, Biddu's orchestra enjoyed a second British hit with 'Rain Forest'.

Tina Charles went on to enjoy three further hits during 1976, namely 'Love Me Like a Lover', which remarkably stalled at No. 28 in the British chart, 'Dance Little Lady Dance' and 'Dr Love', both Top Ten successes and rightly so. Her former group 5000 Volts, meantime, scored a second Top Ten hit with 'Dr Kiss Kiss'.

However, the Charles/Biddu type of disco music had its limitations, and by 1977 Charles was feeling the pinch. She managed two Top Thirty hits – 'Rendezvous' and 'Love Bug-Sweets for my Sweets' – but the following year became her swansong with 'I'll Go Where your Music Takes Me'.

The singer may have bowed out of the music business but her chart-topper wasn't so easy to kill. In 1986, a remixed version, shortened in title to 'I Love to Love' was issued by the Disco Mix Club to become a Top Seventy hit.

The nostalgia circuit sustained Tina Charles's career for a time but her nineties whereabouts are uncertain.

April/May 1976

BROTHERHOOD OF MAN

Save your Kisses for Me

Sweden had Abba; Britain had Brotherhood of Man: both featured mixed doubles, but that was where the real similarity ended. Many believed the British quartet copied Abba so diligently that if the Swedish outfit coughed on record, the British lookalikes would do the same but more so! Yep, Brotherhood of Man became Abba clones from the time they were chosen to represent Britain in the Eurovision Song Contest.

269

They were formed in London by composer Tony Hillier during the late sixties, and lead singer Tony Burrows was late of several pop groups like Edison Lighthouse and The Flower Pot Men. Both enjoyed charting singles with 'Love Grows (Where my Rosemary Goes)' in 1970 and 'Let's Go to San Francisco' in 1967; both were pure commercial sounds.

Signed to the Deram label, the two male/two female line-up of Brotherhood of Man first reached the British chart with 'United We Stand', a Top Ten hit during February 1970. It was a strong, melodic track which was adopted as the gay liberation anthem of the seventies, particularly in America, where it was elevated to a song of defiance against mounting persecution during the early part of the decade. It was a shame that this single of standing was followed by a damp squid called 'Where Are You Going to my Love', a Top Thirty hit during 1970. It marked the quartet's last hit for six years. Nonetheless, Brotherhood of Man continued to work on the club circuit using their limited material and surviving membership changes, until they were chosen to represent Britain in the 1976 Eurovision Song Contest.

The song that received most public votes was the Tony Hillier/Martin Lee/Lee Sheridan composition 'Save your Kisses for Me'. It typified the (mediocre?) standard of the Eurovision Song Contest, telling a sickly tale of a young girl's father going to work and leaving her alone all day. Following Abba's success in 1974 with 'Waterloo', the British quartet appeared with the same double line-up headed by Lee Sheridan and Martin Lee. They also wore bright colours and adopted a simple foot-lifting routine to complement the bouncing music. Predictably, 'Save your Kisses for Me' romped home to become the 1976 winner with the biggest margin in the Contest's history. It then soared to No. 1 in most European countries including Britain where, during April 1976, it dominated the No. 1 position for six weeks. The Americans also supported the song by pushing it into the Top Fifty.

Remarkably, the follow-up, 'My Sweet Rosalie', faltered in the British Top Thirty in June 1976. Rumours of the contest winners' curse began spreading before the Brotherhood of Man fought back. Early in 1977 and following the release of 'Oh Boy (the Mood I'm in)', which reached the Top Ten, the quartet enjoyed their second British chart-topper with 'Angelo', which told of two Mexican lovers running away to die on a beach! Once again written by the composing trio Hillier/Lee/Sheridan, and once more inspired by Abba (this time their 1976 single 'Fernando'), Brotherhood of Man topped the British chart. Their next single was likewise a chart-topper – it was the third penned by the composing trio. Titled 'Figaro', it peaked at No. 1 in the British chart early in 1978, and ended the group's run of Top Five singles.

Two further discs were issued during 1978, namely, 'Beautiful Lover' and 'Middle of the Night', Top Twenty and Top Fifty entrants respectively. To all intents and purposes, Brotherhood of Man were no longer a main attraction, but due to their recent success they had no problem in earning a lucrative living on the nightclub circuit. They had one more stab at the British chart in 1982 with 'Lightning Flash', released by EMI Records. It stalled in the lower section of the listing.

It doesn't need a crystal ball to realise that Brotherhood of Man would have enjoyed longevity if Abba had remained within the boundaries of Sweden and had not stomped across Europe into Britain. Once this quartet had secured its foothold, no other double line-up group stood a chance. Abba simply took no prisoners!

June 1976

THE REAL THING

You to Me Are Everything

'We were lucky to stumble on two good and untapped new writers who were able to write our type of material but with a more commercial flavour to it. It's a great combination.' – Ray Lake

The excitement generated by The Beatles and the like rubbed off on up-and-coming Merseyside groups, who were inspired by them and encouraged by their success. One such group was The Chants who, despite receiving critical acclaim with their handful of singles, just failed to make the grade. Eventually, they disbanded whereupon lead singer, Eddie Amoo, formed The Real Thing with his brother Chris, Ray Lake and Dave Smith. Recorded success was still in the far distance as the group worked steadily in the Northern clubs, establishing a following. Lake said at the time, 'It's certainly been tough surviving . . . soul bands that live here all the time weren't getting the kind of money they were worth.' Much of this, he stressed, stemmed from British black groups emulating their American counterparts on stage, without an original composition or dance routine on offer. The Real Thing had fallen into this category. 'We always have been categorised as a British band playing American music and the Americans were able to do it so much better.

They were past-masters at the old dance routines and the satin suits, so gradually British groups realised that if they were to succeed properly, they would have to become original.'

The Real Thing appeared on the ITV talent show *Opportunity Knocks*, hosted by Hughie Green, and came to the attention of Tony Hall, former Radio Luxembourg DJ. He became their manager and secured a recording deal with Pye Records whereupon they went into the studios with producer Ken Gold who had written 'You to Me Are Everything' with Mickey Deene. This track became The Real Thing's debut single, and much to the surprise of everyone concerned, it raced to the top of the British chart in June 1976, where it stayed for three weeks. In America, though, it was a different story because two other versions of the song were issued at the same time as The Real Thing's interpretation. Chaos ensued. Lake: 'I think the problem lay with the song, we had little or nothing to do with it. We certainly were not in any kind of position to control it and that's how The Broadway and Revelation versions came about.' At first the group was disheartened that American exclusivity was denied to them but, as Lake said, 'We bucked up because we realised that our version was the best and it pleased us to have American groups covering us. It certainly makes up for the amount of times that it's happened the other way around.' However, it meant The Real Thing suffered with split record sales despite their version outselling those by the American acts.

'Can't Get By without You', in much the same mellow mood as the chart-topper, soared to No. 2 in the British chart in September 1976. American sales were good but not sufficient to gain significant chart status. During 1977 the quartet reached the British chart twice, first in February with 'You'll Never Know What You're Missing', a Top Twenty hit, and again in July with 'Love's Such a Wonderful Thing', which reached the Top Forty. The next year, there were three entrants, namely 'Let's Go Disco', and 'Rainin' through my Sunshine', both Top Forty hits, while 'Whenever You Want my Love' reached the Top Twenty.

With these big-selling singles to their credit, The Real Thing noticed a difference in their audiences. Lake: 'We have reached the point where we sing our own songs on stage and people are loving it. It's great to know now that [they] come to see The Real Thing and not a carbon copy of the Four Tops or The Temptations.'

As the eighties loomed, disco music was altering yet again, and groups like The Real Thing had to go with the changing flow. Their first single in 1979 reflected that. Titled 'Can You Feel the Force', it bore the hallmark of the *Star Wars* movie which transported it into the Top Five region, although the follow-up, 'Boogie Down (Get Funky Now)' stalled in the Top Forty.

A change of record company from Pye to Calibre at the end of 1979 produced their first single of the eighties, titled 'She's a Groovy Freak', which struggled into the Top Sixty much to the group's dismay. It was their last British hit for six years.

The Real Thing's return to the chart was thanks to a pair of remixed reissues, released by PRT Records. In March 1986, 'You to Me Are Everything (The Decade Remix 76–86)' soared into the Top Five, then re-entered during June to reach the Top Eighty. The second reissue, 'Can't Get By without You (The Second Decade Remix)' went on to become a No. 6 hit in May.

As these titles attracted new record buyers, 'Can You Feel the Force ('86 Remix)' followed in August 1986 and reached the Top Thirty, while the group itself recorded a new track titled 'Straight to the Heart', released by Jive Records before 1986 closed. It faltered around the Top Seventy; record buyers obviously preferred the group's seventies material!

Nonetheless, during the heady heights of their career, The Real Thing proved they were a reliable unit, musically versatile and lacking only in original material. Not many can say that.

Also No. 1 in June 1976: 'No Charge' by J.J. Barrie; 'Combine Harvester (Brand New Key)' by The Wurzels

July 1976

DEMIS ROUSSOS

The Roussos Phenomenon

He wore long flowing gowns and possessed the most unusual of squeaky voices, yet was hailed as a sex symbol by European women. His immense (pun) popularity also led to him becoming a favourite with impressionists, who, of course, went to great lengths to exaggerate his persona. Ah, the price of fame!

Roussos was born into a musical family in Alexandria, Egypt, on 15 June 1947. His mother was a singer, his father a classical guitarist. While he was studying at an Athens college, Roussos learned to play a variety of instruments that included the organ, double bass and trumpet.

During 1963 he formed the group titled Aphrodite's Child, who five years later enjoyed a Top Thirty British hit with 'Rain and Tears'. The single went on to sell in excess of one million copies. Following this success, Roussos embarked upon a solo career which, after a sluggish start, produced his first European hit album titled 'Forever and Ever'. As a soloist, his debut British hit was 'Happy to Be on an Island in the Sun' released via Philips Records. The single soared into the Top Five during November 1975. The big-selling *Souvenirs* album quickly followed. Despite his success, Roussos was unable to sustain his chart status as the single's follow-up, 'Can't Say How Much I Love You', faltered in the British Top Forty during February 1976. It appeared Roussos was nothing more than a one-hit wonder.

However, he quickly proved the pundits wrong by re-emerging stronger than before with a multi-tracked single titled 'The Roussos Phenomenon'. Featuring the titles 'Forever and Ever', 'Sing an Ode to Love', 'So Dreamy' and 'My Friend the Wind', it became the first extended play (EP) single to top the British chart, in July 1976. If it came to that, Roussos was also the first act of Greek origin to earn the distinction of being a British chart-topper.

The follow-up single, 'When Forever Has Gone', cemented his continuing success by peaking at No. 2 in October, and, of course, exemplified passion for romance which attracted his huge female following. Critics argued it was difficult to believe that such an unlikely man should command this ardent devotion, but he did. So much so that he was elevated to an international sex symbol, which presumably had little to do with his flowing katfan and profusion of hair!

Roussos was to enjoy two further British hits during 1977 but both faltered in the Top Forty, namely 'Because' in March and the 'Kyrila' multi-tracked single three months later.

The recorded phenomenon may have passed, but his concerts remain filled to capacity with adoring females. Looks aren't everything, are they?

August 1976

ELTON JOHN AND KIKI DEE

Don't Go Breaking my Heart

'I guess I want to be remembered as a good musician and a good writer of good songs . . .' – Elton John

Elton John was born Reginald Kenneth Dwight in his grandparents' house in Pinner Hill Road, Pinner, Middlesex, on 25 March 1947 to Sheila and Stanley. His father was a flight-lieutenant and was often away from the family home. John's relationship with his father was abysmal, so much so that he was frightened of his senior. The young boy was not allowed to play like other children: only when his parents later divorced was he able to recapture his youth, and, with his mother's encouragement, pursue his love of music.

Inspired by the likes of Winifred Atwell, John took piano lessons at the age of four. In his fourth year at the Pinner County Grammar School he joined the local group called The Covettes as pianist to play in church halls and local clubs. When the group disbanded, Bluesology was formed, again with John as keyboardist. Their debut professional date was at the Northwood Hills Hotel, in London.

Through his cousin, John secured a position in the warehouse of Mills Music, situated in the heart of London's musicland. The job was poorly paid, yet it introduced John to the music business proper. During 1965, the youngster tested his composing pen with 'Come Back Baby', recorded by Bluesology, and released by Fontana Records during July. A year on, the group issued the 'Mr Frantic' single. Both titles were poor sellers. However, between releases, Bluesology was added to the books of agent Roy Tempest; through him the unit supported visiting American R. & B. acts that included Wilson Pickett, Doris Troy and Patti LaBelle and the Blue Belles. One particular tour was supporting Billy Stewart, which proved to be a nightmare to John, as he told author Philip Norman: 'We started off in the afternoon, playing an American servicemen's club in Lancaster Gate; finished that at four, raced up to Birmingham . . . then came back to London and played The Cue Club in Praed Street the same night.' Not only did John's unit perform, but they had to install and dismantle their equipment, transferring it from stage to van.

As Bluesology grew in status, British blues singer, Long John Baldry, persuaded them to work with him during late 1966 and the membership expanded to nine. Known as the John Baldry Show, they moved onto the cabaret circuit. A year on, John's frustration at his musical limitations reached bursting point; he pined to be a soloist. Answering a newspaper advertisement, he auditioned for Liberty Records, without success. Nonetheless, record company executive Ray Williams gave him a set of lyrics written by Bernie Taupin, born in Lancashire, to work on. This led to approximately twenty tracks being composed by correspondence between the two youngsters, until they

275

met at Dick James's House. The John and Taupin partnership held such potential that they signed a publishing contract with The Hollies' company, Gralto, part of Dick James Music, and worked together from John's family home. When Long John Baldry released the single 'Let the Heartaches Begin' during late 1967, John and Taupin's composition 'Lord You Made the Night Too Long' was the B-side, heralding the partnership's first British chart-topper, although, of course, it's debatable how many people actually listened to it.

Early in 1968, John and Taupin signed as staff writers to Dick James Music, and three months into the deal, John released his debut solo outing on the This Record Company label, via Philips Records. Titled 'I've Been Loving You Too Long', produced by Caleb Quaye, late of the Baldry Show, it bombed.

In 1969, John released 'Lady Samantha', his last single via Philips Records; another bomber. Next on the schedule for Elton John's rise to stardom was his composition with Taupin, 'I Can't Go On Living without You', one of the British entries for the 1969 Eurovision Song Contest. Sung by Lulu on her BBC TV variety show, the title came last; the voting public much preferred the idiotic 'Boom Bang a Bang'. Switching to DJM Records, John's debut single 'It's Me That You Need' was issued during May 1969. Once more, the title bombed, leaving John no option but to move into session singing to earn a living.

His 'Border Song' single welcomed the new decade; another British bomber, while in America, the title struggled into the Top One Hundred. This entrant encouraged the singer to debut in America as support act to David Ackles at the Los Angeles' Troubadour. 'Border Song' was extracted from the album *Elton John,* produced by Gus Dudgeon, which went on to soar into the American Top Five late in 1970 and reached the Top Ten in Britain during early 1971. It was this success that spurred him to embark upon a serious Stateside tour that included dates in New York. John told Joe Smith, 'I think from 1970 onward when I became Elton John, my life changed. I became much happier as a person when I took on Elton John. It became my real name and I could do things I wanted.'

At this juncture, the singer/writer had secured his own permanent group – Dee Murray, Nigel Olsson and Caleb Quaye – with Davey Johnstone completing the membership a year later. However, in 1971, John released his album *Tumbleweed Connection,* featuring his boyhood singing heroine, Dusty Springfield, as a support singer, thereby realising a fantasy ambition. The album soared into the British and American Top Ten, likewise the lifted single. With John's career now on the upward path, Dick James approached John Reid, then Tamla Motown's product manager working from EMI Records' headquarters, to become the singer's manager. The partnership was still current in 1997, at the time of writing.

In 1972, Elton John released 'Rocket Man' as a single, which soared to No. 2 in Britain and No. 6 in America, followed by 'Honky Cat', which surprisingly faltered in the British Top Forty, though it reached the Top Ten in America, while the last of the year, the frenzied 'Crocodile Rock' was a Top Five hit in Britain and John's first American chart-topper. He told the American magazine *Rolling Stone,* 'I always wanted to write a nostalgia song, a rock and roll song, which captured the right sounds. "Crocodile Rock" is just a combination of so many songs . . .' A pair of albums was issued, *Madman across the Water* and *Honky Chateau,* both big-selling items. To change direction and to close 1972, John appeared in Marc Bolan's movie *Born to Boogie,* a box office bomber.

The first album of 1973, *Don't Shoot Me, I'm Only the Piano Player,* reached No. 1 on both sides of the Atlantic. It spawned one of John's most evergreen tracks, 'Daniel', a poignant tale about a blind war veteran. It was No. 4 British hit, and reached No. 2 in America. The single, incidentally, went on to win the Ivor Novello Award in 1974 for the Best Song Musically and Lyrically. Now established in the music market, the singer took a further step, that of opening his own record company, Rocket. The label bore a Toytown railway cartoon and boasted artists like the group Longdancer and Kiki Dee.

From the mellow tone of 'Daniel', John's next single hit the rock. Titled 'Saturday Night's Alright for Fighting', it peaked in the British Top Ten during July, and reached the American Top Twenty. 'Goodbye Yellow Brick Road', the title track from his next album, hit the British Top Ten and was No. 2 in America, rounding off John's single releases for the year. The album, incidentally, shot to the top of the British chart, and a rung lower in America. To promote the album to the fullest, John personally took it to America. The tour was subjected to one of the country's biggest hypes: not that that was really necessary, of course. A giant-sized billboard of the singer posing in top hat and white tie à la Fred Astaire attracted attention along Sunset Boulevard. As for the performances themselves, well, Elton John let no one down. He was outrageous, colourful and spectacular on a monumental scale. Compere Linda Lovelace introduced lookalikes of the Queen of England, Mae West and The Beatles, among others, before John, dressed in white feathers, trotted carefully down a staircase and onto the lid of his blue piano, one of five. As he cautiously jumped to the stage, the piano lids were raised to reveal the letters E LT O N, whereupon 400 white doves flew into the night. The theatrical spectacular led into a two-hour performance. Critics hailed the show as John's finest hour, while the singer likened it to having sex, as he told Philip Norman, 'It's like fucking for two hours and then suddenly finding out there's nothing you can do after that. It's so emotional and so physical, you don't ever want to do anything else.'

John next turned his attention to another field, that belonging to Watford Football Club, when he became chairman late in 1973. He ploughed several million pounds into the failing Fourth Division club from his own pocket or from benefit concerts.

Following the release of the festive title 'Step into Christmas', John released the most endearing single of his entire career. Titled 'Candle in the Wind', it was a personal elegy to the late Marilyn Monroe and became a Top Twenty British hit in March 1974. Not one of the singer's favourite singles, it plagues him to this day; and as recently as 1997, won a listeners' poll on Southern Sound Radio.

By now, the singer was a star; he attracted the trappings of that status, although his screaming, hysterical audiences differed from those following artists like, say, David Cassidy. John's fans did not have a sexual obsession with him; rather they demanded his friendship. He just wasn't a teenybopper icon. 'It's funny to be screamed at, because I'm not your actual sex idol, am I? The only way I ever thought people would scream at me was in horror.'

A month on from 'Candle in the Wind', the singer was forced to abandon a lengthy British tour through exhaustion, yet he rallied to perform a charity concert with Rod Stewart to benefit Watford Football Club. Four singles were issued during 1974, namely, the slow-paced 'Don't Let the Sun Go Down on Me'; 'Whatever Gets You through the Night' (a duet with John Lennon); 'The Bitch Is Back', and 'Lucy in the Sky with Diamonds', a version of The Beatles' track from *Sergeant Pepper's Lonely Hearts Club Band*, recorded at the Caribou Ranch with Lennon attending. The latter title became John's third American chart-topper. Two albums were also issued during the year, the first recorded at the Caribou Ranch in the Colorado mountains, titled (naturally) *Caribou*, and *Elton John's Greatest Hits*, both American chart-toppers.

During April 1975, a single credited to The Elton John Band and composed by the singer for tennis star Billie Jean King and the Philadelphia Freedom World Team Tennis players was issued. The disc was appropriately named 'Philadelphia Freedom' and peaked in the

British Top Twenty, but went all the way in America. King was the coach of the Philadelphia Freedom team, and apparently the singer would attend their matches. The tennis and recording stars struck up a friendship, prompting John to compose the song for her. From the frenetic to the funereal: 'Someone Saved my Life Tonight', loosely connected with the singer's suicide attempt, was issued as follow-up. It was a Top Thirty British hit during July 1975 and made the Top Five in America. 'Island Girl' was the last single of the year; a British Top Twenty hit and an American No. 1. Of the albums issued during 1975, *Captain Fantastic and the Brown Dirt Cowboy*, was No. 2 in Britain and No. 1 in America, faring marginally better than *Rock of the Westies*, Top Five in Britain, and top of the American chart.

During the previous three years, John had spent much time touring America as evidenced by his regular chart-topping status there. His venues usually included the Hollywood Bowl in California, where, on one occasion, he performed before an estimated 25,000-strong audience. He staged charity performances in Los Angeles, raising at one point in excess of $150,000 for UCLA's Jules Stein Eye Institute, and played the Dodger Stadium in Los Angeles, where he was the first act to perform since The Beatles during 1966. Such was his rising status, that all concerts were sold out within days of being announced. It was no surprise when John's health caused concern; he was simply pushing himself too far, to the point of exhaustion. He lived to perfect his art, and it was taking its toll.

In 1976 and following the release of the 'Pinball Wizard' single, lifted from The Who's movie *Tommy* in which he played the pinball wizard, John celebrated his first British chart-topper, but not alone.

Born Pauline Matthews on 6 March 1947, in Bradford, Kiki Dee worked her way through local groups until 1964 when she recorded the title 'Early Night' composed by Mitch Murray. Dee then moved into session singing, notably with Lesley Duncan, to back Dusty Springfield in the recording studios. The results were American-styled, hard-edged tracks, reminiscent of Dee's own single releases that included her version of Tami Lynn's 'I'm Gonna Run Away from You', and a throaty rendition of Aretha Franklin's 'Running out of Fools'. However, nothing Dee recorded dented the British chart, yet she rapidly rose to the ranks of artists' artist.

With Diana Ross's departure from The Supremes dominating the British music press in 1970, the signing of Dee, the first white British artist, to Motown passed by almost unnoticed. Dee: 'I was approached by the company and went over to America for eight days to look around.

279

I met the producers, writers and generally got to know what was going on. I signed the contract the day I left and then returned for two months' recording. They taught me about my voice and how to use it. In fact, I learned so much in a short time, I couldn't believe it.' Plans were in the offing for her to duet with Marvin Gaye, but for an unexplained reason, the project was shelved.

However, during Dee's American stay, she recorded the album *Great Expectations* in July 1970 on Motown's offshoot, Tamla, and performed 'so that the people who were working with me would have some idea of what I was capable of and to give them a chance to decide what material would suit me best. The idea wasn't for the producers to turn me into a soul singer, but rather to record me on material to which I'm most suited.' The album attracted poor sales, although it was highly acclaimed by soul fans. The title 'The Day Will Come between Sunday and Monday' was extracted from the album as the first single in June, while in America, 'Love Makes the World Go Round' charted in the Top Ninety.

Dee then drifted in and out of the cabaret circuit until 1973, when she signed a recording contract with Rocket Records. Elton John produced her album *Loving and Free,* which spawned her debut British hit titled 'Amoureuse', a sweeping ballad, which peaked at No. 13 in the chart. A year later, Dee released the uptempo 'I Got the Music in Me', which reached the Top Twenty. The single was lifted from the album of the same name, although the title nearly wasn't recorded, as producer Gus Dudgeon told Philip Norman. 'Kiki had a bit of a studio complex, and couldn't seem to get the vocal together. While she was doing it, Elton crept in through a back door, hid behind a screen, took off all his clothes and suddenly streaked across the studio, stark naked. Kiki nearly freaked, but kept on singing. That's why the vocal came out so great.' Another year on, her version of the Nancy Wilson classic, titled '(You Don't Know) How Glad I Am' stalled in the British Top Forty. It seemed that Dee's recording career had finally found a healthy footing in the British marketplace, but the true peak was to come when she duetted on vinyl with Elton John. Written by John and Taupin, using the pseudonyms, Ann Orson and Carle Blanche, the couple recorded 'Don't Go Breaking my Heart' in Ontario, Canada. Promoted by a video shot at the actual recording session, the single soared to the top of the British and American charts in August 1976. The American domination lasted for four weeks, while in Britain, it lasted for six. On the fun side, John sang the single with Ms Piggy in an episode of *The Muppet Show,* while more seriously, it won an American Music Award for the Favourite Single Pop/Rock, and for John, the Favourite Male Artist, Pop/Rock.

During September 1976, Dee tried again and released the double A-sided single 'Loving and Free'/'Amoureuse'; the ploy worked, the titles returned her to the Top Twenty, while early in 1977, 'First Thing in the Morning' faltered in the Top Forty. To close the year, she issued her final single under the Rocket Records' logo, titled 'Chicago'; it was a Top Thirty entrant. She also issued the *Kiki Dee* album. During her stay with Rocket, the singer accompanied John on tour, official functions and the like, and was soon known as his token girlfriend. Their friendship survives to this day. Switching to Ariola Records, Dee's debut hit was the snappy 'Star', a Top Twenty hit in February 1981, while her final British hit, 'Perfect Timing', stalled in the Top Seventy in May. In the eighties she released a pair of blinding albums, *Angel Eyes* and *Perfect Timing*, which included a further duet with Elton John, a version of the Four Tops' hit 'Loving You Is Sweeter Than Ever', released as a single during November 1981. Their final duet would be issued during the next decade. Two years later, John co-produced her single 'The Loser Gets to Win', released in September 1983. From recording, Dee turned to acting, performing in *Blood Brothers,* staged in the West End, and her career seemed to be concentrated on the stage through to the nineties.

In 1976, John issued the album *Blue Moves,* his last written by Bernie Taupin, with producer Gus Dudgeon. Taupin told Philip Norman it was a doom-and-gloom project: 'My marriage had broken up, I had a lot of negative thoughts about everything . . . For the first time, when we began to work, I found myself thinking "I don't know if I've got it in me. I don't know if I want to do this any more." ' John's next single was a ballad, 'Sorry Seems to Be the Hardest Word', a Top Twenty British hit, and Top Ten in America. It was during this period that the singer stunned the American public: he broke the house record at Madison Square Garden, earning in excess of $1.25 million in ticket sales, and admitted to an American magazine that he was bisexual. He believed such an admission could damage his career, but cared little: he was tired of living a lie, and told the *Daily Mirror:* 'I realise it's not everyone's cup of tea, and I try not to dwell on it too much . . . But I had to get it off my chest. That's the way I am, and it's no good hiding it.' In fact, he never hid his gayness from his mother who worried more about his future loneliness than his sexuality!

Through to the next decade, the flamboyant character, who had no equal in combination of talent and persona, continued to strut his way through chartbusting titles, although another British No. 1 eluded him for some years, despite excellent attempts. His instrumental 'Song for Guy', recorded in tribute to Rocket Records' messenger, Guy Burchett, proved the point. His first album without Taupin's input – Gary Osbourne filled the vacancy – was titled *A Single Man,* and was produced by John and Clive Franks. It soared into the British and American Top Ten, and was runner-up to *Elton John's Greatest Hits Volume Two.*

In the eighties, the first single, 'Little Jeannie', surprisingly struggled into the British Top Forty, with solid American sales boosting the title to the No. 3. It was swiped from the album *21 at 33* – John's twenty-first album and his thirty-third year – another huge seller. One further single, '(Sartorial Eloquence) Don't You Wanna Play this Game', followed during 1980, stalling in the Top Fifty on both sides of the Atlantic, a poor showing given the singer's status. A year later, the poor sales continued with a live version of The Beatles' track 'I Saw Her Standing There' with John Lennon, and his own compositions 'Nobody Wins' and 'Just Like Belgium'. The album *The Fox* was marginally more successful, with placings in the British Top Twenty and American Top Thirty. It was a blip in his career, because the next outing, during April 1982, 'Blue Eyes', returned the artist to the British Top Ten and the American Top Twenty, whereupon he embarked upon a European tour. Meanwhile, the album *Jump Up!* peaked in the Top Twenty on both sides of the Atlantic, leaving John to tour Britain for approximately two months.

A year later, John and Taupin reunited to release the album *Too Low for Zero,* a Top Ten British hit, Top Thirty in America. A handful of singles, the Top Five British and American hit 'I Guess That's Why They Call It the Blues' and 'I'm Still Standing', followed by 'Kiss the Bride' and 'Cold As Christmas', sustained John as a charting name.

In 1984 John married Renate Blauel, a studio tape engineer, whom he had met in AIR Studios in London. The ceremony was held on Valentine's Day at St Mark's, an Anglican Church in Darling Point, Sydney, Australia, where the singer was touring. They were granted a special waiver to conduct the ceremony which, under New South Wales law, was usually dependent on a thirty-day waiting period. Wedding guests were flown in from America and Britain, although the bride's parents were absent. Blauel wore white silk and Swiss lace, while John preferred white tailcoat and striped shirt, and a boater sat cheekily on his head. Back home in Britain, the tabloids were in their element with headlines and crass statements that included 'Good On Yer, Poofter' (the *Sun*), and quotes from the bride like, 'He's supposed to be bisexual, but that doesn't worry me at all. He's wonderful, the nicest guy I've ever met . . .' While John himself said, 'I'm so happy, and very much in love.' His close friends, likewise, were delighted at the union, claiming Blauel was the perfect partner for the singer. Whatever the reasons for the marriage, they remained personal and rightly so. John took an unusual step in these modern times, by insisting no pre-nuptial agreement be drawn up and indeed, when the couple divorced, Blauel wanted nothing from him.

In the mid-eighties, the singer vocally sparred with the American Queen of Sass, Millie Jackson, to record the 'Act of War' single, a Top Forty staller. He then joined others to perform in the Live Aid gala, staged during July 1985, at Wembley Stadium, duetting with his close friend George Michael on 'Don't Let the Sun Go Down on Me'. A pair of singles subsequently rounded off the year, namely, 'Nikita', which went on to win an Ivor Novello Award for the Best Song Musically and Lyrically, and 'Wrap Her Up', with George Michael. Both were big sellers, and extracted from the mother album *Ice on Fire,* featuring Kiki Dee, among others, on back-up vocals. And once more, John toured, this time a five-month trek across Europe, closing in Belgium.

In 1987, John became actively involved in raising funds for AIDS charities despite his own life being in absolute turmoil. He began the year by being hospitalised in Sydney, Australia, for throat surgery, following his collapse during a concert, before being the victim of daily tabloid persecution in Britain. John was exasperated when one newspaper earmarked him for a remarkable scandal. With no holds barred, the *Sun*'s headline glared 'Elton Ends Sham Marriage'. 'Elton's Five Day Orgy' claimed to be based on personal experiences by young men, claiming to be rent boys, known to the singer. The newspaper raved on, issue after issue. Any lesser artist would have broken down; not so, John. With an unbelievable show of courage, he went on to prove the newspaper articles to be false, resulting in a settlement of £1 million in damages, and the *Sun* printing the headline 'Sorry Elton'.

In the late eighties, John issued his live version of 'Candle in the Wind', recorded with the Melbourne Symphony Orchestra, whereupon all proceeds were donated to AIDS victim Ryan White, whom the singer supported until he died in April 1990. 'Candle in the Wind' returned him to the British Top Five during February 1988, reaching a rung lower in America. Later in the year, John auctioned items of personal memorabilia at Sotheby's in London, much to his fans' delight and astonishment. Of the singles released, the most significant were, 'A Word in Spanish' and 'Healing Hands', while on the album front, *Reg*

Strikes Back and *Sleeping with the Past* were the most successful.

Entering the nineties as a single man, the singer celebrated the new decade with the British chart-topping title 'Sacrifice', his first solo No. 1 in his home country. Royalties from this and, reputedly, other future releases were to be earmarked for numerous AIDS organisations and charities. Also during 1990, John finally came to terms with his self-destructive lifestyle. He voluntarily underwent treatment at a rehabilitation centre, Parkside Lutheran Hospital, in Chicago, Illinos, for his drug and alcohol abuse, and a lengthy battle with bulimia, among other problems. Following a six-week internment, John retired from the music business for approximately one year.

Throughout the decade to date, Elton John tirelessly supported AIDS causes either by performing or attending functions and campaigns. Following the release of the album *Two Rooms – Celebrating the Songs of Elton John and Bernie Taupin,* a compilation of selected artists performing the duo's compositions, John joined forces with Diet Coke to promote the soft drink via extensive advertising. The bulk of 1992 was spent touring – from America, into Europe and back to Britain for dates at Wembley Stadium. He also issued his thirty-first hit album, *The One,* which peaked at No. 2 in Britain and in the Top Ten in America. A year on, the singles 'Simple Life', and another duet with Kiki Dee, 'True Love', sustained his high chart profile. The latter track was extracted from the *Duets* album, a Top Five British hit which reached the Top Seventy in America. The next significant album, *Made in England,* soared to No. 3 in Britain during April 1995, hitting the Top Twenty in America. Interestingly, John had scored higher chart placings in America than in Britain until the mid-nineties. In 1996, two singles charted in Britain; the first, his solo 'Please', the second, 'Live Like Horses', a duet with the mighty Luciano Pavarotti, Top Forty and Top Ten hits respectively.

Although singles are now no longer automatic million-sellers, the singer is guaranteed a charting position. After all, each release marks a special occasion as Elton John has earned his place in the world's music history books. Certainly, the world would be a duller place indeed without him.

(Quotes: *Off the Record* by Joe Smith; *Elton: The Definitive Biography* by Philip Norman)

ABBA

Dancing Queen

'Our difficulty was to get rid of the Eurovision stamp, but I think we've successfully done that now . . . it's been especially hard in England because [it was] used to groups coming over from the Continent and not lasting very long.' – Bjorn Ulvaeus

With two British chart-toppers to their credit ('Waterloo', 1974; 'Mamma Mia', 1976), Abba had finally broken down the barrier erected by the British, who were last in the queue to fall for the group's magic. Europe, Australia and, to a certain extent, America, had supported their music since 1974. Britain had been more cautious.

At the start of 1976, Abba were recording tracks for a further album, but to satisfy worldwide demand, they lifted their version of the Lyngstad solo track 'Fernando' from the sessions for single release. While the title climbed the international charts, the quartet visited Australia where Abbamania was in full grip. Indeed, when they arrived at Melbourne Airport, it was crammed with thousands of hysterical fans, prompting Agnetha Faltskog to say, 'We were so moved by the reception awaiting us.'

Upon their return to Sweden, 'Fernando' topped most European charts, including Britain, a position it held for four weeks from May 1976. The single was hotly chased by the inevitable big seller, the *Greatest Hits* album. In Britain the release had advance orders in excess of 100,000 to catapult it to No. 1 in the album chart, a position it held for a remarkable nine weeks.

By now, the British press seemed to be mellowing slightly, but like all those involved in creating headlines, they remained keen to knock Abba's success. This time, they dissected the membership, especially Faltskog and Lyngstad: 'the beautiful and the ugly'. 'The beautiful' was obviously Faltskog; Anni-Frid Lyngstad (who had shortened her first name to Frida – ABBA to FABB?) was, naturally, furious at her media label. And it was surely remarks like this that added to the personal rift between the two singers. In retrospect, their personalities were totally opposite. Faltskog was introvert, moody and insecure, yet silently delighted she was the favoured one; Lyngstad was vivacious, outgoing, with a wild attitude to life. Her reputed jealousy of Faltskog possibly led to her over-enthusiastic approach to performing. However, whatever their personal attitudes, both ladies acted the true professionals before their public; indeed their closeness on stage, their eye contact and general body language, prompted many a journalist to report they were gay! When this avenue proved a dead end, the scribes moved on, hoping to unearth further scandals. Abba just could not win!

What of Benny Andersson and Bjorn Ulvaeus? They never argued, they said. In actual fact, they could not afford to; without their composing partnership there would be no Abba.

During June 1976, Abba were the only entertainers invited to the wedding of King Carl Gustaf to Silvia Sommerlath in Sweden, where the new Queen was introduced to the world. Many believed that Abba's next single, which they performed at the gala, was composed for her. Not so, the track titled 'Dancing Queen' had been composed several months prior to its release: nonetheless, the title fitted the occasion, so no one was any the wiser!

The majestically presented slice of Abba brilliance, 'Dancing Queen' was quietly aimed at the decade's flourishing disco scene. The subtle dance beat, disguising the group's usual stilted lyrics, was Abba's finest production to date. The selling pattern of previous releases was repeated across Europe and Australia and the track actually went on to top the charts in fifteen countries. This time, Britain likewise bowed down to the quartet's musical expertise. 'Dancing Queen' shot to the top of the chart during September 1976, where it stayed for six long weeks, selling in excess of 800,000 copies. The single also topped the American chart during April 1977.

Before 1976 ended, the group starred in their first television documentary titled (wait for it!) *Abba D'Abba Doo,* filmed during recording sessions, press interviews and at their homes in the Archipelago, Stockholm. Due to international interest, the programme was retitled *Abba – From the Beginning* and rerecorded in English. They visited Poland for the first time, America for the third, and released the album *Arrival* with advance orders in Britain totalling 400,000 copies. It may have taken a while, but Abbamania had now crushed the British in its Swedish fist. *Arrival* was an absolute Abba gem. Andersson: 'It's the best album we've made up until now, but it hasn't been easy and that's the reason [it's] six months late . . . You have to make yourself happy before you can make other people appreciate it. Each song on the album should be strong enough to stand up on its own . . .' Critics agreed (for once): the weekly music newspaper *NME* glowed, '[It] is their most accomplished set to date . . . they deliver their material with such gusto that if you try to turn a deaf ear, they'll just pummel your brain into submission.' The album soared to No. 1 in the chart in January 1977.

British Abba-fever was further confirmed when, following the announcement of their concert date at the Royal Albert Hall, London, during February 1977, the booking office received in excess of three million applications for 11,000 seats! The London date was one of a series of concerts around Britain.

The group's final single of the year, titled 'Money Money Money', lifted from the chart-topping *Greatest Hits* album, rocketed into the British Top Three, breaking the consecutive run of No. 1 singles.

Abba were now constantly under the harsh glare of the world's spotlight, but they defiantly refused to let slip any mention of their private lives or, indeed, any hint of disharmony within the group. If they had, the public would have become aware of the growing gap between 'the beautiful and the ugly'.

Not a good way to sell records!

Also see: 'Waterloo' May 1974; 'Mamma Mia', January 1976; 'Knowing Me Knowing You', April 1977; 'The Name of the Game', November 1977; 'Take a Chance on Me', March 1978

(Quotes: *Abba – The Music Still Goes On: The Complete Story* by Paul Snaith)

October 1976

PUSSYCAT

Mississippi

Here we go again – Europe rules! Thankfully it didn't happen that often. To be fair, though, 'Mississippi' had a particular charm, although two decades later few remember the hookline, let alone the title.

The vocal group Pussycat was born in Limburg, Holland, and was one of the few European acts to break the one-hit wonder mould in Britain. The unit comprised a trio of sisters, Tony Wille, Betty Dragstra and Marianne Henson; Tony's husband, Lou; John Theunissen; Theo Coumans; and Theo Wetzels.

Prior to forming Pussycat, the sisters had worked as telephone operators; Lou Wille was a member of Ricky Rendell and his

Centurions. He then married Tony and formed Sweet Reaction, while the remaining males performed as a trio named Scum.

It was this line-up who signed to EMI Records in Holland, whereupon, for no apparent reason, they adopted the name Pussycat. The vocalists were assigned to producer Eddy Hilberts to record a handful of tracks including 'Mississippi' which Hilberts favoured. The song was six years old, penned by Werner Theunissen, and became Pussycat's debut single, released by Sonet Records in Britain.

'Mississippi' shot to the top of the British chart during October 1976, a position it held for four weeks, before selling in excess of five million copies worldwide.

During December 1976 Pussycat issued the follow-up, 'Smile' which surprisingly peaked at No. 24 in the British chart. It was the group's last hit – not the purrfect way to end a recording career that spanned one year!

November 1976

CHICAGO

If You Leave Me Now

'Chicago is the most successful experiment in group therapy ever to go down in history.' – Robert Lamm

The group began with rock and jazz influences, which were modified and emphasised as their career expanded. The soft fusion of both, against a strong melody, produced one of the decade's most endearing of singles.

Trumpeter Lee Loughnane, born in Chicago on 21 October 1946; drummer Danny Seraphine, born in Chicago on 28 August 1948; and trombonist James Pankow, born in St Louis on 20 August 1947, met fellow student and saxophonist Walter Parazaider, born in Chicago on 14 March 1945, at Chicago's DePaul University. Loughnane, Seraphine and Panknow were members of the group called Jimmy and the Gentlemen, alongside guitarist Terry Kath, born in – yes, that's right! – Chicago, on 31 January 1946.

In time they opted to form their own unit titled The Missing Links, and recruited vocalist Robert Lamm, born in Brooklyn, New York, on 13 October 1944, late of Bobby Charles and The Wanderers. A further name change to The Big Thing, led to dedicated rehearsals early in 1967 which, in turn, secured local club performances. Unhappy with their working name, it was changed once more to The Chicago Transit Authority. As such, they enjoyed a run of prestigious concert dates during 1967, and came to the attention of James William Guercio, who became their producer and manager. Through him, the group supported The Exceptions at a new Chicago club when Peter Cetara (from The Exceptions), born in Chicago (where else?) on 13 September 1944, joined their membership.

Midway through 1968, the group moved to Los Angeles to work solely with Guercio, who had secured them a residency at The Whisky-A-Go-Go nightclub, and had interested CBS Records' Columbia label executives in signing them. In May 1969, the group's debut album, *Chicago Transit Authority,* was issued to soar to No. 17 in the American chart and reach No. 9 in Britain. To promote the release, the group embarked upon an American tour as support act to Jimi Hendrix. Then during July, Mayor Daley, acting on behalf of the Chicago Transport Department, legally demanded the group change its name. They agreed to shorten it, whereupon Chicago was born. A month later, their eponymous double album spawned the single 'Questions 67 and 68', a struggler in the American Top Eighty. Following their participation in the Rock 'n' Roll Gala staged in Toronto, Canada, Chicago toured Europe, beginning and ending with dates in Britain.

Chicago started 1970 touring America, while their next single, 'I'm a Man', swiped from The Spencer Davis Group, became their British debut, charting in the Top Ten during January. A month on, *Chicago* soared to No. 4 in America and No. 6 in Britain. In June, 'Make Me Smile' reached the American Top Ten, followed three months later by the '25 or 6 to 4' which crashed to No. 4 in America, and became their second British hit at No. 7.

During 1971, two albums, *Chicago III* and *Chicago at Carnegie Hall* (a monstrous four-album release) recorded during the group's series of sell-out performances that April, spawned a handful of singles that included the titles 'Lowdown' and 'Beginnings'. All tracks were hits, although it would take Chicago a further five years to enjoy another British hit. These 1971 releases were punctuated by American and European treks. The next year, Chicago recorded and issued the solitary album *Chicago V* which shot to the top of the American chart, a position it dominated for nine long weeks, while stalling in the Top Thirty in Britain. The lifted track 'Saturday in the Park' soared to No. 3 in the American singles chart, while their final 1972 hit, 'Dialogue (Parts I & II)' struggled into the American Top Thirty.

Chicago VI, the only studio album issued during 1973, became an American chart-topper in July, while a pair of singles, including the 'Feelin' Stronger Every Day', reached the Top Ten. The next year, *Chicago VII,* another American chart-topper, spawned a trio of hits, like 'Wishin' You Were Here', featuring members of The Beach Boys.

During the next two years the Roman numerals appeared once more, when *Chicago VIII* was issued, another American chart-topper, likewise *Chicago IX – Chicago's Greatest Hits,* while *Chicago X* stalled at No. 3 in the American chart. Both gave birth to a series of hits backed by touring commitments, including an American trek with The Beach Boys as support act. In October 1976, Chicago's career finally peaked when the smoothest of ballads, titled 'If You Leave Me Now', penned by Peter Cetera, topped the American chart. In November 1976, the single repeated that success in Britain, on its way to European multi-sales. Among the industry awards Chicago received, the most prestigious were won in early 1977 – a Grammy Award for the Favourite Band, Duo or Group in Pop/Rock, while 'If You Leave Me Now' won a Grammy for Best Pop Vocal Performance. Once again, Chicago spent most of 1976 touring the world, including a standing-room-only concert at Madison Square Garden, New York, during October. While 'You Are on my Mind' stalled in the American Top Fifty, 'Baby, What a Big Surprise' reached No. 41 in the British chart.

Tragedy struck the group early the next year. Terry Kath accidentally fatally shot himself. A long-standing collector of guns, he believed he was handling an unloaded gun; the bullet lodged in his head. Deeply saddened by his death, Chicago cancelled all business commitments until April 1978, when a single featuring Kath on lead vocals was issued. Titled 'Little One', it reached the American Top Fifty. Guitarist Donnie Dacus replaced Kath; his stay lasted one year.

By now, Chicago had dissolved their relationship with James Guercio, to secure a management contract with Wald-Nanas Associates, but the company did little to return the group to mega-record-sales status. The majority of releases tended to stall in the Top Sixty, although a trio crawled into the Top Twenty. This state of affairs was likewise reflected in their album sales, culminating in *Chicago 13* which, unlike its precedessors, sold less than one million copies. Maybe the absence of Roman numerals jinxed the release!

In 1981 Chicago switched record companies from CBS Records to Full Moon, a Warner Bros offshoot, via a multi-million-dollar pay cheque. The move worked. *Chicago 16,* released during September 1982, peaked at No. 9 in America and No. 44 in Britain. The lifted single 'Hard to Say I'm Sorry', written by Peter Cetera, returned the group to the top of the American chart. In Britain, the track soared to No. 4 that October. The song was, incidentally, featured in the flop movie *Summer Lovers,* directed by Randal Kleiser, best known for the money-spinning musical *Grease.*

When signing to the Full Moon label, Chicago shuffled its membership to introduce a new group sound. Robert Lamm: '[The music has] an upfront, immediate feel and, if anything, it's more of a group effort.' In 1984, following the release of *Chicago 17,* the lifted single 'Stay the Night' soared into the American Top Twenty, bypassing Britain. It was a mild setback, because in November 'Hard Habit to Break' peaked at No. 8 in Britain following its American release which resulted in a No. 3 hit. Three months later, Chicago enjoyed their final British hit, 'You're the Inspiration', which reached No. 14 in the chart.

Throughout his career with Chicago, founder member Peter Cetera was responsible for much of their success; in 1985, following the release of 'You're the Inspiration', he left the group to embark upon a solo career, a move he had been contemplating for some time. As well as pursuing a singing career, he worked with Amy Grant, and Agnetha Faltskog from Abba, among others. Meanwhile, Chicago, with a further personnel change, moved on.

In 1988, they issued *Chicago 19,* produced by Ron Nevison, while Cetera released his third album, *One More Story.* With group member Bill Champlin elevated to lead vocalist, Chicago, now a Reprise Records' act, returned to the top of the American chart with the Diane Warren composition 'Look Away' in December. The title held that position for two weeks.

In the nineties, Chicago maintained their status as a top touring unit, with spasmodic American recording success. It's interesting to note that Chicago is probably a band that mainstream record buyers would not now recognise by name. When the single 'If You Leave Me Now' is played, those same people would sing along to the melody with great relish, but enquire 'Isn't that by, er . . . ?'

SHOWADDYWADDY

Under the Moon of Love

Dressed resplendently like Teddy Boys, singing cover versions of American rock tracks, this eight-strong group led the way for future recording stars like The Jets and Shakin' Stevens. It was a shame that Showaddywaddy, for all their pioneering ways, were unable to sustain their own chart status.

With guitarists Trevor Oakes and Russ Fields; bass guitarists Rod Teas and Al James; drummers Romeo Challenger and Malcolm Allured and vocalists Billy Gask and Dave Bartram, the group had the image of a showband, in the old fashioned sense of the word.

The eight-piece unit hailed from Leicester, and their first professional break was an appearance on ITV's talent programme *New Faces*. With Mike Hurst (ex-member of The Springfields) as their manager, Showaddywaddy – so named by Bartram 'in a rare moment of normality' – brought rock 'n' roll alive once more.

The group's appearance on *New Faces* led to a recording contract with Bell Records, where they enjoyed a spectacular career with their own interpretation of fifties- and sixties-inspired rock tracks. Their career began with the single 'Hey Rock and Roll', which soared to No. 2 in the British chart during May 1974. This hit was quickly followed by 'Rock 'n' Roll Lady', a Top Twenty British hit. To close the year, Showaddywaddy released the inevitable seasonal track titled 'Hey Mr Christmas', a No. 13 hit.

Through 1975, the group took two cover versions into the British Top Ten, namely, 'Three Steps to Heaven', Eddie Cochran's May 1960 British chart-topper, and 'Heartbeat', Buddy Holly's Top Thirty British hit in January 1959. This pair was complemented by the single 'Sweet Music', a Top Twenty hit, and 'Heavenly', which stalled in the Top Forty. The low chart placing mattered little to Showaddywaddy. They were, by now, guaranteed a young, lively audience who had come to expect fast-moving shows, with the group dancing and singing geared up as Teddy Boys. Bartram told journalist Bill Archer, 'When fame was very, very new and there were lots of nubile young females around every venue we played, the temptation was maybe a little too great to resist and there were some pretty wild parties . . .'

After reaching the No. 2 position twice, Showaddywaddy struck gold to reach the top of the British chart in December 1976 with another cover version titled 'Under the Moon of Love', penned by Tommy Boyce and Curtis Lee, who recorded the original version in 1961 as the follow-up title to the American hit 'Pretty Little Angel Eyes'. Showaddywaddy dominated the British chart for three weeks.

But the group was then absent from the British chart until March 1977 when, following a record company switch from Bell to Aristra Records, they released the single 'When' which took them to No. 3 in Britain. Four months on, the title 'You Got What It Takes' soared one position higher, while the last release of 1977, 'Dancin' Party', hit the Top Five.

During the next two years, Showaddywady retained their high chart status with six singles – 'I Wonder Why'; 'A Little Bit of Soap'; 'Pretty Little Angel Eyes', the group's second Curtis Lee cover version; 'Remember Then'; 'Sweet Little Rock 'n' Roller' and 'A Night at Daddy Gee's' (1979).

In the new decade, dance music was changing. Rock 'n' roll was being replaced by the eighties' beat; British acts were forced to rethink their music, and only the fortunate few continued to be successful. Happily, Showaddywaddy's demise was not immediate. They managed to stagger into the British Top Forty until 1982 with singles that included 'Why Do Lovers Break Each Other's Heart', 'Footsteps' and, as RCA Records' artists, 'Who Put the Bomp (in the Bomp-A-Bomp-A-Bomp)', their final British hit, in August 1982.

Showaddywaddy's brand of rock 'n' roll had become passé – although Shakin' Stevens would rise to incredible heights with his interpretation of British-styled American rock. Nonetheless, Showaddywaddy scooped twenty-three British chart singles from 1974 to 1982; nine reached the Top Ten, one was a chart-topper.

The group did not die; demands for touring sustained them through to the nineties. Bartram: 'The concert tours which we do every two or three years are great. Then there's the "scampi and chips" Northern circuit, with its smoky, dense atmosphere and that can be really hard work.' The Showaddywaddy fans have grown up with them. 'People come along to have a rattling good night and all they want to see is what they saw and enjoyed twenty-odd years ago.'

During 1996, the group recorded a new album in Denmark. Bartram: 'We haven't done a completely new album for seven years, but rather than just hit the fans with a load of new songs, we decided to rerecord some of the old Showaddywaddy classics and do them in a slightly more contemporary way.' The album's highlight was a reworking of Gene Pitney's 1963 British Top Five hit 'Twenty Four Hours from Tulsa', earmarked for single release. Not a bad success story really.

'The thing I've always thought unique about Showaddywaddy is that it's a totally versatile band.' – Dave Bartram

(Quotes: *Lifetime* magazine, interview by Bill Archer, 1996/97)

JOHNNY MATHIS

When a Child Is Born

'I always wanted a career like the giants, Nat "King" Cole, Ella Fitzgerald and Billy Eckstine, those are some of my big heroes.' – Johnny Mathis

Mathis was born in San Francisco, California, on 30 September 1935, into a musically orientated family, and sang at a young age; in fact, he studied opera as a teenager. He excelled at athletics, and intended to become a teacher of physical education. To this end, he was invited to the Olympic try-out sessions. However, ambitions of the athletic kind, were replaced by the musical.

In 1955, Mathis signed a recording contract with Columbia Records, an offshoot of CBS Records in America, where his attempts to establish himself as a jazz singer failed. This did not deter his record company; they simply assigned Mathis to another producer, Mitch Miller. The association resulted in a series of husky-voiced ballads, befitting the Nat 'King' Cole style, which the record-buying public supported. The successful run began with the 1956 single 'Wonderful! Wonderful!', which, after a shaky start, snowballed into a monster American hit. It was followed by 'It's Not for Me to Say', and the double A-sided single 'Chances Are'/Twelfth of Never' during 1957. The latter title soared to No. 4 in America.

Mathis's British career began during 1958 when 'Teacher Teacher' debuted in the chart via the Fontana label, to peak at No. 27. Before the year closed, a further two titles, 'A Certain Smile' and 'Winter Wonderland' reached the Top Five and Top Twenty respectively, while a year on, a pair of singles sustained his British career – 'Someone' and 'The Best of Everything'.

Meanwhile, the singer's homeland popularity showed no signs of faltering as further hit titles ensured his chart presence through to 1962 – 'Come to Me'; 'A Certain Smile'; 'Misty' and 'Gina'. In between these single releases, the singer issued a handful of big-selling albums, including *Johnny Mathis' Greatest Hits* during 1958. This title, incredibly, yo-yoed the American chart for a staggering ten years!

Another notable album during this decade was *Heavenly* which, reputedly, narrowly missed reaching the same high status as the *Greatest Hits* package. Although Mathis was geared towards the middle-of-the-road market, he also crossed over to appeal to the periphery of the R. & B. circle.

By 1963, Mathis's remarkable career began showing signs of deteriorating; so much so, that he left Columbia Records to sign a recording deal with Mercury Records. His final American Top Ten hit was 'What Will Mary Say' in 1963, a Top Fifty hit in Britain, while his last American charter, 'Life Is a Song Worth Singing', floundered in the Top Sixty during 1964. The switch to Mercury was unsuccessful, so he returned to Columbia Records to work with noted composers like Carole King in an attempt to re-establish his career.

In the seventies, Mathis had indeed recharged his musical batteries by moving into a more commercial, contemporary sound. The switch worked remarkably well when he rerecorded The Stylistics' 1972 British Top Ten hit 'I'm Stone in Love with You'. The title became Mathis's biggest British hit since 1960 when it peaked at No. 10 during 1975.

The best was yet to come. Released in November 1976, the single 'When a Child Is Born' was ideal for the festive season. Eager shoppers pushed the title to the top of the British chart in January 1977: when Mathis recorded it as a duet with Gladys Knight five years on, the title re-entered the British chart to peak in the Top Eighty. Regrettably, Mathis was unable to repeat his chart-topping success, although he would come close on one occasion. His American career was yet to reach chart-topping heights, but as the singer told *Billboard* in 1978, he and his producer Jack Gold had recorded the best material on offer to them and 'couldn't figure out how we could do anything any better than we had already done, so we decided to try something different.'

The difference was a duet with Deniece Williams, a soul singer of considerable note, who had enjoyed international success with her 'Free' single during 1976. It was titled 'Too Much, Too Little, Too Late', and Mathis and Williams basked in the glory of their first American chart-topper during June 1978; in Britain, the single hit No. 3.

As 'Too Much, Too Little, Too Late' had captured the public's imagination, Mathis and Williams recorded an album together, from which a second hit track was swiped. Titled 'You're All I Need to Get By', it was their version of the Marvin Gaye and Tammi Terrell 1968 Top Ten British hit. The rerecording faltered in the American and British Top Fifty, whereupon their vocal relationship ended.

To start the eighties and following his solo British Top Twenty hit

'Gone, Gone, Gone', Mathis changed to another singing partner to issue the single 'Different Kinda Different' with Paulette Williams; the title bombed. Two years on, he duetted with Dionne Warwick on 'Friends in Love'; a much healthier seller which reached the American Top Forty, while two years later, Mathis was reunited with Deniece Williams to issue the 'Love Won't Let Me Wait' single. The title bombed.

Mathis recorded the album *The Hollywood Musicals* in 1986, and *Once in a While* two years later, considered by purists as a milestone release, due mainly to producers Pete Bunetta and Rick Chudacoff, and Preston Glass, among others. The material was (naturally) different to his previous work, and included 'Two Strong Hearts', a duet with Dionne Warwick, and 'Ain't No Woman (Like the One I've Got)', a cover version of the Four Tops' No. 4 American hit during 1973. Mathis told journalist David Nathan, 'I wanted to do a record that everyone could get behind, because I feel that I do have a responsibility to them to deliver something that is gratifying.'

The crooner also conceded at this juncture that he made 'a good living doing concerts but, after thirty years, I lost touch with the record-buying public. My albums sell about 250,000 copies each but that's not enough to get excited about.'

In the nineties, Johnny Mathis continued with his lucrative touring career, with spasmodic album releases. He's been affectionately tagged 'The King of Necking Music', and in a more serious tone, equal to Frank Sinatra. Long may he croon . . .

(Quotes: *Blues and Soul* magazine, interview by David Nathan, 1988)

February 1977

JULIE COVINGTON

Don't Cry for Me Argentina

She had the distinction of playing the first Eva Peron: not on the stage but in the recording studios. Yet despite possessing a commercial vocal range, Covington's brush with the bigtime was short.

Born in Britain during 1950, Julie Covington studied at Cambridge University where her appearance in the Footlighters Revue during 1964 led to her television debut. Singing on the *David Frost Show,* she impressed an A. & R. executive from EMI Records sufficiently to be offered a recording contract. Her debut release was the *Beautiful Changes* album released on the EMI subsidiary, Columbia. It bombed.

In 1970, Covington switched her attentions to the theatre until six years later she secured her first major acting role in a television series. Joining Charlotte Cornwell and Rula Lenska, she played the part of a singer in the vocal trio named The Rock Follies, also the name of the television series. The programmes were compulsive viewing, later attracting a cult following. With the series' music penned and produced by Sue Lloyd-Jones and Andy Mackay, The Rock Follies enjoyed a Top Ten British single for real. Titled 'OK?', released by Polydor Records, the title peaked during May 1977.

It was via The Rock Follies that the next step in Covington's career was taken. Tim Rice and Andrew Lloyd Webber were searching for a vocalist to record the soundtrack of their musical *Evita* when they spotted Covington on the small screen. She fulfilled the role to sing a sweeping dramatic ballad titled 'It's Only your Lover Returning'. The result was disastrous; the song was powerless. While in the studios deliberating which move to make, it was decided to simply amend the song's title to 'Don't Cry for Me Argentina' – a stupid title, many felt. Nonetheless, MCA Records issued the track as a single. To everyone's surprise (and horror) it soared to the top of the British chart in February 1977, selling in excess of 970, 000 copies en route! Hot on the heels of this success, Covington released her eponymous album, another big seller. 'Don't Cry for Me Argentina', incidentally, re-entered the British chart during July 1978 when it floundered in the Top Seventy.

With this 1977 chart-topper to her credit, Covington was snapped up as a recording artist by Virgin Records, where her debut single 'Only Women Bleed', a powerful version of the Alice Cooper original, soared to No. 12 in the British chart late in 1977. This was, regrettably, Covington's last British hit, although she continued to record.

During 1979 she was a featured vocalist on *Rise Up Like the Sun* recorded by the Albion Band, and joined Richard and Linda Thompson on their album titled *First Light*. Ten years on, Covington once again recorded as a soloist, this time to sing the theme song from a fifties radio show titled 'When Housewives Had a Choice'.

Covington's career is now confined to the theatre, while 'Don't Cry for Me Argentina' has been rerecorded by countless artists including Elaine Page, who played the role of Eva Peron in the stage version of *Evita,* and Madonna who, in 1996, starred as the dictator's wife in the movie adaptation of the musical. Guess it's true what people say, 'Evita' will live forever!

LEO SAYER

When I Need You

'I want to be as important as Dylan . . . I don't want to be just another rock 'n' roll singer or writer.' – Leo Sayer

Born Gerard Hugh Sayer in Shoreham-by-Sea, Sussex, on 21 May 1948, he studied at Worthing's Art College, where he formed his first group called The Terraplane Blues Band. Leaving college, he enjoyed a short career as a magazine illustrator, while at night he sang and played harmonica in London folk clubs. When there wasn't an opening to perform, he would watch other acts, learning their techniques. Sayer: 'I remember seeing Paul Simon in the folk clubs and followed him everywhere. I talked to him. I followed Donovan around too.'

In 1968 Sayer was forced to return to Sussex following a nervous breakdown. When recovered, he worked in a factory, using spare time to experiment with songwriting. He formed a further group named Jester, later Patches. When David Courtney, late drummer for British singer Adam Faith, placed an advertisement in the *Brighton Evening Argus* newspaper for singers and groups, Patches was among the fifty to be auditioned. Impressed with what he heard, Courtney signed the group to record the solitary single titled 'Living in America' in 1972. The track was never issued, but Courtney and Sayer formed a composing partnership. In time, they interested Adam Faith in their material and he signed the duo to a management deal. Faith was, at the time, involved in the second series of his highly-successful television programme *Budgie*. He wrote in his autobiography, 'The amazing voice I heard was the business . . . I knew I couldn't rest until the whole world agreed with me.'

When Patches disbanded, Faith continued to manage Sayer as a soloist whereupon his first name was amended to Leo because Faith's wife believed the five-foot-four singer with his mass of curly hair resembled a lion cub!

During March 1973 Sayer began his solo career in Roger Daltrey's recording studio. However, as Daltrey was working on a solo album, he secured material penned by Sayer and Courtney before Sayer could record it. Titled *Daltrey*, the album spawned the solo Who's biggest-selling single, titled 'Giving It All Away', which reached No. 5 in April

1973. Sayer told author Joe Smith that when Faith heard the track he wanted to know its origin. Sayer told his manager that it concerned 'somebody walking out on his wife'. In fact, he wanted to escape from Faith's management because he was frustrated with Faith's attitude. 'He kept saying "Wait kid. Don't worry, it's all going to happen. You've got to be patient." I thought, "Well, I'm the boy giving it all away. I'm throwing away my whole creativity to these people who kept telling me to wait." '

Before 1973 closed, Adam Faith negotiated a recording deal for Sayer with Chrysalis Records, where his first single, 'Why Is Everybody Going Home', was issued. It bombed. Sayer then started recording his first album, the autobiographical *Silverbird*, which Faith financed. 'Big mistake. I had no idea what it cost to produce a modern rock album – the thick end of £70,000 plus promotion and manufacturing outlay. Within a short time I was in so deep that Leo Sayer's recording career either became a big success or I was in grave danger of visiting the bankruptcy court.'

Silverbird let no one down. It shot to No. 2 in the British album chart in February 1974, while the lifted track 'The Show Must Go On' also peaked at No. 2 in the singles chart. Incidentally, the track was covered by Three Dog Night who enjoyed a No. 4 American hit.

Not only was Leo Sayer's voice an attraction, but also his garb of sad-faced make-up and a clown costume better suited to a pierrot doll. In actual fact, he had swiped his inspiration from the French movie titled *Children of Paradise*. Britain loved the image; not so America. Nonetheless, he went on to enjoy two chart-toppers there, but as the straight guy.

In July, Sayer issued 'One Man Band', a No. 6 British hit, and three months on 'Long Tall Glasses', which started its life as 'I Can Dance', a No. 4 hit. The latter title was swiped from *Just a Boy*, his second album, also released during October 1974.

Following a lengthy American tour early in 1975, *Just a Boy* and 'Long Tall Glasses' soared into the Top Twenty in their respective charts; and as his next British single titled 'Moonlighting' peaked at No. 2, 'One Man Band' faltered in the American Top One Hundred. Before the year ended, Sayer issued his third album, *Another Year*. As it peaked at No. 8 in Britain and faltered in the lower regions of the American chart, Courtney split up his composing partnership with the singer. Frank Farrell, ex-member of Supertramp, replaced him.

The bulk of 1976 was spent touring Britain, but the year marked the first taster from Los Angeles recording sessions with producer Richard

Perry, who excelled with R. & B. artists. 'You Make Me Feel Like Dancing', penned by the singer and Vini Poncia, held that R. & B. ingredient, heralding a drastic change of musical direction for Sayer who said, 'Some people think I'm falling into an R. & B. trip [but] it's still Leo Sayer music.' Whatever the intention behind the track, 'You Make Me Feel Like Dancing' shot to No. 2 in the British chart during November, and to the top of the American chart in January 1977, selling in excess of one million copies. A year on, the title won the Best R. & B. (!) Song Award at the Grammy Awards ceremony!

The follow-up single, written by Carole Bayer Sager and Albert Hammond, titled 'When I Need You', likewise shot to the top of the American chart. And equally as significant, gave Sayer his first and only British chart-topper in March 1977, a position it maintained for three weeks. Albert Hammond, by the way, originally recorded the track in 1976. Hot on the chart-topper's heels, Sayer released the mother album *Endless Flight,* a No. 4 British hit; No. 10 in America, earning a platinum disc. In April 1977, the chart-topper's follow-up, 'How Much Love', faltered at No. 10 in Britain, while 'Thunder in my Heart' stalled outside the Top Twenty that September.

The next year marked further changes for the singer. In July he hosted his own American television special which led to a British BBC TV series titled *Leo,* screened weekly from that September. A month on, he returned to the British Top Ten with 'I Can't Stop Lovin' You (Though I Try)', while his version of Buddy Holly's 'Raining in my Heart' stalled at No. 21; in America it fared worse, struggling into the Top Fifty. Sayer was losing his way; the decline was imminent, although few wanted to believe that such a talent could crumble so quickly.

The Very Best of Leo Sayer dominated the British album chart for three weeks during 1979, while his new album, *Here,* climbed into the Top Fifty, but his name was absent from the singles chart; it would take until August 1980 before he re-established himself with a cover version of Bobby Vee's 1961 hit 'More Than I Can Say'. The title soared to No. 2 on both sides of the Atlantic.

It took a further two years for Sayer to chart once again. 'Have You Ever Been in Love' reached the British Top Ten during April 1982, followed by a Top Twenty entrant titled 'Heart (Stop Beating in Time)' in July. During 1983, the rot set in once more. He struggled with two poor-selling titles, namely 'Orchard Road' and 'Till You Come Back to Me'; and three years later, 'Unchained Melody' faltered in the Top Sixty. The single was issued because it was featured in the movie *Car Trouble;* it was Sayer's final British hit.

During 1988, with his Chrysalis Records' contract expired, Sayer received a reputed £600,000 from Adam Faith, said to be unpaid royalties. In 1990 he worked with producer Alan Tarney to release the album *Cool Touch* via EMI Records. It bombed. Leo Sayer's recording career had nosedived for the last time. However, Chrysalis Records searched their vaults to release Sayer's *All the Best* compilation, a Top Thirty British hit, while a reissue of 'When I Need You' sailed into the British Top Seventy. It has been rumoured regularly that Leo Sayer intends to return to the spotlight, but to date nothing has materialised.

'I kind of set out in my early songs to romanticize my own life . . . I wanted to make Sussex the centre of the earth.' – Leo Sayer

(Quotes: *Off the Record* by Joe Smith; *Acts of Faith* by Adam Faith)

April 1977

ABBA

Knowing Me Knowing You

While British critics remained relatively tight-lipped when reviewing Abba's concerts, their European counterparts gushed unashamedly: 'Audiences [sat] open-mouthed when they found that Abba could reproduce their music, note for note, without a fault.'

As Abba's album *Arrival* climbed to the top of the international charts and the single 'Money Money Money' rocketed into the British Top Three, the quartet visited London for yet another promotional trip, which included a press reception on the *Mayflower Queen,* moored on the River Thames. The group travelled from Heathrow to the Thames via helicopter, in keeping with the *Arrival* album's artwork. During the reception, Abba received thirty silver, gold and platinum discs representing varying British record sales – the shipping cost to Sweden must have been astronomical but now CBS Records could easily afford it! The group also taped a BBC Radio 1 special to be aired over the pending Christmas season, and conducted exhaustive press interviews, with Bjorn Ulvaeus invariably nominated as the group's spokesman.

The remainder of 1976 was spent rehearsing for the following year's world tour – the make or break disaster/spectacular. Meantime, Abbamania continued, showing no signs of declining.

Once the concerts were announced, the hype got underway. Tickets were sold out, usually in one day, as fans throughout Europe fought to secure a seat. It was a phenomenal slice of music history being made; the likes of which had not been experienced since The Beatles. With this whirlwind came the (usual) killjoy, when rumours circulated the media that the quartet had been killed in a plane crash in West Berlin. Such was the strength of the story, that it could have quashed the tour instantly: Abba issued a forceful denial, Bjorn Ulvaeus appearing on Swedish television.

With a touring entourage of approximately 100 people, including a 12-piece backing group, and costing £9,000 a day, Abba opened their world tour in January 1977 in Sweden. The British dates that included London's Royal Albert Hall were during February, whereupon the group flew to Australia for eleven dates in Sydney, Melbourne, Adelaide and Perth. It was decided that the Australian leg would be filmed for the big screen, an awesome task in itself! *Abba – The Movie* would include onstage and behind-scenes footage, loosely held together by a storyline of a radio DJ's attempts to interview the group within a week's deadline.

The British performance was faultless. Consisting of the obligatory hit singles, the show began with a simulated helicopter landing, and featured the mini-musical 'The Girl with the Golden Hair', where Faltskog and Lyngstad, wearing similar blonde wigs and costumes, sang a selection swiped from *Arrival*. While the remainder of Europe showered unprecedented accolades, British critics were reticent: '[a] clinical disappointment' and 'glib and contrived' were more typical, regrettably, than '[they] are the greatest thing since The Beatles'.

The British performance was also the launching pad for Abba's next single, 'Knowing Me Knowing You' which, thanks to the concentrated promotion, shot to the top of the chart during April 1977, a position it maintained for five weeks. It was slightly autobiographical; if listeners cared to dissect the lyrics, the future break-up of the two couples could have been detected.

The world tour took its toll. Ulvaeus: 'It's a bit of an unsocial life . . . you just eat, sleep, go on stage and nothing more. It kills creativity in a way that I don't like.' Faltskog: 'One day when I woke up . . . I started to think – where am I? And it's terrible.'

Agnetha Faltskog was also the centre of attraction; the role was not of her own making. The media's (rather distasteful) attention surrounded her bum, and when headlines glared 'The sexiest rear in show business', she replied she didn't know if it was true or not, she

303

hadn't seen it! This unwanted attention followed the singer for several years as, of course, did her bum!

With the tour behind (no pun intended) them, a press statement was issued that Abba would not be available for interviews or performances until October 1977, giving them a break of six months. Ulvaeus: 'We are not toys, we have a desperate need to have peace and quiet.' Besides, Faltskog was pregnant with her second child; a carefully planned pregnancy, calculated with her husband, Ulvaeus, not to clash with professional commitments. Sadly, the second child failed to save their marriage.

By the close of 1977, Abba had sold in excess of 20 million singles and 30 million albums worldwide. Not bad for a group, who many believed, would be destined for the 'also-ran' heap, following their 1974 Eurovision Song Contest winner 'Waterloo' which, in all honesty, *was* tailor-made for the garbage bin.

Also see: 'Waterloo', May 1974; 'Mamma Mia', January 1976; 'Dancing Queen', September 1976; 'The Name of the Game', November 1977; 'Take a Chance on Me', March 1978

(Quotes: *Abba – The Music Still Goes On: The Complete Story* by Paul Snaith)

May 1977

DENIECE WILLIAMS

Free

A reluctant singer who enjoyed success almost by default, all Deniece Williams wanted was to be recognised as a composer, but thanks to Stevie Wonder's encouragement she became an international artist instead.

Born Deniece Chandler in Gary, Indiana, on 3 June 1951, to Alma and Lee, Williams sang in the choir of her local gospel church. After leaving Gary College she found a position in a record shop, where she met representatives from countless record labels. One in particular, Clarence Johnson from Toddlin Town Records based in Chicago, went on to record her. 'Lover's Tears' was the only single of note, recorded under the name Deniece Chandler when she was sixteen years old.

At this point in her life, Williams did not intend to pursue music as a full-time career. She attended the Baltimore Morgan State College to study nursing, confining her musical endeavours to evenings when she sang in her local clubs, or as support artist to acts like The Jacksons and The Emotions. Clarence Johnson and Williams worked together once more. This time the result was the single 'Mama I Wish I Stayed at Home', issued on the Lock label, an offshoot of Atlantic Records. This second outing, like its predecessor, bombed.

Early in 1971 Motown recording artist Stevie Wonder held auditions for his vocal backing group Wonderlove. He chanced to hear Williams' Toddlin Town recordings and recruited her to replace the departing Lynda Lawrence, who was joining The Supremes. Williams performed with Wonder for several weeks before returning to nursing – her first love. Wonder had other ideas, and persuaded her to return, whereupon she became a permanent member of Wonderlove for the next three years. During this time, Williams also contributed to his multi-million-selling albums of the seventies, *Innervisions, Fulfillingness First Finale* and *Songs in the Key of Life*. Williams: 'I learned such a lot from working with Stevie. I guess it was really finance that prompted me to take the job but I saw a whole lot of things that I would never have seen in Gary . . . the goal in my mind was to keep the job for as long as I could, but you can't be that unattached to Stevie. As an artist [he] encouraged me to grow in every way.'

By 1975, with this experience behind her, Williams decided to pursue a solo career and moved to Seattle to compose her own material. 'It just seemed like the right time and Stevie gave me his blessing. He realised that it was time for me to put into practice all the things that he had taught me.' She contacted numerous record companies before Maurice White, founder member of the vocal group Earth, Wind and Fire, secured her a recording contract with CBS/Columbia. 'The original idea was to present my songs. I had no real intention of becoming a solo artist. When I sent some demos to Maurice White . . . they weren't really what [he] was looking for but he seemed to like what I had done and suggested I record with him for Kalimba Productions.' The result was her debut album, *This Is Niecy,* released in November 1976, the mother to her first American Top Thirty hit, titled 'Free'. Written by Hank Redd, Nathan Watts, Susaye Green and the singer, 'Free' shot to the top of the British chart during May 1977, where it stayed for two weeks. Williams said at the time, 'I'm honestly surprised by it all. I prayed a lot and I felt it could be right. Maybe it's because it is so different that people have gone for it.' To sustain the single's life and to promote the album, Williams toured America and Britain with Earth, Wind and Fire, further cementing their professional relationship.

'That's What Friends Are For' followed the British chart-topper in August 1977. It bombed in America, but reached No. 8 in Britain. Two months later, her second album, *Songbird,* was issued. It was a poor seller in Britain, yet her last single of the year 'Baby Baby my Love's All for You', reached the Top Forty. Obviously, the British were not that keen to let Deniece Williams fall just yet.

However, her career was to take a twist when she duetted with Johnny Mathis on 'Too Much, Too Little, Too Late'. Mathis told *Billboard* in 1978, '[I] knew Deniece was big in the R. & B. area so I said, "Maybe we can get some of the R. & B. diehards to listen to some of my music." We decided the best way was to get someone who was already accepted in that area and see what happens.' Williams rose to Mathis's somewhat selfish challenge, but was unaware the song had been intended for single release until she heard it on the radio. 'Too Much, Too Little, Too Late' raced to the top of the American chart in June 1978, attaining the No. 3 position in Britain. An album of duets followed, titled *That's What Friends Are For,* spawning their next single, 'You're All I Need to Get By'. This cover version of the Marvin Gaye and Tammi Terrell original faltered in both the American and British Top Fifty. The album, on the other hand, sold better, reaching the Top Twenty in both countries!

By now Deniece Williams was in demand, not only as a vocalist (she worked with Michael Zager on 'Time Heals Every Wound' for example) but as a composer as numerous acts approached her for material, like The Whispers and The Emotions. Meanwhile, with her eye on her own recording career, she switched record labels from Columbia to ARC Records, newly formed by Maurice White and distributed via CBS Records. Her debut album *When Love Comes Calling* was co-produced by Ray Parker Jr (founder of the group Raydio and composer/performer of 'Ghostbusters', the title track from the 1984 movie). Despite the heavyweight presence, the album bombed, leaving Williams bewildered as to where to turn next.

During 1981 she decided on her musical course and worked with Thom Bell, who had established himself with productions for The Stylistics, among others. The result was the album *My Melody* from which the single 'Silly' was lifted. Both titles were minor American hits. Nonetheless, a year later the two collaborated further on the *Niecy* album, a thoughtfully conceived and presented collection, a view shared by the American public, who pushed it into the Top Twenty. The album spawned 'It's Gonna Take a Miracle', a version of the Royalettes' sixties hit which re-established Williams as a Top Ten American artist. Public support for this single initially surprised the singer, although upon reflection she felt its lyrical content was the main selling factor. 'The title depicts the way a lot of people feel about the situation today – it really is gonna take a miracle! Socially and economically. It's a very strange time in history . . . as a nation and as a people. There are things happening today that have not happened before.'

Returning to the major record company Columbia Records during 1983, Williams recorded the album *I'm So Proud*, produced by George Duke. For some inexplicable reason it stalled in the American Top Sixty. A year later, Williams recorded a pair of singles with Johnny Mathis, 'Love Won't Let Me Wait', previously recorded by Major Lance, and 'Without Us', later adopted as the theme to the American television series *Family Ties*. Once more, Williams was a top-league artist and this time it was to be capitalised upon when she recorded and released the Tom Snow/Dean Pitchford composition 'Let's Hear It for the Boy'. It was to be her contribution to the soundtrack of *Footloose*, the dance movie released during May 1984, and was the second of five singles to be lifted. Williams's first recording of the track was rejected by the composers because it was too twee. She rerecorded it in twenty minutes and it was that version that became an American chart-topper, reaching No. 2 in Britain. Williams: 'I had no idea where the song fitted in the film so I was a little anxious. I was thrilled to find out that it came at the highpoint . . . I could relate to [the film] in many ways because it's about young people who rebel against the kind of strict moral codes in a little town. I grew up at a time when that was very much the way – girls weren't encouraged to wear make-up or go out on dates and it was all very strict . . . I think audiences love to see people win.'

Unprepared for this unexpected success, Willams compiled and released the cash-in album *Let's Hear It for the Boy*. Lacking forethought and dedication, the album faltered in the American Top Thirty, while the lifted single 'Next Love' struggled into the Top Ninety.

Through to the close of the eighties, Williams's mainstream success was negligible, although her staunch soul following continued to support her via albums like *Hot on the Trail* in 1986 and *Water under the Bridge* a year later. For her gospel fans she recorded for the Sparrow Records label during 1988, before recording the album *This Is As Good As It Gets*, released by MGM Records.

As Deniece Williams's recording career to date has been inconsistent to say the least, there's every reason to suppose that she will once again enjoy a British hit. In the light of nineties' music trends this might prove difficult, but that extra-special single often creeps through as if to prove good music never dies, it simply sleeps awhile.

(Quotes: *Blues and Soul* magazine, interviews by John Abbey/David Nathan)

June 1977

THE JACKSONS

Show You the Way to Go

'We have always been a very loyal and affectionate group . . .' – Michael Jackson

Jackie, born Sigmund Esco, on 4 May 1951; Tito, born Toriano Adaryll, on 15 October 1953, and Jermaine La Juane, born on 11 December 1954, all in Gary, Indiana, were the three eldest children of Joe and Katharine Jackson. While youngsters, and with their parents' encouragement, they performed locally under the name The Jackson Family. Marlon David, born on 12 March 1957, and Michael Joseph, born on 29 August 1958, also in Gary, likewise were encouraged to perform with their elder brothers, whereupon they became known as The Jackson 5.

In the fifties, Joe Jackson was guitarist with The Falcons, a Chicago-based blues band. Jackson: 'I was married very young and while my wife was having our nine kids I still wanted to see out my ambition to be a musician. I joined The Falcons and used to rehearse in the kitchen while the kids were crawling around the floor . . . But it takes a lot of money and time to get any group off the ground and I realised that my time was going to have to go one way or another. So I decided to transfer my interest in music to my family, not that they needed much encouragement. In Gary with all the steel mills the kids didn't have anything to do except go to school and come home. So I had them learn to sing or play some kind of instrument and they worked for four hours every day. My goal was to get them on stage where they could perform with other amateurs at talent shows. It took about a year until I felt they were good enough.' The brothers based their act on The Miracles and The Temptations, from whom they pinched stage routines and songs. Eight-year-old Michael was the lead singer, leaving his brothers to play the instruments and provide backing vocals. Remembering the evenings after school when rehearsals were obligatory, Michael wrote in his autobiography, 'If you messed up you got hit . . . My father was real strict with us.' Indeed, playing family games and so on happened in other family homes, never in the Jackson household. Instead, their entire leisure time was spent learning and rehearsing. Michael: 'I remember my childhood as mostly work, even though I loved to sing. I wasn't forced into this business by stage parents the way Judy Garland was. I did it because I enjoyed it.'

The group, with the addition of drummer, Johnny Jackson and pianist, Ronnie Rancifer, first performed before a paying audience at Mr Lucky's, where they earned $5 collected from punters pitching coins on the floor. They then began winning talent shows, for which their mother designed and made their stage suits, before progressing to the club circuit, which they played during the school holidays. The youngsters' local singing reputation spread sufficiently for them to be booked to tour with Gladys Knight and The Pips, and The Temptations.

The Jackson 5's first single titled 'I'm a Big Boy Now', produced by Gordon Keith, was issued by Steeltown Records during 1968, followed by 'Some Girls Want Me for their Love'. The recording contract secured the brothers for six months, allowing Joe Jackson to scout for a further deal. When Diana Ross was invited by Gary's mayor, Richard Hatcher, to visit the city, she attended a Jackson 5 show. Liking the performance, she reputedly persuaded Motown's founder Berry Gordy to buy the brothers out of their Steeltown contract. With the Jackson 5 now a Motown act, they were groomed for future stardom by Suzanne de Passe, her cousin Tony Jones, and Gordy, who left nothing to chance. He formed and worked with what he called The Corporation, comprising at any one time producers and composers Freddie Perren, Fonzie Mizell and Deke Richards, for two reasons. Firstly, he knew the importance and success of a songwriting team – Holland, Dozier and Holland had proved that – and, secondly, he wanted to avoid one writer/producer taking credit for the Jackson 5's rise to fame. Gordy desperately needed the young brothers to succeed because he had been unable to find a unit to match the success of The Temptations, the Four Tops and The Supremes. The Jackson 5 lived up to all expectations, as their young soul/pop sound lasted for several years under Motown's banner, while on stage, they held their audiences spellbound with their vividly coloured suits and tight dance routines.

Under the group's one-year recording contract with Motown, they received 6 per cent of 90 per cent of a record's gross price, which, in turn, would be split five ways. Clauses were also included to specify unique royalty provisions, and to prevent the brothers recording for another company within a specified time limit.

The phenomenon of the brothers' success was through an ingenious publicity campaign which ensured them maximum exposure. Motown told the media that Diana Ross had discovered the group and had adopted its members as her protégés. They were introduced to 350 journalists at a gala party held at the Daisy, one of the 'in' clubs in Beverly Hills, California. Of her so-called discovery Ross said glowingly, 'I'm very happy to have been able to give a nationally well-deserving group an opportunity to perform because that's how we, The Supremes, got our big chance. Had it not been for Berry Gordy searching for talent in our black community we wouldn't have been discovered.' The ex-Supreme also gave the brothers their national television debut in October, when she hosted the *Hollywood Palace Show.* Her name was even featured on the group's first album, *Diana Ross Presents the Jackson 5.*

The truth did not emerge that this was all part of a sophisticated marketing campaign until much later in the group's career, when Michael retorted that if anyone discovered them it was their parents. 'We were in Chicago at a theatre called The Regal, which was a kind of audition place for Motown, and Motown decided to use Diana Ross's name to introduce us to the public. But she never discovered us. We were an established professional act long before we ever signed to Motown.' However, prior to the Jackson 5's performance, both Gladys Knight and Bobby Taylor had tried in vain to persuade Berry Gordy to sign them.

The Jackson 5's debut single, 'I Want You Back', composed by The Corporation, had originally been written for Gladys Knight and The Pips. Should they reject it, the track would be offered to The Supremes. Before that could happen, the Jackson 5 recorded it. Released in October 1969, 'I Want You Back' soared to the top of the American chart, reaching No. 2 in Britain in February 1970. It was the first in a succession of million-selling singles and albums. The Jackson parents and the younger children – Randy, born Stephen Randall Jackson, on 29 October 1962; Rebbie, born Maureen Jackson on 29 May 1960; Latoya, born on 29 May 1965; and Janet, born on 16 May 1966, would occasionally join the five brothers on stage.

In April 1970, the follow-up to 'I Want You Back' was issued. Titled 'ABC' from the same composing team, it likewise soared to the top of the American chart, reaching the Top Ten in Britain. Two months on, 'The Love You Save' became their third American chart-topping single, and third million-seller, hitting the Top Ten in Britain. As the single ascended, the brothers' second album, *ABC*, soared into the American Top Five and the British Top Thirty, while the group performed selected dates on America's East Coast.

In October, following a last-ditch decision by Berry Gordy to can the title 'Mama's Pearl', (a musical clone of the group's previous work), the slow-paced single 'I'll Be There' was issued instead. The Jackson 5 enjoyed their fourth American No. 1 single. It held top spot for five weeks, selling in excess of four million copies, earning the distinction of becoming Motown's biggest-selling single (to date). In Britain the title peaked in the Top Five.

Early in 1971, 'Mama's Pearl' was finally issued, reaching No. 2 in America and No. 25 in Britain. The single was prevented from reaching the top in America by The Osmonds' 'One Bad Apple', which Berry Gordy had previously rejected, thinking it was too childish. Naturally, he was astonished at the single's success, while Joe Jackson told author J. Randy Taraborrelli, 'He handed those white boys a song we should have recorded. To me, that's fuckin' unbelievable. And Mormons too . . . Every time I hear those white boys imitating my sons, I cringe.' Competition between the Jackson 5 and The Osmonds hotted up, and although in retrospect they attracted a different fan following, each group considered the other a threat. Taraborrelli further reported that Motown's vice-president, Ewart Abner, released a press statement that said, 'This is an older white group . . . We here at Motown are not mad at anybody. We wish them luck, while we go on doing our thing, and they go on doing – our thing.' Crazy but true!

On 18 April 1971, the Jackson 5 linked up with Diana Ross for her debut solo television special *Diana!*, participating in comedy sketches and duets. At this time the Jackson family moved to California, buying an estate at 4641 Hayvenhurst, Encino, at a cost of $250,000.

In May, the next single 'Never Can Say Goodbye', marked a change of musical pace to the slow lane: nonetheless, the title soared to the American No. 2 position, reaching the Top Forty in Britain. Controversy then surrounded its follow-up, 'Maybe Tomorrow'. Reputedly, the track was written by Deke Richards for the newly-signed Motown artist Sammy Davis Jr. Berry Gordy thought otherwise and insisted the Jackson 5 record it. The result? The title stalled in the American Top Twenty in August, selling less than 850,000 copies, which to other acts would represent a monumental sales figure, but for the Jackson 5 was pretty low key. The single was also the title of their next album, a No. 15 American hit: poor singles performance equalled sluggish album sales.

This year of 1971 also marked the Jackson 5's debut ABC TV special *Goin' Back to Indiana*; a programme that included performances and footage shot during the brothers' return to Gary. The subsequent soundtrack album, released before the year-end, reached the American Top Twenty. This national television exposure led to the group's longest American tour to date; beginning in North Carolina in July, closing in Honolulu during September. The Commodores were support act throughout the trek. The run was mayhem from start to finish. Audiences stormed the stage to grab at the young brothers; young fans screamed, cried, pushed and fainted, while security personnel were pushed to the limit trying to separate artists from public. The Jackson 5 usually had no choice but to abandon the stage prior to the show's end to enable them to be smuggled from the theatre. The Commodores' main vocalist, Lionel Richie, praised Michael Jackson for his fearless approach to hysterical audiences, particularly when he pleaded for order to be maintained. Yes, indeed, these were heady, exciting and exhilarating days for the brothers who, of course, had not been prepared for such an undiluted show of passion from fans no older than themselves!

The Jackson 5 also hit the small screen each Saturday morning – as cartoons! Via a contract between Motown and Videocraft, the series featured the group's recordings, while actors provided the dialogue, although fans were hard pressed to distinguish the difference. Well, to be honest, the public was not told. The brothers were reputedly paid $3,500 per episode. The series was later screened in Britain.

Meantime, Berry Gordy had a further headache. Donny Osmond released his debut solo single 'Sweet and Innocent' in June 1971. Following hasty discussions, Gordy agreed Michael should record a ballad originally composed for the Jackson 5. Titled 'Got to Be There', and issued in October 1971, the title shot to No. 4 in America and No. 5 in Britain. Donny Osmond's single peaked at No. 7 in America.

'Sugar Daddy' was the Jackson 5's first single of 1972, a Top Ten American hit, while the follow-up was their version of Thurston Harris's frenetic 'Little Bitty Pretty One', a Top Twenty American hit. The future seemed bleak, no longer were the million-sellers guaranteed. As this latter single charted, Michael's second solo outing, the similar-sounding 'Rockin' Robin', previously recorded by Bobby Day in 1958, likewise stalled in the American Top Twenty, but reached No. 3 in Britain. The Jackson 5 were on the decline as Michael ascended. As remarkable as it seemed, the group's popularity on vinyl was dropping; the fans demanded the lead singer.

On the personal front, Tito was the first Jackson brother to marry. Following a short engagement, the eighteen-year-old married seventeen-year-old Dee Dee Martes on 17 June 1972. His parents were so against the union that they ensured a pre-nuptial agreement was signed by Martes.

In August 1972, the group's album *Lookin' through the Windows* was issued, and the title track was swiped for single release to reach, once again, the American Top Twenty. It made the Top Ten in Britain during December 1972. The mother album soared to No. 7 in America, No. 16 in Britain. The compilation *Jackson 5 Greatest Hits* was released in Britain to reach the Top Thirty, in preparation for the brothers' appearance on the Royal Variety Show in November. This performance was the highlight of a hastily arranged two-week European trek, where, inevitably, the brothers were mobbed at every move. When their plane landed at Heathrow, London, thousands of fans waited in welcome. A Motown statement said, 'Tito was bruised and shaken by the stampede of the thundering herd. Randy nearly panicked when frenzied females devoured him . . . It was near chaos. It was frightening. It was Jacksonmania.' Indeed, it was also the result of record company hype. During their British stay, mobs of fans followed them, made camp outside the Churchill Hotel in London's Portman Square, and caused total mayhem outside the Talk of the Town where Motown/EMI Records hosted their first British press reception. As the brothers sneaked away from a theatre side door, the media fought to escape from the front exits, despite the heavy presence of police who, doubtless, find these incidents totally unnecessary. Likewise, the Jackson 5's guests!

Jacksonmania held Britain in its grasp; even when they returned to America, the furore refused to subside. Motown/EMI Records' offices remained under siege for days; only the promise of group merchandise dispersed the young fans, who should have been attending school.

Jermaine Jackson was the second brother to embark upon a solo career, while remaining a member of the group. His single 'That's How Love Goes', issued in November 1972, reached the American Top Fifty, and was lifted from his eponymous album, a Top Thirty American hit. Before the year closed, the Jackson 5 issued the single 'Corner of the Sky', a song borrowed from the Broadway musical *Pippin*. Berry Gordy had financed the musical, and Motown went on to release the soundtrack album. Once again, the brothers' single had poor sales, struggling into the American Top Twenty. The team of composers and producers known as The Corporation had by now disbanded, which many felt was the reason the Jackson 5 were suffering.

The lesson was not learned; the first single of 1973 was a version of Jackson Browne's 'Doctor my Eyes', which bypassed America but hit the British Top Ten. Meanwhile, across the Atlantic, Jermaine's solo 'Daddy's Home' peaked at No. 9 during March. This title was another cover version; this time of a Shep and The Limelites 1961 hit.

The *Skywriter* album, released in March 1973, was hard pushed to sell 200,000 copies, and was the brothers' lowest-selling American album to date. The lifted single 'Hallelujah Day', peaked in the American Top Thirty and at No. 20 in Britain. The single reportedly sold less than 250,000 units, and the more Joe Jackson complained to Motown, the worse the situation became. 'Ewart Abner cared for nothing but the bottom line. If sales figures were low and the Jackson 5 was losing its audience, it was the group's fault, not Motown's. Perhaps Abner reasoned the group's success had run its course.' Whatever the reason, the vice-president's attitude widened the already growing gap between Motown and Joe Jackson. Defection was inevitable.

During mid-1973, the Jackson 5 toured Japan and Australia, before embarking upon a lengthy American tour which closed during September, the same month as 'Skywriter' reached the Top Thirty in Britain. In October, the title track from the brothers' next album, *Get It Together*, was issued as a single to falter in the American Top Thirty. A month on, brother Jackie issued his debut eponymous album; it bombed. Likewise, Jermaine's 'You're in Good Hands' single. However, his single's title was apt: on 15 December he married Berry Gordy's daughter, Hazel, in a ceremony held at the Beverly Hills Hotel, before 100 guests. A further 500 guests were invited to the reception decked with artificial snow-covered pine trees, where white doves fluttered in white cages, and hundreds upon hundreds of white flowers, including carnations and camellias, complemented the bride and groom's . . . ah . . . white clothes. Berry Gordy paid the final bill of $234,000. Following the wedding, Jermaine's mother, Katharine departed the family home, having discovered her husband's adultery. Within a short while, Jermaine would be faced with a decision he had hoped to avoid.

During February 1974, the Jackson 5 were back in action, touring the Republic of Senegal in Africa, where they were shocked rigid at the level of poverty. Yet, when their accommodation failed to reach their sumptuous expectations, the tour was cut short. Double standards indeed!

A further song was lifted from *Get It Together* in May 1974, namely 'Dancing Machine'. Thankfully, the title soared to No. 2 in America, selling in excess of 710,000 copies, postponing any moves by Motown to drop the group. This success ensured that capacity audiences watched the Jackson 5's season in Las Vegas, where they were joined on stage by their sisters Janet and Latoya. When Berry Gordy heard of the brothers' triumph, he dispatched numerous company executives to Las Vegas to demonstrate the company's continued, enthusiastic commitment. It was too late.

In 1975 the unthinkable occurred; decisions were finally made, careers re-formed. Joe Jackson had been secretly scouting other record companies. Following an unsuccessful meeting between Michael Jackson and Berry Gordy, the Jackson 5 announced to the world they were leaving Motown for CBS Records' Epic subsidiary. The financial details of the new agreement were publicised as being a signing fee of $750,000, plus a guaranteed payment of $350,000 per album. Royalties were said to be 27 per cent of the gross record price. Although the rest of the family was aware of their father's negotiations, Jermaine, by the very nature of his marital situation, was not. There was an instant conflict of interest, culminating in Jermaine refusing to sign the CBS Records' contract. Undeterred, the remaining brothers switched companies without him. Jermaine preferred to stay at Motown as a solo artist. Jermaine: 'Berry gave me the confidence to know that I could go places if I stayed with him and the company. I believed him. I didn't believe anything my father had to say.' Despite media reports, the Jackson family did not escape Motown unscathed. In their 1968 recording contract, there was a stipulation that Motown owned all rights, title and interest in the group's name. This was further secured in 1973 when Berry Gordy registered the name and logo with the United States Patent Office, reputedly unbeknown to Joe Jackson. It remained debatable how Gordy was able to register a name that had been in use by the brothers prior to their joining Motown.

On 30 June 1975, the group, in which Randy had replaced Jermaine, announced that a new deal with the Epic label would commence on 10 March 1976, the same day as their Motown contract ended. Berry Gordy commenced legal action against the Jackson 5, Joe Jackson and CBS Records for the sum of $5 million, for concluding the new deal while still signed as a Motown act. (He would later receive the reduced figure of $600,000 in compensation.) In retaliation, Joe Jackson sued Motown for unpaid royalties and advances.

As the group was legally unable to record for CBS Records for eight months, Motown issued the first of several albums taken from the 300 unreleased tracks they held. Titled *Moving Violation*, it peaked in the American Top Forty, while the lifted single, a cover version of The

Supremes' 1968 hit 'Forever Came Today' stalled in the Top Sixty. Meanwhile, unable to use the name 'The Jackson 5', the brothers became known as The Jacksons.

Before the astonishing events of 1975 came to a close, another of a more personal nature was announced. Following a marriage of only nine months, Jackie and his wife Enid Jackson began divorce proceedings. However, when Jackie discovered the financial implications involved, he relented and remained married for a further eleven years. But there was more to come. In January 1976, brother Marlon told his family that he had married Carol Parker four months earlier. He had kept his secret to avoid his father's interference. His action cast further doubt on trust and confidence within the family circle, particularly when Joe Jackson remained the group's manager.

Unable to record, The Jacksons agreed to host a series of four variety programmes screened by ABC TV during June 1970. Titled *The Jacksons,* the programmes featured all the family members, except Jermaine, as singers and comedians. Despite Michael's earlier reservations, the series was a success and subsequently launched their new career. Meantime, before 1976 ended, Motown issued the three-album compilation *Jackson 5 Anthology* and Jermaine's *My Name Is Jermaine,* from which 'Let's Be Young Tonight' was lifted as the first single to reach the American Top Sixty.

Early the next year and following a second television series, The Jacksons finally released their eponymous debut album, produced by Kenny Gamble and Leon Huff. The title reached the American and British Top Forty, while the swiped track 'Enjoy Yourself' soared to No. 6 in America, only reaching the Top Fifty in Britain. Midway through the year, the brothers toured Britain, their first visit for over five years. Audiences had stayed true; reaction was as hysterical, although not as violent as during their young teen idol mayhem. To coincide with the visit the single 'Show You the Way to Go' was issued. Michael: '[It] showed what a good regard the Epic people had for our singing. We were all over that record and it was the best one we did.' The group's public agreed. Boosted by their concerts, 'Show You the Way to Go', penned by Gamble and Huff, topped the British chart during June 1977; their only British chart-topper. Within a month of the single's release, *The Jacksons* peaked in the British Top Sixty.

With his brothers' success underway once more, Michael accepted, much against his father's wishes, the role of Scarecrow in the film *The Wiz.* His co-star, in a cast of notable artists, was Diana Ross.

Before 1977 ended, another track, 'Dreamer' was swiped from the mother album, a Top Thirty British hit, while the title track from their pending album *Goin' Places* likewise stalled in the Top Thirty, only reaching the Top Sixty in America. The album proper went on to reach the British Top Fifty and the American Top Seventy, worrying for a group like The Jacksons whose heritage was glittered with million-sellers and in whom much had been invested. The tide was to change.

Over on the Motown label, brother Jermaine struggled with his *Feel the Fire* album; eventually he would briefly return to his former high-selling glory.

Before the decade closed, The Jacksons once again proved their selling power with a pair of Top Five British singles, namely, 'Blame It on the Boogie' in 1978, and 'Shake your Body (Down to the Ground)', which passed platinum sales in America a year later. Both titles were lifted from the magnificent *Destiny* album, itself a Top Forty hit in Britain and a Top Ten smash in America, selling in excess of one million copies on the way. The 'Destiny' tour of America followed; it was riddled with problems, the most serious of which concerned Michael. He lost his voice through singing excessively: he even resorted to lipsynching to Marlon's voice on stage but that was ineffective. Eventually, the tour was abandoned.

It was also during 1979 that Michael departed from the restrictive confines of the group to record and release his first solo album for CBS Records. Titled *Off the Wall,* produced by Quincy Jones, and issued during October, it spawned the single 'Don't Stop 'til You Get Enough', which soared into the British Top Three and topped the American chart the same month. This success pushed the mother album into the Top Five on both sides of the Atlantic, while its title track 'Off the Wall' was released to reach the British Top Ten. The album went on to sell in excess of ten million copies. With his first major success, Michael had freed himself from his father's thinking, which often conflicted with his own plans. All the youngster craved was to control his life and to pursue his career as a group member and solo artist. Michael: 'In 1979 I turned twenty-one years old and began to take full control of my career. My father's personal management contract with me ran out around this time, and although it was a hard decision, the contract was not renewed.'

In 1980, The Jacksons kept a low profile. Indeed, the public waited until October 1980 for their album *Triumph* to be issued: it hit the Top Twenty in Britain, and the Top Ten in America. 'Lovely One' was swiped as a single to reach the British Top Thirty and the American Top Twenty. Despite the lack of group recordings this year, there was much activity from individual family members. Michael released the singles 'Rock with You', 'She's out of my Life' and 'Girlfriend', penned for Jackson by Paul McCartney. All titles were uncontrollable million-sellers. Meantime, over at Motown, Jermaine enjoyed his biggest success as a solo artist with 'Let's Get Serious', a track penned for him by Stevie Wonder (who was also featured on the single). The disc was the title track from the album, which went on to spawn two further singles, 'Burnin' Hot' and 'You're Supposed to Keep your Love for Me'. All were charting songs. Hot on the brothers' heels, sister LaToya released her eponymous debut album via Polydor Records. Busy bees indeed!

To kick in 1981, The Jacksons issued a further track from *Triumph*. Titled 'Heartbreak Hotel', it stalled in the British Top Fifty and the American Top Thirty. The follow-up, 'Can You Feel It', fared much better in Britain by steaming into the Top Ten. Across the Atlantic, the title struggled into the Top Eighty. Once again, The Jacksons took their new musical project on tour through America. The 'Triumph' trek spanned thirty-six dates, grossing in excess of $5 million. Michael was determined the performances would be their finest yet. To this end, he recruited the services of magician Doug Henning, who devised a way for him to disappear in smoke at the close of 'Don't Stop 'til You Get Enough'. 'We were competing with bands like Earth, Wind and Fire and the Commodores for the position of top band in the country.' The result was a spectacular showcase of pyrotechnics, lights and talent.

Prior to the tour's start, Michael underwent the second in a series of operations on his nose. The first one had resulted in the singer experiencing breathing problems; the second operation was to rectify that. Michael enjoyed an unexpected British chart-topper in 1981 on Motown, with the dated title 'One Day in your Life'. This was instantly followed by 'We're Almost There', itself another gem.

The year of 1982 belonged to Michael Jackson. He started working on the audio story book based on Steven Spielberg's movie *ET*. The end product would be issued early during 1983 via MCA Records under the title *ET – The Extra-Terrestrial*. Then with Quincy Jones and a host of the finest musicians in the music business, Michael issued the album *Thriller*, which went on to spawn seven American Top Ten singles, while itself topping the American chart for an unprecedented thirty-seven weeks, to surpass all previous milestones achieved by any artist, finally becoming the biggest-ever-selling album in the world with sales in excess of forty million (1996). Indeed, at one juncture, *Thriller* sold a staggering 500,000 copies weekly, while his record company eventually recouped approximately $60 million in profit. The title 'The Girl Is

Mine', a duet with Paul McCartney, was the first extracted from *Thriller* as a single, followed by 'Billie Jean', which shot to the top on both sides of the Atlantic, and was accompanied by a promotional video showing Michael at his ultimate best; a combination of intricate choreography with a visual storyline. The follow-up single, 'Beat It', which Michael wrote for schoolchildren – 'Its message, that we should abhor violence, is something I believe deeply. It tells kids to be smart and avoid trouble' – zoomed to No. 3 in Britain in April, and hit No. 1 in America. Once again, a forthright video boosted sales; this time, Michael was accompanied by a group that included members of Los Angeles' street gangs, who frenetically danced their way through the single. Before 1983 closed, further singles included 'Wanna Be Startin' Somethin'', 'Human Nature', 'Say Say Say' (a further duet with McCartney) and the album's title track 'Thriller', featuring the voice of horror movie king, Vincent Price. Its fourteen-minute video was inspired by the movie *An American Werewolf in London* and cost $600,000 to film. So successful was this smack of unreal horror, that a commercial video was issued, *The Making of Thriller*. However, so concerned was Michael that he would offend religious communities that he issued a disclaimer on the video: 'Due to my personal convictions, I wish to stress that this film in no way endorses a belief in the occult.' Remarkably, he had created a monster and would spend the rest of his life trying to destroy it.

It was obvious that, by now, Michael had left his brothers behind, and they also realised (probably to their disbelief) that their popularity was, in the main, due solely to their little brother. Standing alone, The Jacksons were no better or worse than any American vocal group of the time. Instead of abandoning the group, Michael felt a certain twinge of responsibility towards his family, and stayed the day of execution until they had sufficient money to survive without him.

Meanwhile, The Jacksons' next significant milestone was their appearance on Motown's twenty-fifth anniversary gala staged in 1983, alongside company acts, past and present. For their spectacular performance, Jermaine was reunited with his brothers to perform a brief Jackson 5 sequence, before Michael lipsynched and moonwalked his way through 'Billie Jean'. This appearance led to Jermaine joining the group for the 1984 'Victory' tour, having severed his recording ties with Motown to sign with Arista Records. Certainly, 1984 was The Jacksons' year, both professionally and financially.

To help the multi-million-dollar tour hype, The Jacksons promoted Pepsi, who was sponsoring the 'Victory' trek, through television commercials and other avenues. During the shooting of the commercial before 3,000 people at Los Angeles' Shrine Auditorium, Michael suffered second-degree burns on his head when a magnesium flash light accidentally exploded and set his hair alight. He was rushed to the Brotman Memorial Hospital, Culver City, for treatment; Pepsi paid him $1.5 million in compensation, which he donated to the hospital.

So to the 'Victory' tour itself. Comprising forty-two dates, the trek was fraught with controversy before the brothers stepped on stage. Tour promoter Don King and Michael crossed; Michael did not trust him or want him to represent his interests. Ticket prices were too high at $30 each, and were sold in lots of four only. It was estimated that if a member of the public wanted to buy a ticket for the show by mail order, it would cost $120, plus the fee of the postal order and $2 administration charge for each ticket. Michael was incensed; from the outset, he had insisted $20 per ticket be the maximum charge. However, despite all the behind-scenes arguments, some over Michael's unhappiness at being a party to a touring sham, all concerts were sold out. Audiences were treated to the group's biggest singles and solo spots by both Jermaine and Michael. Highly lucrative as the tour was, and despite the enjoyment experienced by Jackson fans, who never believed the brothers would actually perform together again, at the final concert staged in Los Angeles during December 1984, Michael announced to the audience, and to the surprise of his brothers, that this was to be his last show with them. He then went on to donate his $5 million pay cheque to several charities, while plans to take the 'Victory' tour to Europe were scrapped.

The next Jacksons' album was issued in July 1989. Titled *2300 Jackson Street,* it was the first not to feature Michael. His achievements included collaborating with artists like Stevie Wonder; publishing his autobiography *Moonwalk;* and releasing the album *Bad,* which gave birth to a handful of hit singles. The Jacksons' album title was borrowed from the street where the family lived in Gary, Indiana, and the music featured Tito, Jermaine, Randy, Jackie and Marlon, with LaToya, Rebbie, Janet, and a host of relatives. Michael did, however, contribute to the album's title track. The first single lifted, 'Nothin' That (Compares 2 U)' faltered in the British Top Forty and the American Top Eighty. Meantime, Jermaine's solo outing, titled 'Don't Take It Personal', struggled into the British and American Top Seventy. Yes, The Jacksons' bubble had burst: the public wanted only Michael.

Personally speaking, Randy was ordered to pay $3,000 a month in child support to his girlfriend, before being jailed for one month after beating his wife and daughter. This and other behind-scenes misdemeanours, were, many believed, the result of the Jackson's bitter-sweet childhood. Indeed, most of the Jackson children had married young and were, by now, either divorced, separated or remarried. A tragedy.

In 1992, a five-hour television mini-series titled *The Jacksons: An American Dream* attempted to tell the story of the group's rise to stardom. Part-biographical, part-fantasy, the series was approved by most members of the Jackson family. Two years on, *The Jackson Family Honours* television special was aired by NBC TV from a Las Vegas venue. The audience felt deceived when Michael did not perform as promised, but made a brief appearance instead. By 1996, the Jackson brothers were *history,* ironically the title of Michael's 1995 CD box set, featuring past and current material. However, the Jacksons' magic did rub off on the siblings, when Tito's three sons, known as 3T, were signed to Michael's MJJ Records to record the single 'Anything', which soared to No. 2 in the British chart during March 1996. Meantime, Michael himself had somehow survived child abuse allegations and had married and divorced Elvis Presley's daughter, Lisa Marie, before marrying Debbie Row, who carried the singer's son, born early in 1997. A picture of him holding Prince Michael Junior carried a $1 million price tag for any magazine wanting to print it. Professionally speaking, Jackson issued the *Blood on the Dance Floor* CD containing five new tracks and eight remixes from *History.* The CD's title was lifted for single release, while the project was supported by a world tour which included dates in Britain during July 1997.

What a family; what a story. And it's not over yet . . .

(Quotes: *Moonwalk* by Michael Jackson; *Motown: The History* by Sharon Davis; *Michael Jackson – The Magic and the Madness* by J. Randy Taraborrelli)

July 1977

HOT CHOCOLATE

So You Win Again

The group's style was integrated music from white and black cultures. So successful was the combination that Hot Chocolate enjoyed eleven Top Ten and twenty-one Top Thirty hits during their life. The group's songs were classed timeless, due to Errol Brown's talent for striking a memorable hookline: 'I'm very fortunate because if I come up with a good title, it seems to inspire a melody in my brain.'

Patrick Olive, born in Grenada, on 22 March 1947, with Franklyn De Allie and Ian King, formed the nucleus of Hot Chocolate during 1969. However, to ensure the group was self-contained, a further trio joined the membership, namely, Larry Ferguson, born in Nassau, Bahamas, on 14 April 1948; Tony Wilson, born in Trinidad, on 8 October 1948, and Errol Brown, born in Kingston, Jamaica, on 12 November 1948.

It was Brown who transformed the band from an everyday musical unit into one of imagination and flair. He told *Blues and Soul* magazine: 'There I was working at the Treasury drinking tea all day. I left because I had words and melodies in my head. I met the co-founder of the band who said we should start to write together. It was then I found my natural niche in life.'

Before 1969 ended, the group was fortunate to secure a one-off single release on The Beatles' Apple record label. The title was a reggae reworking of John Lennon's 'Give Peace a Chance'. As the band was nameless at this point, a record company employee chose The Hot Chocolate Band; when the single bombed, the label lost interest in the group. No further material was released.

Brown and Wilson soon established themselves in a songwriting partnership and approached Mickie Most, founder of RAK Records, with a handful of their compositions. One title, 'Bet yer Life I Do', was recorded by Herman's Hermits, and Most signed The Hot Chocolate Band to his company in 1970. He suggested their debut single should be 'Love Is Life' with him as producer. The record label carried the name 'Hot Chocolate', and introduced the public to the multi-racial group's distinctive sound which secured them a high status in British music. The public also encountered Errol Brown's shaved head – a style he maintains to this day!

'Love Is Life' shot to No. 6 in Britain during September 1970. Before the year ended, the group membership had expanded to include Harvey Hinsley, born in Northampton on 19 January 1948.

Hot Chocolate's second single was released early in 1971. Titled 'You Could Have Been a Lady', it stalled in the Top Thirty, while the next release, 'I Believe (in Love)', re-established the group in the Top Ten. Hot Chocolate suffered a setback early the next year with 'Mary-Anne'; but by the end of 1972 they retrieved their standing with 'You'll Always Be a Friend', a Top Thirty hit.

In a further membership change, King departed to be replaced by Tony Conner, born in Romford, Essex, on 6 April 1947. The group issued their debut 1973 single, 'Brother Louie', for which Brown swiped the hookline from The Kingsmen's 1963 'Louie Louie' single. The strongly-worded song, dealing with racism and its appalling repercussions, shot to No. 7 in the British chart. A reworking of the single by The Stories soared to the top of the American chart in August 1973.

Inspired by their minor American success, Hot Chocolate embarked upon a lengthy tour there, followed by a multi-date concert trek of Britain and Europe. By now, Hot Chocolate had established themselves as theatre-fillers; they had a good presentation on stage, although it was true to say front man Errol Brown commanded the most attention with his static and well-groomed image. Brown: 'When I go on television there's a stylist who looks after my clothes for me because I'm terrible with these things. I love smart and designer clothes, and dress the same off stage as I do on.' This dedication to fashion, he said, stemmed from his teenage years. 'When I was twelve or thirteen, my mother took me out of secondary modern school to attend private school. Everybody there was very wealthy and I came to appreciate good clothes and good food. You could say I was a teenage yuppy!'

'Emma' shot to No. 3 in the British chart during 1974, reaching the Top Ten in America. This title was hotly followed by the group's belated debut album, titled *Cicero Park*. Despite their encouraging singles success, the album bombed.

Five further singles were issued in 1974–75, including 'Cheri Babe', which made the Top Forty; 'Disco Queen', the group's first stab at dance music which reached the Top Twenty, and, in complete contrast, 'A Child's Prayer', which soared to No. 7. A more serious appeal at the dancefloor audience, 'You Sexy Thing' catapulted to No. 2 at the close of 1975, and hit No. 3 in America, the group's top-selling single, selling in excess of one million copies. During this time, the group suffered a disruption, when Wilson departed to embark upon a solo career.

A trio of charting singles sustained Hot Chocolate's high profile in 1976, namely, 'Don't Stop It Now', 'Man to Man' and 'Heaven Is the Back Seat of my Cadillac'. The group issued their album *Man to Man*, and at the close of the year, the compilation titled *Hot Chocolate: 14 Greatest Hits* was the monster seller it deserved to be, selling in excess of 510,000 copies in Britain.

The Hot Chocolate sound was well established; a potpourri of dance and soul with a commercial slant, guaranteeing instant recognition by the public. Those ingredients were mixed together in the Russ Ballard composition 'So You Win Again', when it topped the British chart during July 1977, a position it held for three weeks; the group's only British chart-topper. In America, the title stalled in the Top Forty. The follow-up single, 'Put your Love in Me', issued at the close of the year, reached the British Top Ten.

Midway through 1978, the album *Every 1's a Winner* shed its title track for single release to peak at No. 12, while the album reached the Top Thirty. When released in America early in 1979, *Every 1's a Winner* soared into the Top Ten, selling in excess of one million copies en route. Further titles were issued before the decade ended, including Hot Chocolate's debut twelve-inch single 'Mindless Boogie', and 'Going through the Motions', also the title of their next album, which bombed.

Before the seventies closed and inspired by their American success, Hot Chocolate embarked upon a lengthy tour there, followed by a multi-date concert trek across Europe and Britain. While the group was engrossed with stage work, their compilation *20 Hottest Hits* soared to No. 3 in Britain, selling more than 500,000 copies thanks to concentrated television advertising.

In the eighties, a trio of charting singles sustained Hot Chocolate's chart profile with the titles 'No Doubt about It', 'Are You Getting Enough of What Makes You Happy' and 'Love Me to Sleep'. The last two titles were lifted from the group's poor selling album *Class*. For the next five years the group issued an average of three singles yearly; the titles either soared into the Top Ten or struggled for a placing in the Top Forty. The most notable, though, were their final single 'I Gave You my Heart (Didn't I)'; a remixed dance track of the 1975 hit 'You Sexy Thing', a Top Ten hit; and the 1978 title 'Every 1's a Winner', a Top Seventy staller. For album success, the outfit once more relied on a compilation, *The Very Best of Hot Chocolate*, which passed sales of 250,000 copies to top the British chart.

In May 1987, Errol Brown embarked upon a solo career as a WEA Records artist. Brown: 'We took everything pretty lightly for twelve years, but at the end of the day, the laughter turned into animosity . . . when the jealousies came to the surface, there was no other way out. When you are the writer of the group, you are also more or less in charge because you are the sound. That writer takes the group through the different musical changes, which basically rises or falls on the writer's ability. It got to the point where I thought about going solo two years before I made the move.' Regrettably, once Brown took the step, the remaining group members broke off all contact with him. 'When these things happen everything gets exaggerated . . . I think it's fair to say, I gave that group a lot.'

Teaming up with producers Steve Jolley and Tony Swain, Brown issued his debut solo single titled 'Personal Touch', which peaked in the British Top Thirty during August 1987. The singer was quietly surprised at the success. 'When you make your first single after leaving a group situation, it makes you very nervous, but happy. I'm not really a confident person and that doesn't go with making music. You have to believe in yourself because there's one thing you cannot take for granted and that's the public.'

'Body Rockin'' was the follow-up single, a Top Sixty hit. Both titles were lifted from Brown's first solo album *That's How Love Is,* released in 1990, which, not surprisingly, critics declared was reminiscent of the Hot Chocolate sound. Brown: 'I've been asked why this should be so. The truth is, all the years I was with Hot Chocolate I wrote all the songs, so of course I'll now write songs that will sound like something else, like "Emma" or "It Started with a Kiss". There will be this resemblance from time to time and I don't think I should disown it.'

Unfortunately, Brown's career declined until he disappeared from the music scene entirely. However, Hot Chocolate's recorded work showed no signs of dying; as recently as 1990, a further compilation titled *Their Greatest Hits* was issued to become a big seller. There really is no reason why these releases should ever dry up, particularly with the CD explosion.

'I'm an only child and have learned to survive.' - Errol Brown

(Quotes: *Blues and Soul* magazine, interview by Sharon Davis)

August 1977

DONNA SUMMER

I Feel Love

'Let's face it, it's in every woman to be seductive, whether she's a teacher or a whore.' – Donna Summer

La Donna Andrea Gaines was born in Dorchester, Massachusetts, on 31 December 1948 into a family of six girls and one boy. Her father, Ernest, was a butcher by trade, and the family enjoyed a strict middle-class upbringing. Neither Donna nor her sisters were allowed to wear make-up, attend dances or parties. Their free time was spent singing.

By the age of eighteen, Donna had passed through several local groups, including one named The Crow, before auditioning for an understudy position to Melba Moore in the Broadway stage musical *Hair.* The teenager joined the show's touring company, before accepting the role of Sheila in a German production of the musical. Moving to Munich, she remained with the company for over a year, and during free time was a session singer which led to her being offered roles in two further musicals, namely *Porgy and Bess* and *Showboat.* To earn extra money, Donna was, during her first days in Munich, also an artist's model. She tells the story of sitting in a café drinking coffee, when she became aware of a man staring at her. Eventually, he rose and stood behind her, while shouting 'the perfect behind'! It was the German artist Klaus Fuchs; he invited the singer to pose for him. She agreed, until 'the great man's interest in my behind seemed to grow beyond his canvass and oils. I think his wife noticed that too, so I thought it best to take me and my behind right on back home.'

During 1968, she moved to Austria, where she married Helmut Sommer. In 1970 Donna, now using a variation of her married name, 'Summer', performed in the German production of *Godspell* and continued her career as a session singer in the Musicland Studios in Munich. It was during one of these sessions that she befriended record producers Giorgio Moroder and Pete Bellotte, who had previously worked with Chicory Tip, among others. Moroder was sufficiently impressed with Summer's voice and vocal styling to sign her to his Oasis label to record a trio of titles, 'Virgin Mary', 'The Hostage' and 'Lady of the Night'. Of the last track, Summer said, 'It's all about a prostitute, although the word never actually occurs in the song. It's all about the normality of the woman's life and it's really a tender song.' The latter pair of titles became European hit singles, establishing Summer's name as a recording artist in her own right. None were issued in Britain or America.

Giorgio Moroder was anxious to secure worldwide distribution for his Oasis label, and mailed copies of Summer's fourth and as yet, unreleased single to countless American and British record companies. One copy was heard by Neil Bogart, president of the Los Angeles-based Casablanca Records. Bogart was stirred by Summer's single and to test public reaction, played it during a Beverly Hills party. Such was the response that Bogart contacted Moroder, requesting a twenty-minute version of the track. Moroder believed the Casablanca president to be mad, but nonetheless, hauled Summer into the studio to recut the track as a 16 minute 50 second monster.

Casablanca Records gave nightclub DJs the full-length version of the title, while editing it to three minutes-plus for commercial single release. Early in 1976, 'Love to Love You Baby' raced to No. 2 in the American chart, passing gold status. When released in Britain, the title soared to No. 4 via the GTO Records label. The bulk of British sales resulted from club airplay, not the radio. 'Love to Love You Baby' was banned outright from every radio station; it was classified as pure sex at its most explicit – slight, enjoyable sighs were replaced by heavier moans until climax was reached; nothing was left to the listener's imagination, while the single's title was breathily repeated time and again. To the broad-minded, the single was a fun song. Although Summer could not understand why the title was banned, she was glad it happened, 'because it will get a lot more publicity than it would have otherwise done . . . I truly don't understand where the problem is unless people have got dirty minds and hear something in there that I didn't intend.'

The singer admitted, however, that she found the track difficult to complete, having to sing softly and almost in a whisper. 'When we first started, there were no lyrics other than "love to love you baby" so I made it up as I went along, in the hope that what I was saying fitted the mood of the music . . . people have actually asked me if I was touching myself when I was singing . . . I was seduced by the music.'

Whether Summer intended to create shock waves or not, 'Love to Love You Baby' branded her as a sexual figure, rather than a recording artist. Hot on the lips, er . . . heels of the single came the album *Love to Love You Baby* in 1976, which soared to No. 11 in America and No. 16 in Britain. In May, Summer's second single 'Could It Be Magic', a version of Barry Manilow's original and therefore free from eroticism, lifted from her album *A Love Trilogy*, faltered in the American Top Sixty and the British Top Forty. Sex sold singles; slush didn't (in this instance). The album itself reached the American Top Sixty, and British Top Fifty, and was, Summer said, a chance for her to expand musically. Before the close of 1976, she issued her most adventurous album *Four Seasons of Love*. Housing only four tracks, each side related to one of the four seasons. On the calendar that accompanied the release, the singer posed appropriately for each season. Two lifted tracks became American hits, namely, 'Winter Melody' and 'Spring Affair' ('Winter Melody' reached the British Top Thirty early in 1977).

In the space of one year, Summer had issued a trio of top-selling albums, whose message was primarily sex. Summer said 'What is wrong with making love?' Why spoil a successful run? She obviously thought the same, as her next album carried the same message. Titled *I Remember Yesterday*, and released during 1977, it spawned her first and only British chart-topper. 'I Feel Love', co-written by the singer with Moroder and Bellotte, was seventies' disco at its very best. The pioneering single topped the chart in August, a position it held for four weeks, selling in excess of 750,000 copies. The album, meantime, shot to No. 3 in Britain. In American, 'I Feel Love' soared to No. 6 during November 1977.

With this chart-topper, Summer became the standard bearer of disco music. Her name would remain synonymous with dance through to the nineties, once she had swiped the title from Gloria Gaynor who was, in actual fact, crowned the first Queen of Disco in 1975 by the International Association of Discotheque Disc Jockeys. Nonetheless, future dance vocalists owed their ability to succeed to Summer, although few would acknowledge her as their mentor. But the music Summer had created would be rejected by her in 1980, a stand that dismayed her loyal followers, particularly those in the gay fraternity.

The follow-up single to her 1977 British chart-topper was the theme from the movie *The Deep*, starring Jaqueline Bisset and Nick Nolte. 'Down Deep Inside' soared into the British Top Five during September. Meanwhile, on the personal front, Summer divorced her Austrian actor husband. The marriage had produced a daughter, Mimi. Before 1977 closed, the album *Once Upon a Time*, described as 'Cinderella set to disco', reached the American and British Top Thirty.

In 1978, four singles were big sellers on both sides of the Atlantic: 'I Love You', 'Rumour Has It', 'Love's Unkind' and 'Back in Love Again'. While these titles were released, Summer was filming her first feature movie titled *Thank God It's Friday*. Summer said the movie was in fact an extension of her own life; one of the highlights was her trying to prove to a DJ that she could really sing. During July 1978, the single 'Last Dance' was lifted from the movie's soundtrack album to reach the American Top Three, while in Britain it stalled in the Top Sixty. The single went on to win an Oscar for the Best Film Song of 1978.

Hot on the soundtrack's heels, Summer released double-album *Live and More:* three sides featured her in concert at California's Universal Amphitheatre, while the fourth contained the solitary track, her version of Richard Harris's 1968 hit 'MacArthur Park', written by Jimmy Webb, and recorded by a host of acts including the Four Tops. Summer's version spanned twenty-nine minutes on the album. Edited to under four minutes, the track was issued as a single to reach No. 5 in Britain in October, and top the American chart a month on.

In 1979 she won a host of disco awards at the annual American Music Awards ceremony, which confirmed beyond doubt her status as a dance original. Five singles issued during the year ensured Summer's dominance of the disco scene; all were classics – 'Heaven Knows', 'Hot Stuff', 'Bad Girls', 'Dim All the Lights' and 'No More Tears (Enough Is Enough)', a duet with Barbra Streisand. A pair of best-selling albums, *Bad Girls* and *On the Radio – Greatest Hits Volumes I and II,* spawned them all.

In the new decade, Summer scooped a further Grammy award, and instigated a legal action against Casablanca Records, whom she'd signed with 1977, and others for $10 million, alleging misrepresentation and fraud. Subsequently, she was dropped by Casablanca, and joined Geffen Records, the first artist to be signed to the company by its founder David Geffen. The appropriately titled 'Walk Away' was her final single for Casablanca Records; it faltered in the American Top Forty. However, on the upside, the singer married Brooklyn Dreams' member, Bruce Sudano, in Los Angeles during July 1980, a month before her Geffen debut single titled 'The Wanderer' stalled in the British Top Fifty. In November, the single raced into the American Top Three, while *The Wanderer* album peaked in the Top Twenty.

Donna Summer had shrugged off her past career; the sex and sauce were part of yesterday, as she told the *Los Angeles Times:* 'There were times when I hated the image. Reporters would come to interview me and I'd see them shaking as they opened their notebooks. They were so hyped up by the sex goddess image.' The monster she had so willingly created began to eat her away. She developed stomach ulcers and was hospitalised. She also suffered extreme paranoia. 'I was so afraid of living and dying that I was on these heavy, heavy anti-depressants. They were the kind that you give people who are seriously schizophrenic.' It was, she said, at this juncture that she found God. 'I recommitted my life and I asked God to help me to be a productive person, someone with good, positive attributes. And overnight, literally, I went from being this anxious paranoid person to this person who was truly joyful.'

In 1981, Summer changed more than her attitude towards music. Now a born-again Christian, she publicly condemned gay people, alleging that gays were sinners and AIDS was the disease from God's hand sent to obliterate them. The singer later claimed she was misquoted, but it was too late. Her listening and buying public was reduced to half. In all honesty, without the support from gay nighteries, the work of Donna Summer would have remained either unreleased, or stacked on record store shelves. The singer had not only cast aside her past career for personal reasons, but had grossly prejudiced her future selling power. In 1987, she spoke again on the subject to journalist David Nathan: 'As a loving person, it wouldn't be consistent for me to point fingers. Apart from which, if I'm someone who wants a public career, I'm not going to say things like that. I feel like I'm representing God, I have to demonstrate that – and you don't do that by finger pointing.'

A year later, Summer gave birth to another daughter, Amanda Grace, while her single 'Love Is in Control (Finger on the Trigger)' reached the British Top Twenty and the American Top Ten. Her solitary album of the year, *Donna Summer,* likewise became a Top Twenty British hit, while in America the title passed gold status. A star-studded cast that included Lionel Richie, Dionne Warwick, Stevie Wonder and Michael Jackson assisted on her next single, titled 'State of Independence'. The title stalled in the American Top Fifty, but fared better in Britain, peaking at No. 14 during November 1982.

For the following five years, Summer maintained her chart status on both sides of the Atlantic via titles like 'She Works Hard for the Money' single and album, and 'Dinner with Gershwin', swiped from the *All Systems Go* album.

Unhappy with her recording career, the singer spent the bulk of her time during this five-year period devoted to family life, but by 1989, with a renewed enthusiasm for her art, she became one of several artists to record a Stock, Aitken, Waterman composition titled 'This Time I Know It's for Real'. Fans who had remained loyal throughout her career, despite her AIDS comments, were horrified at her choice of composer/producers, who were responsible for British pop at its finest, creating teen idols like Kylie Minogue and Jason Donovan. Irrespective of their opinion, the single shot in No. 3 in Britain and No. 7 in America. The title's mother album, *Another Place and Time,* likewise became a big-selling item. In total, four tracks were swiped from the album for hit single release: the British No. 3 hit; 'I Don't Wanna Get Hurt'; 'Love's About to Change my Heart', and 'When Love Takes Over You'.

In 1990, while a remixed version of 'State of Independence' entered the British Top Fifty and her compilation album titled *The Best of Donna Summer* became a Top Thirty hit, the singer was engrossed in exhibiting her paintings and lithographs in Beverly Hills. It was a lucrative exhibition, as people rushed to purchase Donna Summer originals.

In 1991, a further pair of minor British hits, 'Breakaway' and 'Work that Magic', were issued, while during 1993 her recorded work was confined to re-releases. A year later, the new track 'Melody of Love (Wanna Be Loved)' lifted from *Endless Summer – Greatest Hits,* reached the British Top Thirty. In 1996, Summer returned to the American touring circuit, recorded a duet with Liza Minelli titled 'Does He Love You', and a further remix of 'State of Independence' climbed the British chart into the Top Twenty.

Without a major record company to promote her at the time of writing, Donna Summer's career is devoted to live performances, television guest spots and hit memories. The Queen of Disco has certainly mellowed and matured, but despite all, whether she likes it or not, she will be remembered for her unashamed vinyl sexual experiences.

'I can sing songs like "Love to Love You Baby" but I can also sing ballads, light opera, musical comedies, church hymns, all kinds of songs.' – Donna Summer

(Quotes: *Blues and Soul* magazine, interviews by John Abbey, 1976, and Graham Betts, 1980)

September 1977

ELVIS PRESLEY

Way Down

'Elvis Presley's death deprives our country of a part of itself. He was unique and irreplaceable.' – President Jimmy Carter.

In 1972 Presley once more fulfilled his annual commitment in Las Vegas, where he spent four weeks performing to full houses at the renamed Hilton Hotel. During his stay, the title 'I Just Can't Help Believing', swiped from the soundtrack of *Elvis: That's the Way It Is* became a No. 6 British single. Meanwhile, on the personal front, Presley and his wife Priscilla separated; she had fallen into a relationship with karate instructor, Mike Stone, whom she had first met during one of Presley's Las Vegas seasons. During the months following Priscilla's departure from Graceland, Presley reportedly bombarded her with threats of the most evil kind, but she never returned. His personal life now in absolute turmoil – he never believed Priscilla would leave him despite his indiscretions and complicated lifestyle – Presley sought solace in his increasing drug intake, which he still referred to as medication usage, while his erratic moods caused his immediate staff considerable concern.

During March 1972, Presley received a Lifetime Achievement Grammy Award, before embarking upon a further American tour, which included his debut performances at Madison Square Garden, New York, before an estimated 80,000 people, earning in excess of $720,000 for four concerts. Of the singles issued this year, his live recording of 'An American Trilogy' faltered in the American Top Seventy, while faring much better in Britain, where it soared into the Top Ten during July. However, the title 'Burning Love' quickly re-established him as an American million-seller; reaching No. 7 in Britain. Before 1972 ended, strong rumours circulated music business circles that Presley's presence in Britain was imminent; but Colonel Tom Parker killed any hint of a visit, claiming Britain had no suitable venue for his artist. Instead, Presley hit the American trail.

Elvis: Aloha from Hawaii, a benefit concert for writer/singer Kuiokalakani Lee, who died in 1966, and which subsequently raised $75,000 for his Cancer Trust Fund, was transmitted live from the Honolulu International Centre Arena via the Intelsat IV satellite to countries that included Australia, New Zealand, Hong Kong and Malaysia, leaving America and Europe to view a taped version. An estimated one billion people watched the concert in January 1973; Britain decided not to partake. The double-album release of the concert reached the British Top Twenty in March 1973, while, two months on, it topped the American chart. Presley then released the 'Separate Ways' single, recognised as an admission that his marriage was finished; the title reached the American Top Twenty, hitting No. 9 in Britain as the B-side to 'Alway's on my Mind'.

The bulk of 1973 was spent touring America, following his annual visit to Las Vegas, where James Caughley witnessed Presley shoot a gold-engraved pistol sufficient times to demolish one of the hotel's chandeliers. He also fired the gun at his current girlfriend, Linda Thompson. Caughley told author John Parker, 'Elvis did crazy things, but you can't blame it all on the drugs. He had a very emotional temper . . . Nobody would stand up and tell him "no".'

It was also during this Las Vegas stint that the first of the star's publicised hospitalisations caused concern among his fans, who were ignorant of his failing health. The second internment followed his divorce being finally settled, with Priscilla reputedly receiving a solitary payment of $100,000, alimony and child support, monthly payments of $1,500, plus other expenses. Having had no prior experience of handling money, Priscilla soon realised the settlement was grossly inadequate. She hired a Los Angeles lawyer who was, among other things, horrified that Presley had dictated the terms of her financial pay-off, ignoring the law of an automatic 50/50 settlement. A suit was subsequently filed in the Californian superior court, claiming intrinsic fraud, and that Priscilla had been wrongly advised.

Presley conceded and paid her a $1.5 million settlement; half paid immediately, the remainder by instalment; her alimony and child support payments were also increased, and she received a 5 per cent holding in a handful of her ex-husband's music companies, responsible for record royalties. Presley was unable to settle the court judgment in its entirety because he did not have sufficient funds.

From 1973 until Presley's death on 16 August 1977, his career was consumed with American tours; during each he would be taken ill and hospitalised, usually suffering from exhaustion. He also recorded. Of the albums he released during this four-year period, the most significant were *Elvis – A Legendary Performer Volume 1* and *Good Times*, (1974); *Promised Land* and *The Elvis Presley Sun Collection*, (1975); and *Elvis – The Legendary Performer Volume 2*, (1976). On the singles front, the most notable titles were 'If You Talk in your Sleep', (1974) and 'Promised Land', (1975).

From 1973 onwards, Presley's health worsened. He was battling against obesity and high blood pressure, plus his dependency on drugs to sleep, wake and perform. He also needed medication for recurring throat ailments and painkillers for sprained muscles following a performance. His emotional problems, instigated by personal and professional stress, likewise required medication. All in all, Presley was said to be a self-contained pharmacist. It was during this time that Dr Nichopoulos, 'Dr Nick', was integrated into the singer's personal entourage, alongside his dentist and countless, nameless doctors. Linda Thompson told John Parker that she saw Presley swallow as many as thirty pills during the course of an evening and 'he periodically used injections, some were vitamins B12 but I think a lot of them were amphetamines, the Dr Feelgood mixture . . . His behaviour was constantly erratic. His temperament was volatile and variable, but . . . a lot of the time quite loveable.'

By 1974, Presley had reached the ultimate downer. He collapsed while on tour and was hospitalised for the third time, forcing Colonel Tom Parker to cancel forthcoming concerts. Presley was admitted into the Baptist Memorial Hospital, Memphis, where, Parker reported, he was placed on a detoxification programme and therapy. His doctors were astonished when, after they administered sleeping pills, Presley remained fully awake for four days. Eventually, he was given a knock-out shot. Presley's father, Vernon, now at desperation level with his son's drug habit, hired John O'Grady, an ex-Los Angeles law enforcement officer, to investigate his son's suppliers and drug usage. He successfully unearthed information and told Parker, '[Presley] was in a bad way; it was obvious . . . He was a human being under the influence of drugs, suffering a deep debilitation caused by the use of narcotics . . . Of all the cases I've worked on . . . I have never seen so many drugs prescribed for one person ever before.'

Following the release of a pair of hit cover versions, namely 'Green, Green Grass of Home', previously a British chart-topper for Tom Jones in 1966, and 'Hurt', a Timi Yuro 1961 original, Presley issued the first album to be recorded in his Graceland studio, titled *From Elvis Presley Boulevard, Memphis* in July 1976. It was a Top Forty American hit; Top Twenty in Britain. Three months on, his 1960 hit 'The Girl of my Best Friend' was reissued in Britain to soar into the Top Ten.

In early 1977, his 1972 release, 'Suspicion', was reissued in Britain to peak in the Top Ten, while the follow-up single, 'Moody Blue', struggled into the American Top Forty during March. A month later, the title shot to No. 6 in the British chart. Also during April, the singer was readmitted to the Baptist Memorial Hospital in Memphis for five days, said to be suffering from exhaustion and influenza. Within days of being discharged, Presley recorded what would be his last material, while in June he performed his last concert at the Market Square Arena in Indianapolis. A month later, two former employees published the book he dreaded titled *Elvis: What Happened?* which dug deeply into the unsavoury side of his lifestyle.

By now, the Presley dynasty was falling apart. How the singer maintained his gruelling concert schedules was a mystery. Perhaps sheer willpower, because he needed to perform to pay the bills that now included a new Convair 880 plane, used to fly over 100 passengers and crew. Presley purchased the aircraft for $300,000 (the bulk of which was raised via loans), then stripped and refurbished it at a further cost of approximately $350,000. Not only was the star neck-deep in debt, but the immediate staff he had relied on left his employment, likewise Linda Thompson, his girlfriend of four years. Thompson, however, was hastily replaced by Ginger Alden. According to reports, it was she who found Presley's body in his bathroom on 16 August 1977. Thousands of words have been written about the singer's death and the lead-up to it. Investigations during the nineties, included those headed by John Parker, who published his findings in *Elvis: Murdered by the Mob* in 1993. Briefly, the scenario was along these lines.

In the early afternoon of 16 August 1977, paramedics were dispatched to Graceland, having no idea they were to treat Presley. They were whisked through Presley's untidy bedroom into his bathroom, where a woman was leaning over a body, giving mouth to mouth resuscitation. The paramedics rushed the body to the Baptist Memorial Hospital, where Presley was pronounced dead. He was forty-two years old.

Prior to the autopsy, it was announced that a press conference would be held. Once the body had been opened, the procedure should have included analysis of the stomach contents. Parker reported that in Presley's case, this was not done. Instead, the stomach was pumped, its contents flushed away. Later tests proved that fourteen chemical substances were present in Presley's body. There were signs of hypertension, with his arteries in no worse condition than for any man of his age. Based on these findings, the cause of Presley's death was given at the press conference as 'cardiac arrhythmia . . . due to undermined heartbeat [but] there is no evidence of chronic drug abuse whatsoever.' From the time the press conference ended, it was clear a cover-up was in progress; even Vernon Presley believed his son died from the hand of another by poisoning or lethal injection.

Following discussions between Vernon Presley and medical personnel from the Baptist Memorial Hospital, and following a further autopsy at his request, which resulted in the cause of death being given as an ingestion of multiple drugs, a further press conference was held to confirm Presley's death was due to 'hypertensive heart disease with coronary artery disease as a contributing factor'. The body was then sewn up in preparation for its final return to Graceland. Once again, the autopsy report was not made publicly available. Two years on, further evidence indicated that the cumulative effect of the drugs in his body caused his demise – but at whose hand?

The events surrounding Presley's death were, to say the very least, controversial and suspicious. Nothing added up. When rumours circulated that Presley was the victim of foul play, had been murdered because of his involvement with the Mafia, they were not denied. In fact, nothing was denied or confirmed. Presley was dead: that was the end of it. What was true, however, was that the star was worth more dead than alive, having amassed huge debts during the latter years of his life. Vernon Presley and Colonel Tom Parker took control and would eventually transform those debts into credits. Within days of the tragedy,

335

Parker concluded a deal with Factors Inc to exclusively manufacture merchandise in the late singer's image, while Parker himself unearthed rolls of archive film footage, to be sold to the highest bidder. Even Presley's record company, RCA Records, was reputedly saved from pending bankruptcy when an unprecedented demand for his recorded work necessitated the record presses producing discs day and night. Yes indeed, in death Presley was worth a fortune.

Within hours of star's death being announced, thousands of American fans converged on Memphis, while those from overseas set out on their final pilgrimage. On 17 August, thousands more filed past Presley's coffin at Graceland, while the following day, at his funeral service, 150 attended while approximately 80,000 more stood outside Graceland's front gates. Presley's last journey through Memphis took him to the Forest Hill Cemetery to be entombed in a marble crypt with his mother, who had died in 1958. During October, both mother and son were removed to rest next to each other in the Meditation Centre at Graceland, following attempts to steal both bodies from the cemetery. A month on, the Meditation Centre was opened to the public.

By the close of August, Elvis Presley albums re-entered the world's charts by the dozen, including in Britain, where titles like *G I Blues* and the *Elvis Golden Records* trilogy were big sellers once more. Singles likewise returned to the chart, notably 'All Shook Up', 'Crying in the Chapel' and 'The Wonder of You'. But it was the title 'Way Down', issued prior to his death, that shot to the top of the British chart during September 1977, where it stayed for a staggering five weeks, also reaching No. 18 in America. Composed by Layng Martine Jr, the disc carried Presley's name as co-producer, and was among those tracks included in the October 1976 recording sessions at Graceland's studio. The same month, the album *Moody Blue* soared to No. 3 in the British and American charts.

And still the reissued product swamped the international charts. Before 1977 ended, the single 'My Way', a live cover version of the Frank Sinatra 1969 classic, peaked in the American Top Thirty, while early the next year, the title shot into the British Top Ten. The Presley dynasty lived on under the guidance of Colonel Tom Parker, who ensured his late client remained big business.

During June 1979, Elvis's father, Vernon, died from a heart attack in Tulepo. His body was laid to rest next to his wife and son in Graceland's Meditation Centre. Midway through 1980, 'Dr Nick', responsible for the bulk of Presley's prescriptions during his lifetime, was indicted on fourteen counts of over-prescription of medication and drugs to eleven patients, notably Elvis Presley. He was later cleared of all charges.

In September 1980, an ambitious eight-album box set titled *Elvis Aaron Presley,* featuring previously unreleased tracks, was issued. Only 250,000 sets were pressed for worldwide distribution, and it spawned Presley's final Top Five British hit, titled 'It's Only Love'.

Among the countless publications following Presley's death, Priscilla Presley penned *Elvis and Me,* which was adapted for American television, before she joined the small-screen cast of *Dynasty.* Among the films, *This Is Elvis,* a documentary featuring concert footage linked by actors, was one of the most significant.

During June 1982, the Graceland mansion and grounds were opened to the public on the authority of Priscilla and the director of Elvis Presley Enterprises. Through the eighties, Presley lookalikes appeared by the thousands, while rumours of the star himself being seen were believed by those wishing it to be true. In the nineties, Presley merchandising continued as a multi-million-dollar concern; genuine memorabilia was auctioned for exorbitant prices, while tacky souvenirs were sold from Memphis stores. Further investigations into the circumstances of Presley's death continued, notably *The Elvis Conspiracy* screened on TV in 1992. In excess of 100 platinum and gold discs were presented to the Presley estate representing sales since the singer's death.

In 1993, America paid a national tribute to its star with the Elvis Presley postage stamp, and a year on, stood in disbelief when Elvis and Priscilla's only daughter, Lisa Marie, married for the second time to Michael Jackson. (Her first marriage was to musician Danny Keough in October 1988, with whom she had one daughter and one son.) The couple married in May 1994 and divorced in 1996 at Lisa Marie's instigation, citing 'irreconcilable differences'.

To the present day, publications and investigations abound with new evidence of Presley's death – in much the same way as Monroe's untimely and sinister death in 1962 – but nothing can alter the fact: the King of rock 'n' roll died on 16 August 1977, leaving a huge void in the world of entertainment, and the British population feeling they had been cheated of his personal presence.

Long live the King!

Also see: 'The Wonder of You', September 1970

(Quotes: *Elvis: Murdered by the Mob* by John Parker)

BACCARA

Yes Sir I Can Boogie

Disco had no barriers. Success was not confined to American or indeed British acts, because Europe had quite a healthy presence on the dancefloor. Sustaining that success was the problem; European productions, while sounding samey, tended to concentrate on singles, not artist longevity. Baccara was a prime example.

This chart-topper had European-wide influence. Mayte Mateus and Maria Mendiola, known as Baccara, were Spanish. 'Yes Sir I Can Boogie' was written and produced by two Dutchmen, Rolf Soja and Frank Dostal. The single was sung in English. The throwaway disc earned Baccara the distinction of being the first Spanish duo to reach the top in Britain.

Released by RCA Records, 'Yes Sir I Can Boogie' topped the British chart in October 1977. Thankfully, the British public was not that crazy over this ridiculous little track; it stayed at the top for only one week.

The follow-up, 'Sorry I'm a Lady' was equally nondescript, peaking in the Top Twenty. Both tracks were swiped from the *Baccara* album and happily represented the duo's only British successes.

Where Baccara are now is anyone's guess!

Also a No. 1 single in October 1977: 'Silver Lady' by David Soul

November 1977

ABBA

The Name of the Game

'We see no reason to be alarmed about our future . . . So many stars who allow themselves to become too much of a public property find themselves burned out in a glare of publicity.' – Bjorn Ulvaeus

During their six-month break following the exhausting world tour, Abba issued their sixth British chart-topper. 'The Name of the Game' topped the chart in November 1977, where it stayed for four weeks.

Most music critics claimed the title was a bomber; once again they were proved wrong. The beat was lazy; the lyrics a little more complex than previous singles, but it was the Abba production that sold the song. As the quartet were engrossed in recording their next album, they did not personally promote 'The Name of the Game'. Instead they used a video directed by Lasse Hallstrom, who was responsible for filming the group's Australian tour of 1977 for *Abba: The Movie*, yet to be premiered, and the group's previous promotional film for 'Knowing Me Knowing You'.

Needless to say, 'The Name of the Game' topped European charts, where still the group could do little wrong. The title was to be included in the next album, originally planned to be issued alongside *Abba: The Movie*. However, as advance orders for the album were massive, Abba's several record companies were unable to press sufficient copies for the scheduled December 1977 release date. The same applied to the movie: could enough copies be available to meet cinema demand?

However, before either could be released, Agnetha Faltskog gave birth to her second child, a son, on 4 December, thirteen days before *Abba: The Movie* was premiered in Amsterdam's City Theatre. Meantime, it was decided that the album, now titled *Abba: The Album*, would be released in Sweden only, to coincide with the film's premiere there.

Abba: The Album was issued in Britain during February 1978; critics' views were mixed but 'Abba's least satisfactory album' tended to be the general reaction. Once again, though, the record-buying public thought otherwise; the album entered the chart at No. 1, thanks to advance orders in excess of one million copies. The title would eventually pass triple platinum status in Britain alone and gold status in America.

Also in February, *Abba: The Movie* was premiered in London. Critics were generally generous – 'This movie will stun you' – but occasionally uncompromising - 'This full-blown epic is shockingly bad!' Meanwhile, back home in Sweden, the finishing touches were made to their own Polar Music record studio in Stockholm, built to Andersson and Ulvaeus's specifications. Andersson: 'It has many facilities that you cannot find in any other studio anywhere else.'

By releasing both the movie and album at the start of 1978, Abba were able to use the remainder of the year for other work and, of course, their valued home life. Both projects would sustain the group's high public profile until new material was available. As promoters from across the world clustered to request concert dates, Abba holidayed. Agnetha Faltskog, Bjorn Ulvaeus and their family stayed in the Caribbean, while Frida Lyngstad and Benny Andersson chose the Virgin Islands. In their absence, the Abba empire jogged on; no one glanced ahead to peek at the slow descent of both their professional and personal lives.

Also see: 'Waterloo', May 1974; 'Mamma Mia', January 1976; 'Dancing Queen', September 1976; 'Knowing Me Knowing You', April 1977; 'Take a Chance on Me', March 1978

(Quotes: *Abba – The Music Still Goes On: The Complete Story* by Paul Snaith)

December 1977/January 1978

WINGS

Mull of Kintyre

'The Beatles was always four of us. People will say we could get someone else in, but it's still not the same. The Beatles was The Beatles.' – Paul McCartney

As The Beatles finished their last album as a group, *Let It Be*, Paul McCartney, born in Liverpool, Lancashire, on 18 June 1942, had completed his first solo album. For some time, the group's relationships had been strained, particularly when John Lennon introduced Yoko Ono into the group's inner sanctum. When the situation became irreversible – George Harrison, for example, was frustrated at not having his compositions recorded, while Ringo Starr attempted to control and/or override the disagreements which dogged recording sessions and filming schedules – The Beatles publicly disbanded during 1970. McCartney was blamed for the breakdown of the world's most famous group because of the growing rift between him and the remaining three. Yet, Lennon had already recorded independently with The Plastic Ono Band.

Before 1970 ended, McCartney filed a suit in London's High Court for the dissolution of The Beatles and Co partnership, and engaged a receiver to investigate the group's financial situation, while Allen Klein remained as the remaining trio's financial advisor. A year on, McCartney won his action; the partnership was officially dissolved.

McCartney then released his eponymous solo album which, not surprisingly, soared to No. 2 in the British chart in May 1970 and hit No. 1 in America, a position it held for three weeks. The swiped track,

'Another Day', was released early in 1971, to (again) reach No. 2 in Britain, and No. 5 in America.

Midway through 1971, McCartney issued the album *Ram* bearing his wife's name. Born Linda Louise Eastman in Scarsdale, New York, on 24 September 1942, she met McCartney at the London club, Bag O'Nails, where she was photographing the performing group, Traffic. They married in 1969. Her inclusion dismayed McCartney's fans – how could a non-musician suddenly contribute to an ex-Beatle's work? However, as the dust settled, McCartney formed a new group, Wings, comprising Denny Laine, late of The Moody Blues, Denny Seiwell, Linda and himself. Henry McCullough, late of The Grease Band, completed the line-up early in 1972. By all accounts, the group's name came as a flash of inspiration to McCartney when he was waiting in London's King College Hospital for his daughter Mary to be born.

Before the end of 1971, Wings released 'Back Seat of my Car', which stalled in the British Top Forty, while 'Uncle Albert'/'Admiral Halsey' released in American became a chart-topper. Uncle Albert was based on a member of McCartney's family, who used to read the bible when he was drunk – the only time he did! The album *Wings Wildlife* followed: Top Twenty in Britain, Top Ten in America.

In 1972, Wings embarked upon their first British tour; a low-key affair, with performances confined to the college circuit. McCartney's intention was to return to his roots, to play for the people, and probably also to test the public's reaction to his new group, an unknown quantity when compared to The Beatles. Interestingly, McCartney's music was totally unlike the material he composed for, and performed with, The Fab Four. His was now more basic, far less musically cluttered, prompting critics to declare Lennon was the innovator in their previous partnership. In time, though, McCartney's music became more adventurous, albeit often smacking of middle-of-the-road influences.

Horrified at the carnage associated with the bloody conflict in Northern Ireland, more particularly the Bloody Sunday Massacre, the ex-Beatle wrote and released 'Give Ireland Back to the Irish', a strongly-worded single, publicly airing the views of so many. Needless to say, BBC Radio 1 failed to share his stand by banning the single outright, while sales pushed the title into the Top Twenty on both sides of the Atlantic. In retaliation to the ban, the singer released the nursery rhyme 'Mary Had a Little Lamb' set to music. No one found offence with this, enabling the inane track to peak in the British Top Ten during June 1972 and the Top Thirty in America. McCartney had vented his anger! Before the year closed, though, he was banned once more, this time for the innocuously-titled single 'Hi Hi Hi'. With a BBC Radio 1 blackout, the furious singer flipped the disc to allow 'C Moon' to soar into the British Top Five, while in America with no such restrictions on airplay, the topside shot into the Top Ten.

As a member of The Beatles, McCartney was hounded by the police, hunting for drugs. One imagined that when he said on TV that The Beatles had used LSD to record *Sergeant Pepper's Lonely Hearts Club Band* – the album that turned the music business into a more exciting world – he opened the gates for future surveillance. Police attention was at its most diligent at the close of 1972, when he and Linda were arrested twice; once in Sweden, and then again in their Scottish home, for possession of cannabis. His British drug record went on to cause immense problems when he applied for an American visa. In the eighties, McCartney and the law clashed once again, this time in Japan. He was arrested for possession of one half-pound of marijuana at the Narita International Airport, and subsequently jailed for nine days in Tokyo. The Japanese customs officers originally believed the marijuana to be Linda's, before McCartney confirmed it was indeed his. The intended Japanese tour was cancelled, and McCartney was extradited from the country, with all charges dropped, following the intervention of the British Consulate.

During 1973, Wings released the solitary album, *Red Rose Speedway:* a No. 5 British hit, No. 1 in America. A year later, their finest work to date, recorded in Nigeria and titled *Band on the Run*, was issued. This magnificent release with the star-studded packaging went on to sell in excess of six million copies internationally, and rightly topped both the British and American charts. Wings released the haunting 'My Love', one of the most endearing ballads of the decade. The title peaked in the British Top Ten, but soared to the top in America. Hot on its heels came a complete musical contrast as McCartney was asked to compose and record the theme to the forthcoming James Bond movie *Live and Let Die*, a thundering track, befitting the Bond musical formula, which Brenda Arnau actually sang on the film's soundtrack. McCartney's version, however, peaked in the British Top Ten during June 1973, and reached No. 2 Stateside.

The hell-on-wheels single, properly titled 'Helen Wheels', reached the British Top Twenty and the American Top Ten. McCartney's jeep had been the inspiration, while his dog was responsible for the follow-up single, 'Jet'. The title was a Top Ten hit on both sides of the Atlantic.

In 1974 Geoff Britton joined Wings. A pair of charting singles sustained McCartney's high profile as a recording entity through to the end of the year, 'Band on the Run', a No. 3 British hit, American chart-topper and winner of the Grammy Award for Best Pop Vocal Performance by a Duo, Group or Chorus, and 'Junior's Farm', a Top Twenty British hit which reached the Top Three in America.

In 1975 Geoff Britton was replaced by Joe English, and McCartney released *Venus and Mars,* another album crammed with blinding material. One track in particular attracted special attention: as unlikely as it seemed, the track was the theme to the television soap series *Crossroads,* which introduced the programmes from June 1975. Meanwhile, *Venus and Mars* and the lifted single 'Listen to What the Man Said' topped the respective American charts simultaneously, while the single contented itself with a British Top Ten placing, as the album became Britain's No. 1 seller. To capitalise on this success and that throughout the world, Wings embarked upon a long-overdue and much needed year's tour, starting in Britain, including ten countries, with the 'Wings over America' leg proving the most arduous. Wings performed before two million people, which surely cemented their international popularity. In their absence, the singles 'Letting Go', 'Silly Love Songs' and 'Let 'Em In' were released, and the album *Wings at the Speed of Sound* were all big sellers.

In 1977, McCulloch and English departed from Wings, and McCartney composed and recorded the biggest-selling single in Britain up to that time with sales surpassing the three million mark. He would probably have held this distinction for longer but for 'Do They Know It's Christmas?' recorded by Band Aid and issued in 1984. Nonetheless, the ex-Beatle's 'Mull of Kintyre', a Scottish anthem, lazy and relaxing, was inspired by the tip of the Kintyre peninsula, situated eleven miles from the singer's Campbeltown family farmhouse. With twenty-one bagpipers accompanying the group, 'Mull of Kintyre' topped the British chart for a remarkable nine weeks, yet bombed in America. Instead, they settled for 'Girl's School', McCartney's thoughts about porno-graphic film advertising, hidden away on the B-side, which faltered in the Top Forty. The artist had created a monstrous sound with the topside, which sold beyond his wildest ambitions. From the vinyl came the honours, including the Ivor Novello Award for the Best Selling A-Side Single.

Following such a monumental single was impossible, so it was no surprise when the sprightly 'With a Little Luck' was issued without a bagpipe to be heard! The title soared into the British Top Five, selling in excess of 2.5 million copies, and reached No. 1 in America, the ex-Beatles' sixth single to reach that position. Flushed once more with

343

success, the album *London Town* (originally titled *Water Wings* and largely recorded on a yacht moored in the Virgin Islands) followed. It was another big seller. With Wings reduced to a trio, McCartney continued his consistent chart run with singles like 'I've Had Enough', 'Goodnight Tonight' and 'Old Siam Sir'. Also issued were a pair of albums, namely, *Wings Greatest* and *Back to the Egg*.

Now the recipient of a rhodium medallion, presented during a *Guinness Book of Records* awards ceremony in recognition of his composing career that spanned 43 songs from 1962 through to 1978, and recognised as the most successful composer of all time, McCartney started the eighties with his first solo single in nine years titled 'Wonderful Christmas'; a Top Ten British hit.

In 1980, McCartney returned to the top of the British chart with his *McCartney II* album, and worked with The Beatles' mentor, George Martin, to record the track 'We All Stand Together' for future release. Instead of the Abbey Road Studios, where Martin oversaw the bulk of The Beatles' recordings, they worked in his own studio, AIR in London. 'We All Stand Together', bearing the label credit Paul McCartney and The Frog Chorus, was issued to become a No. 3 British hit late in 1984. Accompanied by an animated video based on the *Daily Express* newspaper cartoon series Rupert Bear, which McCartney owned, the song remained a children's favourite through to the next decade. Of his other singles during 1980, 'Coming Up' was the biggest seller of all, peaking at No. 2 in Britain. Yes, McCartney could do little wrong at this juncture. His star was shining brightly as one burned out. John Lennon was murdered on 8 December outside the Dakota Building in New York. His killer, Mark Chapman, a Lennon fanatic, became famous.

Wings now disbanded, leaving its founder to duet with Stevie Wonder on 'Ebony and Ivory', a plea for racial harmony. When McCartney issued *Red Rose Speedway*, he had the words 'We love you' inscribed for Wonder in Braille on the upper left-hand corner of the disc's packaging. Wonder received the message, and years later learned that McCartney had composed a track for him. The pair subsequently recorded it in Montserrat in the West Indies. 'Ebony and Ivory' shot to the top of the British chart; it was Wonder's first chart-topper. Sales were boosted by a promotional video filmed on both sides of the Atlantic. Wonder was superimposed on video in America; the artists were not actually filmed together. Nobody knew the difference! The unique duet likewise topped the American chart during May 1982, a position it held for seven weeks. During the same month, McCartney issued his album *Tug of War*; yes . . . a British and American chart-topper!

The duet with Motown's top-selling male soloist encouraged McCartney to record with Michael Jackson. Following lengthy deliberations, the two singers recorded 'The Girl Is Mine', swiped from Jackson's *Thriller* album, to reach the British Top Ten; and hit No. 2 in America. During November 1983, their second duet, 'Say Say Say', peaked just one position from the top in Britain while in America it went all the way, where it stayed for six weeks.

To start 1984, McCartney's historical tribute, namely, 'Pipes of Peace' became a British chart-topper, supported by a thoughtful video depicting the Christmas Day Truce of 1914 during the First World War. The single helped the eponymous album to No. 4 in Britain and into the Top Twenty in America, while the follow-up single, 'No More Lonely Nights' soared to No. 2 in Britain. It was the theme from McCartney's debut feature film in which he starred with Linda and Ringo Starr, titled *Give my Regards to Broad Street*. With promotion advertising the film as something it was not, McCartney suffered a box office disaster. This return to the film world surprised many, bearing in mind McCartney's past failure with The Beatles' *Magical Mystery Tour*. Guess he had to try it one more time!

The next year was one of mixed emotions. A highpoint was McCartney's performance of 'Let It Be' during his contribution to Live Aid. All proceeds were earmarked for the victims of Ethiopia famine. A lowpoint was his inability to purchase ATV Music, owner of Northern Songs, responsible for 263 Beatles tracks. McCartney was outbid by Michael Jackson, whom he had held in high esteem as a friend and artist; McCartney viewed Jackson's move as a betrayal of that position. Jackson reputedly paid $53 million for the music catalogues which meant, in theory, that each time, say, McCartney wanted to use one of his own compositions, he legally had to pay for the privilege. Before the Jackson acquisition, the titles were guarded and rarely was permission granted for commercial usage, particularly in television advertisements. Jackson appeared not to share that same respect; another aspect that annoyed McCartney and, needless to say, the remaining Beatles and their stalwart fans, who believe such compositions are sacred. Years on, McCartney tried desperately to buy back the music, but Jackson refused to acknowledge his offers, saying the matter was controlled by his managers.

Through to the end of the decade McCartney issued his obligatory greatest hits compilations *All the Best!* and *Flowers in the Dirt*, while singles included 'Once upon a Long Ago', 'This One' and 'Figure of Eight'. All were charting titles. He also contributed to the charity single

'Ferry 'cross the Mersey' with fellow Liverpudlians, The Christians, Holly Johnson and Gerry Marsden. All royalties from the single's sales went to the Hillsborough Disaster Fund, which happily were large due to the song's chart-topping status.

However, it was McCartney's 1989 world tour that excited the public most; his first trek for around thirteen years. The tour started in Sweden during September. It included North America, where during one show Stevie Wonder joined him on stage to sing 'Ebony and Ivory'. His concert in Rio de Janeiro, Brazil, won him an entry in the *Guinness Book of Records,* for playing before a staggering 184,000-strong audience. When the trek ended in Chicago, McCartney had performed in 46 cities and presented approximately 100 concerts, several of which were recorded for the album *Tripping the Live Fantastic,* released in December 1990 and a Top Twenty British hit, Top Thirty in America. The trip earned the singer a fortune, a proportion of which he donated to charity, including $100,000 to Friends of the Earth.

In the new decade, McCartney contributed his version of the Presley classic 'It's Now or Never' to the compilation *The Last Temptation of Elvis;* all proceeds went to Nordoff Robbins Music Therapy. His first single of the nineties, 'Put It There', faltered in the British Top Forty. A year on, he diversified musically, when following a low-key concert at the Mean Fiddler, London, he composed the classical piece 'Liverpool Oratorio', performed by the Royal Liverpool Philharmonic Orchestra at the city's cathedral during June 1991. The work was later premiered in America during November, conducted by Carl Davis, while a month later the album *Paul McCartney's Liverpool Oratorio Conducted by Carl Davis* was issued.

Through 1992 and 1993, with his home city still foremost in his mind, McCartney donated £500,000 to the Liverpool Institute for the Performing Arts, designed to teach young people to dance. The total sum eventually donated by the singer was said to be twice the original figure and included £110,000 he received from King Carl Gustaf of Sweden during a ceremony staged in Sweden by the Royal Swedish Academy for his imaginative contribution to music during thirty years. In 1993, *Off the Ground,* recorded at his home studio at Rye, East Sussex, where the McCartney family now spent much of their time, was issued. The swiped track, 'Hope of Deliverance', peaked in the British Top Twenty during January; and reached the Top Ninety in America. As the album peaked in the British Top Five, the singer embarked upon a further world tour. During this stint, McCartney contributed to the 'Earth Day' concert, staged at the Hollywood Bowl, joining artists like

k. d. lang and Steve Miller. All proceeds went to Greenpeace, PETA (People for the Ethical Treatment of Animals) and Friends of the Earth.

Early in 1994, McCartney inducted the late John Lennon into the Rock 'n' Roll Hall of Fame, during a ceremony staged at the Waldof Astoria Hotel, New York. His speech was one of public emotion for his lost friend: 'I love him to this day and I always did love him.'

A year later, McCartney shifted musical gear once more, when he performed at a charity dinner to benefit the Royal College of Music in London. His set included excerpts from his 'Liverpool Oratorio' and The Beatles' 'Lady Madonna', with the Brodsky Quartet as support. In May, he directed *Oobu Joobu,* a thirteen-part radio series aired in America via Westwood One Radio, which included previously unheard Beatles' interviews and recordings. However, behind scenes and for over a year, McCartney had been mulling over a television project called *The Beatles Anthology,* the life and times of the group. The original plan was for him to collaborate with Ringo Starr and George Harrison to provide incidental music for the proposed series. Once the trio began experimenting in the recording studio, the plan changed. McCartney told journalist Nick Bradshaw: 'Even if we hit something really great it would still be George, Ringo and myself, and that's not quite as much fun as if, somehow, John could be in on it.' To this end, he contacted Lennon's widow, Yoko Ono, who played him a tape of demo tracks which included 'Free as a Bird', 'Real Love' and 'Grow Old with Me'. McCartney believed the first title was workable: 'I took the tapes back to England, got copies made for the guys. They liked it, so we decided to do it.' What Lennon would have felt when a demo track that he obviously had considered unsuitable for release was finally issued as a new Beatles' track, is probably unthinkable. Nonetheless, the pure historical interest of 'Free as a Bird' was overwhelming, although it failed to reach the top of the British chart, peaking at No. 2. The title 'Real Love' followed.

Meanwhile, Chip Chipperfield had completed the film *The Beatles Anthology,* assisted by a support team of ten, and using approximately 10,000 pieces of music and footage. Screened by ITV in Britain, the six-part series began in November 1995, hotly followed by the three-double-CD package, housing unreleased tracks, obscure items, re-recordings and narration. Videos and sundry publications followed. Obviously Beatle hype was at full strength to promote both the singles and the television series. The three remaining group members were prominent on the promotional roundabout which the bulk of the British public gratefully received. The Beatles were back, with the complete membership!

While McCartney was publicly turning dreams into reality, behind-scenes his family suffered anguish when Linda was diagnosed with breast cancer. She was treated privately in America with her husband by her side. Following an operation and months of chemotherapy, she joined McCartney to be filmed for their acceptance speech after winning an award from PETA.

The ex-Beatle's life now appears to be one of husband and father first, with musician and singer a close second. He has remained level-headed throughout his career, despite selling 150 million singles during the past 30 years, and, unlike some, has always been approachable by media and public alike. His family are vegetarians – Linda has spearheaded her own range of vegetarian dishes with Ross Foods – while their daughters' upbringing does not reflect too strongly McCartney's vast wealth, estimated at £420 million. McCartney: 'People find it hard to accept that I am an ordinary bloke because I have a lot of money.'

His many tireless contributions to charity functions and funds were finally recognised in March 1997 when he was knighted by the Queen at Buckingham Palace. He said he accepted the second honour (he is already a recipient of the MBE) on behalf of The Beatles and all the people living in Liverpool, while stressing he would remain 'Paul' and not Sir Paul McCartney! Also during 1997, McCartney issued his first collection of new tracks since 1993 under the title *Flaming Pie*. The single 'Young Boy' was the first to be swiped for release in May. Both titles were best-sellers.

'I don't actually want to be a living legend.' – Paul McCartney

(Quotes: *The Beatles: Day by Day – 1962–1989* by Mark Lewisohn)

ALTHIA AND DONNA

Uptown Top Ranking

How singles like 'Uptown Top Ranking' managed to dominate British music remains a mystery. A week's compulsive buying was usually to blame following a solid radio brainwashing session. Apparently, the single was originally conceived as an instrumental, but Althia and Donna decided to add lyrics – such as they were. The result was, many believed, tiresome and banal.

As reggae fans were in a minority, very few singles charted in Britain. Commercial reggae was different, it wasn't an ethnic sound, therefore it fell into the pop or mainstream music category. Like, say, Dave and Ansil Collins before them, these young Jamaican schoolgirls – Althia Forest and Donna Reid – caught the public's imagination, though they had only a short stab at stardom.

Released on the Lightning Records label and penned by the singers with Errol Thompson, 'Uptown Top Ranking' soared to the top of the British chart in February 1978, It was, needless to say, their only hit, although the spin-off album, *Uptown Top Ranking*, enjoyed considerable success.

Regrettably (or not) Althia and Donna were unable to follow up their one-week chart-topper and became a one-hit wonder.

The seventies took no prisoners.

March 1978

ABBA

Take a Chance on Me

'Everything has to end sometime. We have doubts each time we release a record . . . If we produced something that we really believed in and it made no impact on the charts, we'd be scared.'– Benny Andersson

As a recording group, Abba had achieved more than any other

contemporary musical unit. *Abba: The Album* had easily passed the one million mark in Britain, and *Abba: The Movie* had been more successful than was originally anticipated. What more could this Swedish quartet desire? A stable personal life perhaps, because for some time tempers had been frayed. By 1978, their behind-scenes story was bitter-sweet. When Andersson and Frida Lyngstad finally married in October, Bjorn Ulvaeus and Agnetha Faltskog filed for divorce. All agreed, however, the show had to go on. And it did. 'Take a Chance on Me', with its a cappella introduction, soared to the top of the British singles chart in March 1978, and later reached the Top Three in America. The title was the group's third consecutive British chart-topper.

Early 1979, the group sang the plaintive ballad 'Chiquitita' at the 'Music for UNICEF Concert' staged in New York as part of the celebrations for the International Year of the Child. All proceeds from the subsequent sale of the 'Chiquitita' single went to UNICEF. The title shot to No. 2 in the British chart during February, and reached the Top Thirty in America in 1980. Two months later, the unlikely choice of the mid-paced rocker 'Does your Mother Know?' was issued as a single to soar to No. 4, and into the American Top Twenty. This single was the lead-in to the group's first album to be recorded in Polar Music's state-of-the-art studio, *Voulez-Vous*. It entered the British chart at the top, selling one million copies. As it slowly descended, two titles were swiped as a double A-sided single, namely, 'Angeleyes'/'Voulez-Vous' (an unusual move for Abba, who generally earmarked specific titles for single release). Whatever the reason, the single peaked at No. 3 in Britain. 'Voulez-Vous' staggered into the Top Eighty in America during the September, the same month as the group toured there. A month on, the title 'Angeleyes' fared marginally better to reach the Top Seventy.

In October 1979, Abba toured Britain once more, where the inevitable mayhem and fan hysteria shadowed their every move. During the shows they previewed their next single 'Gimme Gimme Gimme (a Man after Midnight)', which rose to No. 3 in Britain during November. Also during this month, Abba entered the *Guinness Book of Records* under the heading the Biggest Selling Group in Music History. With the voices of the International School of Stockholm as support, Abba's final single of the year was 'I Have a Dream'; a Top Two British hit.

In 1980, the compilation *Greatest Hits Volume 2* peaked in the American Top Fifty, while the single 'The Winner Takes It All' returned the quartet to the top of the British chart during August 1980: the group's first chart-topper since 'Take a Chance on Me' in 1978. Before the year ended, the *Super Trouper* album followed its predecessors to the top of the British chart. Advance orders for the album topped one million copies; once on sale it sold 160,000 copies in one day! The album went on to sell seven million copies worldwide. As *Super Trouper* dominated the European charts, Andersson publicly announced that his marriage to Frida Lyngstad had ended; he cited his girlfriend Mona Norklit as the reason. The statement said, 'The decision has been taken after considerable consideration and mutual agreement . . . This step won't affect our partnership in Abba. It is of a completely private nature.'

Abba further suffered when an anonymous note was delivered to Polar Music claiming the safety of the group and their children was in jeopardy. Faltskog: 'Whoever's writing the notes said that if we went on tour they'd hurt our children.' Swedish police treated the threat seriously, while the quartet cancelled touring plans to remain in Stockholm.

During the next year, Abba released a pair of British singles, 'Lay All your Love on Me', a dance track pressed as a twelve-inch single, which reached the Top Ten, and the slower-paced 'One of Us', a No. 3 hit. Their next album, *The Visitors,* with advance orders of 700,000 in Britain, shot to No. 1 in December, ironically marking the beginning of the disintegration of the group. What was to be their last concert was staged in Stockholm, and the 'Head over Heels' single stalled in the British Top Thirty in March 1982.

As Abba celebrated their tenth anniversary in the music business, 'The Day Before You Came' struggled into the Top Forty British singles chart. Lyngstad had moved to London and released her big-selling solo album *Somethin's Going On,* from which the Top Fifty single 'I Know There's Something Going On' was lifted.

On the personal front, Andersson and his new wife, Mona, had a son, while Ulvaeus and his new wife, Lena, celebrated the birth of their daughter. They later moved to Britain to live in Henley-on-Thames. Ulvaeus said, 'In Sweden I felt the lack of freedom and that so many decisions were taken away from me by politicians. For example, they take more than 80 per cent of income in tax. It wasn't that the remaining 20 per cent wouldn't have been enough, it was the fact that I couldn't make my own decisions about what to do with my own money.'

On the professional front, Abba and Russia were at loggerheads. Russian authorities banned the group and its recorded work when the promotional video for 'When All Is Said and Done' was used in an American television documentary where artists protested against the Russian foray in Poland. Andersson admitted the group would suffer financially but added, 'We are worried about our fans being denied the chance to hear our music.'

The history book was finally closed in November 1982 when Abba issued the double compilation *The Singles: The First Ten Years,* their final British chart-topping album. The title 'Under Attack' was swiped for single release, but faltered in the British Top Thirty a month later. Although no statement was issued regarding the group's demise, it became apparent when Agnetha Faltskog followed in Lyngstad's footsteps and recorded the solo album *The Heat Is On,* while Andersson and Ulvaeus collaborated with Tim Rice to compose the 1985 musical *Chess.* Andersson: 'For a long time Bjorn and I have been talking about how great it would be if there was a chance for us to move into the music theatre. So when Tim came to us in Stockholm and asked if we wanted to collaborate with him, we seized the chance.' Two British hit singles were lifted from the musical's soundtrack, namely, 'I Know Him So Well', a duet between Elaine Page and Barbara Dickson, and 'One Night in Bangkok' by Murray Head.

With Lyngstad and Faltskog concentrating on solo careers, the final Abba single to chart in Britain was released. Titled 'Thank You for the Music', the title reached the Top Forty late in 1983. With the group disbanded, their manager, Stig Anderson, sold Polar Music, building a bigger gulf between him and Abba. When the Swedish Inland Revenue investigated the group's financial affairs, it was estimated that Faltskog and Ulvaeus owed £1 million each in back taxes. Share prices in their company were plummeting. Stig Anderson was blamed for mismanaging their various financial investments; Abba sued Polar Music for loss of earnings reputed to be worth £16 million under a contract both parties had signed in 1983. Eventually, the group and Polar reached a private settlement, but publicly, reputations had been smeared, even to the extent that the media suggested Abba should be jailed for tax evasion!

In the nineties, Faltskog remarried, and appeared to retire from the music business. Lyngstad went on to marry a German architect; she also abandoned music to concentrate on environmental issues. Only Andersson and Ulvaeus remained active in music. In 1992, when the bulk of Abba's recording contracts around the world had expired, including that with CBS Records in Britain, Polydor Records purchased the rights to the group's back catalogue and issued 'Dancing Queen', the first Abba single in ten years. While the title climbed the European charts, the compilation *Abba Gold* passed platinum status in twenty countries, selling approximately five million copies. With this remarkable achievement, rumours obviously abounded that Abba would re-form. Hah, not so. Ulvaeus: 'When we split up in 1982 that was it . . . I don't believe in making any half-assed comebacks. I think it is so pathetic when old bands who have broken up, go back on the road again.'

In 1993, the compilation *More Abba Gold* was released to repeat the success of its sister record. Who on earth was buying these discs? Surely, everyone who wanted an Abba title had purchased it first time round? True, the introduction of CDs obviously helped sales; but even so! Polydor Records who in actual fact took a tremendous risk buying Abba's tried and tested material, must have been hysterical with delight. Two years on, the four-CD box set titled *Thank You for the Music* and *Abba Gold – Greatest Hits* were multi-million sellers. Ulvaeus: 'I realise that millions of records are being sold out there, and that it has something to do with me . . . It was another time and I was another person.'

The Swedish quartet also lives on through tributes from other artists and musical clones. For instance, Erasure released the *Abbaesque* EP in June 1992, while Abba's worst nightmare turned to reality when Bjorn Again, Australian impersonators, toured the world earning more than a lucrative living!

Obviously, Abba's music will continue to live on into the next millennium, but what will that new generation think of the group's stage clothes? Not a lot!

'I don't know if there is anything more to achieve. How could there be?' – Benny Andersson

'I really don't miss all the fame and success of Abba.' – Agnetha Faltskog

Also see: 'Waterloo', May 1974; 'Mamma Mia', January 1976; 'Dancing Queen', September 1976; 'Knowing Me Knowing You', April 1977; 'The Name of the Game', November 1977

(Quotes: *Abba: The Music Still Goes On – The Complete Story* by Paul Snaith)

KATE BUSH

Wuthering Heights

This young singer's impact on British music was not only due to her innovative recordings, but her extraordinary visual imagination. She became established as one of Britain's foremost singer/songwriters, respected by the media and public; quite a rare combination during this musically volatile decade.

Born Catherine Bush on 30 July 1958, in Bexleyheath, Kent, she mastered the piano and violin by the age of eleven years, while attending St Joseph's Convent Grammar School. Her interest in music expanded to composing, which sufficiently excited a family friend to finance a recording session for the young enthusiast. Among the titles she recorded were 'Berlin' and 'The Man with the Child in his Eyes', later heard by Pink Floyd member, Dave Gilmour. Gilmour passed the recorded work to Bob Mercer, one of EMI Records' more adventurous directors during the seventies. Mercer instantly recognised Bush's raw exciting talent as a singer and composer, and signed her to a recording and publishing contract, offering to finance her development as an artist.

Bush put the money to excellent use to learn voice and dance techniques, and to attend Lindsay Kemp's Mime School. Bush: 'He taught me that you can express with your body, and when your body is awake so is your mind.' The entire process spanned three years, during which time she also performed, heading the K T Bush Band on the London circuit.

Having paid her dues, Bush released her debut single for EMI Records during 1978. The lyrical content was inspired by Emily Bronte's novel *Wuthering Heights,* and the song was unique, and perhaps alien, to the decade's singles market. Indeed, Mercer was unsure how to present the title to the public, feeling it to be too adventurous for British pop. To test the reaction, he circulated 'Wuthering Heights' to the media via an expensive press reception and marketing campaign. The result was staggering, proving the company's investment was solid. 'Wuthering Heights' shot to the top of the British chart during April 1978, a position it held for four weeks, whereupon the success was repeated throughout Europe and in Australia. It is true to say Bush's vocal styling was individualistic; her soprano presentation against a lavish orchestral backdrop took courage and determination for one so young. The beauty of her recordings was actually in her voice and the depth of her intense lyrical verses. Bush: 'The reason I sang "Wuthering Heights" so high is that I felt it called for it. The book has a mood of mystery and I wanted to reflect it.' Nonetheless, as was expected, the media slated her 'squeaky, high pitched' voice, believing it to be no more than a gimmick, but as future releases proved, Bush was no mere product of record company hype.

Her debut album quickly followed. Titled *The Kick Inside* and featuring Dave Gilmour's experienced contribution to tracks she had composed during the previous three-year period, it shot to No. 3 in Britain, a position doubtless encouraged by its sleeve being splashed across the backs of a hundred-strong London buses!

The British chart-topper's follow-up was the tortured 'The Man with the Child in his Eyes', a Top Ten hit during July, which made a poor showing in the American Top Ninety in March 1979. The next single, 'Hammer Horror', a complete musical contrast, stalled in the British Top Fifty; nonetheless, the title proved the artist's broad musical taste. Before the year ended, Bush's second album *Lionheart*, a Top Six hit, went further to prove her growing talent.

With the security of the British hits behind her, Bush embarked upon her first, and long-awaited, nationwide tour. The lengthy trek, using the banner 'Tour of Life', saw the artist on stage for approximately three hours, where she surprised and delighted audiences with a tireless combination of song, dance and mime. She then took the tour to Europe, where, once again, sold-out venues greeted her.

Sadly, this tour was the singer's last; the experience took its toll, it was one experience she refused to repeat.

The single 'Wow' followed the 'Tour of Life' to reach No. 14 in the British chart in March 1979, while the *Kate Bush on Stage* EP soared into the Top Ten during October. She won an Ivor Novello Award for 'The Man with the Child in his Eyes', and performed with other EMI Records' acts in a charity gala. The proceeds of this concert went to the family of a lighting engineer tragically killed in a theatre accident.

In the new decade, Bush remained a formidable recording force; her first single of 1980 covered another hard-hitting topic, the devastation resulting from a nuclear holocaust. Titled 'Breathing', it reached the Top Twenty in May. Three months on, 'Babooshka' returned her to the Top Five, while in September, her album *Never for Ever* crashed into the chart at the top. The title 'Army Dreamers', lifted from the album, peaked in the Top Twenty, before Bush's contribution to the festive season, 'December Will Be Magic Again' became her second-lowest-selling single to date, stalling in the Top Thirty.

During the next two years, Bush's public profile was more or less confined to her recording work. In 1981, the single 'Sat in your Lap' soared into the Top Twenty, and the title track of her pending album *The Dreaming* stalled in the Top Fifty a year later. The mother album, incidentally, grew legs by peaking at No. 3 in its chart. Joining the artist on this album were Dave Gilmour, Rolf Harris playing the didgeridoo (honest) and her boyfriend, Del Palmer, who first played with her in the K T Bush Band.

A second album track titled 'There Goes a Tenner' bombed: an unexpected blip in her career, yet one she would eradicate during 1985, having spent 1984 away from the spotlight to supervise the completion of her recording studio in her London farmhouse home. She was conspicuous by her absence, and the media intimated Bush had lost her talent; she was burned out. They choked when she proved them wrong.

In the autumn of 1985, the title 'Running Up That Hill' was issued as a single, returning her to the British Top Three, and reaching the Top Thirty in America. Her new album, *Hounds of Love,* entered the British chart at the top. Boy, how those media critics must have swallowed hard!

Throughout her career, Kate Bush was an innovator in the promotional video field. She hired the best to produce storyboard tales to accompany her single releases; always having the final decision. Indeed, a collection was issued late in 1983 under the title *The Single File,* showcasing her individual style in visual art. One of the finest accompanied her 1985 single 'Cloudbursting', a Top Twenty British hit, where the singer secured the services of actor Donald Sutherland. During 1986, a further video collection titled *Hair of the Hound* was issued.

In 1986, a trio of singles sustained her position, 'Hounds of Love', 'The Big Sky' and 'Experiment IV'; apart from the first, which peaked in the Top Twenty, the others stalled in the British Top Forty. A year on, the much-awaited compilation of her biggest-selling titles was issued, *The Whole Story,* which shot straight to the top of the chart, while the accompanying video package did likewise. Bush was regarded as a recluse, preferring to sustain her career through her music and film, and the occasional public appearance.

By the close of the decade, she chose a different musical path to release the album *The Sensual World,* inspired by the Bulgarian folk unit Trio Bulgarka, a No. 2 charter. The album's title track reached the Top Twenty, while a further lifted song 'This Woman's Work' stalled in the Top Thirty.

In the nineties a further, more far-reaching compilation of her top recordings was issued. Appropriately titled *This Woman's Work,* it proved to be a huge catalogue seller. A further year passed before Bush recorded the solitary title 'Rocket Man' as her contribution to a compilation celebrating the work of Elton John and Bernie Taupin. Lifted as a single, it peaked at No. 12 in the British chart late in 1991.

In 1993, Bush issued her belated album *The Red Shoes,* once more featuring Gilmour, to peak No. 2 in Britain and in the Top Thirty in America. A pair of singles was released that year, 'Rubberband Girl' and 'Moments of Pleasure'; Top Twenty and Top Thirty hits respectively. In the next year, the album's title track was swiped as a single to reach No. 21 in the chart, followed by 'The Man I Love' and 'And So Is Love'; both Top Thirty hits.

As the nineties draw on, Kate Bush is rarely seen or heard. A new album is reputedly in the planning stages but to date (1997) no material has been released. The quality of Bush's work has never been questioned; the regularity of her releases has.

'I always enjoy reaching notes that I can't quite reach. A week later you'll be on top of that one, and trying to reach the one above it.' – Kate Bush

(Quotes: *NME Rock and Roll Years*)

May 1978

THE BEE GEES

Night Fever

'*Saturday Night Fever* is like an albatross around our neck.' – Maurice Gibb

Barry Gibb was born on 1 September 1947, and his twin brothers Maurice and Robin were born on 22 December two years later, all in Douglas, Isle of Man. Their mother, Barbara, was a singer, while their father, Hughie, was the leader of his own orchestra on the Mecca circuit. The family moved to Lancashire, before emigrating to Australia where Andy, their fourth son, was born. Before leaving Britain, the brothers had already performed before an audience, usually at the Manchester Gaumont's Saturday picture shows, where, known as The Rattlesnakes, they sang the then current songs. Maurice Gibb: 'The three of us knew what we wanted to do from day one. I can remember us walking down the street in Manchester and we were all saying we wanted to be appreciated for what we do in music.'

Once settled in Australia the brothers, still using the name The Rattlesnakes, befriended Bill Good, organiser of The Speedway Circus in Brisbane, where they performed between races, and 4KQ Radio's DJ Bill Gates, who played their taped material on air. In fact, the brothers took their name from Bill Gates and Bill Good's initials to become the BGs, although years later Maurice Gibb denied this. 'It stands for "Brothers Gibb". That's where the Bee Gees came from. We never knew if Andy was going to join us or not.'

Their first television appearance on *Anything Goes* in 1960 led to other spot performances before they secured a residency at Brisbane's Beachcomber Hotel. Two years on, they moved to Sydney, where one of their first performances was supporting Chubby Checker at the city's stadium. They also started flexing their composing hand to write 'Let Me Love You', followed by 'Starlight of Love' which was recorded by the Australian vocalist Col Joyce.

Most of 1963 was taken up with a residency at a Queensland nightclub, but between performances the BGs signed a recording deal with Festival Records. Their debut was 'Three Kisses of Love', while 'Wine and Women' became their first hit two years later. Switching to Spin Records, they recorded a series of minor Australian hits until 'Spicks and Specks', released late in 1966, became their first Australian chart-topper.

Early in 1967, the BGs decided they wanted to return to Britain. Maurice: 'We went as far as we could go in Australia. We were sort of like a dirty version of The Osmonds.' Also, he admitted, the brothers were in love with The Beatles and wanted to be 'where all the action was'. The timing was perfect because *Sergeant Pepper's Lonely Hearts Club Band* had just broken worldwide. Despite their parents' initial reluctance Hughie Gibb posted copies of his sons' Australian album to numerous notable British management companies, including NEMS Enterprises, once owned by Brian Epstein, now controlled by Robert Stigwood. Stigwood agreed to audition the BGs upon their arrival; this led to a recording contract with Polydor Records.

'New York Mining Disaster 1941' was The Bee Gees' debut Beatles' soundalike British single – and the first to be recorded outside Australia – released during May 1967. It also marked two additions to the brothers' line-up: guitarist Vince Melouney and drummer Colin Petersen, both Australians. The three-part harmony on 'New York Mining Disaster 1941' pushed the single to No. 12 in the British chart; No. 14 in America. During its life the disc sold in excess of one million copies. Interestingly, the initial copies of the single were circulated to the media bearing no artist credit. It was probably the intention to confuse radio DJs into thinking that maybe this was a Beatles' disc, and as such should be afforded maximum airplay. When the truth was out, many still actually believed it was The Beatles recording under another name. In fact, two members of the Fab Four were at the single's recording session. While The Bee Gees were in America midway through 1967 to promote 'New York Mining Disaster 1941', they wrote a song for Otis Redding. However, instead of giving it to him, they opted to record it themselves. Titled 'To Love Somebody' it peaked at No. 41 in Britain and No. 17 in America, but more importantly, it became one of the most covered Bee Gees' songs. Nina Simone, Janis Joplin, Jimmy Somerville and Michael Bolton, among others, rerecorded it.

Another track penned during their first American trip was 'Massachusetts', and when released in 1967 it became The Bee Gees' first British No. 1 single during November. It also soared into the American Top Twenty. Once more, it was the superb three-part harmonising that made the song so compelling, and it was this that sustained the trio's popularity for years to come. It was often the point of ridicule by impressionists – but who laughed all the way to the bank? Before the end of 1967, The Bee Gees' fourth single, 'World', was a Top Ten British hit, establishing them among the biggest-selling acts of the year.

The Bee Gees' sixties' success turned them into top-league artists within months, and the pressures that went hand in hand with such elevation were beginning to show by 1968. Minor disagreements within the group were usually disposed of, but when Barry Gibb announced he wanted to leave the line-up to concentrate on a movie career, the remaining brothers knew his vacancy could not be filled. And when Robin Gibb collapsed from exhaustion during a British tour and was admitted into a London nursing home, they realised their lifestyle needed to be modified. Robin's illness postponed their pending American tour for a month, until August 1968, and meant they would not be able to properly promote their next British single, 'I've Gotta Get a Message to You'. The track told a chilling tale of a man on death row whose only future was the electric chair. The public loved it and pushed it to No. 1 in September 1968; it peaked at No. 8 across the Atlantic. This was to have been the last single to feature Barry.

During November, midway through a German and Austrian tour, Robin and Barry Gibb were taken ill and ordered to rest. Their remaining dates were cancelled. Then musicians Vince Melouney and Colin Petersen announced their intention to leave. The disagreements within the trio worsened, probably heightened by their excessive drinking binges. 'I Started a Joke' was the brothers' first single of 1969, a No. 6 American hit, and was the last to feature Melouney and Petersen. It also marked the final single for Robin Gibb who, tired of constant arguments with Maurice, left the trio. Robin did, however, forget his differences by being best man at Maurice's wedding to Scottish singer, Lulu, in April 1969. Maurice said the marriage was 'good fun for about five years'.

As a duo, Maurice and Barry Gibb became involved in the *Cucumber Castle* project, a film starring Frankie Howerd, Spike Milligan and Lulu, among others. 'Don't Forget to Remember', lifted from the soundtrack, was issued during September 1969 to reach No. 2 in Britain, but in America sales were abysmally low as the single floundered in the Top Eighty. Following a period where each brother became involved in his own ventures, The Bee Gees re-formed late in 1970 at Robin's instigation. 'If we hadn't been related, we would probably never have gotten back together.' The British were slow to support them this time, as reflected by their first single, titled 'Lonely Days', which stalled in the Top Forty. The Americans, on the other hand, pushed the single to No. 3.

From 1971 through to 1974 The Bee Gees toured the world and released Top Twenty singles on both sides of the Atlantic. But music was changing; the public wanted to dance. The seventies were slowly being strangled by disco music, and artists not previously associated with dance were cashing in, many losing credibility on the way. Nonetheless, disco was booming, new acts were becoming big sellers as the beat dictated. And The Bee Gees were responsible for changing, or, as many believed at the time, destroying the good name of the dance.

In August 1975, the brothers released 'Jive Talkin' ', a fiery stuttered dance track conceived while Barry Gibb and his wife Lynda drove across railroad tracks; the tyres 'chuka chuka'd' on the metal, prompting Lynda to comment the sound was likened to 'drive talking'. The sound subsequently introduced the single which soared into the British Top Five and topped the American chart. The song was lifted from the brothers' album *Main Course,* recorded in New York and Miami with producer Arif Mardin, who was a genius with R. & B. acts. A second track, 'Nights on Broadway', was lifted to become a Top Ten American hit during December 1975.

A year later 'You Should Be Dancing', swiped from the *Children of the World* album, smashed into the world's charts, peaking at No. 5 in Britain, while topping the American chart, giving The Bee Gees their third No. 1 single there. Indeed, the brothers had returned to the music business with a new sound the trio tagged 'New York R. & B.', but which others called 'disco'. There was more to come.

During February and March 1977, Robert Stigwood, now owner of his own RSO Records, was interested in producing a movie based on an article by Nik Cohn, published in the *New Yorker*. Cohn had headlined his piece 'Tribal Rites of the New Saturday Night' and highlighted the disco explosion that compelled dancers to 'dress in their best to strut their stuff' on a nightclub dancefloor. Stigwood approached John Travolta, late of the American television series *Welcome Back Kotter* to play the starring role, and The Bee Gees for songs. At the time, the trio were planning material for a new album they were recording in the Chateau D'Herouville Studios, near Paris. Maurice Gibb: 'We wrote "How Deep Is your Love", "If I Can't Have You" and "Stayin' Alive" and Robert Stigwood . . . said he needed five songs for this film he was doing . . . When someone offers you the chance to have your music in a motion picture, it really freaks you.' The trio played him the aforementioned titles; he wanted them all. The brothers had earmarked 'How Deep Is your Love' for American vocalist Yvonne Elliman, but when Stigwood insisted The Bee Bees sing it on the soundtrack, they gave her 'If I Can't Have You' instead (which went on to become the fourth American chart-topper from the movie's soundtrack). A further title, 'More Than a Woman', was recorded by both The Bee Gees and the soul group Tavares: both versions were featured in the movie and both released as singles. The movie was called *Saturday Night,* but when The Bee Gees told Stigwood they had already composed a track titled 'Night Fever', he agreed on a compromise. *Saturday Night Fever* was premiered in New York during December 1977. Thanks to The Bee Gees' compositions, disco music would never be the same.

'How Deep Is your Love' was the first single to be lifted from the soundtrack. It peaked at No. 3 in the British chart in December 1977 and reached No. 1 in America, where it went on to sell one million copies. The title also won a 1978 Grammy Award for the Best Pop Vocal

Performance by a Duo, Group or Chorus, and an Ivor Novello Award for Best Pop Song and Best Film Music or Song.

Early in 1978 the double soundtrack album from *Saturday Night Fever* was issued to immediately top the American chart. During February, 'Stayin' Alive' was issued as a single; another American chart-topper. A month later the title soared to No. 4 in the British chart. The follow-up was 'Night Fever', which shot to the top in America during March 1979, a position it held for a remarkable eight weeks. When released in Britain it likewise shot to the top in May for a two-week stay. The soundtrack album, also a British chart-topper (naturally), went on to sell in excess of thirty million copies worldwide to top charts in most countries.

Saturday Night Fever was an absolute monster, from the music to the John Travolta lookalikes in white suits perfecting solo dance routines. They could be spotted on nightclub dancefloors, strutting their Travolta stuff, right arm raised in the air, finger pointing, body jerking, oblivious to the hidden smiles from other dancers. And the lookalikes roamed into the nineties; very sad. Maurice: 'The *Fever* thing was a phenomenon that just happened. All the world wanted to dance . . . All we did was just write these songs for our new album. "Disco" to us was Donna Summer . . .'

Once the furore surrounding *Saturday Night Fever* had subsided, The Bee Gees were blamed (predictably) for killing disco music. However, the film was a curse on them also, a millstone around their necks that they had to carry into the next decade and beyond. Ironically, their next movie bombed, but not so their music.

Also see: 'Tragedy', March 1979

(Quotes: *We Had Joy We Had Fun* by Barry Scott)

June 1978

BONEY M

Rivers of Babylon

This was a quartet the public loved or loathed, there was no in-between. Soul music fans believed they had 'sold out' – recording garbage yet upholding their true colour, while pop music buyers were reticent when asked if they had a Boney M record in their collection. Well, someone must have bought their discs because the group enjoyed two British chart-toppers and a career that spanned more than six years.

Boney M – vocalists Bobby Farrell, born in Aruba, West Indies, on 6 October 1949; Maizie Williams, born in Monserrat, West Indies, on 25 March 1951; Liz Mitchell, born in Clarendon, Jamaica, on 12 July 1952, and Marcia Barrett, born in Jamaica on 14 October 1948 – was formed in Germany where they were based throughout their career. The four were in fact studio session singers working for disco composer/producer Frank Farian. In 1976, when he needed a focal point for his material, he pushed the quartet, now known as Boney M, into the spotlight. Maizie Williams said at the time, 'Frank does all the preparation, but then we have to physically sing and present the songs. We have to tour and promote the Boney M sound, and we have to sell the act to the public. Or put it another way, without us, there remains only a series of backing tracks . . .'

Farian's dance style, based on electronics, was typified by the group's first single 'Baby Do You Wanna Bump', a European hit, but more so by 'Daddy Cool' later released by Atlantic Records. It soared to No. 6 in the British chart early in 1977, and reached the Top Sixty in America. While that title was on the descent, 'Sunny', a cover version of Bobby Hebbs's 1966 Top Twenty British hit, fared better in the British chart by peaking at No. 3 in April 1977. The group's album *Take the Heat Off Me* quickly followed to reach the Top Forty.

Boney M singles were becoming addictive. No matter how ridiculous they looked while performing, the public support was growing, and when the ludicrously titled 'Ma Baker' became a No. 2 British hit in July 1977, the group was well established on the music scene. The single went on to top most of the European charts. The last single of the year was 'Belfast', which Marcia Barrett had stored on tape for three years. 'It was Frank's idea that we should do it but it's strictly non-political and is certainly not provocative in any way . . . People in Britain could have gone against it, but happily [they] have given us the benefit of the doubt and first listened to the words and then decided that the song is valid.' There were countless listeners – 'Belfast' peaked in the Top Twenty.

It was during the following year that Boney M showed their true selling muscle when they rerecorded a non-copyrighted traditional reggae song, 'Rivers of Babylon'. The title was released with 'Brown Girl in the Ring' on the flipside. No one could escape the power of these two songs; they really made compulsive listening. 'Rivers of Babylon' shot to the top of the British chart in June 1978, a position it held for five long weeks. It also became the group's best-selling American single when it reached the Top Thirty.

During September 1978, when the chart-topper was on the descent, radio DJs flipped it to play 'Brown Girl in the Ring' and the chart climb started over again, finally ending when the title peaked at No. 2 in Britain. Both titles sold in excess of two million copies in Britain alone, and it became the second biggest-selling single of all-time (to date). Both 'Rivers of Babylon' and 'Brown Girl in the Ring' were lifted from the album *Night Flight to Venus,* which itself topped the British listing in September 1978.

It was during this period that soul music fans aired their views, declaring Boney M's music to be crass, undiluted drivel; a black group could not record commercial slush while proclaiming they 'kept the faith'. The comments did not pass unnoticed by the group. Williams: 'It used to worry us. After all, we're only human and we have worked extremely hard to reach the position we are in today. But I do feel some of the more extreme comments are unwarranted and unfair. After all, someone is buying our records and coming to our concerts, so we must be doing something right.' Williams also stressed that their music was not, in any case, aimed at the limited soul market. 'We have not deliberately avoided any one area, but attempted to create an overall market appeal. In cold facts, a record sale is equally valid from anyone. The "Black" thing is not really a consideration in terms of professional success.'

At this juncture in their career, many in the music business believed Boney M should move to America, the heart of the disco explosion, to take their chances on the international market. The group declined, stating the high competition and abundant talent would swallow them up. Plus, Germany needed them, as Barrett explained. 'You rarely hear pop music at all on the radio over there and with so many British and American servicemen and families there, they have to be catered for. And since most Germans learn [only] a little English, they can concentrate completely on the rhythm content of a record.'

In October 1978 'Rasputin' was issued as the follow-up to 'Brown Girl in the Ring'. As its title suggested, it was a disco version of a Cossack dance, yet despite the dubious musical mix, the single soared to No. 2 in Britain. Before the year was ended, the group enjoyed their second British chart-topper with 'Mary's Boy Child – Oh my Lord'. The first title was their cover version of Harry Belafonte's fifties' hit which was reworked into Frank Farian's own style, thereby guaranteeing him a royalty percentage – and a high one at that! The single sold in excess of one million copies to top the chart for four weeks, while in America it struggled into the Top Ninety, representing their last charter there.

The start of 1979 saw Boney M in the Top Ten with 'Painter Man' before 'Hooray! Hooray! It's a Holi-Holiday' soared to No. 3, its calypso feel obviously attracting the disco record buyers despite its flimsy beat. In September 1979, the follow-up, 'Gotta Go Home', reached the Top Twelve and was the group's last single of the year. Early 1980 heralded the beginning of Boney M's chart struggle, although 'I'm Born Again' secured a healthy-enough position in the British Top Forty. However, by the group's standards it was a poor seller. In May 1980 the situation worsened when 'My Friend Jack', a cover version of Smoke's 1967 Top Fifty hit, stalled in the Top Sixty. Nine months later, the group was further humiliated when 'Children of Paradise' faltered in the Top Seventy. The Frank Farian German disco sound had danced itself out, dragging Boney M with it.

The vocalists disappeared from the spotlight, returning briefly in December 1981 with 'We Kill the World (Don't Kill the World)', which re-established them in the British Top Forty. Frank Farian then appeared to abandon Boney M altogether to turn his attention to other acts. But compilation albums were issued, including *The Best of 10 Years* in 1986.

In the late eighties and early nineties Boney M resurfaced thanks to the dancefloor hits 'Megamix – Mary's Boy Child' and 'Boney M Megamix' which, when they crossed over from the dance chart into mainstream music, became a Top Sixty and Top Ten hit respectively.

Recorded success subsequently petered out, but that did not prevent Liz Mitchell from touring Britain during 1993 promoting the Boney M sound to push their current *Greatest Hits* album into the Top Twenty. Regrettably, the Boney M of the nineties fell a thousand miles short of the hit-making group. Their act was loud, cluttered and tuneless; little wonder they were confined to the holiday camp circuit.

JOHN TRAVOLTA AND
OLIVIA NEWTON-JOHN

You're the One that I Want

Starting its life as a 1972 Broadway stage show, *Grease* successfully transferred to the cinema screen to grow into the second-biggest-grossing film of its time behind *Saturday Night Fever*. It was the perfect example of a nostalgic rock 'n' roll movie.

Born in Englewood, New Jersey on 18 February 1954, the sixth child of Helen and Samuel, John Travolta play-acted with his mother from an early age. He was an avid movie and television buff, and when his sister Ellen secured a role in the touring show *Gypsy* starring Ethel Merman, he learned all the roles by heart. Subsequently, when a branch of the New York City-based Actors' Studio opened in Englewood, Travolta was among the first to enrol and be offered a role in the drama *Who'll Save the Ploughboy?* Travolta told author Wensley Clarkson, 'Nobody pushed me into showbusiness. I was aching for it!'

Travolta's passion for the theatre obviously affected his education at Dwight Morrow High School, and when he was offered the second lead in *Bye Bye Birdie* during 1970, for the weekly wage of $50, the sixteen-year-old and the education system parted company. This role led to further acting parts including that of Doody in the national touring production of *Grease*. To ease the monotony of the nine-month stint, Travolta guested on television shows like *Owen Marshall*. When *Grease* closed, he transferred his Doody to the Broadway version of the show before auditioning for the Jack Nicholson movie *The Last Detail*. He lost out to Randy Quaid, but secured a role in The Andrews Sisters' stage show *Over Here*.

Further stage and television work led to Travolta being offered the role of Vinnie Barbarino in the forthcoming television series *Welcome Back Kotter*. Travolta: 'I thought it was a hot role . . . Vinnie was an Italian kid who dreamed of one day being a Mafia leader. It was a good role.' *Welcome Back Kotter* debuted on ABC TV during September 1975 and was an immediate hit with viewers catapulting Travolta to stardom, even though he wasn't the main star! Travolta: 'It doesn't bother me that I'm not prominent on the show each week or that I'm not paid a great deal. The series has been good for me.' The television series eventually ran for three years, although Travolta was often missing from episodes due to acting commitments elsewhere. For instance, he played Billy Nolan in *Carrie*, starring Sissy Spacek.

Following a scat version of The Beach Boys' 'Barbara Ann' in *Welcome Back Kotter*, Travolta secured a recording contract with Midland International Records in 1976. His debut single, 'Let Her In', became an American Top Ten hit; his eponymous album quickly followed, categorised as 'a bland rock album tailored to sub-teens'. Two further singles, namely, 'Whenever I'm Away from You' and 'All Strung Out on You' reached the American Top Forty and Seventy respectively, while his second album, *Can't Let You Go*, likewise stalled in the Top Seventy during 1977.

On the personal front, Travolta was romantically involved with Diana Hyland, his co-star in the television movie *The Boy in the Plastic Bubble*. Hyland was forty-one years old with a four-year-old son, Zachery. Travolta was twenty-two. Sadly, Hyland was battling against cancer and would eventually die from the disease in March 1977. The tragedy devastated Travolta.

Meanwhile, behind scenes, Australian entrepreneur Robert Stigwood had two projects in the pipeline, namely *Sergeant Pepper's Lonely Hearts Club Band* and *Grease*. However, due to contractual stipulations, the film version of *Grease* could not be released prior to Easter 1978. Having studied Travolta in his television role of Barbarino, Stigwood wanted him to star in *Grease*. Travolta agreed to a three-movie deal with Stigwood, the first of which launched the young actor into international stardom. In *Saturday Night Fever*, Travolta played the lead role of Tony Manero in the dance movie based on an article written by British journalist Nik Cohn, telling the tale of a group of young people who worked the week in dull jobs simply to pay for their Saturday night dancing at local nightclubs. The Bee Gees composed the movie soundtrack, which spawned numerous million-selling singles, the album selling in excess of 25 million copies, while the film grossed $18 million during its first 16 weeks on American release, becoming the third highest-grossing adult feature movie, taking in excess of $350 million (1996). *Grease*, therefore, was the natural follow-up to *Saturday Night Fever*, and Travolta was the obvious choice for the lead character Danny Zuko.

Born in Cambridge on 26 September 1948, Olivia Newton-John later moved with her family to Melbourne, Australia. As a teenager, she sang in a folk group, and duetted with Pat Carroll on regular television spots.

In 1964, the duo won the Johnny O'Keefe talent contest, where the first prize was a trip to Britain. Newton-John told author Joe Smith, 'I didn't really want to go, but my mother . . . said, "We need to broaden your horizons. You should go to Europe" . . . I didn't want to leave my boyfriend. I was very young and I thought Australia was everything.' Once Newton-John had reached eighteen and had completed her education, she and Carroll hit British soil, where they performed on the folk circuit until Carroll's visa expired, forcing her to return to Australia.

Newton-John remained in Britain, working as a soloist. She secured a recording contract with Decca Records and issued her version of Jackie De Shannon's 'Till You Say You'll Be Mine' in 1966. At this juncture, she befriended and began dating Bruce Welch, a member of The Shadows, Cliff Richard's backing group. Welch offered her a role in Richard's forthcoming *Cinderella* pantomime; she declined, preferring to return to Australia. Her stay was short-lived; she returned to live with Welch in London.

Following a spell with the quartet Toomorrow, also the name of a science fiction musical, Newton-John duetted with Cliff Richard on 'Don't Move Away' early during 1971. In April, she recorded her second single, 'If Not for You'. It was another cover version, this time of the Bob Dylan classic. Produced by John Farrar, married to her one-time duettist Pat Carroll and a member of the breakaway Shadows trio, Marvin, Welch and Farrar, 'If Not for You' soared to No. 7 in the British chart, reaching No. 25 in America. Before the year was out, 'Banks of the Ohio' hit No. 6 in Britain and made the American Top One Hundred.

During 1972, Newton-John released two singles, namely 'What Is Life', a Top Twenty British hit, and 'Just a Little Too Much'. She guested weekly on Cliff Richard's long-running BBC TV shows, while on the personal front, her relationship with Bruce Welch ended. For the next two years, Newton-John was a regular charting name with titles like 'Take Me Home Country Roads' and 'Let Me Be There', her first American million-seller and winner of the Grammy Award in 1974 for the Best Country Vocal Performance, Female. In April 1974, Newton-John represented Britain in the Eurovision Song Contest staged in Brighton, East Sussex, with the track 'Long Live Love': Abba won with 'Waterloo'. Two months on, the singer switched to EMI Records based in London, where 'I Honestly Love You' peaked at No. 22 in the British chart and made No. 1 in America.

Early in 1975, Newton-John, with her new manager and partner, Lee

Kramer, and John Farrar, her regular composer/producer, moved to California, where she was enjoying the bulk of her recorded success. Newton-John: 'Helen Reddy and Jeff Wald took me under their wing. They said, "If you want to have a big hit in America, you have to be here. You have to concentrate on this country." . . . I decided they were right.'

For the following three years, she was one of the country's most successful acts, recording a succession of million-selling titles like 'Have You Ever Been Mellow' and 'Please Mr Please', and collecting awards and trophies by the armful. On the personal front, her relationship with Kramer ended; he subsequently resigned as her manager.

In May 1977, following her debut at the Metropolitan Opera House, New York, Newton-John was dining with Reddy and Wald when she met Allan Carr. Newton-John: 'He was goofing about at the table and started talking about me doing *Grease*. I had seen the show in London and Richard Gere as the lead. When Allan asked me to do it, I got very nervous, but I did it.'

As *Saturday Night Fever* was such an unexpected runaway success, Robert Stigwood injected further cash into *Grease,* raising the budget to $6 million. Originally, Travolta had informed Stigwood he was unhappy with the script and with being typecast in the role of a working-class punk. The script was subsequently rewritten, and when Newton-John, with her distinct Australian accent, accepted the role of Sandy, her character was amended from an American to an Australian import!

Filming together instigated media rumours that Travolta and Newton-John were romantically involved off-set. She said at the time, 'The hand holding and kissing are for the cameras only. We've just become very good friends. And that friendship is working to capture the love we must have for the cameras.' But still the rumour-mongers persisted!

Grease was premiered amidst a mammoth publicity campaign during June 1978, and eventually grossed $150 million in box office receipts, while the soundtrack album sold in excess of 24 million copies, topping both the American and British charts, earning it the distinction of being the second best-selling film soundtrack behind *Saturday Night Fever.*

John Farrar composed the film's biggest hits, the first being 'You're the One that I Want', a duet between Travolta and Newton-John. The title soared to the top of the American chart in June 1978, selling in excess of two million copies, while in Britain it shot to the top for an incredible nine-week stay.

Frankie Valli, late of the Four Seasons, also joined the *Grease* merry-go-round by recording the film's title. The track shot to the top of the American chart in August 1978, presenting the singer with his first American chart-topper in sixteen years. 'Grease' was the second single lifted from the soundtrack to reach the top of the American chart. In Britain, the disc became a Top Three hit.

*Grease*mania was everywhere; dress styles changed to match those of Danny and Sandy, while the stars behind the characters were musical sensations. There was more to come – and quickly.

Also see: 'Summer Nights', October 1978

(Quotes: *John Travolta: Back in Character* by Wensley Clarkson; *Off the Record* by Joe Smith)

September 1978

COMMODORES

Three Times a Lady

'Personally speaking, "Three Times a Lady" has given me so much personal satisfaction. I think it's a songwriter's dream to be totally accepted.' – Lionel Richie

In 1968, the future Commodores were freshmen at Tuskegee Institute. Prior to becoming the world-famous group, Lionel Richie, born on 20 June 1949, in Tuskegee; Thomas McClary, born on 6 October 1950 in Florida, and William King, born on 30 January 1949, in Alabama, sang James Brown material as members of The Mystics. The unit's biggest rival at the time was another home-based band, The Jays, of which Milan Williams, born 28 March 1948, in Mississippi, was a member. When a disagreement led to the disintegration of The Jays, the two units merged.

By 1969, the renamed Commodores were combining their studies with their musical career; their grades were steady as their audience following grew. Also this year, the membership was shuffled, to include drummer Walter 'Clyde' Orange, born on 10 December 1947, in Florida, and bass guitarist Ronald LePread, born on 4 September 1946, in Alabama. King: 'The essence for the group was, and always has been, that we were ready to experiment when it was necessary. We were a black group and we had grown up at the time when The Temptations, Supremes and Miracles were at their peak. What we wanted to know was why The Temptations, as good and as hot as they were, could not put 25,000 people in a stadium on their own. And yet a Beatles or a Led Zeppelin didn't even have to put out a record. All they had to say was that they'd be in town on such a such a day, the tickets would be $20 and it would be a sell-out within 24 hours. How come no black group could do it?' The Commodores were determined to change this situation, although the struggle for recognition would be tougher than anticipated.

By 1970, the Commodores recorded an album for Atlantic Records titled *Rise Up* with Jerry Williams, better known as Swamp Dog. It was never released. The album was said to comprise instrumentals which the group used as demo tapes and upon which Richie played the saxophone. The title 'Keep On Dancin' ' was the only single issued.

When college studies allowed, the Commodores continued to tour their locality, playing the Boston, New York and Carolina circuit. Yet still they lacked a solid recording deal. They turned to friend Benny Ashburn for help. He arranged a New York showcase for them at Lloyd Price's Turntable Club on Broadway and 50th, inviting record business personnel and the media. After a disastrous journey, the Commodores arrived hot, tired and hungry, thirty minutes late for their performance. However, their show convinced Motown's attending A. & R. executive Suzanne de Passe to secure the group for a forthcoming Jackson 5 tour. The two groups toured together for approximately three years before the Commodores worked with The O'Jays, The Temptations and The Rolling Stones.

During 1972, the Commodores signed a recording contract with Motown Records, where their recordings would initially be issued via the company's newly-formed Mowest label. The group debuted in March with 'The Zoo (the Human Zoo)', written and produced by Pam Sawyer and Gloria Jones. The follow-up single, 'Don't You Be Worried' early in 1973, emulated its predecessor's performance and bombed. However, for their third release, the Commodores switched to the Motown label proper, where their success began. It was Motown's policy for new acts to be assigned to in-house staff for recording purposes, a perfect arrangement for inexperienced bands, but not for the Commodores, who felt stifled at not being able to record their own material. Nonetheless, they accepted the guidance offered by Sawyer and Jones until such time as they were able to branch out alone, first with the funky, instrumental dancer 'Machine Gun' (originally titled

'The Ram'). Williams originally wrote lyrics for the track, but their producer James Anthony Carmichael insisted that as the trend was for synthesized instrumentals without lyrics, they should follow suit. The single, released on the Motown label during April 1974, peaked in the American Top Thirty and the British Top Twenty, before achieving high positions in Asia and Africa, among other territories. This unexpected but welcomed success prompted Benny Ashburn to become the group's full-time manager, and it was with his guidance that international status was finally reached, fulfilling the group's ambitions to become the Black Beatles. Before 1974 ended, the single 'I Feel Sanctified' stalled in the American Top Eighty; a minor setback in the overall plan.

Early the next year, the Commodores issued their second album, titled *Caught in the Act* (their first was *Machine Gun*), while their next single, swiped from that second album, was issued during mid-1975. Titled 'Slippery When Wet', it entered the American Top Twenty. At the year's close, the group had released their third album, *Movin' On;* won the Bronze Prize at Tokyo's 1975 Music Festival; headlined an American tour, and issued the first in a series of ballads titled 'Sweet Love', from the pen of Lionel Richie. Always more comfortable with slow-paced tracks, Richie would earn the reputation of the world's top balladeer within a few months when his success surpassed even his rash ambitions.

The year of 1976 was relatively quiet, with the release of Richie's second ballad, 'Just to Be Close to You', a Top Ten American hit. However, the next year saw the Commodores' career catapult. They co-starred with Donna Summer in the disco movie *Thank God It's Friday* and contributed to its soundtrack; issued four singles during the year – 'Fancy Dancer', 'Easy', 'Brickhouse' and 'Too Hot Ta Trot'. All were big sellers, and following the release of their eponymous album, the group embarked upon an extensive European tour, which included dates in Britain. Audiences were greeted with on-stage fireworks and musicianship at its finest, during an act that combined funk and ballad, against a frenetic and moody backdrop.

At this stage in their career, the group was still attempting to expand their music outside the black buying market, despite the restrictions of American radio stations. Williams: 'Certain stations considered our music too black for listeners. "Just to Be Close to You" was one. But if that tune was too black to be played on a pop station, then how the hell did it get to No. 7 in the national chart?' McClary: 'Statements about music being too black are hindering the people that are listening to the music and they are also hindering the artist. Whatever we create should be accepted and rejected by people as a whole. Why should we have to sell 800,000 copies at No. 1 in the R. & B. chart before we get accepted as pop? When people make those kinds of statements it's because of the fact that they are usually afraid to make a step.' Richie: 'What we're dealing with is that age-old problem of people's hang-ups. In the music business you'll find that musicians are universal people. We can go to Japan, Colombia, South Carolina, and I can meet someone I've never seen before in my life and immediately we have something we can identify with and that's music. The problem is musicians are very open-minded people dealing with a very closely-minded society!'

The group's problem was to resolve itself in June 1978 when the emotional love ballad 'Three Times a Lady' was released. The title reached the top of the American chart during August and it was a British chart-topper in September, a position it held for five wonderful weeks. This runaway success was repeated in all quarters of the world, and when newspaper headlines dubbed the Commodores 'The Black Beatles', the group's ambitions had been realised.

'Three Times a Lady' (the very title conjures up romantic thoughts!) went on to win most of 1978's prestigious awards and honours. Not bad for a song Richie composed as an album track for their *Natural High* album, released simultaneously in Britain and America during May 1978. Richie: 'I attended my parents' wedding anniversary and my father made a speech about how much he loved my mother and appreciated the way she had stood by him for thirty-five years. It was beautiful, but started me thinking about my own life, and how my wife, Brenda, stands by me, and how she does so many things without being asked or thanked. So I wrote "Three Times a Lady" for her. I think my next-door neighbour summed it up when she said that if any man wanted to buy her a gift, all he need do was buy her this record and he wouldn't have to say anything else. From the masses of awards that the song has won, it seemed the whole world really does love it, and it's a great feeling.'

The Commodores were touring America when the single broke. Richie: 'It started out as a sixty-eight-day tour and we had to extend it by another forty days. We found more and more dates coming in, and in places that groups like us don't usually play. That was primarily because the single got into every possible market, including country and western. Now the trick is to hold on to all of those newly found fans.' The Commodores stayed at the top for eighteen months but never repeated the success of 'Three Times a Lady'.

As it would have been impossible to follow the international chart-topper, the group refused to try. The next American single, 'Flying High', faltered in the Top Forty during November 1978. In Britain, the ballad 'Just to Be Close to You' struggled into the Top Seventy.

In July 1979, the Commodores' *Midnight Magic* album was released on both sides of the Atlantic, and during August and September the group undertook a world tour. There was now standing room only at their concerts, thanks to the spate of million-selling records. King: 'In the last two years we've done more money in attendances than any black group has ever done. Our plan has always been to surpass The Beatles. I feel they are the epitome of pop music, the strongest entity to ever exist in the entertainment world. They changed the world and we want to surpass them. But they missed out on a couple of things purely by timing. For example, the R. & B. crowd would never touch The Beatles – even if they liked them – because they came during the conflict between black and white. You don't see Beatles records all over the floor of the average black home, like you do today to a small extent with The Bee Gees. Times have now changed because it doesn't matter a helluva lot what colour you are.' He illustrated his point by citing The Commodores' recent American mid-west tour where 80 per cent of the audience was white.

The group devoted the bulk of 1980 to touring America, which assisted sales of their next album, *Heroes*. The spiritual album spawned the American Top Twenty hit 'Old-Fashion Love' during July. The album's title track was then issued as follow-up to stall in the American Top Sixty, three months on. Richie, meantime, branched out from the group to work with the country and western singer, Kenny Rogers, when he recorded one of his finest ballads, 'Lady'. The title went on to sell in excess of 16 million copies, earned Richie $1 million and part-share in a cosmetics range bearing the single's name. The collaboration was possible because one of the Commodores was injured in a motorbike accident, forcing the group to cancel the backend of their American tour. With his solo work, rumblings of him leaving the Commodores were rife. Even though the rumours were strenuously denied at this time, it was a move Richie would make within a year.

Of the Commodores' ten albums, all passed gold status in America; two albums reached platinum, one album double-platinum and two albums triple-platinum. The initial slump in sales of *Heroes* was worrying, yet it did not affect the group's concert attendances. Richie: 'It isn't all about a hit record anymore; all of a sudden it's about personalities that people can hang something on. That's where the Commodores are trying to go now. Hit records are one thing but they are a year by year thing. Personalities are forever. We have to develop personalities so that when we write and sing a specific song people will say, "I know why they wrote that".'

Early in 1981, the group recorded the title theme for the *Underground Aces* movie; this, in turn, led to Richie duetting with Diana Ross on 'Endless Love', the title song from the movie of the same name, starring Brooke Shields. It was nominated for a Grammy Award, topped the American chart for nine consecutive weeks, and reached No. 7 in Britain. By the close of 1981, Richie was represented in the American Top One Hundred with six singles, 'Endless Love'; the Commodores' 'Oh No' (which he wrote and co-produced) and 'Lady (You Bring Me Up)' (co-produced by him); Kenny Rogers' 'I Don't Need You' and follow-up 'Share your Love', and 'Still', rerecorded by John Schneider.

Also in June 1981, the Commodores' released their album *In the Pocket*, and Richie hired a public relations company to handle his image, once more fuelling rumours of his imminent departure from the group. Richie said the new album afforded Clyde Orange the opportunity to express his talent. 'Before the Commodores made it in terms of records, Clyde was the lead vocalist. I was the horn holder and the shoop-shoop guy. For the past few years because I wrote the songs I came to the front as being the lead singer. On this album, he's now coming to light as the great performer he is . . . We have six arrangers, six producers, six writers and six performers.' However, as cynics correctly guessed, Richie was ensuring that when he left the group, it would safely survive without him as lead singer, and by the group membership contributing more, the absence of his compositions would not be so apparent.

With the release of his first solo single, titled 'Truly', and his eponymous album in September 1982, Lionel Richie confirmed his intention to concentrate on his own career. With the Commodores' career on the decline, he was (naturally) criticised for not recording those songs planned for his solo album with the group membership. But the group believed Richie's departure would affect them personally more than professionally. King: 'He was family and to us he's still a Commodore, and maybe down the line we'll get back and do something.' Richie: 'I never wanted to leave the Commodores in the first place. It was stifling in the group, particularly when it got to the point where all of us wanted to write and produce . . . I do miss the Commodores but we knew it wasn't going to work, particularly when the friction started.'

Celebrating their fifteenth anniversary in the music business, the Commodores visited Britain once more in September 1983 as their album, *13*, their first without Richie, was released. Unlike the Commodores' previous work, producer James Anthony Carmichael was not involved: he was working on Richie's second solo album.

In November 1984, Thomas McClary became the second Commodore to pursue a solo career. He issued his first self-produced eponymous album, which had spawned the singles 'Thin Walls', featuring Lionel Richie, and 'Man in the Middle'. McClary: 'I had 15 great years with the Commodores and I think we accomplished all the goals we set out to do and we'll certainly go down in history for what we achieved. However, there has always been this dream inside of me to grow and to attain new goals.' McClary's success was limited. The Commodores issued their first and only Top Three hit on both sides of the Atlantic after the departure of Richie. Titled 'Nightshift', the poignant dedication to the late Jackie Wilson and Marvin Gaye boosted the group's flagging career by winning a Grammy Award in the Best R. & B. Vocal, Duo or Group category. The album *Nightshift* followed early in 1985; a disappointing release, falling into the rock and contemporary pop category. However, the group, now with ex-Heatwave member, James D Nichols, born on 12 April 1952, in Watford, Herts, as Richie's official replacement, were happy with the album. The second track to be swiped as a single, 'Animal Instinct', followed in April 1985.

With no further hit material, the Commodores' strained relationship with Motown ended, and the group switched to Polygram Records. Their debut single titled 'Goin' to the Bank', a track lifted from their pending album *United*, was issued during autumn 1986. LePread left the line-up to pursue other interests; the Commodores continued as a quartet.

In the nineties the group, reduced to a trio of William King, Clyde Orange and J.D. Nichols, continued as a touring unit, particularly in Britain where they headlined a nationwide trek with the former ladies of The Supremes.

Lionel Richie's career reached spectacular heights, until he too left Motown in 1992 to join Mercury Records, where his debut album *Louder Than Words* spawned the 'Don't Wanna Lose You' single. Richie will doubtless return to his former stardom; he's too precious a talent to decline. The Commodores, on the other hand, would benefit from a return to the world's charts to regain their status. Now, maybe if the two combined musical forces . . .

(Quotes: *Motown: The History* by Sharon Davis)

JOHN TRAVOLTA AND
OLIVIA NEWTON-JOHN

Summer Nights

'When *Grease* hit, I was accepted . . . It meant I could have a hit movie with hit songs and a new image.' – Olivia Newton-John

When Newton-John accepted the role of Sandy in the musical movie *Grease,* she had no qualms regarding the character's initial image – an innocent, sweet girl with a ponytail. However, she was concerned that her fans would not accept the raunchier image towards the close of the film, namely as a leather-clad, gum-chewing biker's tart. A lengthy telephone conversation with her co-star John Travolta calmed her anxiety. 'My image had been so white bread, so milk shake, and *Grease* was a chance to do something different. I didn't want to be forty years old and still be the girl next door.' Travolta, on the other hand, had no qualms. 'There aren't that many musicals around to do. Who knows when I'll ever do another. So I thought it was a good move for me.'

The couple's second duet was swiped from the *Grease* soundtrack album as follow-up to the international chart-topper 'You're the One that I Want'. Titled 'Summer Nights', the track was once again a mega-seller, although it faltered at No. 5 in America. *Grease*mania was still rife in Britain and 'Summer Nights' shot to the top of the chart in October 1978, a position it held for a remarkable seven weeks, with sales of one million plus. Meanwhile, the movie's soundtrack became Britain's top-selling album for a staggering twelve weeks.

During October 1978, the soundtrack was further milked. Travolta's solo 'Greased Lightnin' ' was issued as a single, reaching the American Top Fifty, and the British Top Twenty, while 'Sandy' soared to No. 2 in the British chart, kept from the top spot by 'Summer Nights'. Incidentally, when the Boomtown Rats eventually replaced the title at the top of the chart, group leader Bob Geldof destroyed a poster of Travolta and Newton-John before the television cameras filming the BBC TV's music programme *Top of the Pops.* Childish or what!

Early in 1979, Travolta's album *Sandy* was issued as a last-ditch attempt to capitalise on the high-flying movie. The album struggled into the British Top Forty. In America, though, the hype went further when both of his albums were re-packaged as a double under the title *Travolta Fever.*

As *Sandy* lived, Travolta was shooting *Moment to Moment* with Lily Tomalin. This was the last of the trio of films he was contracted to do for Robert Stigwood. The movie bombed, whereupon he went into exile, convinced his film career was finished. His retirement was short-lived; he accepted the lead role in *Urban Cowboy,* playing a young Houston chemical worker whose nights were devoted to his cowboy fantasies. Directed by James Bridges, *Urban Cowboy* was critically acclaimed.

Further movies like *Blow Out* led to *Stayin' Alive,* the long-awaited sequel to *Saturday Night Fever.* Working with Sylvester Stallone, Travolta undertook seven months of gymnastic training to portray a muscle-bound torso on the cinema screen. So enthusiastic was he over his new body, that he published the keep-fit book titled *John Travolta – Staying Fit.* The movie *Two of a Kind* followed, co-starring Olivia Newton-John; it bombed. Subsequently, Travolta kept a low profile until he was offered the role of a big-hearted taxi driver in *Look Who's Talking,* co-starring Kirstie Alley and the voice of Bruce Willis. This time the movie was a runaway success and should have relaunched Travolta's crumbling career. Critics dictated otherwise, saying the film was 'cute' and his role was 'too goody', adding the film was only successful because no other blockbusters were on release at the same time, and that it rode on the back of *Three Men and a Baby!* Nonetheless, *Look Who's Talking* earned in excess of $133 million in America alone, whereupon Travolta was signed to star in the sequel, *Look Who's Talking Too.* At the time, though, he just could not win against the Hollywood backstabbers.

Once again Travolta retreated to devote his time to his lifetime hobby, piloting planes and flying. 'I recognised my career might have started to decline irreparably. It wasn't that I'd lost faith in my own potential . . . but I was seeing . . . that my career as an actor had come to an end.' However, that was to change in September 1991 – he married Kelly Preston, which coincided with his acting career taking an upward turn. He accepted the role of Vincent Vega in the black comedy *Pulp Fiction* for the low fee of £100,000. Travolta's character was a middle-aged hitman with a huge appetite for heroin. Despite his abhorrence of drugs and violence in real life, Travolta played an extremely convincing role, earning him both critical and public praise. He was once again in demand in Hollywood: in 1995 he starred in the film *Get Shorty* with Danny DeVito and Gene Hackman, and a year on, in *Broken Arrow* and *White Man's Burden.* John Travolta was finally back on the right track . . .

In 1978, following the release of 'Summer Nights', Olivia Newton-John issued her solo track from *Grease,* titled 'Hopelessly Devoted to You'. The ballad soared to No. 3 in America in September; three months later, it fared better in Britain at No. 2. In the early eighties, Newton-John was a sought-after property, but with acting still in her veins she returned to the movie world to co-star with Gene Kelly in the musical *Xanadu*. It was a multi-million-dollar affair, with special effects of mindblowing proportions, which cinema goers hated. However, the music (thankfully) survived, due many believed, to The Electric Light Orchestra's involvement. The *Xanadu* soundtrack sold in excess of one million copies and spawned five Top Twenty American singles, the first being Newton-John's 'Magic', composed and produced by John Farrer, in August 1980. The remaining four were 'Xanadu' by Newton-John and The Electric Light Orchestra; 'Suddenly', a Newton-John duet with Cliff Richard, and 'I'm Alive' and 'All over the World' by The Electric Light Orchestra. All titles were big-selling British hits.

While filming *Xanadu,* Newton-John met Matt Lattanzi, whom she married in 1985. Newton-John's image changed dramatically, as she swopped her milkshake persona for that of an independent woman of the eighties. A risky business, but one that worked for her. 'Physical' shot to the top of the American chart in the November 1981, a position it dominated for ten long weeks. Newton-John: 'I wasn't in the mood for tender ballads. I wanted peppy stuff because that's how I was feeling. We thought it was a great title because of the [then current] keep-fit craze.' Despite its innocence as an aerobics class track, 'Physical' was banned by several radio stations due to its sexual innuendoes. Suggestive or not, 'Physical' sold in excess of two million copies in America and soared to No. 7 in Britain. In December, the *Physical* album followed; another million-seller and Top Ten album on both sides of the Atlantic. By the way, the so-called controversial single remained linked to aerobic classes and work-outs a decade later!

Remaining a high-profile singer, Newton-John returned to acting to co-star with John Travolta in *Two of a Kind*. Early in 1984, the film's soundtrack album was issued; 'Twist of Fate' was the first title to be lifted as a single by Newton-John.

She maintained her recording career through to 1989 when she was elected Goodwill Ambassador for the United Nations Environment Programme. Now a mother to daughter Chloe, she secured a recording deal with Geffen Records to issue an album of children's songs and standards under the title *Warm and Tender* in 1990. The next year, with a pair of remixed compilations, namely, 'Grease Megamix' and 'Grease

– The Dream Mix' becoming British hits, Newton-John capitalised on the success and released the album titled *Back to Basics: The Essential Collection 1971–1992*. Following her appearance on *A Call to Action in the War Against AIDS,* an American television special screened in 1992, the singer announced she had breast cancer. Following treatment, she was in remission in 1993. A year on, she returned to the Australian stage to participate in a gala concert where all proceeds went to the Queensland farmers. She also returned to the film world, starring in CBS TV's *A Christmas Romance.*

In 1995 she once again duetted with Cliff Richard on the single 'Had to Be', lifted from the stage show *Heathcliff* in which Richard had the starring role, and returned to the recording studio to record the *Gaia (One Woman's Journey),* a Top Forty British album.

'Had it not been for *Grease,* I don't know if I ever could have gotten away with "Physical".' – Olivia Newton-John

'What's wrong with doing a light musical? Brando did a musical, *Guys and Dolls,* very early in his career.' – John Travolta

Grease lives on as a stage musical. So protective were the backers and producers behind the London show that in 1996 they forbade amateur and school productions of the musical being performed, fearing they would take audiences away from the London box office. As ridiculous as this sounds, they were completely serious!

Also see: 'You're the One that I Want', July/August 1978

(Quotes: *John Travolta: Back in Character* by Wensley Clarkson, *Off the Record* by Joe Smith)

November 1978

BOOMTOWN RATS

Rat Trap

'People seemed to think we were taking the piss out of the whole business just because we'd mess about, and indeed we were.' – Bob Geldof

Bob Geldof, born in Dublin, Eire, on 5 October 1954, had two elder sisters, Cleo and Lynn. Living in a Catholic household, he was raised by his sisters following the early death of his mother, and his father's absences from home due to work commitments. Geldof attended Blackrock College, where in later years, he grew into an educated rebel. Regular trips to the local Murray's Record Centre exposed him to various American musical styles, notably the blues, which inspired him to learn to play the harmonica.

He left the college with no qualifications, and worked his way through countless jobs, beginning with a position in a photo-processing plant. After working with Irish labourers on the construction of the M25 motorway, he headed to London, where he stayed with others in a Tufnell Park squat. The highspots of his existence were seeing acts like The Rolling Stones and Rod Stewart perform. During his stay in Tufnell Park, Geldof experimented with a variety of drugs to add colour to his drab home surroundings, while in the daytime he worked as a hotdog seller, among other soul-destroying jobs.

In time, with desperation his influence, Geldof and a friend travelled to Spain where, among other things, they taught English to Spanish students. Eventually, though, they returned to Dublin, through Madrid and Paris. Back home, Geldof reluctantly worked in an abattoir, where he witnessed unspeakable atrocities to screaming, doomed animals.

Sickened by his stay at the abattoir, Geldof moved with a girlfriend to Canada, where they travelled extensively, financing their journey with part-time work. His intention was to stay in Canada, but when he was faced with immigration problems he had little choice but to return to Dublin, where he became a contributor to the *New Musical Express,* and befriended musicians with ambitions. In time, Geldof formed the group known occasionally as Mark Skid and The Y-Fronts, later The Nightlife Things, and finally the Boomtown Rats; so named after Geldof had read Woody Guthrie's autobiography *Bound for Glory.* The line-up of the future hit band read Pete Briquette, Johnny Fingers, Simon Crowe, Gary Cott, Gerry Roberts, and Geldof as the reluctant lead singer. The Boomtown Rats became a regular audience-puller on the club circuit, leaving other Dublin groups bewildered at their success. When animosity occurred, Geldof turned it to his advantage, as he wrote in his autobiography: 'I was enjoying myself. The band was becoming notorious. We began to appear in the gossip columns of both the alternative and the established press . . . People began to ask for autographs.'

Following dates in Dublin, ending at the 2,000-seated National Stadium, the Boomtown Rats visited Holland. By this time, Geldof had received numerous offers from British record companies, including Decca and Chiswick. With such interest, the group decided to move to

London to negotiate their own recording contract. Following a trek that spanned Phonogram Records and United Artists, the group were offered a recording contract and a £1 million advance with Virgin Records, committing them to ten albums during a five-year period. When Geldof had calculated an album by album breakdown, the group members would actually receive £4,500 each! Meantime, also in the running was DJ Chris Hill and Nigel Grange's new label, Ensign Records. Eventually, Geldof was sufficiently impressed with their enthusiasm and company set-up, that he signed the Boomtown Rats to the company during 1976, whereupon the band joined bitter-sweet competition with The Sex Pistols, The Damned, and other punk acts riding high on the New Wave musical tide. By luck or judgement, the Boomtown Rats carried the tag of 'punk band', and, like their fellow groups, worked clubland to the point of exhaustion.

In September 1977, the Boomtown Rats issued their debut single for Ensign Records, 'Looking After No. 1'. The title soared to No. 11 in the British chart and was lifted from their Top Twenty album *The Boomtown Rats*. The title, which Geldof had penned while in Ireland, together with the other album tracks, took seventy-eight takes to perfect. 'Most of the songs were about people I'd known, or about Dublin', he said, while the single itself was 'a quintessential seventies song for the "me" decade.' Before 1977 closed, the group's second single, 'Mary of the Fourth Form' reached the British Top Twenty. The Boomtown Rats were on their way!

The first single of the new year, titled 'She's So Modern' was, in Geldof's opinion, the group's worst outing. Nonetheless, it was another Top Twenty British hit. The next title, 'Like Clockwork', was the group's debut Top Ten entrant, as was their second album *A Tonic for the Troops*. Geldof: '[The album] made a million pounds and went gold. This is not what punk bands were supposed to do.'

When the Boomtown Rats performed at the Music Machine in Camden, London, before an audience of aggressive punks, glasses were dropped from the theatre balcony into the audience below, causing countless injuries, whereupon fighting erupted between different punk packs, and a member of the previous performing group walked on stage and punched Geldof in the face. Geldof fell against a cameraman, one of several, filming the performances for American television. Wiping blood from his eyes, Geldof continued the show. Next day, pictures of the blooded singer were splashed across the various music papers! Not the kind of publicity he intended his family to see!

Before the year closed, the Boomtown Rats topped the British chart;

again, an unheard of achievement for a punk outfit. 'Rat Trap' shot to the top during November, a position it held for two weeks. All credibility with the glass-throwing fighters was lost.

On the personal front, Geldof had met Paula Yates, daughter of Jesse, who had hosted the religiously-slanted television programme *Stars on Sunday* until he was publicly disgraced following an affair with a divorcee. Geldof and Yates first met at a media party for the Boomtown Rats' 'Looking After No. 1'. With the success of the group's chart-topper, the couple holidayed in the West Indies, while Yates, now publicly acknowledged as Geldof's partner, utilised her position to become a newspaper and magazine columnist.

'In one and a half years my life had changed utterly and totally. It seemed ridiculous, but I was now a "pop star".' – Geldof

Also see: 'I Don't Like Mondays', August 1979

(Quotes: *Is That It?* by Bob Geldof)

December 1978

ROD STEWART

Da Ya Think I'm Sexy?

'I love women . . . I have a great appreciation of them and I'm not denying that in the past I've made the most of my opportunities.' – Rod Stewart

Following his recent two Top Five British hits, 'Hotlegs' and 'Ole Ole (Muhler Brasileira)' featuring the Scottish World Cup Football Squad, Rod Stewart released the dancer 'Da Ya Think I'm Sexy?' lifted from the *Blondes Have More Fun* album. The track was directly aimed at the disco boom of the decade, not an unusual move for artists of his calibre, but he found it difficult to return to his tried and tested formula of rock/pop. More worrying, though, his credibility was disintegrating as his manager Arnold Stiefel said: 'He had this terrible image problem. His image became this glitzy guy with Britt Ekland and beautiful blonde girls who wore fabulous things and drove fabulous cars. I told him that we had to take four to six years to . . . rebuild him without ever admitting to the world that there was any rebuilding to be done.' Stiefel also felt that 'Da Ya Think I'm Sexy?' 'offended and eroded his core male audience.' He was probably right: indeed when impersonators play Stewart it's usually that song they chose, using, of course, highly exaggerated movements.

'Da Ya Think I'm Sexy?' was written by Stewart and Carmine Appice, but composer Jorge Ben believed they had swiped his song 'Taj Mahal', written in tribute to the blues artist who had named himself after the Indian monument. When Stewart performed the track at the 'Song for UNICEF' concert staged in January 1979, he donated the royalties to UNICEF, thereby presumably wiping out any financial account to Ben.

On the personal front, Britt Ekland had left him following his public statement that he had no plans to marry her. Stewart returned to his womanising, adding fuel to the belief he was destined to become the music business's most wealthy and eligible bachelor. It was a short-lived image because, following the rise of the 'offending and eroding' single to the top of the American chart in February 1979, Stewart married Alana Hamilton, ex-wife of actor George Hamilton, in Beverly Hills. The marriage produced two children and lasted only five years despite the singer saying, 'I have always had a weakness for long legged blondes but since I'm married to the best I'm not going to be interested any more in testing for any other fish in the sea.'

Before 1979 ended, Stewart issued a pair of singles, 'Ain't Love a Bitch', a Top Twenty British hit, and 'Blondes (Have More Fun)' which stalled in the Top Seventy, and toured America with the final date in California. During the first four years of the new decade, Stewart's British chart success wavered. He began 1980 with 'If Loving You Is Wrong (I Don't Want to Be Right)', again drawing on his love of black soul music, which staggered into the Top Thirty, while 'My Girl' became a Top Forty entrant. However, during 1983 he re-established himself as a chart-topping artist when 'Baby Jane' became a No. 1 single in Britain during July. Reminiscent of his earlier work like 'You Wear It Well', this was obviously the formula his public wanted.

By 1984 his marriage to Alana had ended, and on the professional front he issued the album *Camouflage,* from which the Top Thirty British hit 'Infatuation', featuring Jeff Beck, was lifted. 'Some Guys Have All the Luck' followed to reach the Top Twenty. Two years later, Stewart recorded 'Love Touch' for the movie *Legal Eagles,* starring Robert Redford and Debra Winger. Later released as a single, it struggled into the Top Thirty. Its follow-up, 'Every Beat of my Heart', however, soared to No. 2 in July 1986. Through to the end of the eighties, the singer maintained regular chart appearances and embarked upon extensive world tours, thereby maintaining his superstar status.

In 1990 Stewart was the subject of two lawsuits, both the result of his practice of kicking footballs into the audience during performances. A splendid idea until a ball lands! He enjoyed a Top Ten hit with 'Downtown Train', and then recorded the Marvin Gaye and Kim Weston Motown classic 'It Takes Two' with Tina Turner. The novelty element of two giant voices and the marketing muscle of Pepsi Cola, who used it to advertise their soft drink on television, pushed the single to No. 5.

Before 1990 was out Stewart remarried. His new wife, Rachel Hunter, was a New Zealand model. Meanwhile his former live-in girl friend Kelly Emberg filed a multi-million-dollar palimony suit against him. Stewart's love of women cost him dearly. Then his best friend, Elton John, took his recent marriage one step further when he dressed up as a bride to join Stewart on stage during a concert at Wembley.

Rod Stewart was now in vogue. His British tours guaranteed sell-out venues, while his American hikes ensured million of dollars in pay cheques. During 1991, his British chart success was his most impressive for some time. 'Rhythm of the Night' and 'The Motown Song', featuring The Temptations, were both Top Ten singles, the latter boasting an animated promotional video that included selected Motown artists. His next Top Tenner, 'Tom Traubert's Blues (Waltzing Matilda)', was issued in 1992, while a year later in 1993 'Have I Told You Lately' soared into the Top Five and its follow-up 'People Get Ready' made it into the Top Fifty. Early in 1994, Stewart was inducted into the Rock 'n' Roll Hall of Fame during a ceremony held in New York before being presented with the Michael Jackson International Artist Award during the American Music Awards gala in February. The remainder of 1994 was spent touring America, while on the singles front 'All for Love' bolted to No. 2 in the British chart and No. 1 in the America. Joining Stewart on this title were Sting and Bryan Adams. For the next two years Stewart toured, taking in British dates, including those staged at Wembley Arena late in 1995. And so it goes on . . .

Rod Stewart, with his blond spiky hair, remains one of Britain's more colourful artists. His name is as familiar as his football team, and his throaty voice is an acceptable sound of rock/pop music, while his bizarre reputation has supplied the tabloids with many a blazing headline!

Also see: 'Maggie May', November 1971; 'You Wear It Well', September 1972; 'Sailing', September 1975

VILLAGE PEOPLE

YMCA

With Christmas over and the New Year festivities a hazy memory, what better way to shake off 1978's hangover than with a bunch of all-American guys with a mission? Let's face it, music was fun with the Village People. Those wacky macho outfits, the obligatory short haircuts, chest hair and thick moustaches. Nothing was that serious with these guys except, of course, their music. And sometimes, one wondered . . .

Amid the plethora of disco, the gay population recognised and supported tracks that were potential crossover hits long before straight club DJs knew the discs' titles. And it was this that prompted French record producer Jacques Morali's brainwave. His idea was to combine the two markets by creating a male group that would have crossover appeal. To this end, he toured the wildest of New York's gay nighteries, devoured the atmosphere and dress style of trendy males until he was satisfied that a biker, a policeman, cowboy and indian, a construction worker (complete with hard hat) and a soldier adequately typified the macho American male stereotypes. These creations would form the basis for a song and dance act that would flaunt campness, yet would appeal to gays and straights.

Morali's first recruit was lead vocalist Victor Willis, quickly followed by support singers and dancers Alex Briley, Randy Jones, David Hodo, Felipe Rose and Glenn Hughes. The name of Village People was swiped from New York's Greenwich Village. And it was this package that Morali signed to his company, Can't Stop Productions, distributed by Casablanca Records, while in Britain, Phonogram's Mercury Records released the bulk of their product.

The next stage of the producer's plan was to find top notch composer/producers, and to this end he hired Phil Hurtt, Henri Belolo and Pete White, among others. They were instructed to conceive tracks that held gay themes without being too overt.

During October 1977, the Village People were presented to the public via their eponymous album which peaked in the American Top Sixty, later selling sufficient copies to pass gold status. The first single to be lifted, 'San Franciso (You've Got Me)' released on the DJM label, became their debut British hit, reaching the Top Fifty. The group's blending of hard-hitting vocals and music carried them through a series of hit singles – it was unique, and coupled with their macho choreography, won them public support from both sectors.

In 1978, Casablanca Records and Motown Records joined forces to produce the disco movie *Thank God It's Friday,* principally starring disco queen Donna Summer, and supported by The Commodores, among others. The Village People contributed two songs, 'I Am What I Am' and 'Hollywood' to the soundtrack. The movie was based around a nightclub's activities, offering unlimited scope for non-stop dancing and singing against a weak storyline.

Tinged with gay attitudes, *Macho Man* was the Village People's second album, issued during August 1978. The public rushed to buy it, pushing its sales beyond one million copies, qualifying it for a platinum disc. The album's title was lifted as a single, reaching the American Top Thirty.

The momentum of this risqué group grew until they reached the pinnacle of their career, with 'YMCA'. Penned by Morali, Belolo and Willis, it first blistered its way through disco dancefloors before crossing over into mainstream music. It soared to the top of the American chart in January 1979 before repeating that success in Britain during the same month, a position it held for three weeks. 'YMCA' sold in excess of two million copies Stateside, while in Britain it went on to sell 1.5 million, an incredible feat for an act who flaunted gayness, although it was accepted that certain sectors of the public treated the group with ridicule. However, it is probably these same people who almost two decades later, can be seen emulating the chart-topper's dance routine of enacting with hands and arms the letters in the single's title. For surely, gays would not want to be reminded of their sexuality being flaunted in such an absurd manner.

A month on from the chart-topper, the Village People's album *Cruisin',* from which 'YMCA' was lifted, soared into the British Top Thirty, and reached the Top Three in America; another milestone in seventies gay dance music.

Possibly the boys' most outrageous of singles was the follow-up to 'YMCA'. Titled 'In the Navy', its lyrics held two interpretations; neither needed a college degree to decipher. Once more, the public rose to the call to push the single to No. 3 in America, and No. 2 in Britain during March 1979. Remarkably, the US Navy intended to adopt the single as a recruitment aid, but once the full implications of the lyrics were taken into account, the higher ranks dropped the idea! However, before the year was out, Billy Connolly, Scottish singer/comic, rose to the bait to record a take-off single 'In the Brownies' which, alarmingly, scored sufficient sales to give him a Top Forty hit, thus proving that British record buyers were permitted errors of judgement.

Throughout their career so far, The Village People had craved acceptance for their music, and respect for its presentation. Although it had been unprecedently successful, they felt it was considered lightweight and, at the very worst, treated as a joke. Britain's most popular music weekly, *NME,* responded in print: 'The boys in Village People may complain that people are only interested in whether or not they're gay, but they should have thought about that before they started putting on such butch costumes and started singing songs like 'Macho Man', 'YMCA', and 'I Am What I Am' with lyrics so camp they have to be held down with tent pegs.'

Meanwhile, the authentic Village People issued the single 'Go West'; this time the chart positions were lower – Top Forty in America, Top Twenty in Britain. The group was on the verge of losing its selling power. When their next single, 'Ready for the 80s' issued late in 1979, crawled into the American Top Sixty, the end was in sight. Victor Willis must have sensed pending doom, because he left the group in December and was replaced by Ray Simpson, brother of composer/singer Valerie Simpson, one half of the duo Ashford & Simpson.

The Village People were, however, destined to enjoy two further British hits before their career ground to a halt. The first, 'Can't Stop the Music' was lifted from the movie soundtrack of the same name to reach No. 11 in the chart in August 1980. The second and final hit was five years later when 'Sex over the Phone' reached the Top Sixty.

By this time, the Village People had undergone several upheavals. They had switched companies to RCA Records, where they dropped their macho image in favour of the New Romantic/Punk fashion, complete with shorn hair and face make-up. It was with this company that they issued their last charting album, *Renaissance,* offering a combination of rock and camp. But unsure which audience to appeal to, the album floundered in the lower rungs of the American Top One Hundred.

Although disco music remained prevalent, the style was changing; fashions grew and died overnight and the Village People were lost in their attempts to regain status. Sadly, by the mid-eighties the group conceded defeat.

During 1991 Jacques Morali died at the age of forty-four from an AIDS related illness. The following year the Village People re-formed to perform on the nostalgia circuit and (naturally) in gay clubs, while in 1993, 'YMCA' rose again to re-establish itself in the British Top Twenty. Although the record label carried the title 'YMCA '93 (Remix)' everyone recognised and supported the 1979 hit that had represented both outrage and fun. Five months later a remixed version of 'In the Navy' peaked in the British Top Forty, marking the final hit from the group.

The Village People didn't take themselves that seriously, they rose above the criticism and presented the public with a brand new dance music that was irresistible. And oh! – those costumes!

Also No. 1 in January 1979: 'Hit Me with your Rhythm Stick' by Ian Dury and The Blockheads

February 1979

BLONDIE

Heart of Glass

'[The song] came very easily and very naturally. It just toppled into place . . . I think Chris [Stein] came up with the "heart of glass" phrase.' – Debbie Harry

Born Deborah Harry in Miami, Florida, on 1 July 1945, she was adopted as a toddler by Catherine and Richard, and the family moved to Hawthorne in New Jersey. Deborah's first taste of show business proper came when she joined the Flower Power group, Wind in the Willows, who recorded an eponymous album during 1968 for Capitol Records.

Harry shifted career direction to become a Playboy bunny at Max's Kansas City in New York, where apart from waiting on table she was able to socialise with visiting musicians. From here, she joined a trio known as The Stilettos, who were involved in the New Wave musical movement.

Chris Stein, born in Brooklyn, New York, on 5 January 1950, was a student at New York City's School of Visual Art. Upon graduation, he joined The Stilettos. In time, The Stilettos disbanded, whereupon Harry and Stein, now lovers, formed a new musical unit called Angel and The

Snakes, the nucleus of the future Blondie. Prior to the creation of Blondie, the hitmaking group, musicians drifted through varying line-ups, including, Billy O'Conner on drums, Fred Smith on bass, and various female back-up singers. The group was a success on the punk club circuit. During 1976 and known as Blondie – with the permanent line-up of drummer Clem Burke, keyboardist Jimmy Destri, bass player Gary Valentine and Fred Smith – they secured a recording contract with Private Stock Records. Late in 1976, Blondie's debut single titled 'X-Offender' was issued, swiped from the *Blondie* album. Both were poor sellers. However, on the strength of these releases, the group toured America, before visiting Britain. Then more upheaval hit the membership, when Valentine departed to concentrate on his own group called Know. His replacement, Frank Infante, late of World War II, joined in time to move with Blondie to Chrysalis Records to record and release the *Plastic Letters* album.

In 1978, Blondie cracked the pop scene when their single 'Denis', a revamped, updated version of the Randy and The Rainbows' 1953 American hit, soared to No. 2 in Britain. The *Plastic Letters* album became a big seller. The second single '(I'm Always Touched by Your) Presence Dear', likewise extracted from the album, reached the British Top Ten. It was an excellent start for an American group in an overseas territory. Pity public support wasn't as strong at home!

Following these releases, Blondie teamed up with British record producer Mike Chapman, who had first seen the group perform in 1977 at the Whisky Club, where Tom Petty was support act. In fact, so smitten was Chapman that he watched the show four times in total. The bonding was instant and extremely profitable.

Blondie's next single, 'Picture This' hotly followed a British tour, to reach the Top Twenty, while 'Hanging on the Telephone', soared into the British Top Five before 1978 ended. In between releases, Harry had diversified into the movie world to appear in *The Foreigner*. As it was abundantly clear she was now the band's trophy, the figurehead, she was cultivated and exploited to glow with the image of a blonde sex kitten as singer and actress. Eventually, she would openly criticise the 'cheesecake' image, but for the time being was content with the view 'that sex sells and I do exploit my sexuality.'

With Britain and Europe securely in Blondie's grasp, they concentrated on their home country, where to date, their success had been negligible. The group's next single 'Heart of Glass', lifted from their pending album *Parallel Lines*, was released in February 1979. Aimed squarely at the powerful dance scene and not inspired by new wave/punk demands, the title shot to the top of the British chart, a position it held for four weeks, thanks to sales in excess of one million copies. Two months on, 'Heart of Glass' stormed up the American chart to the top, taking both group and record company by surprise. Stein: 'We didn't expect the song to be that big. We did it as a novelty item . . .' The single's climb to the top may have been helped by a threatened radio station ban, due to the opening lyrics which included the word 'ass'. A further version was recorded for those lily-livered stations. Blondie refused to be concerned. Harry: 'Any kind of controversy causes excitement and more interest in the long run.'

The group had included 'Heart of Glass' in their stage act for several months prior to recording it. Harry, who composed it with Stein, said at the time, 'I was so tired of hearing girl singers write or sing about being beaten by love, and I just sort of said . . . I think there are a lot of girls who walk away.'

Parallel Lines, the result of their studio sessions with Mike Chapman, soared to the top of the British album chart during 1979, before selling in excess of 19 million copies worldwide. Harry: 'Mike is a real hot chili pepper and very energetic and enthusiastic.' Chapman's enthusiasm and the group's popularity provided a further British chart-topper and three more in America, the country they found so difficult to crack. Chapman told author Joe Smith, 'Debbie Harry was, and probably still is, one of the most extraordinary and unusual artists that you could hope to come across.'

Also see: 'Sunday Girl', June 1979

(Quotes: *Creem* magazine 1979; *Off the Record* by Joe Smith; *Rock 'n' Roll Babylon* by Gary Herman)

March 1979

THE BEE GEES

Tragedy

'We don't like being labelled as something because our music was put to a motion picture, and everybody labelling us with the "John Travolta" look.' – Maurice Gibb

Prior to becoming involved with *Saturday Night Fever,* The Bee Gees were actually working on their own movie. Titled *Sgt Pepper's Lonely Hearts Club Band,* it was based on The Beatles' innovative, mind-bending recording project and featured the brothers as composers and actors. This was premiered in America in July 1978. The soundtrack peaked in the British Top Forty the same month, before soaring into the American Top Five in August. Compared to the John Travolta blockbusting disco film, *Sgt Pepper's Lonely Hearts Club Band* bombed. So devastating were the financial implications that it contributed to the downfall of RSO Records, The Bee Gees' record company, owned by Robert Stigwood.

Instead of bemoaning their failure, The Bee Gees returned to the recording studios to work on their first studio album since 1976. Locked within the walls of the Criteria Studios in Miami for nearly a year, the task before the trio was awesome; how could they hope to follow the biggest-selling album of all time (to date), namely *Saturday Night Fever*?

The brothers nearly did it with the magnificent *Spirits (Having Flown)* from which 'Too Much Heaven' was swiped as the debut single. Released in 1978, it soared to No. 3 in the British chart, and early in 1979 topped the American chart. While it dominated the top spot, The Bee Gees performed at The Music for UNICEF gala concert, celebrating the International Year of the Child, held in New York. NBC TV went on to broadcast the gala, and the brothers donated all the royalties from 'Too Much Heaven' to UNICEF.

In March 1979 a further track from *Spirits (Having Flown)* titled 'Tragedy' shot to the top of the British chart, where it stayed for two weeks. This success was repeated in America. 'Tragedy', an impassioned, complex track, featured Barry Gibb's lead falsetto voice pushed to the limit and beyond. The close of the title featured an explosion; not an authentic sound but rather Barry cupping his hands over the studio microphone while their keyboard player simultaneously thumped the lower keys of a piano. This was then over-taped several times to produce the big 'bang'.

'Tragedy' marked the trio's final British Top Ten hit, although America continued to support them with multi-million sales, for example 'Love You Inside Out', The Bee Gees' sixth consecutive No. 1 single, tying them with their musical heroes The Beatles. The single was also the third consecutive chart-topper from *Spirits (Having Flown)* and the ninth American No. 1 (in total) for the brothers. Unhappily, the story was less stunning in Britain. 'Love You Inside Out' only managed a Top

Twenty placing late in 1979, marking the end of an unprecedented career for the most successful group of the seventies. Ah, such is the uncertainty and fickleness of the most exciting industry in the world – that of music! But The Bee Gees were destined to return to more dizzy heights – as composers and producers.

Using the vocals of Barbra Streisand, the trio wrote and produced the album *Guilty*, from which 'Woman in Love' was lifted as an American and British chart-topper during October 1980. The album likewise topped both countries' charts. A further single, 'Guilty', soared to No. 3 in America, reaching the Top Forty in Britain. Late in 1981, The Bee Gees issued a taster from their next album *Living Eyes*. Titled 'He's a Liar', the single stalled in the American Top Thirty. Maurice Gibb believed the project was an error on their part because, at the time, they were experiencing personal traumas. 'Robert Stigwood was trying to sue us and we were suing him . . . We never went to court. It was just blown all out of proportion, especially by the rubbish press.' The finances involved in the legal action were, however, far from 'rubbish'. The trio filed the biggest lawsuit in the history of the music business. Accusing Stigwood of misrepresentation of their financial affairs, the brothers filed a suit for $75 million against their record company, Polygram, and a staggering $125 million against Stigwood himself and his family of companies. Stigwood called their action 'a cheap stunt' before the rift was healed. The action also meant, of course, that The Bee Gees were now without a record company.

During 1982, after composing 'Heart (Stop Beating in Time)' for British singer Leo Sayer (a Top Thirty hit), Barry Gibb produced the *Heartbreaker* album for Dionne Warwick, from which the hit singles 'Heartbreaker' and 'All the Love in the World' were lifted. The next year, the brothers composed material for the movie *Staying Alive*, produced by Sylvester Stallone and the sequel to *Saturday Night Fever*. It paled by comparison. Maurice Gibb: 'Halfway through the movie we wanted to pull out because Stallone unfortunately knew nothing about music. They edited all our music to pieces.' The trio believed the film was actually a vehicle for Stallone's brother Frank who enjoyed an American Top Ten hit with 'Far from Over'.

With The Bee Gees' own career still uncertain, Robin Gibb embarked upon a solo career. He was relatively successful: 'Another Lonely Night in New York' was a minor British single hit in June 1983. Later that year, Barry Gibb produced *Eyes that See in the Dark* for country singer Kenny Rogers, before releasing his own debut solo album *Now Voyager*. During 1985, he worked with another star, Diana Ross. The result,

Eaten Alive, spawned 'Chain Reaction' as a single. The title was Ms Ross's second solo British chart-topper, in January 1986.

The Bee Gees were destined to return with a vengeance. In 1987, with a new recording contract with Warner Bros Records, they issued their strongest album for some time, titled *ESP.* The lifted single, 'You Win Again', returned the brothers to the top spot in Britain during November 1987, while in America it struggled into the Top Eighty. My, how the tables had turned! The trio had, of course, won their freedom from RSO Records and a $200 million out-of-court settlement with Robert Stigwood.

The youngest Gibb brother, Andy, died from an inflammatory heart virus in the John Radcliffe Hospital, Oxford, on 10 March 1988. He had, like his brothers, enjoyed a spectacular American career that included two chart-toppers, '(Love Is) Thicker Than Water' and 'Shadow Dancing', both in 1978; had married actress Victoria Principal, who had starred as Pamela Ewing in the highly compulsive soap opera *Dallas,* and who had succumbed to the attraction of drug taking.

In the nineties, The Bee Gees continued to make their presence felt via prestigious live performances, and they retrieved much of their past stardom with British hits that included 'How Can You Mend a Broken Heart?' in 1990, 'Secret Love' (1991), 'Paying the Price of Love' and 'For Whom the Bell Tolls' in 1993.

The Bee Gees are now celebrating their third decade in the music business. Without doubt they were the international leaders of the seventies, whose strength lay in their willingness to experiment with music that ranged from sultry ballads to vital disco or to slices of R. & B. Their constant quest for self-perfection is a lesson others could learn.

Maurice Gibb: 'People tend to get this image of us with the hairy chests and the medallions and white trousers and all that sort of rubbish . . .'

Well?

Also see: 'Night Fever', May 1978

(Quotes: *We Had Joy We Had Fun* by Barry Scott)

GLORIA GAYNOR

I Will Survive

'Once I was afraid, I was petrified . . .' My, how those lyrics sent shivers down the spine as the disco revolution continued, subsequently crowning Gloria Gaynor the Queen of Disco. Two decades on, the single still lives!

Gaynor was born on 7 September 1947 in Newark, New Jersey, to Queenie May Fowles. Gaynor's father, Daniel Fowles, was a vaudeville artist who abandoned Queenie May when she was five months pregnant. During her high school years, Gaynor took college preparatory courses to study to be a teacher. She graduated with honours, but, unable to find a job to support her while at college proper, her plans to be a teacher were dropped. It was at this juncture she decided her future was singing, but realising this too could prove fruitless, she attended a beauty culture school, learning hairdressing, and business college to learn secretarial and bookkeeping skills.

With education behind her, eighteen-year-old Gaynor worked at Bambergers Department Store as a sales auditor. By night, she and her brother Arthur would frequent the local nightspots. One evening, while at the Cadillac Club, she was asked by Eddie McClendon of The Pacesetters to sing with them on stage. This led to a two-week tour of Canadian clubs, and Bamberger's store upon her return. Gaynor wrote in her autobiography, 'Arthur would pretend that I was this great singer from out of town and tell them that if they wanted him to, he might be able to coax me into singing for them. And it worked!'

After winning a local talent contest at the Blue Mirror Night Club, beating Dionne Warwick to second place, Gaynor secured a singing spot at the Orbit Lounge. While there, she was offered an audition for Johnny Nash's Joda record label, where she recorded the solitary title 'She'll Be Sorry', changing her name to Gaynor at Nash's insistence to enjoy a minor hit. Before 'She'll Be Sorry' could gain momentum, Joda folded!

Plans to pursue her solo career were postponed, whereupon she joined Cleave Nickerson and The Soul Satisfiers, a local New Jersey group. From there, she formed her own band named City Life (billed as 'City Life with Gloria Gaynor') to perform on the nightclub circuit. During one of these concerts, entrepreneur Jay Ellis Leberman offered her a management deal, and within months had secured her a recording contract with CBS Records' Columbia offshoot. Gaynor: 'Clive Davis [president of Columbia Records] decided to record me but not, unfortunately, with City Life. It made things a bit difficult between us.'

Gaynor's debut single for the Columbia label, 'Honey Bee', penned by Mervyn and Melvin Steel, produced by Norman Harris, was recorded in Philadelphia, the home of sweet soul music, during December 1973. Despite not being credited on the record label, City Life promoted the title with Gaynor in live appearances. Then the unexpected occurred. Clive Davis left Columbia Records and those acts he signed were not of interest to his replacement. 'Honey Bee' was therefore neglected. But the title would not die. Thanks to the support from nightclub DJs, the single became a dancefloor hit. Jay Ellis Leberman, incensed that the single had failed to reach its full potential, purchased the tapes from CBS Records to lease them to MGM Records, a Polydor Records' subsidiary. In 1971, Gloria Gaynor became an MGM Records artist. Gaynor: 'I invited Bruce Greenberg (from MGM) to hear us performing "Never Can Say Goodbye" because I was convinced that it should be my next single . . . They saw I was right. We did it.' The updated version of the Jackson 5's 1971 hit soared to No. 2 in the British chart in December 1974; the American Top Ten in January 1975. The title introduced the record-buying public to the Gaynor sound: a beefy disco style that subtly romped, without running. This was carried through to her second British hit, titled 'Reach Out, I'll Be There', another Motown cover version, of the Four Tops' 1966 chart-topper. Gaynor's interpretation peaked at No. 14 during March 1975.

Issued between this pair of singles was the singer's debut album *Never Can Say Goodbye,* on which one side consisted of the three segued tracks, 'Honey Bee', 'Never Can Say Goodbye' and 'Reach Out, I'll Be There'. Obviously, this was a runaway hit with club DJs who could leave the side playing, maintain a dancefloor, and do whatever DJs do when not spinning vinyl. On a small scale, though, home dancers could practise and perfect their dance steps and dancefloor staying power in private! On the strength of this solitary album and her success to date, Gaynor was quickly linked to the disco explosion of 1974, by being elected 'Queen of the Discos of 1975' by the International Association of Discotheque Disc Jockeys. She was crowned in March 1975 at New York's Club Les Jardins. Gaynor: 'It was a terrific, glamorous occasion and drew so much international press attention they had to rope off the streets to keep back the crowds.' Two further albums followed, *Experience Gloria Gaynor* and *'I've Got You'*.

Meantime, in the market place, disco competition was intensifying; new artists were emerging almost daily as dance fanatics purchased records for their beaty sound, rather than the artists performing them. Nonetheless, Gaynor looked set to retain her crown as no other female artist neared her popularity. However, her career did peter off because of hospitalisation for a back injury sustained when she fell from stage, and the aftermath of her mother's death. While Gaynor was indisposed, rising star Donna Summer snatched her crown in 1976. Gaynor said at the time: 'It doesn't really bother me because there is no competition between us. Nobody goes into a store and only buys one record, so it's not that significant. In some ways, it's all good for publicity and promotion to have something like that going on.'

Luckily, before Gaynor could be categorised as a disco casualty, she enjoyed two further British hits, 'All I Need Is your Sweet Lovin'' in August 1975, and her version of Benny Goodman's 1940 track 'How High the Moon' in January 1976. The latter title was her last chart placing for three years. Gaynor and her manager Leberman parted company, as a result of conflicting interests. Linwood Simon, whom she married in 1979, stepped in as her business manager.

When Gaynor returned to the recording studio to work with Dino Fekaris and Freddie Perren, they played her their 'I Will Survive', one of several tracks to be included on the album *Love Tracks*. 'Substitute', with 'I Will Survive' on the B-side, was the first single from those sessions to be released. Gaynor believed 'I Will Survive' the better track; she felt the lyrics represented a woman's strength. Club DJs shared her feeling and flipped the disc. It was this support that forced her record company to repress the single. With its renewed life, 'I Will Survive' shot to the top of the American chart during March 1979; a month on, the title repeated that success in Britain, and dominated the chart for four weeks.

Gaynor's belief was on target. Women of the world identified with the song's theme of the abused or jilted woman who had little hope until she regained self-confidence and esteem. Gaynor: 'I knew [the song] was a hit when I read the lyrics. I knew it was an international and "now" lyric, one that people could get into. It became innovative as a disco anthem and I know that contributed to its acceptance . . . It's nice to know that I've lent some strength and self-reliance to the whole concept of women being able to continue on without being treated wrongly and without respect.' While the title lived, Gaynor performed six sell-out performances at the London Palladium. The singer could have sold out twice the amount of dates, but the venue was unavailable.

'I Will Survive' was the biggest-selling single of 1979; seven million copies were sold worldwide, with three million in America alone. The phenomenal success of this title rubbed off on its mother album *Love Tracks,* which passed platinum status. Yes indeed, the Queen of Disco had returned; this time, she said, she intended to wear her crown a little longer. Gaynor: 'Discos play a very important role in my life. I don't see them dying out because they are performing a valuable service to the people.' From the music industry's viewpoint, 'I Will Survive' threatened the very concept of disco music; the driving beat had replaced the thumping rhythm that had dictated the timing. Gaynor was smooth, not cruel; and the monster she had created she had to tolerate or destroy. Ultimately, the public was judge and jury, and they made the decision swiftly when 'Let Me Know (I Have the Right)' marked her final British charter for four years.

Meantime, like so many of her ilk, Gaynor's success had a downside; massive doses of insecurity and bewilderment. 'I couldn't hold on to a relationship. I was going in with whatever other people did, drugs and alcohol. I was sure they only liked me because I was a singer.' From 1978 to 1982 the singer and her husband were earning substantial amounts of money through her recordings and his business interests. 'We were hiring limousines and driving around with champagne in the back of the car, just having great fun. Linwood loved the fast cars, he loved the crazy night and day parties that sometimes went on for weeks, and he loved all the attention he was getting from all sorts of women.' In time, the lifestyle proved unacceptable to Gaynor; she attempted to remove herself from the fast-lane temptations. Attending church regularly only isolated her from the 'partying', so she returned to her fun friends. 'The god-fearing side of me slowly began to get the upper hand and I was staying more and more in my room and ignoring the parties we would have.' Finally, she said 'enough'; her husband partied elsewhere.

Following an eight-year stay as a Polydor artist, Gaynor switched companies to join Atlantic Records in 1982. The move was hitless. Gaynor: 'I was disappointed. I thought the product was excellent.' Also during 1982, she returned to her Bible readings; two years later she attended a Christian Convention at the Nassau Coliseum, New York, where she was baptised in the Holy Spirit.

Moving on to Joel Diamond's Silver Blue label, distributed by Chrysalis Records in Britain, Gaynor re-established herself as a powerful act. In December 1983 she released the forceful 'I Am What I Am', the Act 1 finale lifted from the movie *La Cage Aux Folles*, which crashed to No. 13 in the British chart, bringing with it the Gaynor sound lost for so long. Gaynor: 'I just wanted to be recognisable in my style and yet be able to advance at the same time. So I tried to keep the "I Will Survive" sound and yet make it a little more rocky.'

Like 'I Will Survive' before it, 'I Am What I Am' was adopted by the gay population as an international anthem, boosting the already healthy sales of both titles. Gaynor: 'I can understand gay people taking it up because I know that they feel suppressed. I guess it's an obvious song for them.' Yet, she echoed the comments of rival Donna Summer, when during the eighties she offended her gay fans who had interpreted her 'I Will Survive' as a defiant stand against AIDS, by referring to gayness as 'an abomination'. The singer told *The Times* in 1995: 'I believe every word in the Bible, but who am I to judge? Many of my friends are gay.' Will these singers never learn? Without the loyal support of the gay world, neither Summer nor Gaynor would have enjoyed the success and wealth they now possess. Thankfully, there was one songstress who would in the nineties openly acknowledge her gay following.

The disco movement changed direction and burned out, leaving artists like Gaynor to flounder. She did not abandon recording altogether, merely altered course to record tracks with religious themes. Between 1989 and 1992, she hosted six series of *The Gospel Train,* a weekly BBC Radio 2 programme. Gaynor: 'It was my best yet opportunity to share the knowledge and love of Christ with my fans in Britain.' In 1995, she published her autobiography, the aptly titled *Soul Survivor,* while confining her concerts to the nightclub and gospel circuits.

Despite Gloria Gaynor's mixed feelings regarding 'I Will Survive', the song remains synonymous with her, although another superstar came close to snatching that away from her. In February 1996, Diana Ross recorded her version of the chart-topper, as a way of thanking the gay communities for their continued, loyal support. The single peaked in the British Top Ten, while the accompanying promotional video featured Ross, her many lookalikes, drag queen RuPaul, and in excess of 300 fans and millions of sequins, parading through the streets of Los Angeles!

With so many connotations within its lyrics, 'I Will Survive' will do just that – and live on forever!

(Quotes: *Soul Survivor* by Gloria Gaynor)

ART GARFUNKEL

Bright Eyes

Following his break-up with Paul Simon, Art Garfunkel re-established himself as a chart-topping name with his solo version of The Flamingos' 1959 American hit 'I Only Have Eyes for You'. Incidentally, Ben Selvin first recorded the song in 1934.

Simon and Garfunkel no longer recorded as a duo, though they would occasionally perform together, usually for fundraising concerts. At one juncture, they even embarked upon a fully fledged, sell-out European tour which included dates in London.

'Bright Eyes', lifted from Garfunkel's album *Fate for Breakfast*, released in 1979, was the follow-up British hit to 'I Only Have Eyes for You'. The single soared to the top of the chart in May, dominating the position for a staggering six weeks. Penned and produced by British writer Mike Batt (the force behind The Wombles, the unlikely but lovable furry creatures who lived on Wimbledon Common, whose remarkable success began in 1974 with 'The Wombling Song'), Garfunkel's 'Bright Eyes' was *the* song from *Watership Down,* an animated movie based on Richard Adams's novel, first published in 1972. It was the author's intention to write an adult novel for children, and when transferred to the big screen the result was exciting and beautiful, happy and sad, occasionally frightening. The story told of the adventures of a small group of rabbits led by the courageous Hazel, the impetuous warrior Bigwig and the prophet Fiver. All the ingredients necessary for a blockbusting movie!

However, Art Garfunkel wasn't convinced. His initial reaction to the project was to keep 'Bright Eyes' hidden as an album track, believing it did not represent the individual musical style perfected by him during the past few years. He was to change his mind when he became aware of the runaway popularity of *Watership Down* and its furry characters. More to the point, probably, he could smell the cash register! His wise decision ensured 'Bright Eyes' claimed the position of No. 1 selling single of the year and repeated chart-topping success throughout Europe. Ironically, the title bombed in his home country!

The follow-up single, 'Since I Don't Have You', released in July 1979 failed miserably by comparison, stalling in the British and American Top Forty. It marked his last British chart entrant.

Following the suicide of his girlfriend and the release of his *Scissors Cut* album midway through 1981, Garfunkel released a further single 'In Cars' featuring Paul Simon, who had also contributed to the album. Regrettably, both the album and single were poor sellers by his standards, but Garfunkel maintained his high public profile by reuniting with Paul Simon for a Central Park concert in New York, before returning to the movie world in 1986 to appear as a teacher in the film *Good to Go*.

Art Garfunkel's career through to the end of the eighties included spasmodic recording success and emotional struggles, plus an inclusion in Disney's cable channel programme *Mother Goose Rock 'n' Rhyme*. In 1990, Garfunkel joined Paul Simon on stage at the Rock 'n' Roll Hall of Fame ceremony to sing 'Bridge over Troubled Water' before playing a handful of concerts. These appearances may have been selective, but Garfunkel performed to full houses.

While the world awaits another Simon and Garfunkel recorded reunion, Art Garfunkel's solo career will be remembered for 'Bright Eyes' (whether he likes it or not!) and the lovable rabbits – Hazel, Bigwig, Fiver and friends. And, of course, the joke that accompanied the movie, obviously conceived by a carnivore: 'A sign hanging outside a butcher's shop: "You've read the book. You've seen the movie. Now eat the cast"!'

Also see: 'I Only Have Eyes for You', October 1975

June 1979

BLONDIE

Sunday Girl

When she was given the title of the decade's most exciting sex kitten, Debbie Harry was less than amused. 'In America they put girls into two categories. Either you're a sweet, clean-cut girl or a real nasty bitch. And I know which one they've figured me out to be.'

Following their British and American chart-topper 'Heart of Glass' earlier in 1979, swiped from their best-selling album *Parallel Lines*, Blondie enjoyed their second British No. 1 single in June. Titled 'Sunday Girl', composed by Harry's lover Chris Stein, the single topped the British chart for three weeks. Two months later, the group's next album *Eat to the Beat* likewise shot to the top of its chart, and was a further result of the group's sessions with Mike Chapman. The album peaked in the American Top Twenty.

In October, the single 'Dreaming' soared to No. 2 in Britain and reached the Top Thirty in America, and before the decade ended, 'Union City Blue' became a Top Twenty entrant. This title was taken from the movie *Union City*, starring Harry.

Blondie had a further British chart-topper in March 1980 with 'Atomic', which reached the Top Forty in America. This was another track lifted from *Eat to the Beat*. And there was more. 'Call Me' reached No. 1 in both Britain and America. Written and produced by Giorgio Moroder for the Paul Schrader movie *American Gigolo*, starring Richard Gere, the title dominated the American chart for six long weeks. The track was originally conceived by Moroder as 'Machine Man', before Harry attended a rough screening of the movie which included the musical track, and then wrote the lyrics herself. Her next movie involvement was with *Roadie;* Meatloaf was her co-star. The year ended on a further high note when Blondie's version of 'The Tide Is High' by the Jamaican group, The Paragons, became a British chart-topper for two weeks; it was a No. 1 hit in America early in 1981. It was written by John Holt, and Blondie first heard the track on a cassette given to them during a visit to London. Harry: 'Chris fell madly in love with the song, as did I, and we just decided to do it. We thought it was a potential hit song.' The title was swiped from their *Autoamerican* album, which marked the group's return to the producing talents of Mike Chapman; it was a No. 3 British hit and a Top Ten American entrant.

As 'Rapture', the follow-up single to 'The Tide Is High', soared into the British Top Five, Harry recorded a solo album titled *Koo Koo* with Chic members Nile Rodgers and Bernard Edwards, cementing rumours of her intention to leave the group. The first single lifted, 'Backfired', stalled in the British Top Forty, while the album itself soared into the Top Ten. In 1982 the inescapable record company marketing ploy, *Best of Blondie*, was released. This held back the group's next album proper, featuring all group members, titled *The Hunter*, which peaked in the British Top Ten. A pair of singles lifted from this Chapman-produced project, namely, 'Island of Lost Souls' and 'War Child', floundered in the Top Fifty on both sides of the Atlantic. These titles heralded the decline of the group, much to the regret of the music industry who believed there remained much mileage in the membership.

Through to 1986, Debbie Harry concentrated on her film career, appearing in *Hairspray,* for example, and as a stage actress in the off-Broadway comedy *Trafford Tanzi.* Chris Stein, on the other hand, opened his own record outlet, Animal, distributed by Chrysalis Records in Britain, before suffering from pemphigus, a genetic disorder which forced him to be hospitalised and in need of care for several long months. When Stein was sufficiently recovered, he and Harry composed together once more. Chapman: '[Debbie] had this intense relationship with Chris Stein, and the two of them were unbelievably talented. They did some incredible things . . . drugs and what-have-you destroyed all that.'

Late in 1986, Harry's single 'French Kissin' (in the USA)' re-established her as a charting act: it reached the Top Ten in Britain and the Top Sixty in America. This title, and its follow-up 'Free to Fall', a poor-selling item, were lifted from her album *Rockbird,* itself a good seller. Harry's solo career crawled on with the album *Once More into the Bleach* in 1989, a performance at London's Borderline Club, and further dates during June 1990 at the Brixton Academy. The venues were pint-sized compared to those played during Blondie's heyday; nonetheless, Harry performed before loyal and enthusiastic audiences.

Before the eighties closed, the singer was earmarked to star in the Disney movie *Mother Goose Rock 'n' Rhyme,* and issued her album *Def, Dumb and Blonde,* which reunited her with producer Mike Chapman. A couple of lifted singles were issued to become British hits, namely, 'I Want That Man', and 'Sweet and Low'.

In the nineties and following the release of two further albums, *Dead City Radio* and *Red Hot + Blue,* a compilation titled *The Complete Picture – the Very Best of Deborah Harry and Blondie,* featuring group and solo material, soared to No. 3 in Britain. Once more, Harry performed in Britain, where the highlight was a concert at Wembley Stadium, before returning to the film world to appear in *The Killbillies* and *Intimate Stranger.*

Switching from Chrysalis Records to Sire Records during 1993, Harry issued the album *Debravation,* a Top Thirty hit, while a couple of lifted singles included the title 'I Can See Clearly', a mediocre seller. Two years on, Harry alternated as soloist, actress and group leader, while Blondie lived again when their 1979 British chart-topper 'Heart of Glass', albeit a remix, returned to the British chart as a Top Twenty hit!

And that was that!

Also see: - 'Heart of Glass', February 1979

(Quotes: *Off the Record* by Joe Smith)

ANITA WARD

Ring my Bell

'Ring my Bell' was as compulsive as it was annoying: '. . . yooo can ringma beeell, ringma bel . . .' Yet it pushed unknown Anita Ward into the international spotlight. When the bell rang no more, the campanologist disappeared.

Born on 20 December 1957 in Memphis, Tennessee, Ward was one of five children. She spent much of her early years singing in local gospel choirs. Indeed, one of her first significant recordings was as lead a cappella singer with the Rust College Choir featuring Leontyne Price, a noted opera singer. Ward: 'It was all such perfect training for my voice. I studied gospel as well and that has given me range.'

To finance her fledgling singing career, Ward worked as a teacher in elementary schools until she met Chuck Holmes, who offered her a management deal. Holmes introduced her to composer/singer Frederick Knight (whose most significant British hit was his Stax Records release 'I've Been Lonely for So Long' in 1972) who, in 1977, secured her to a recording contract with Juana Records, an offshoot of TK Records, owned by Henry Stone.

Frederick Knight's original intention was to experiment with Ward on a pair of pre-chosen tracks, but he decided instead to record an album with her, not wanting to lose her talent to another record company. When the album, *Songs of Love,* was completed, Knight felt an uptempo track was needed to add balance to the project. He unearthed a song he had originally penned for eleven-year-old Stacy Lattisaw who was earmarked to be contracted to him, but who instead had signed a recording contract with Cotillion Records.

Due to Lattisaw's tender age, Knight's composition was aimed at the teenage market, telling the tale of kids constantly chatting inanely on the telephone. Hence the title 'Ring my Bell'. To cater for Ward's adult approach, Knight rewrote the lyrics to appeal to an older audience, leaving the storyline ambiguous to enable listeners to form their own conclusions. Ward immediately disliked the song, but agreed to record it. The session took forty-eight hours. Frederick Knight played percussion on the track and sang back-ups, together with Cheryl Bundy and Valerie Williams.

To introduce Anita Ward as a new artist to a wider audience, 'Spoiled by your Love' was first lifted from the album as a single. Ward: 'It got played in the Memphis area but didn't do too much.' The follow-up did. When released in Britain, 'Ring my Bell' shot to the top of the chart in July 1979, a position it held for two weeks. Then it repeated its chart-topping success in America. Naturally, the singer was needed to promote the single but she refused to resign from her school teaching because, 'I never really believed in my making it as a singer. I never took it that seriously. Entertaining would always be just a job to me [and] I wouldn't let [it] have any kind of influence on me. I am basically just a naive, shy little church girl.'

Anita Ward became a seventies one-hit wonder, unable to repeat any resemblance of a hit in Britain, though in America 'Don't Drop my Love' reached the Top Ninety. Ward: 'I [had] no intention of ever trying to be a disco queen. I accept that as a phase I have to go through to get where I'm going.' Exactly where that was remained unclear. Sadly, the music business failed to support her. She went no further, returning to the teaching profession full-time except for the occasional club performance in Britain.

That's show business!

(Quotes *Blues and Soul* magazine, 1979)

August 1979

BOOMTOWN RATS

I Don't Like Mondays

'We were sure we had another hit with "Mondays" though I thought it was no more than a decent B-side.' – Bob Geldof

With the Boomtown Rats' British career at its peak with a trio of big-selling singles and a 1978 chart-topper with 'Rat Trap', the group needed to crack the lucrative American market. Their previous releases had been critically acclaimed, but had not sold sufficient quantities to chart. Now was the time, Geldof believed, to promote their second album, *Tonic for the Troops*.

Mercury Records had issued the group's first discs, but had, according to their lead singer, not invested sufficient money and dedication in them. Following a visit to the record company's American offices, when Geldof threatened to systematically trash the president's office, the Boomtown Rats were dropped from the artist roster, enabling them to join Columbia Records.

Columbia instantly scheduled a one-month promotional trek for the group to include radio and television spots, record store and one-off appearances. The Boomtown Rats' presence was felt. They repeated the exercise throughout Europe, hoping that their status as Britain's top-selling band would rub off.

During April 1979, the group returned to America to embark upon a fully-fledged tour. Geldof intended to conquer the country, as he wrote in his autobiography: 'Vanity, arrogance and ambition were all caught up in this. I wanted to impress these people.' One of the concerts was staged in San Diego, where four months previously, a young girl named Brenda Spencer had leaned from her bedroom window, brandishing a gun, systematically shooting the people below her. During the massacre, a reporter asked her via a telephone connection why she was murdering innocent school children. She answered, 'I don't like Mondays.'

Geldof composed the Boomtown Rats' future British chart-topper during the American trek. 'I tried to picture the girl. I tried to visualise the scene: the police captains, the bullhorns, the playground, the parents.' Produced by Phil Wainman, 'I Don't Like Mondays' shot to the top of the British chart during August 1979, a position it held for four weeks, to become the group's biggest-selling single ever. When the American media became aware of the title's lyrical content, radio stations slashed it from their airplay schedules, while Brenda Spencer's parents threatened legal action against both the group and its record company. The single was actually on sale for only one week because Columbia Records feared a lengthy and expensive legal entanglement; nonetheless, 'I Don't Like Mondays' reached the Top Eighty, whereupon the Boomtown Rats' American career disintegrated. On the other hand, Brenda Spencer, serving a twenty-five-year prison sentence, was delighted Geldof had elevated her to stardom. Despite the (natural) American attitude, the single went on to win a pair of Ivor Novello Awards for the Outstanding Lyric and Best Pop Song of 1979.

In November, the album *The Fine Art of Surfacing* soared into the British Top Ten, while during December, the follow-up single 'Diamond Smiles' peaked in the Top Twenty. In 1980, the single 'Someone's Looking at You' shot to No. 4 in Britain, but the Boomtown Rats were unable to enjoy the success due to overseas touring commitments that included a trip to Japan. During their stay there, they experienced a new culture for the first time. However, during the tour Geldof suffered food poisoning yet continued performing – leaving the stage at regular intervals to vomit. From Japan, the group visited Australia and New Zealand. Meantime, back in Britain, their single 'Banana Republic' closed the year by soaring to No. 3.

In 1981, 'The Elephants' Graveyard (Guilty)', swiped from the group's next album, *Mondo Bongo,* stalled in the British Top Thirty, while the album itself fared better in the Top Ten. The second lifted single, 'Never in a Million', closed the year by struggling into the Top Seventy. A poor showing to close the decade, especially with two British chart-toppers to the group's credit.

With the Boomtown Rats' touring commitments fulfilled, Geldof secured a part in the Pink Floyd movie *The Wall.* 'My character was a manic depressive . . . I was churlish, snappy and desperately miserable at home with Paula [his girlfriend] in the evenings.' Although he was desperate to work outside the confines of the Boomtown Rats and the music business generally, filming *The Wall* was a strain on Geldof's emotional state. When the movie was finally completed, he refused to attend the screenings but consented to join in the Cannes' Film Festival hype.

In 1983, now signed to Phonogram, the Boomtown Rats issued two singles, 'House on Fire', which made the Top Thirty, and 'Charmed Lives', which bombed. In 1984, a further pair of singles, 'Tonight' and 'Drag Me Down' both struggled into the lower region of the British chart, dragging Geldof into further despair. Towards the close of the year, Geldof, like most British television viewers, watched horrific reports of the most appalling famine in Ethiopia. Geldof: 'The pictures were of people who were so shrunken by starvation that they looked like beings from another planet.' As the British public cried in disbelief, Geldof took his grief one step further, by formulating plans to raise funds for the famine victims.

Geldof, as he mulled over the Boomtown Rats' pending album, which he predicted would bomb, decided to record a single to help raise funds for Ethiopia. The planning involved was unimaginably extensive and exhaustive; not only was there a host of British artists to be recruited, but a recording studio, record company, record retailers and so on to be won over, who, in the end, either gave their services free or offered healthy discounts. Geldof then recorded a demo tape of the track he planned to use titled 'Do They Know It's Christmas?'

Approximately thirty-six acts, including Boy George and Jon Moss from Culture Club, George Michael, Paul Young, Duran Duran, Annie Lennox, Phil Collins and Bananarama, gathered in London's SARM

Studio to record the track penned by Geldof and produced by Midge Ure. Collectively known as Band Aid, 'Do They Know It's Christmas?' was launched at the Royal Albert Hall during a benefit gala sponsored by the Save the Children Fund. In December 1984, Mercury Records issued the single, which entered the British chart at No. 1, a position it held for five weeks, selling in excess of three million copies, earning the distinction of becoming Britain's top-selling single of all time. When released in America early in 1985, 'Do They Know It's Christmas?' reached the Top Twenty.

The single was followed by the Live Aid concert staged at Wembley Stadium in Middlesex on 13 July 1985. Once again, a selection of British acts performed, while its sister concert in Philadelphia offered an impressive array of American artists. The two-set gala was watched by an estimated two-billion-strong audience in twenty-two countries. In excess of $70 million was raised to help the starving Ethiopian nation, and all thanks to the determined Bob Geldof. His tireless and selfless work earned him countless awards and, in 1986, an honorary knighthood: Bob Geldof KBE.

Meantime, 'Do They Know It's Christmas?' re-entered the British chart to reach the No. 3 in December 1985, and four years on, was rerecorded by the Stock-Aitken-Waterman house of acts, including Jason Donovan, Cliff Richard and Kylie Minogue, under the name Band Aid II, to become a British chart-topper.

Early in the nineties, an amount exceeding $144 million had been raised, with guarantees that no more than 2 per cent of the sum had been earmarked for administration costs.

In 1986, Geldof, now a prime media attraction embarked upon a solo career as a Mercury Records artist. His debut single, 'This Is the World Calling', reached the British Top Twenty and was swiped from his album *Deep in the Heart of Nowhere,* released in November. Prior to these releases, and despite public protestations to the contrary, Geldof married Paula Yates, now the mother of his daughter Fifi Trixibelle. Since the couple had become a public item, the press coverage they attracted had been questionable. Author Gary Herman reported that Geldof was particularly upset at the attitude of the music press. 'They were really nasty about Paula,' [Geldof] said. 'They'd say, "Geldof made an appearance with that ugly cow he calls a girlfriend", or "They're so boring, who do they think they are? The Rod and Britt of the new wave?" '

On the other hand, the couple had not avoided media interest; indeed, they had purposely attracted it. Items appeared in the tabloid press until

Geldof lost his self-confidence: he no longer could tolerate derogatory statements concerning the Boomtown Rats, and refused to conduct media interviews.

In the nineties, a pair of Geldof singles charted in Britain, 'Love Like a Rocket' and 'The Great Song of Indifference', Top Seventy and Top Twenty hits respectively. By 1993, he had issued further albums including *The Vegetarians of Love* and *The Happy Club,* while a year on, the compilation *Loudmouth – The Best of the Boomtown Rats* paid tribute to the group's material.

Bob Geldof continued to maintain a high public profile, sadly not for his music, but for the aftermath of Band Aid and his stormy marriage, which eventually ended when Paula's affair with Michael Hutchence, member of INXS, was made public. When Paula became pregnant by Hutchence, a legal battle ensued in 1996 regarding her children with Geldof. The personal saga continues, but Geldof will rise above it all.

'The Boomtown Rats became enormously successful and were then eclipsed. If the Rats had still been a success, I might never have managed to start on the enterprise.' – Bob Geldof

Also see: 'Rat Trap', November 1978

(Quotes: *Is That It?* by Bob Geldof; *Rock 'n' Roll Babylon* by Gary Herman)

September 1979

CLIFF RICHARD

We Don't Talk Anymore

'I've done everything I could possibly want to do and possibly everything anybody could want to do . . . So if it all ended for me, the one thing I could say is that I've lived a fuller life than most people will ever do.' – Cliff Richard

Cliff Richard was born Harry Roger Webb in Lucknow, India, on 14 October 1940, to Roger and Dorothy. In 1948 the family emigrated to Britain with £5 between them. Initially times were hard as Harry's father was unemployed. In 1950, his luck changed when he was hired by Ferguson's Radio in Enfield, Middlesex, while his wife found factory work in Broxbourne. The family – now including Webb's three sisters

Donella, Jacqueline and Joan – settled in Cheshunt, Hertfordshire. After Webb failed his eleven-plus examination, he attended the Chesthunt Secondary Modern School, where his life was consumed with amateur dramatics and rock 'n' roll music: in fact, the youngster often played truant to watch touring shows by American artists.

In 1957, Webb left school with one GCE 'O' Level in English, and formed a skiffle group called The Quintones with school friends, which soon disbanded. Webb worked at Atlas Lamps, Enfield, as a credit control clerk. During his spare time, he joined Terry Smart and others in the Dick Teague Skiffle Group. He soon formed a rock 'n' roll group named The Drifters, and came to the attention of John Foster, who offered to manage them. Harry Webb and The Drifters held little magic for prospective booking agents, and John Foster chose the name Cliff Richard. In the summer of 1958 Cliff Richard recorded his first demo record, and was soon signed by Norrie Paramor, A. & R. manager for the Columbia record label, owned by EMI Records. His first single, 'Move It', reached No. 2 in the British chart during September 1958. The group, with Richard dressed in a pink jacket and black tapered trousers, debuted on national television on Jack Good's popular *Oh Boy* music show.

By 1959 The Drifters had become The Shadows, with the line-up of Hank Marvin, Jet Harris, Bruce Welsh and Tony Meehan. 'Living Doll' was the first No. 1 single, lifted from the soundtrack of Cliff Richard's first film, *Serious Charge*. In his second film, *Expresso Bongo,* he played an eighteen-year-old rock 'n' roll artist waiting for stardom. It also spawned successful singles.

Cliff Richard's rise to fame was remarkable. His career appeared to follow that of his idol, Elvis Presley, inasmuch as both turned from singer to actor; they both combined ballad and rock in their material, and both had the support of effective management. Richard was quick to credit Presley as his inspiration, from the curling of the lip to the sexual gyrations on stage. Indeed, such was the similarity that Richard was to be dubbed 'The British Presley'. Alongside the stardom came the fans, uncontrollable and hysterical, whipped to a frenzy at sell-out concerts, while merchandising, tacky but expensive, bore the singer's likeness and name in a range of items.

With the close of the fifties, Richard had won most of the prestigious industry awards, ranging from silver and gold discs to Ivor Novello Awards. He was voted Best British Male Vocalist on countless occasions, and had appeared regularly on stage and television. He was now as popular on the small screen as he was on the cinema circuit, and in the singing stakes he could do little wrong. In the first two years of his career, Cliff Richard sold a staggering 5.5 million singles. The best was yet to come. Richard had a string of huge hits throughout the sixties, ultimately without The Shadows. In 1962, 'The Young Ones', from the soundtrack of the film of the same name, entered the British chart at No. 1, a position it held for a staggering six weeks, earning the singer a gold disc. 'Bachelor Boy' sold in excess of 900,000 copies to soar to the top of the British chart during January 1963.

Although Elvis Presley's influence on Richard's public image was well known by now, Richard did not fall into the trap of starring in movies with indistinguishable themes and lightweight storylines and music. Instead, he concentrated on quality; *Summer Holiday*, in 1963, was a perfect example. The film was a box office success, the single raced to the top of the British chart and the soundtrack dominated the album chart for an incredible fourteen weeks.

By 1965, Richard had discovered Christianity by joining a group of North London school teachers who did 'simple things'. He said, 'I had been rejuvenated and my career seemed uninteresting. At the same time, the success of The Beatles and The Stones had shelved me and The Shadows. We were now the oldsters.' But Richard would use his faith to help his career, and through that, others. His success continued. In 1968 'Congratulations' became the singer's first chart-topper for three years and his last for seven. The title was Britain's entry in the Eurovision Song Contest, and he had recorded it in numerous languages, helping it to sell in excess of one million copies in Europe. The single went on to become a universal song, on a par with, say, 'Happy Birthday'. Even Charles and Diana swayed to it on their wedding day – for all the good it did!

To start the new decade, the singer hosted his own BBC TV series, and issued a duet with Hank Marvin, the theme tune of the television shows, titled 'The Joy of Living'. The single peaked at No. 25 in March. In between the release of two singles – 'Goodbye Sam, Hello Samantha' (his fiftieth single in Britain) and 'I Ain't Got Time Anymore', Richard debuted in a straight stage role in *Five Finger Exercise*, presented in Kent, and issued a trio of albums, *Cliff Live at the Talk of the Town*, *About that Man* and *Tracks 'n' Grooves*.

In 1971 he presented a further BBC TV series, *It's Cliff Richard;* this time his resident guests were Una Stubbs and Hank Marvin. Following the release of 'Sunny Honey Girl', a Top Twenty hit single in February 1971, Richard recorded the Hank Marvin composition 'Silvery Rain', a Top Thirty hit. A further pair of singles were also issued in 1971, namely 'Flying Machine' and 'Sing a Song of Freedom', Top Forty and Top Twenty hits respectively. In between recording, Richard returned to tread the boards at Sadlers Wells Theatre, London, to appear in *The Potting Shed,* before contributing to the gala concert in tribute to the late Dickie Valentine at The London Palladium.

To add to his ever expanding collection of awards, honours and trophies, Richard received the prestigious Ivor Novello Award for his Outstanding Services to British Music in a ceremony staged in Juan Les Pins.

In similar fashion to the previous two years, 1972 began with a BBC TV series, *It's Cliff Richard,* with resident guests The Flirtations and Olivia Newton-John, with whom he was reputedly romantically involved. A trio of singles was also issued during the year, including 'A Brand New Song', his first title not to reach the Top Fifty. It was a minor hiccup which no one heeded that much, particularly when in 1973 Richard once again represented Britain in the Eurovision Song Contest. The title chosen this time was 'Power to All our Friends'; Richard lost to the Luxembourg entry. Nonetheless, Richard's title soared to No. 4 in the British chart during March.

During the following two years, Richard's star continued to shine brightly as an actor and singer. He first starred in the movie *Take Me High,* with co-stars George Cole and Debbie Watling, before playing the character, Bottom, in his old school production of *A Midsummer's Night Dream.* A series of singles and albums ensured his chart presence, although he experienced one scare with the 1975 release '(There's a) Honky Tonk Angel (Who Will Take Me Back in)'. When Richard discovered the lyrics glorified the virtues of prostitution, he withdrew the title from sale.

However, it was a year later that his most significant album of the decade was issued. The material was vital and current, due primarily to Bruce Welch producing the recording sessions. Titled *I'm Nearly Famous,* and released in June 1976, supported by a massive promotion campaign, the album soared to No. 5 in the chart, spawning a handful of hit singles en route, namely 'Miss You Nights', 'Devil Woman' and 'I Can't Ask for Anymore Than You'. The album was also issued in Russia, alongside *The Best of Cliff Richard,* earning the singer the distinction of being one of the few British acts to release material in that country. In September, Richard toured the country, starting with a sell-out concert in Leningrad (now St Petersburg), followed by a reception at the British Embassy in Moscow.

In the next year Richard continued with his fresh musical direction and image, releasing *Every Face Tells a Story,* another Top Ten seller. Once more, a run of singles, including 'My Kinda Life', sustained his hit status. It was also a year of prestigious awards: the British Phonographic Institute presented him with the Britannia Award for the Best British Male Solo Artist of the Last 25 Years, and the Song Writers' Guild of Great Britain honoured him with a Gold Badge Award. It's anyone's guess where he stored them all! Before 1977 closed, he received a gold disc for the double-album package titled *40 Golden Greats,* one of several in EMI Records' 'greatest hits' series. Thanks to maximum television advertising, *40 Golden Greats* shot to the top of the album chart in November; his first chart-topper since *Summer Holiday* in 1963.

Twentieth anniversary celebrations started with a two-week stint at the London Palladium at the beginning of 1978, and ended at the Royal Albert Hall, in December. To personally celebrate twenty years in show business, Richard was reunited on tour with The Shadows, while in March he issued the religious album titled *Small Corners,* from which the poor-selling single 'Yes, He Lives' was extracted. Two months on, he received the Silver Clef Award for Outstanding Services to British Music during a ceremony hosted by HRH Duchess of Gloucester. In October he released his next secular album, *Green Light,* a Top Thirty hit.

When a particular single attracted poor sales, the follow-up invariably re-established him in the chart. This was indeed the case in 1979. 'Green Light' bombed by his standards, yet the Alan Tarney composition 'We Don't Talk Anymore' which followed, shot to the top of the British chart in September, a position it held for four weeks. The title, produced by Bruce Welch, was Richard's first British chart-topper since 'Congratulations' in 1968, and became 1979's biggest-selling disc with sales in excess of five million copies. Released the same month was his *Rock 'n' Roll Juvenile* album, a No. 3 seller. Then true to form, the chart-topper's follow-up, 'Hot Shot', swiped from the album, struggled into the Top Fifty. Anyway, to complete the successful year, Richard led more than 30,000 people in a carol concert staged outside Buckingham Palace, London, in aid of the International Year of the Child.

In the eighties, Cliff Richard, a major contributor to British entertainment for more than two decades, a dedicated charity worker and, whether he liked it or not, a significant part of the British Establishment, was included in the Queen's New Year Honour list to receive an OBE. He continued relentlessly to record. During the early part of the new decade, he issued top-selling albums that included the chart-topping compilations *Love Songs, Wired for Sound, Now You See Me . . . Now You Don't, Dressed for the Occasion* and *Silver*. The last title represented twenty-five years as a recording artist. A series of singles were extracted from these titles, that included 'Daddy's Home', 'The Only Way Out', 'She Means Nothing to Me' (a duet with Phil Everly), and his first dance track to be pressed as a twelve-inch single, 'Never Say Die (Give a Little Bit More)'.

Following the release in 1984 of a trio of poor-selling singles – 'Baby You're Dynamite', 'Two to the Power' (a duet with Janet Jackson) and 'Shooting from the Heart', Richard announced his intention to star in the Dave Clark's stage musical *Time*. April 1986 was the month the musical opened at the Dominion Theatre, London; Richard's year-long stay attracted capacity audiences, while two singles in particular became charting titles. The first, 'She's So Beautiful', featured Richard on vocals and Stevie Wonder as producer and solitary musician; the second, 'It's in Every One of Us', was composed by David Pomeranz. When Richard left the musical to resume his recording career, David Cassidy stepped in to replace him.

While Richard played the London stage he enjoyed (if that's the right word, under the circumstances!) his second British chart-topper in seven years with a spoof version of 'Living Doll'. Accompanying him on the 1986 version were The Young Ones, then leaders of British alternative comedy, and Hank Marvin as guitarist. 'Living Doll' topped the British chart for three weeks and sold in excess of 600,000 copies, with all proceeds destined for the Comic Relief charity.

Before 1985 ended, the *Time* soundtrack album was issued, featuring Dionne Warwick and Freddie Mercury, among others; plus two Richard duets were issued as singles – 'All I Ask of You' with Sarah Brightman, borrowed from Andrew Lloyd Webber's musical *The Phantom of the Opera*, and 'Slow Rivers' with Elton John. The first title soared into the Top Three; the second title didn't.

As Richard signed a new lucrative recording contract with EMI Records in 1987, with special provisions for his charitable contributions, his next album, titled *Always Guaranteed,* was issued. Produced by Alan Tarney, it shot to No. 5 in the chart, reaching platinum status, and earned the distinction of being Richard's best-selling album to date. Two singles of note were swiped for release, 'Some People' and 'Remember Me'; the first catapulted into the Top Three, the second struggled in the Top Forty.

In 1988 Richard celebrated the thirtieth anniversary of his debut hit

'Move It'; had a Christmas chart-topper titled 'Mistletoe and Wine'; and released a double album, *Private Collection,* which went on to pass quadruple platinum status with sales in excess of one million. Then, in 1989, Richard was honoured at the BRIT Awards, staged at the Royal Albert Hall, for his Outstanding Contribution to British Music; released his hundredth British single, titled 'The Best of Me', which entered the chart at No. 2 but which could go no higher; staged 'Cliff Richard – The Event' at Wembley Stadium before 72,000 people; recorded his first Stock, Aitken, Waterman composition, 'I Just Don't Have the Heart', and duetted with Van Morrison on 'Whenever God Shines His Light', a Top Twenty hit in December.

The 1990s saw Cliff Richard, the recording artist, entertainer and all-round celebrity, rise to even greater heights, if that was possible. He was in demand in all sectors of the entertainment business. His 'Access All Areas '92 Tour' spanned a staggering thirteen sell-out dates at Birmingham's NEC; a series of concerts at the Sheffield Arena and Glasgow SECC, plus an unprecedented sixteen dates at Wembley Arena!

During October 1995, Richard visited Buckingham Palace for the second time. With his sisters, Jacqui, Donna and Joan, the singer received a knighthood from the Queen for his tireless charity work. Richard told *Today* newspaper, 'What I am proud of is that I have received this for nothing to do with politics, commerce, or even rock 'n' roll.' Sir Cliff Richard indeed! 'I guess I never will really get used to it.'

In 1962, while Richard was filming *Summer Holiday,* he told a journalist his acting ambition was to play Heathcliff in *Wuthering Heights.* Thirty-four years on, his ambition was realised. He joined the cast of the Tim Rice/John Farrar musical adaptation of the Emily Brontë novel. With a $2 million investment from Richard, capacity audiences watched the musical during a six-month tour of Britain. Richard spent much time studying the role of Heathcliff, including visiting Brontë country, particularly Top Withers, the building said to have inspired the author. Richard: 'All that's left are the four walls and a couple of doorways, but the ruin stands on the crest of a hill which rolls into moorland. The isolation and bleakness sums up the story of the unhappy hero Heathcliff and his doomed romance with Catherine Earnshaw.'

The more the critics belittled his performance, the more the public flocked to see him. Heathcliff was the total opposite of Richard's pure, squeaky clean image, and the singer was keen to discard the mantle of upright citizen and adopt the role of the damaged character. Richard:

'In one scene I beat my stage wife, Isabella, and I'll be doing it with great pleasure. The fact that in many people's eyes I am Mr Goody Two-Shoes will make it seem so much more disgusting and I think that will work in my favour.' It did. One newspaper headline glared, 'Mean and moody, snarling and stubbly. Yes, this really is Sir Cliff!'

Cliff Richard will last forever! But will he want to?

(Quotes: *The Biography – Cliff Richard* by Steve Turner; *The Complete Chronicle: Cliff Richard* by Mike Read, Nigel Goodall and Peter Lewry)

October 1979

POLICE

Message in a Bottle

'We were energetic, loud and noisy, and as the punk bands fell by the wayside, for various reasons we stayed and survived.' – Sting

Stewart Copeland, born in Alexandria, Virginia, on 16 July 1952, was the son of an American CIA agent and spent much of his younger life in the Middle East. He attended college in California before moving to Britain and perfecting his art as a drummer to perform with the group Curved Air. The group's manager was Miles, Stewart's brother.

Sting was born Gordon Matthew Sumner in Wallsend, Tyne and Wear, on 2 October 1951. He told author Joe Smith, 'I ended up at the age of fifteen, sixteen, playing with guys . . . who had been playing since the fifties.' He would play jazz standards rather than learn Led Zeppelin riffs, a move that would stand him in good stead later in his career. Holding various jobs that included ditch digger, civil servant and primary school teacher, he worked his way through groups that included Earthrise, the River City Jazz Band and The Ronnie Pierson Trio. The nickname 'Sting' was given to him by Gordon Soloman, a local jazz player, because he wore yellow and black striped jumpers.

Copeland and Sting first met in Newcastle when Sting was in the group Last Exit. When they met again in London during 1977, they decided to form their own group of musicians. Recruiting guitarist, Henri Padovani, they began rehearsing in earnest, usually at Copeland's own studio in Mayfair. The first results of this musical liaison included the title 'Fall Out', which was issued on the Illegal label, Copeland's own, in May 1977. Sales pushed the title into the Indie chart. Meantime, the group were linked to the American singer, Cherry Vanilla, touring Britain's clubs with her and Johnny Thunders & The Heart-breakers. A European tour with Wayne County's Electric Chairs followed.

During this period, Copeland and Sting befriended guitarist, Andy Summers, born Andrew James Summers, in Poulton-Le-Fylde, Lancashire, on 31 December 1942. In June he officially joined the group, now known as Police, performing at the Marquee Club, and the Music Machine in London. Before 1977 closed, Padovani left the line-up, leaving the trio to appear for the first time without him at Rebecca's Club, Birmingham, before supporting Eberhard Schoener on his album *Video Flashback,* recorded in Munich, Germany.

Early in 1978, Police began recording their first album until touring commitments in Britain as support act to the American group, Spirit, took precedence. While the trio was on the road, Miles Copeland secured a one-off recording deal for their single 'Roxanne'. Sting: 'Being brought up in jazz, I was locked out when I started going around record companies. I went to every major record company with my songs, and they all said it wasn't commercial enough.'

Police needed an identity and as the punk movement was exploding at the time, Sting opted to steer the group at that market, in much the same way as Bob Geldof had reluctantly guided his Boomtown Rats. Indeed, Police went on to appear in an American Wrigley's Chewing Gum television advertisement because of their reputed association with the punk fraternity. Sting believed Police's music to be mellow, yet it contained the anger that was needed to revolutionise the music industry, so they 'flew that banner for a while'.

During March 1978, Miles Copeland secured a recording contract with A&M Records, where the title 'Roxanne' was their debut single; it failed to make the mainstream chart. (It was later covered by comedian actor Eddie Murphy.) Seven months on, Police issued their second single, 'Can't Stand Losing You', a Top Fifty British hit. The title probably would have charted higher if the trio had been on hand for promotion purposes. Instead, they had embarked upon an American tour. In November, their album *Outlandos D'Amour,* recorded for the princely sum of £3,000, rose into the British Top Ten, from which the track 'So Lonely' had already been swiped for single release.

Early in 1979, Police returned to America for a further lengthy tour. In their absence from home ground, 'Roxanne' was reissued. This time it soared to No. 12 in Britain and made the Top Forty in America. Persistence had paid off, the public finally succumbed. Hot on the heels of the single's success, the trio embarked upon their first fully fledged

British tour, which included an appearance at the Reading Rock Festival, staged in Berkshire.

With no titles suitable for single release, the group's second single, 'Can't Stand Losing You' was reissued during August to shoot to No. 2 in Britain. At this juncture, Sting starred in the movie *Quadrophenia,* playing the role of Ace. This short diversion fuelled rumours of further acting roles; however, any that might have been in the pipeline were shelved to enable Sting to concentrate on his music career and, more immediately, Police's next single.

Using a pending British tour to publicise the title, 'Message in a Bottle' soared to the top of the British chart during October 1979, a position it held for two weeks. When issued in America in December, the track faltered in the Top Eighty. The British chart-topper and its follow-up, another Sting composition, 'Walking on the Moon', were both swiped from the group's second album *Reggatta De Blanc,* released in October to crash through the chart to peak at the top, where it stayed for four weeks, also reaching the Top Thirty in America. The album went on to win the Grammy Award for the Best Rock Instrumental Performance. 'Walking on the Moon' topped the British chart thanks to the innovative promotional video filmed at Houston's Kennedy Space Centre. Police, like Queen, were masters of the video, believing visuals were as important as the music itself. Yet nothing matched the hands-on promotion touring provided, when group and audience gelled. Police's audiences were becoming uncontrollable, to say the least, as the group was elevated to a teenybop sensation; a strange position to be in, considering their previous struggles to win any kind of acceptance. Indeed, fan hysteria instigated riot situations during their concerts, prompting Summers to tell the *NME*: 'I never thought we'd get that kind of teenage audience . . . but we haven't compromised at all. Some of our music is definitely not teenage-orientated, but I don't mind. You get a tremendous amount of enthusiasm with kids of that age.' Sting, as prime singer and focal point, was the teenybop pin-up: 'To a lot of people, teenyboppers are a sub-species not even to be entertained. I don't agree. If you can transcend the screaming, you can take a generation with you into something else. It's a real challenge.'

In 1980 Police embarked on their first world tour, covering nineteen countries, including a concert in Bombay, the first Western group to do so. So important was the Indian visit, that a film crew accompanied them. Sting: 'We are doing this for a charity, and we're actually promoting a few rupees for the people. We can sort of salve our conscience with that.'

Following the tour and the release of *Six Pack,* a collection of singles pressed in blue vinyl which reached the British Top Twenty, Police returned to the recording studio to work on their third album. They also performed at a pair of significant concerts; a benefit concert in Milton Keynes, Buckinghamshire, and the Dalymount Festival in Dublin. After a lengthy European tour, the trio released their next single, 'Don't Stand So Close to Me'. The title became a British chart-topper in September 1980, a position it held for four weeks, and reached Top Ten in America in April 1981. Before 1980 ended, their album *Zenyatta Mondatta* soared to the top of the chart; they embarked upon a North American and Canadian tour, and issued the single 'De Do Do Do, De Da Da Da', during a fit of the stutters, to hit the British Top Five and become a Top Ten American hit.

Sting then turned to the film world once more, to do the preliminary work on BBC TV's drama *Artemis 81,* before winning an Ivor Novello Award for Songwriter of the Year. His two careers seemed to run easily together, and this would stay true when Police disbanded.

Moving to Montserrat, the trio began recording their next album, *Ghost in the Machine,* from which the title 'Invisible Sun' was swiped for single release. The track soared to No. 2 in Britain amidst public outrage because the accompanying promotional video was shot in war-torn Belfast. Every care was taken to ensure the result was non-partisan, but still the public heaved in dismay. Needless to say, Police need not have bothered to put visuals to tape; the video was banned. Sting: 'The video . . . could be misinterpreted and said to convey meanings which are not present in the lyrics.' Meanwhile, *Ghost in the Machine* grew legs to shoot to the top of the British chart.

In complete contrast to the serious statement within the lyrics of 'Invisible Sun', the trio released 'Every Little Thing She Does Is Magic', a title which nobody could object to. So popular was this perky slice of pop music that it became a British chart-topper in 1981, reaching the Top Three in America; the follow-up 'Spirits in the Material World' peaked in the British Top Twenty and hit No. 11 Stateside a year on.

Early in 1982, Police took the unusual step of raising funds for Freddie Laker's innovative but doomed airline, by performing at San Francisco's Fillmore Stadium; then went on to win the Best British Group Award at the BRIT ceremony held in London, one of several awards the group received that year.

As Sting continued to expand his movie career, he also released his debut solo single titled 'Spread a Little Happiness'. The track reached the British Top Twenty, and heralded the start of his future lucrative career. The other two members of Police likewise had pursued their own projects; Copeland had written the film score for *Rumble Fish* and was engrossed on the music for an American ballet version of *King Lear,* while Summers went on to issue his own instrumental album, *I Advance Masked.*

Midway through 1983, Police topped the British chart once more; this time with 'Every Breath You Take'. The single held the position for four weeks, and the success was repeated in America. The mother album, *Synchronicity,* likewise roared to chart-topping status in both countries. Before the close of the year, the trio entered the chart twice; with 'Wrapped around your Finger', and 'Synchronicity II'; both Top Twenty British and American hits.

From 1984 through to 1986, the members of Police continued to pursue individual careers. Summers released his second album, *Bewitched,* while Copeland issued *The Rhythmatist.* Sting, on the other hand, went from strength to strength as songwriter, actor and solo performer. He longed to tour. To this end, he formed a new line-up of musicians, The Blue Turtles Band, released an album, *The Dream of the Blue Turtles,* then took 'The Dream of the Blue Turtles World Tour' on the road. Following this tour, Sting was reunited with Copeland and Summers to perform at the Amnesty International gala staged in Atlanta and prepare for a new Police album. The recording sessions were never completed. Instead, the compilation *Every Breath You Take: The Singles* was issued in 1986. During the next two years the members of Police pursued individual careers, until they dropped from the public eye altogether.

Sting married Trudie Styler, the mother of his three children, during August 1992, where the entertainment was a brief set from a reunited Police.

Professionally speaking, the trio was reunited on record two months later, when the *Greatest Hits* compilation soared into the British Top Ten. A year on, a specially-compiled four-CD box set which featured sundry tracks and their five albums, titled *Message in a Box: The Complete Recordings,* was issued. A *Live* album followed in mid-1995 to reach the British Top Thirty.

With Police far behind him, Sting has emerged the most dedicated and, perhaps, adventurous group member. Maybe his constant high media profile has secured his status. Whatever, he is an active supporter of human rights campaigns and environmental issues. His music is as far reaching as his political views, while his tours, always a major provider of funds for his beliefs, play before standing-room-only audiences. Suffice to say, Sting is a wealthy man in talent and convictions; certainly he's classed as a figurehead of the decade.

'At the beginning . . . Police was all fantasy. We fantasised having a No. 1 hit . . . I did not imagine we would become as mega as we did.' – Sting

(Quotes: *Off the Record* by Joe Smith)

November 1979

DR HOOK

When You're in Love (with a Beautiful Woman)

Like the Commodores with 'Three Times a Lady', this group recorded one of the decades most lingering of love songs. The only pity was, Dr Hook was unable to sustain the attack.

In 1968 vocalist/guitarist Ray Sawyer, born in Chickasaw, Alabama, on 1 February 1937, and guitarist Dennis Locorriere, born in Union City, New Jersey, on 13 June 1949, were the instigators of a group that was to become Dr Hook and The Medicine Show. For the time being, though, they searched for further musicians to complete their line-up. After extensive auditions the pair recruited guitarists Rik Elswit, George Cummings and Jance Garfat; drummer John Wolters and keyboardist Bill Francis. All selected were also vocalists. The group played the local club circuit, using various names, unable to decide on a permanent tag. The decision was eventually taken by a club owner who, inspired by Sawyer's black eye pitch, hiding the loss of his right eye in a car accident, named them Dr Hook and The Medicine Show.

During 1970 the group secured its first major professional break when they performed 'Last Morning' in the movie *Who Is Harry Kellerman and Why Is He Saying Those Terrible Things*. The film's producer, Ron Haffkine, was impressed with the group's performance and negotiated a recording contract for them with CBS Records. Inspired by possible future success, the group perfected their stage act and enlarged their repertoire before recording and releasing the Shel Silverstein composition 'Sylvia's Mother', telling the tale of a lover's painful long-distance telephone call not with his girlfriend Sylvia but her mother! The single, for all its faults, soared to No. 5 in the American chart in June 1972, selling in excess of one million copies on the way.

However, it fared much better in Britain when two months later it became a No. 2 hit, indicating the public had a higher tolerance level for insane lyrics!

This surprising success added impetus to the group's debut album, *Dr Hook and The Medicine Show,* issued between the two single release dates, while 'Carry Me, Carrie' was the follow-up single in September 1972. Its unexpected failure on both sides of the Atlantic returned the group to square one.

Early in 1973, Dr Hook and The Medicine Show's second album, *Sloppy Seconds,* faltered in the American Top Forty, while during March, they hit a major – and unwarranted British setback. Their third single, 'The Cover of Rolling Stone', referred to the indispensable American music magazine. This prompted BBC Radio 1 to ban all airplay, claiming it was a blatant advertising ploy. Across the Atlantic, however, there were no such ethical dilemmas, as the title peaked in the Top Ten. Not to be beaten by British bureaucracy Dr Hook and The Medicine Show recut the track for British release retitling it 'The Cover of the Radio Times'! The ploy backfired; the single still bombed, although the group achieved a professional ambition by actually appearing on the cover of *Rolling Stone* magazine!

Two further singles became minor American hits before the end of 1973, namely, 'Roland the Roadie and Gertrude the Groupie' (!) and 'Life Ain't Easy', plus the poor-selling *Belly Up!* album. In the group's declining state, CBS Records dropped them from its artist roster. It was a temporary setback, thankfully.

In 1975, now known as Dr Hook, the group signed a one-year recording contract with Capitol Records, the American offshoot of EMI Records in Britain. In September their debut single 'The Millionaire', lifted from the album *Bankrupt,* was issued to falter outside the American Top One Hundred. However, with the confidence of the record company behind them, Dr Hook battled on. During 1976 they released 'Only Sixteen', a cover version of Sam Cooke's Top Thirty British hit in August 1959. As their updated interpretation climbed the American chart, their one-year contract with Capitol expired. Nevertheless, the record company supported the single, which became a Top Twenty entrant, and extended their recording arrangement with the group. 'A Little Bit More' was issued as the follow-up single in August 1976; it was a Top Twenty American hit and reached No. 2 in Britain. The eponymous album quickly followed; though a poor American seller, British sales pushed it into the Top Five. The final single of the year, 'If Not You', likewise hit No. 5 in Britain, while

American sales were disappointing, only achieving a niche in the Top Sixty.

During 1977 Ray Sawyer diversified to release a solo album, while Dr Hook issued two, namely, *Revisited* and *Making Love and Music*. Chart success avoided them during the next year except for a solitary British hit titled 'More Like the Movies', a Top Twenty single in April. The group was in despair; following such an encouraging start to their career with Capitol Records, nothing now appeared to work. But the climate was destined to change.

In 1979 and following the release of a pair of singles 'Sharing the Night Together' and 'All the Time in the World', Dr Hook released the Even Stevens' composition 'When You're in Love (with a Beautiful Woman)'. The easy-listening title raced to No. 6 in America in August 1979, while three months later it dominated the top of the British chart, a position it held for three weeks. After several attempts, Dr Hook had finally made it!

Early in 1980 'Better Love Next Time' was issued as the chart-topper's follow-up to reach the American Top Twenty and No. 8 in Britain. Dr Hook was now an established name and they maintained their power with the next single, 'Sexy Eyes', a Top Five hit on both sides of the Atlantic. With their third single of the year, 'Years from Now', however, the struggle began once more as the title slithered into the American and British Top Fifty. This prompted a record company move from Capitol Records to Casablanca Records. To pre-empt any new material emanating from the new deal, the Capitol label issued 'Sharing the Night Together' in Britain, originally released as an American single in 1979. It reached the Top Fifty in Britain but, sadly, heralded the end of Dr Hook's charting career.

Into the new decade, Dr Hook continued to enjoy spasmodic American success but nothing compared to their previous achievements. Midway through 1982, with little work and a zero bank balance, the group disbanded, leaving Ray Sawyer and Dennis Locorriere to pursue solo careers. By 1988, though, prompted by public interest, Sawyer headed a new membership of Dr Hook to tour Britain, the country that had supported their music so loyally.

During the early part of the nineties 'When You're in Love (with a Beautiful Woman)' rose again to peak at No. 44 in the British chart, while its follow-up, 'A Little Bit More', likewise peaked in the Top Fifty. Capitol Records just could not resist squeezing that last drop! Dr Hook compilation albums are reissued with regularity, while the group, under various memberships, continue to tour upon demand.

PINK FLOYD

Another Brick in the Wall (Part II)

Pink Floyd began their career as an underground group, and developed into a progressive rock phenomenon, with record sales in excess of twenty million. Their stage sets were as adventurous as their music; their creativity far ahead of its time.

Roger Waters, born in Great Bookham, Surrey, on 6 September 1944, befriended Nick Mason, born in Birmingham, Worcestershire, on 27 January 1945, at London's Regent Street Polytechnic. Together they formed their first group called Sigma 6, with Keith Noble, Juliette Gale and Clive Metcalf. They later became known as The Architectural Abdabs.

A short time after the name change, Syd Barrett, born Roger Barrett, in Cambridge on 6 January 1946, joined the group, following stints with a pair of outfits including The Hollering Blues. With his arrival, the group changed its name once more to The Pink Floyd Sound, swiped from the Carolina bluesmen Pink Anderson and Floyd Council. During 1965, the group performed its first professional date at London's Countdown Club. This led to regular spots at the Marquee Club on Sunday afternoons, where they gradually changed their repertoire from R&B to original Barrett compositions and lengthy instrumentals, leaning towards psychedelia. During October 1966, the group, with The Soft Machine, performed at the Roundhouse, Chalk Farm, London, as part of the celebrations surrounding the launch of the *International Times* newspaper. Two thousand people were handed sugar cubes as they watched and mingled. Author Pete Frame, who contributed to the publication *Pink Floyd*, wrote, 'The bands got noticed, particularly the Floyd who blew up the power during their set and consequently ended the evening's entertainment.' Following this 'explosive' performance, Pink Floyd (the 'Sound' had been dropped) signed a six-way management contract with Peter Jenner and Andrew King, calling the company Blackhill Enterprises.

Early in 1967, Pink Floyd performed at the UFO Club, the first regular underground venue, where their true value was finally realised. They were more fashionable than some of the charting acts at the time, although they had yet to release a record and their popularity was confined to the London area. Nonetheless, Pink Floyd was red hot; record companies climbed over each other to wave recording contracts and eventually EMI Records succeeded. The deal, including a reputed £5,000 advance, was one of the highest at the time. The record company believed in the group, and promoted their music enthusiastically.

Pink Floyd's debut single was 'Arnold Layne', which they had recorded prior to signing to EMI Records. However, due to the dubious lyrical content of the single, which referred to a transvestite, securing radio airplay was sticky. Thankfully, the pirate station Radio Caroline carried no such restrictions, and plugged it incessantly. Unfortunately, that was not enough to ensure Pink Floyd a chart hit beyond No. 20 during April 1967. In July, their second single, 'See Emily Play', was issued to soar to No. 6 in the chart. It was originally composed by Barrett as 'Games for May' for inclusion at a concert the group played at the Queen Elizabeth Hall in London. Barrett: 'We had an incredible light show by then as well, and the concert, which was the first pop show ever held in the Hall, was just unbelievable.'

The Piper at the Gates of Dawn, Pink Floyd's debut album, was issued during August to peak in the Top Ten. The album's name was borrowed from a chapter in *The Wind in the Willows,* the children's classic written by Kenneth Graeme. A month on, the group toured Ireland, before embarking upon an American trek. However, that trip was cut short when Barrett, now a regular user of the drug LSD, refused to lipsynch to 'Arnold Layne' and blanked a television interview with Pat Boone. By the start of 1968, Barrett was replaced in the group by Dave Gilmour, born in Cambridge on 6 March 1947, a late member of The Jokers Wild. With Barrett's departure, Pete Jenner and Andrew King relinquished their part of the Pink Floyd partnership. 'Basically, the Floyd left us because they thought we'd have no confidence in them without Syd, which was true . . . We just couldn't conceive how they would be able to make it without Syd, who put all the creativity in the group.' How wrong they were! Before 1968 closed, Pink Floyd released a pair of singles, namely, 'It Would Be So Nice' and 'Point Me at the Sky', both of which bombed, plus an album, *A Saucerful of Secrets,* which soared into the Top Ten. The group also performed at the first free rock gala held in Hyde Park, London, alongside acts that included Tyrannosaurus Rex.

In 1969, Pink Floyd participated in several prestigious concerts, including the National Jazz, Pop and Blues Festival, and released two albums, *More,* the soundtrack to the movie bearing the same name, and the double album *Ummagumma,* which shot into the Top Five during October 1969. Meanwhile, Syd Barrett was signed as a soloist to EMI Records' Harvest label, where the single 'Octopus' was released during December. Gilmour told journalist Roy Shipson in 1969, 'The group has changed a lot since the early days, and come a long way. The worst period was after the two hit singles; we went right down then, because people expected us to do them and we wouldn't.' The guitarist also complained that it took the group longer than most to record an entire album, due primarily to their inability to book block sessions in the recording studios. 'We get in the studio for a couple of days, then someone else, like The Beatles, wants to record and we get shoved out. So a couple of weeks later we go back and we've forgotten the mood.' Despite these comments, Pink Floyd's next album, *Atom Heart Mother,* previewed at the Bath Festival of Blues and Progressive Music, shot to the top of the chart during October 1970. This release gave the first insight into the group's future musical direction and was one which Mason called 'an amazing feat of brilliance'.

Hotly following the group's chart-topping album, Roger Waters issued *Music from the Body* and Barrett his eponymous album. When the latter bombed, he retired from music, despite requests from the group to reverse his decision. Midway through 1971, Pink Floyd toured the Far East, before EMI Records issued their album *Relics,* which included 'Arnold Layne' and 'See Emily Play', on its budget-priced label, Regal Zonophone. In November, Pink Floyd released their next album proper, titled *Meddle,* which included the track 'Echoes'; this spanned the entire second side of the album. Gilmour: 'At the end of "Echoes" is this kind of guitar orchestra going on, about four different parts all joining together to create a sound. I still think that is wonderful.' *Meddle* peaked No. 3 in Britain, catapulting Pink Floyd to top group of the year behind Emerson, Lake and Palmer.

Most of 1972 was spent touring Britain, Europe and America, interrupted only by the release of their top-selling album *Obscured by Clouds* in June, the soundtrack to the movie *The Valley.* But nothing would compare to their most significant album to date, scheduled for release in April 1973. Composed and produced by Pink Floyd, *Dark Side of the Moon* explored the inner, rather than the outer, space, highlighting death, madness and insecurity, against a musical cacophony of eerie melodies and spacy technology. The project, then called *Eclipse,* because Medicine Head had already issued an album titled *The Dark Side of the Moon,* was actually first played live in 1972; the group wanted to test audience reaction before taking the project into the studio. Pink Floyd changed the title to *Dark Side of the Moon* when Medicine Head's album bombed. Gilmour: '*Dark Side of the Moon* is an allusion to the moon and lunacy. The dark side is generally related to what goes on inside people's heads – the subconscious and the unknown.'

Overnight, Pink Floyd became recording megastars. The album shot to No. 1 in America in April 1973, to remain in the chart for a staggering 741 weeks (1996). British release the same month saw the group enjoying the No. 2 position, whereupon the title remained on the album chart for a total of 301 weeks (1996). *Dark Side of the Moon* went on to sell in excess of 20 million vinyl copies. With the baby flown from the nest, Pink Floyd spent the remainder of the year touring, performing the project in its entirety.

Two years on, the group's long-awaited follow-up was completed. Titled *Wish You Were Here,* the album crashed both the American and British charts at the top in the October. The album featured Roy Harper singing 'Shine On You Crazy Diamond', a tribute to the group's former member, Syd Barrett, and did not disappoint the waiting Floyd followers. Before the year closed, Pink Floyd switched American record companies from Capitol Records to CBS Records for a reputed $1 million advance.

Early in 1976, the group was locked once more in the recording studios working on their next album, *Animals,* which was, they said, released due to their material greed. It was a four-track album and was, as the music weekly *Record Mirror* said, 'an allegorical LP [which] will inevitably be compared to *Dark Side of the Moon.* The words are strong, bitter and they ask questions. The instrumental interludes are at times powerful, Gilmour's guitar work does predominate.' When the album's cover artwork was being shot at Battersea Power Station, the forty-foot tall inflatable pink pig (later used for the group's live performances) flying above the station broke loose. It was said that pilots using London's airspace were warned by the Civil Aviation Authority to look out for this pink pig on the run, placing a whole new meaning to the well-worn phrase 'pigs might fly'!

Pink Floyd took *Animals* to the stage for a European and Canadian tour. The latter dates were staged in baseball stadiums with audiences of 50,000 plus, who were so removed from the stage they were unable to see or hear the group performing. Roger Waters: 'It was hell, it made me very angry.' In Montreal, their last show, members of the 80,000-strong audience were crushed under the stage itself. In February 1977, the album peaked at No. 3 in America and No. 2 in Britain.

Until they regrouped for their next project, the membership divided to work on individual projects. David Gilmour released his solo album in May 1978, prior to working with EMI Records' new signing, Kate Bush, on her debut album, while Rick Wright issued his solo debut *Wet Dream*.

It took almost two years for Pink Floyd to reunite in the recording studio, to work on their next album, *The Wall*, conceived by Waters during a hiatus following the Canadian trek. He intended to construct a wall, separating the audience from the group. 'The wall was the foundation. Everybody puts bricks in their own wall at different times of their life.' Part one of the project was autobiographical; part two featured the destruction of rock stars. It was at this juncture, in 1979, that Waters admitted Pink Floyd was no longer based on democratic rule. He told journalist Janet Huck, 'We have been pretending we are all jolly good chaps together. It's a load of rubbish. Ten years ago it was true, but not for the last six or seven years.' He simply called the group together, played his project to them and they recorded it; communicating through technology, by exchanging tapes of individual ideas.

Spanning two albums, *The Wall* was issued late in 1979, peaking at No. 3 in Britain in December. The same month, 'Another Brick in the Wall (Part II)' was swiped as a single to soar to the top of the British chart, a position it held for five weeks; the group's first hit since 1967 with 'See Emily Play'. The single likewise became an American chart-topper in March 1980; it held the position for four weeks. Meanwhile, the mother album had peaked at the top of the American chart during January 1980, dominating the chart for a remarkable fifteen weeks. Pink Floyd did not rest on their success; they introduced the Wall to the paying public, with the most adventurous and costly pieces of stage equipment, namely a 30-feet-high, 160-feet-long brick wall, which separated group from audience. Partway through the concert, the wall was destroyed. Following twenty-nine appearances, it was considered too pricey to transport, build and rebuild, so was dropped from the group's stage shows. Next, Rick Wright left the group following a history of disagreements with Roger Waters. Rumours circulated the media regarding his sudden departure until Waters dispelled the speculations: 'The story that gets out is that it was a personal whim of mine which is a load of bollocks.' Arguing that Wright's musical contribution to the group was practically zero, Waters had threatened to dump *The Wall* if Wright remained with the group. On the other hand, Rick Wright insisted he planned to leave anyhow!

In July 1982, the movie *The Wall,* starring Bob Geldof in the role of Pink, a burned-out rock star, and directed by Alan Parsons, with a profusion of Gerald Scarfe's monstrous animations, was premiered in London. Brian Mulligan wrote in *Record Business,* 'A truly nasty film, relentless in its pursuit of depicting the worst excesses of human behaviours, a study of madness and the corrupting effects of violence and alienation. Roger Waters' view of mankind is totally and morbidly hopeless.'

The next year, the group released their third British chart-topping album, *The Final Cut,* a project yet again conceived by Waters. The album stalled at No. 6 in America during April. A month on, the track 'Not Now John' was lifted as a single to reach the British Top Thirty. It was Pink Floyd's fifth hit single in a career of sixteen years!

In the mid-eighties, Roger Waters and David Gilmour earnestly embarked upon solo careers once more. In 1986, Waters, now working on a solo project, instigated legal action against Gilmour, Rick Wright and Nick Mason to prevent them using the name Pink Floyd for recording and touring purposes. In November, the trio publicly announced the group had no intention of disbanding and was planning a new album using the Pink Floyd name. Waters retaliated, claiming they had no right to use Pink Floyd, whereupon a temporary judgment granted the trio permission to use the name. Meantime, Waters spent the bulk of 1987 touring America, while Pink Floyd issued the album *A Momentary Lapse of Reason,* from which the title 'Only Learning to Fly' was swiped as a single. Remarkably, the track bombed, but the album peaked in the Top Three on both sides of the Atlantic. Despite renewed threats from Waters, Pink Floyd embarked upon a world tour, and before 1987 closed, a second single lifted from the album, 'On the Turning Away', struggled into the British Top Sixty. The third single, 'I Slip', issued during June 1988, faltered in the Top Fifty.

When Pink Floyd's 'The Momentary Lapse of Reason' tour finished its year's trek, in excess of 10 million people spanning fifteen countries had seen them perform. Before the close of the eighties, the group issued *The Delicate Sound of Thunder,* which peaked in the American and British Top Twenty.

In the nineties, Waters performed before 210,000 fans on the site of the Berlin Wall in Potzdamer Platz, Berlin. With selected fellow acts including Bryan Ferry, Marianne Faithfull and Van Morrison, among others, Waters destroyed an artificial wall, while performing *The Wall* in its entirety. Broadcast worldwide, the event raised money for Leonard Cheshire's Memorial Fund for Disaster Relief.

To add to the countless awards and honours received by Pink Floyd, the nineties offered more. In 1991, they were inducted into the second annual Brick Hall of Fame celebrations held in New York, in thanks for their services to the brick industry via *The Wall;* and in 1992, at the annual Ivor Novello Awards ceremony, the group was presented with the Outstanding Contribution to British Music Award. Two years on, Pink Floyd embarked upon an extensive American tour, covering fifty-nine dates and three million-plus people, before touring Europe and performing in Prague, Czechoslovakia. Upon their return, they opened a British tour at Earl's Court, London. The concert was fated though; a seating area collapsed injuring members of the audience. The injured were compensated from the group's pocket. Before 1994 closed, the album *The Dark Side of the Moon* passed sales of thirteen million copies, and by 1996, Pink Floyd's total album sales were phenomenal. *Wish You Were Here* had sold in excess of five million copies, while *The Wall* topped ten million sales.

Compilations and reissues continue to keep Pink Floyd in the public eye. Despite losing two prime members, Barrett and Waters, they remain a musical force not to be ignored. In fact, Pink Floyd's music speaks for itself – whether it's animals, walls or moons!

(Quotes: *Pink Floyd* by Bruno MacDonald)